INDUSTRIAL PROBLEMS AND DISPUTES

INDUSTRIAL PROBLEMS AND DISPUTES

BY LORD ASKWITH
(George R. A. Askwith)

BOOKS FOR LIBRARIES PRESS
FREEPORT, NEW YORK

First Published 1920
Reprinted 1971

INTERNATIONAL STANDARD BOOK NUMBER:
0-8369-6631-7

LIBRARY OF CONGRESS CATALOG CARD NUMBER:
72-179502

PRINTED IN THE UNITED STATES OF AMERICA
BY
NEW WORLD BOOK MANUFACTURING CO., INC.
HALLANDALE, FLORIDA 33009

FOREWORD

In publishing this work, I have no ambition to be a prophet of the future relations between Capital and Labour, but to state, however imperfectly, facts within my own knowledge, with some views upon certain of the problems which have arisen.

These facts may help in some small measure to throw light upon events of the present day and the problem of industrial peace. We have no guide to the future except our experience of the past.

I would like to record my gratitude to the staff who worked so hard and loyally with me for long years and through the War—men and women. Mr. I. Haig Mitchell and Mr. D. Cummings, as chief lieutenants, with Mr. Sidney Clarke, my first private secretary, and Mr. H. J. Wilson, who succeeded him, worked with me through many strenuous days, of which these pages give some record.

There are, too, many conciliators and arbitrators, men like Sir W. W. Mackenzie, Sir William Robinson, the late Mr. T. Smith, and Professor J. B. Baillie, as well as my colleagues on the Committee on Production, who have given unwearying service to the cause of industrial peace. I should add that Professor Baillie materially aided me with the chapters on Socialism and Syndicalism.

Askwith.

v

CONTENTS

INDUSTRIAL PROBLEMS AND DISPUTES

CHAPTER I

THE LAD

LET any man imagine himself a boy again, and throw back his thoughts to those days of which the memory remains so keen and vivid throughout the whole of life. He will remember his ambition to excel in games or in work; his desire for the goodwill and friendship of others, possibly of all with whom he comes in contact; his hope for enjoyment of life; his interest in every plan he makes. Every day all that he does seems to result in something of direct and immediate interest to himself. He is always going forward, in mind as in age and strength; and even though he may never pause to sum up results, he feels and senses them, and acts upon the experience gradually coming to him. In great or little measure education gives him knowledge. Some things he is told that it is necessary for him to learn, and as all the other boys and girls are learning them, he follows the rule and finds results. According to his nature, the influence and skill of his teachers, and the incentive of competition he may achieve some success. Spurred on by results, he becomes a leader of others, and may discover, almost without knowing it, fitness for particular kinds of learning or pursuits beyond the general knowledge commonly impressed on all.

Most lads are full of life and hope, eager to succeed, without much prevision or any knowledge of the different lines of life which may be open to them; but they do find that effort produces results and that the results affect them individually. Their zest is not thrown away; they become eager to follow the paths of success. Other lads, of course, there are who do not wish through their surroundings even to arrive at a basis of a general education or to apprenticeship of any kind. "The laddie was terrible against being made a gentleman," as Sir James Barrie says, "and when he saw the kind o' life he would hae to lead—clean hands, clean dickies, and no gutters on his breeks—his heart took mair scunner at genteelity than ever, and he ran hame."

One may turn to the parents of these young people. Whatever standard of life the parents may have reached, they are anxious that their children should not fail to have at least as good a standard. For years, now, more and better education has been called for. Vast sums have been spent by successive Governments in improving and extending education, and at the present time wide schemes are before the country. Parents have spent their means and harassed their minds in the endeavour to obtain the best possible result for their children. They want them to learn as much as possible and to have their intelligence developed with a view to success in life and improvement of their condition. Year by year thousands and thousands of young people are thus being educated, and have to start out on some means of earning their own living and reaching a position which will enable them to marry and have children of their own.

It is extraordinary that, with all this yearning desire for advancement, there is at the present day so little a knowledge of the possibilities of different careers both among old and young, and such little guidance as to careers. A lad's chance of choice is generally so narrow that he is very likely to take up some form of unsuitable work. When the time comes, lads start on what they can get, some following their father's trade, some taking the first employment which offers itself, some joining a trade which their friends may be seeking to follow, or which happens to be the main trade of the district in which they live. The selected work may be work for which the lad is mentally and physically unfitted, or work which offers few opportunities of a satisfactory career. How can any lad know that there are more than sixty main occupations, each with many subdivisions, and in each subdivision employment for workers, whether skilled, semi-skilled, or unskilled ? It is at least one step forward if that fact is realised by a lad before he considers or examines several of them with a view to selection of the most suitable. The most suitable will probably be that occupation where the good and not the weak qualities which he possesses will be most useful : in that direction the best chances of his success will lie.

If he has a strong interest in anything, the idea will come to him, with little examination, which callings may possibly be entered. If he has no strong interests, he may be equally fitted—or perhaps it should be said, not unsuitable—for several kinds of employment, and may try to ascertain what occupations are open, and examine as best he can, by reading or by talking to persons engaged in the work, or, if possible, seeing the place of work, the nature of the work which he proposes to undertake. For both classes of lads knowledge alone, forethought alone, can give some glimpse of the chances of the future. Few can find out much by themselves before taking the leap in the dark.

Many are the questions that might be asked, both as to occupations and as to the circumstances of occupations. Some occupations are given in a list at the end of this chapter. Is such a list or choice often brought before a lad ? Useful questions are also given. Are such questions ever asked, when a random choice is hinted at by lads necessarily, by their age, without any experience of actual facts or future possibilities, or any power of wise judgment ? If lads cannot get the answers for themselves, it is not too much to say that educational authorities, boys' clubs or associations, or even employers, may well prepare information that can be readily accessible to those who desire to know. Every boy kept from an unsuitable occupation is likely to be a more contented citizen. Guidance and encouragement in using any available training facilities and exercising judgment will not be thrown away.

It seems to be very usually supposed that general remarks about the value of education are sufficient for lads—sermons on their duty and the usefulness of knowledge. As a matter of fact, they are of little or no use. It has to be brought home to the lad as an individual that self-improvement is an advantage to himself before he will be prepared to make much effort to obtain it. As Solomon very truly wrote, "The beginning of wisdom is the desire for discipline." The first thing is to establish the desire. When desire exists, opportunities may be more easily seen and more quickly taken. The ground is prepared for advice on the course of training to be followed and for information on the occupations in which a boy is interested. The boy will be in a position to consider for himself such vital questions as whether he is suited for the work, whether the wages are satisfactory, whether the employment is regular, and whether there are fair chances of promotion. All these four questions are elementary questions which every boy should have brought before him and should try to exercise his intelligence in answering. He should know that, if he is an apprentice or learner in commerce and industry, his path is more or less defined, but that if, as a boy, he joins the army of unskilled workers in works, offices, or factories, or starts in employments which lead nowhere, blind-alley employments, he may be amongst the few, the very few, who reach as adults the ranks of skilled industry; he may be absorbed among the unskilled or semi-skilled who are attached to an industry; or he is very likely to have to leave and seek other employment, because there is no room in that industry for his services as an adult. It is an outstanding feature of employment in the unskilled and blind-alley employments that after a time the lad must leave and seek other employments for which he has had little or no training. The remedy lies in preparation and training, only too difficult to obtain and too slightly given. A generation of lads is now growing up, many of whom, owing to the war, have not had the control of fathers or elder brothers, and often not of mothers. In their hands will lie the decisions and work of the future, the fate of the nation. There is available at our very doors a vast field for effort and service. The world urgently needs effective workers, and offers them good rewards. Conditions in a workshop or an office are so exacting that none but intelligent persons with knowledge of their work can hope for success. General intelligence is the chief requisite, knowledge beyond the small piece of work a man may first be engaged on is the second, if a lad is to have a real chance of advancement and promotion. It is a platitude that education to an intelligent man never ceases during his life, that every addition to his knowledge is an asset of advantage or pleasure to himself. It is at no period of life more important than in the period of his youth that this lesson should be learned, and that teachers should bring it before the individual lad. And yet how seldom is it done! Lord Rosebery is reported to have said that there was one thing which age could never teach—experience. If the implication is that the young must and will find out for themselves, the saying may have truth when applied to some facts of life; but at least it must be qualified by saying that there are facts in life, the whole career of a man, on which it is desirable to raise and encourage curiosity, and for which experience may give guiding lights of value.

The industrial problems of the present day, the problems of years past, are closely connected with the use which we make of our lads; the chances we give them to advance, and by advancing to assist others by service and example; the avoidance of putting them in wrong places; their opportunity of getting a fair chance according to their efforts and brains, and of understanding the position of others and not seeking or imagining misunderstanding.

Women may well say, "We are giving you sons year by year. What are you doing with them?"

Occupations of the World

Agriculture.—General farmer, stock farmer, dairy farmer, fruit farmer, poultry farmer, gardener.

Commerce.—*Wholesale and Retail Shopkeepers.*—Bakers and confectioners; booksellers; butchers and meat salesmen; chemists and druggists; drapery, wholesale and retail; dealers in dress: boot and shoe dealers, hosiers and haberdashers, outfitters and clothiers; fishmongers; poulterers; game dealers; florists; greengrocers; fruiterers; grocery; ironmongery and hardware; hairdressers and barbers; milk-sellers and dairymen; newsagents; oil and colour men; pawnbrokers; stationers; tobacconists; warehousemen. *Offices.*—Banks; insurances; shipping; railways; carriers; agencies; counting-houses; manufacturing works.

INDUSTRY.—Building trades; engineering; textiles; mining; metal-working; precious metal and instrument-making; glass; chemicals; paper and printing; pottery; woodworking and furniture; leather, skin, and hair.

PROFESSIONS.—Minister; doctor; dentist; teacher; lawyer; architect; army; navy; police.

PUBLIC SERVICES.—Civil service; municipal service; gas; electricity; water-supply; tramways; roads; sanitation; health.

There are more than sixty main occupations, most of them with many divisions, open to young people leaving school.

WHAT A BOY SHOULD KNOW ABOUT AN OCCUPATION HE WISHES TO ENTER

1. The size and importance of the occupation.
2. Is the occupation growing or diminishing? (E.g., is it becoming mainly work for semi-skilled, or is it actually decreasing in importance?)
3. Is the occupation crowded, or is there a scarcity of high-class workers?
4. Is the occupation stable, or is it subject to frequent changes?
5. What is the length of the working-day? Is overtime frequent, and is it paid for?
6. Is payment by time or by the piece?
7. What are the different kinds of work in the occupation? He should know the names of the different branches, the kind of work, and the pay in each branch.
8. Is it an occupation which employs a large proportion of boy-labour? If this is so, the boy should know that he will probably be dismissed when he reaches seventeen or eighteen years of age.
9. Is the occupation a healthy one, and is it carried on under good conditions?
10. The average age of entry.
11. Is there any need of training before entrance?
12. Where this training can be obtained.
13. The wages at entrance. Are they small at first and slowly increasing to high wages, or comparatively high at

first, with a small rate of increase—the maximum reached in a few years ?

14. Have all beginners the opportunity to learn more than one operation or process ?
15. What is the number of apprentices or learners ?
16. How are the skilled workers recruited ?
17. What are the opportunities for technical training ?

CHAPTER II

THE LAD IN EMPLOYMENT

ONE of the first results, when a lad enters employment, is apt to be the disillusionment of youth. I am not speaking of blind-alley employments, such as messenger, errand- and van-boys, newsboys and street-sellers, into which a boy may have drifted by the necessity of earning money or ignorance of the danger of starting in blind-alley work. In such work fairly good wages may be obtainable at the start, but lads will generally find that they have to give place to others before they become men, and must change their occupation when it is too late to learn more skilled work. After several years of blind-alley work, a youth of eighteen is generally unfitted for learning skilled work. He cannot apply himself to the task or will not submit to the discipline and control necessary for learning a trade. He will not take a boy's job, and cannot get a man's job ; and a few weeks spent in looking for a job is often sufficient to make him degenerate into a casual worker or a loafer. At most he may as a young man be able to get work in an unskilled trade, with the prospect before him that in times of trade-depression the unskilled workmen are the first to be dismissed, and the last to be taken on, and by force of circumstances have to be the chief applicants for relief.

Even in these occupations, at the most impressionable period of their life, when the general education which they have received might be a basis on which to build, they enter a new school, and are left to shift for themselves.

In a lesser degree, the same principle appertains in the skilled trades, and will appertain in those trades and under those employers where the worker is only regarded as a mere element in the cost of production : with the system of restriction to one machine or one process, and no training in his industry or in several sections of his industry. The young lad, on entering a workshop or taking up almost any form of manual labour, finds his position curiously changed. He may not realise it at first, but it cannot be long before the fact is borne in upon him, either by his own experience or the instruction of his colleagues. Instead of everything being done for them, with parents harassing themselves to give them the best possible education and insurance for progress, and teachers endeavouring to get the best results from the development of their brains, these young lads are only too often put in a position where development is curtailed. They have been full of zeal and ambition, underrating difficulties, believing that the world was before them, and that, given a good education, fair brain, and hard work, they must be able to make their way. Perhaps at school they had gained prizes and were encouraged to believe that progress and advancement were not only possible, but even easy. But they find out that in the new world this is not so. They may begin by making every effort to get on and, by conscientious work, try to get out of the ruck. It is not to be done. There is no ladder, no open door. In the majority of cases they never have a chance. As trainers say of young horses when spurred to greater effort than they can accomplish, " Their hearts are broken." Good work and bad work, steady effort or slacking, lead to no result, no difference in their remuneration, no real chance for the future.

The lads are not taught a trade or how to take interest in a trade, but only a process or part of a process. They are encouraged to become proficient in one or a few operations, not to gain a general knowledge of a trade or its interest. They are not taught the continuance of education or how to effect it, but become an element in the costs of production. Occasionally some may be promoted and may rise, but the majority find the door closed to them. Their efforts are restrained to becoming machines graded to produce a particular type of article, but nothing else, with no direct interest in their work or the result of their work. They are against a wall which they cannot climb, and are not encouraged to try to climb. Why ? The answer is obvious. The lad is out of the hands of teachers whose business it is to expand and develop his growing mind and intelligence, and who make their livelihood by following that pursuit or business. The lad is transferred to the custody of persons whose business it is to produce, not to continue general training. Their business is to make the best use of the factors within their reach, and they do not want to spend their time, energy, and money in teaching. Teaching of that kind might be philanthropic, but it is not their business, any more than to teach young children. Proficiency of a narrow, specialised kind is most conducive to their undertakings, and, so they think, to their production. As individuals they select what they require for production; and as production is their business, no blame should be attached to them for that reason. They have started with that object; they have directed their brains and their money, large or small in amount as it may be, to that object; and they wish to make use of every opportunity and of every person whom they can employ in furtherance of that object. What is the result? The young lad leaving his general school-training finds that the specialised operations common in workshops are to be his lot in life. His hopes may be great, his ambition may be soaring. For some time he may trust in possibilities. He does not like to admit to himself that he is not being trained as an engineer, a ship-builder, or a house-builder, but to become an operative. But in a brief time to the majority comes disillusionment; and when once a man is disillusioned, bitterness is a very natural result, and antagonism to the system which he deems to be the cause. He has to turn elsewhere, and in place of a business career he may see the chief prizes are to be got by becoming a leader amongst his fellows and by finding, in opposition to the system, a career which does not lead to production from which he gains his daily or weekly wage, but which does lead to direct results to himself, with possibilities of high advancement. Slowly or quickly he finds himself opposed to the employer, and opposed to the very prospects which that employer holds most dear. His hopes of success lie in bleeding the employer rather than in joint effort to increase production and gain the best possible results for both.

In the workshops the lad, who was led, while at school, to believe that all was possible and within his reach, finds himself in an atmosphere where he soon discovers that the belief exists that his chances lie not in prospects of success in his trade and co-operation with his employer, but in something outside and in opposition to that employer. If he has served an apprenticeship in the trade, and spent years and money in learning two or three processes, he will soon realise that the knowledge of such processes is his trade possession, and is all he knows. Jealously will he guard the very pigeonhole in which he finds himself—any infringement of rules or restrictions, rates or methods, he will resent and fight against, because, as far as trade is concerned, he is fighting for his sole possession, his only vested interest; and he will thus aid in maintaining those trade union restrictions which are so continually denounced by those who consider them to be a bar to production. Then, again, lads cannot desire that any in the same state as themselves should do work which would raise the level which they are expected to reach. As soon as the day's work is over they are only too ready to put on their coats and leave, however important the result of their work may be to their employers. They will band together and support any movement which shows a chance of the general level of their remuneration being raised. They will listen to any teaching which holds out a prospect of taking something from somebody else, and of sharing in greater measure the supposed results of the production of goods or the supposed capital embarked in the support of an enterprise. Some will accept the position and, engaged in domestic affairs, or games, or betting, or simply from want of enterprise, will follow what others suggest in the matter of trade movements, and agree with the behests of delegates either elected or self-constituted. Others will take no interest until cost of living or some requirement of their lives stings them to support claims which they would otherwise regard with apathy. Others, who cannot reconcile themselves to the lack of opportunity, seek it in obtaining leadership over their colleagues, in active support of their trade union meetings, and in the endeavour to become trade union leaders, or leaders of any movement which interests their minds and shows direct results for themselves. And against whom or what are their efforts directed? Their claims, their promotion, the use of their education, the chance of advancement in new and untried paths, all appear to them to be blocked by the employers who have placed them in particular work, and keep them at that work and that work only, and to be hampered by the system which has that result and fixes in particular ways the distribution of the results of their toil. The result is that there is suspicion and, from time to time, war: suspicion and war continuously fostered by propaganda.

Women might again ask: "Is this what you are doing with the sons we are giving to you?"

CHAPTER III

THE EMPLOYER

The boy who, by succession, education, or wealth, becomes in the ordinary course of events an employer or manager knows little or nothing, and as a rule thinks little, of the fate that is in store for him. He is occupied with the interests and aims of a boy's life, and acquiring information on various items of a general education. If he shows any liking for the Army or Navy or the University, his parents, if well enough off, may endeavour to satisfy him and help him to the career of a profession. In any event most parents will strain to send him to the best school they can manage. The ever-increasing lists of boys to be entered for our public schools show the earnest desire for education, and preferably for that which is supposed to give good schooling, in addition to the advantages derived from membership of a great institution, comradeship in thought and games, and friendships lasting throughout life. When the time comes to leave school, it is the parent who looks round and consults others as to what he can do for his boy. If he has a business himself, in nine cases out of ten the boy goes into it as a natural path where the resistance is least: or he is placed in a similar business run by a friend. Then, under the eye of a trusted clerk or with some watching by his father, he proceeds to learn as much as he can of the working of it, in an eager or desultory way according to his inclinations and the nature of his tuition. He may loathe it from the first day of his entrance, but it is difficult to break away, and he is continually told, and feels, that he has no experience, and that he must earn his own livelihood, and perhaps livelihood for others. If the business is run in a particular groove, he has to follow that groove or tradition, and finds little encouragement to break away.

Employers of this class are only a type. Side by side with them in the same trade will be found a limited number of men who have risen from the ranks, and by intelligence, luck, or strong will attained to the government of a business. Others will be managers acting on behalf of companies, associations, municipalities, or the State, restricted in varying degrees by Boards, committees, or governing bodies.

It is not my purpose to define the varieties of the employing classes. They, like the wage-earning classes, must vary in intellect, physical attributes, and character. They do not form a homogeneous whole moulded to satisfy the stock phrase "Capital and Labour." There are vast numbers of anomalies and fluctuations, gradations, interlocking of interests, schemes of management, and divisions of rank and authority. But even if these facts are true and a wide generalisation is difficult, the broad point remains that the man who aspires to be a successful employer aims, in the course of his competition with others, at production and the right to profit by his own exertion. He is not up against a stone wall beyond which he cannot advance. His aim is gain, success, advancement, so that he may have means for himself and means to hand on to his children. He is a competitive individualist, limited by such restrictions of association with others as, in his judgment, will aid his own success, and sometimes also influenced by philanthropic or educational aims selected by fancy, sympathy, or ambition. The familiar phrase "Business is business" covers many a design, good or bad in intention or result. Nobody ever heard of a workingman making use of or relying upon that cover or explanation of his objects. To the employer it has become a commonplace proverb.

When the employer considers the best method of improving his business, he may bring into the estimate a large number of factors; but it is safe to say that, as a rule, a very small factor in guiding his judgment would be the idea that it might be his business to teach, or to continue the general training and open the doors of a career to, the working-class lad entering his employment. The lad is useful to him in proportion to his value as one of the items of the costs of production. The employer will even lament that during the period spent in acquiring knowledge of one or two processes the lad costs more than he is worth. One hears the remark over and over again: "They are always moving just as they are beginning to be useful." Of course they are. It is the attempt of the lad, by himself or through the advice or need of his parents, to better himself and to go where he thinks there are higher wages, better conditions, or more chances of advancement. It is the same spirit of movement which may lead some lads to seek a new continent or go to the Colonies.

The employer himself, as a rule, does not want to move. He may open new branches, and the new branches may overshadow the original business. But when once he is established in a place or amid particular surroundings, his object is generally to develop in that locality. He is tied by buildings, occupation or ownership of land, contracts, goodwill, machinery, etc., and is practically unable to change as the humour seizes him. An old-established business is not lightly scrapped.

The workman, too, is not a migratory person any more than an employer. He does not want to move away from his home, and go among strangers or to an unknown country-side. There must be an incentive before he is stirred to action; and the greatest incentive of all is the lack of opportunity or the pressure of circumstances in the district from which he comes. The restive spirit of youth may be moved by prospects of high wages and greater independence; and by the hearsay reports of what others are doing. The desire for change and adventure may be a lure, and the wish to test his ability or value in other places, with the hope of better openings, may speed departure. Hence the attraction arising from developments of iron or of coal, and such startling results as the increase of the population of Glamorganshire from 70,879 in 1801 to 1,120,910 in 1911, or of the port of Barry from about 100 in 1881 to over 13,000 in 1891.

If, then, quick changes are not the usual desire of employers or employed, it might have been supposed that the difficulties and disadvantages of movement would tend to better acquaintance, friendship, and mutual interests between parties who would prefer to stay where they were and cultivate that intense love of home which is so strong in British minds. In some, perhaps in many, instances such results may have been attained, but can it be said that in the majority of businesses any such relation exists, particularly in large cities ?

Whatever may have been the philanthropic or paternal interest in their workpeople which has been evinced from time to time in businesses run by one man or a family, the tendency of late years has not been in the direction of interest by acquaintance or friendship. The cold entity of a joint-stock company or a huge combine does not lead to it. The workmen become numbers, grouped on processes, driven into pigeon-holes at the very time when education and more education is pressed upon the people and better educated lads are being turned out by their tens of thousands.

In England in January 1918 there were nearly 5½ million, and in Wales over 466,000, scholars on the books of the ordinary public elementary schools, higher elementary schools, special schools and certified efficient schools. During 1917 the number of pupils of both sexes in secondary schools recognised as efficient was, in England, 242,024 (128,709 boys), as compared with 203,540 (110,118 boys) in 1914. The vast majority of these children and lads must necessarily seek their livelihood in industry of one kind or another. The number is continually increasing. Where will the employers be if there is no outlet for them to go forward, and if their chances of a career are continually stopped by a wall ? The cry is daily for more and better education. The Government itself has proclaimed "the need for a complete and systematic plan of elementary education in each area, properly related to elementary and secondary schools and universities, adapted to local needs and particularly to industrial needs, and offering to every student facilities for a graduated and progressive course of instruction suited to his or her requirements."

In that the working-classes see the chance for the better fitness of their children to take part in the work of life : but the children, with wider views than their ancestors, will not be satisfied with a life limited artificially in its opportunities, and controlled by the dictation of a few. They want to have an open chance ; and will generally desire to see a direct interest in the result of their work. Without such incentives they will not do the work as it ought to be done, or give the production which is necessary for the future of the nation.

It may be said that the employers themselves are becoming more and more limited in freedom. These are the days when the process of handing over the conduct of business to joint-stock companies is rapidly continuing, and employers act as trustees for others. These are also the days when huge combines in every class of industry are being effected. Such amalgamations are devised for economy of working, and in some measure allow more openings for those connected with them than the "one chief" business. But there is the great difference that, when employers come under such limitation, the limitation is voluntary. The employer joins if it is to his advantage to join. He can choose for himself, except so far as pressure of competition may impose the practical necessity upon him. But the existence of these bodies does not lessen the utility of considering the importance of an open chance or of a direct interest in the result of work, both for employers and their workpeople. A tribute to those principles may be given in the words of a recent report of a successful company:

"We try to give all our employees an equal opportunity of advancement, and the growth and success of our business prove the soundness of this policy. The path is open to them, even up to the directorate."

CHAPTER IV

EDUCATION

If the preceding suggestions are not entirely incorrect, and if the nation or employers or both are perplexed with the seething mass of proposals for betterment put forward on behalf of equally perplexed workers under the guise of ideals, it may not be out of place to ask them to pay more attention to the subject of youth.

The present practice not only stunts the proper growth of our youths, but tilts their activities in a wrong direction. Nothing has been so marked during the last thirty years as the growth of labour troubles. Reams of paper have been consumed in dealing with it. Labour troubles vied with the war as a nightmare troubling everybody, and since the war have oppressed the nation. Are they not largely the result of a system, or, rather, the lack of a system? And are not the majority of labour troubles due to a movement of the young men ?

Let it be admitted that the education of children has been progressive, that the good education of twenty years ago was not equal to that of ten years ago, that the education of ten years ago fell short of the education of to-day, and that the training of our children from five to fifteen years of age is being constantly improved. Let it be allowed that there is a general desire to equip the rising generations as thoroughly as possible for the battle of life, and that large sums (a fact only too obvious) are annually spent in the perfecting of this equipment. The tendency is in the direction of education and still more education. For eight or ten years in the life of our children the aim of our National Education is to broaden, develop, and expand their minds and latent capabilities, an endeavour generally endorsed as right and proper, even though a strong volume of opinion may exist that, as a nation, we are still far behind what is required if the best results are to be obtained and our children are to get that chance which their natural abilities demand.

And yet, in comparison with this attitude, public sentiment, so far as the training of our young workpeople after they leave school is concerned, is one of surprising neglect. Much has been said and written of the extreme impressionability of the youth of both sexes between the years of fifteen and twenty. Whether these years are the most impressionable or not does not matter. They are at least sufficiently impressionable to make the after-life of the youth largely dependent upon the use which is made of these years. What generally happens ? At the risk of repetition, is it not the fact that the general practice is to place these young people with some private employer whose business is not training, but production ? No doubt there is in the mind of the parents a hope that the broad education begun at school will be followed by a comprehensive training in the trade which the youth has chosen. In actual fact nothing of the kind occurs. Let us suppose that a lad enters a trade through the medium of a large manufacturing business. The lad finds that the line taken with his education while he was at school is reversed. At school the whole endeavour was to broaden and expand his mind, so much so that he frequently wondered to what use he could put the different branches of knowledge which he was encouraged to study. In his new business a contrary line is taken. His work is narrowed, confined, and restricted; he is encouraged to become proficient in one or a few operations, not to acquire a general knowledge of a trade.

It does not require much reflection to see that no other result could come from the system at present followed in industrial education. Until a comparatively recent date, industrial education was left, with some confidence, almost entirely to employers under the apprenticeship systems. Whatever may be said of this training in the past—and it may have been suitable a century ago—it is certainly wholly inadequate now. There are, of course, exceptions in the case of firms which have taken special care about the subject. A particularly successful firm tells that they "have nineteen apprentices who are instructed in a special tool-room in the operation of all machine tools; their work consists in making jigs, fixtures, special tools, parts of machine tools that need replacing, a certain amount of millwright work, and any work of an exceptional nature. Each apprentice carries through his work from the commencement to the finish, and repetition is avoided as much as possible. Their progress has been quite satisfactory. Three of them have left our employ to take positions as competent toolmakers. The remainder are probably better workmen than the majority of men who come to us as skilled mechanics.

"In addition to the regular shop-work, they receive instruction in mathematics, physics, and machine drawing, the classes being held three evenings a week from the middle of September to the middle of May. The classes are held from 5.45 to 7.45 p.m. We have four classes in elementary mathematics on Tuesdays and Fridays, one class on advanced mathematics on Fridays, and the same pupils attend the class in physics on Thursdays. The two last-mentioned classes are conducted so as to furnish material for each other—i.e. a portion of the mathematics relates to the physics being studied at that time, and special attention is given in the physics classes to provide material to demonstrate the applicability of their mathematics.

"Up to January last we had two classes in machine drawing each week, but we found that we could keep up the interest and accomplish more by giving the youths one long session from 5.30 to 8.30, during the first portion of which they receive their instruction, after which they devote their time, under the supervision of the teacher, to work which would otherwise be done at home under less favourable conditions.

"The books and materials required for the classes are provided by us, and we also provide the accommodation free of charge. The instructors are provided by the county educational committee."

The method of production in the earlier half of the nineteenth century, with its small factory and workshop, its limited orders and its lack of specialisation, lent itself to the general training of the apprentice; he had to do everything within the compass of the business. To-day that system is changed, or at least the only thing that appears to remain is the belief that a lad can enter a large shipyard, engineering works, or building establishment, and learn his trade.

It would seem that either such a belief exists, or that, with a complacency which is even more dangerous, the nation is content to leave matters to right themselves. In either event an incorrect theory clouds clear thinking. A lad entering his apprenticeship to-day does *not* learn his trade, and matters, if allowed to go on, will not right themselves, for the simple reason that all tendencies and interests are the other way.

An employer, when he engages a lad, however much he may be concerned with the mental, moral, industrial, and physical development of the boy, is much more concerned with making his own business a success, and, naturally, whatever he may do for the boy is circumscribed by his larger and more important aim. Many, in fact, pay little attention to the lad except as an aid to their business. In any case the modern employer does not want his works filled with all-round highly-skilled mechanics or artisans. He requires many specialised workmen capable of handling the machines as specialists, and executing the parts of the special kind of work he is engaged in manufacturing. Any training he gives his apprentices will naturally tend in the direction of turning out men equipped for the special operation he will require them to do. Thus thousands of young men become highly expert in one, or at most a few operations, and narrowed, in outlook as well as capability, long before they are out of their apprenticeship. It would be remarkable if it were otherwise; an employer no more accepts responsibility for the training of our youths than he does for the training of our children. Indeed, when children were entrusted to him he made a bad mess of it, as the history of the factory laws so clearly establishes.

The effect of this narrow scope of work has been already mentioned. The lad becomes disillusioned, embittered, and finally antagonistic to the whole system. A few, aided by influence, struggle on and win through, but the great bulk look for other fields for their endeavours. Work-people are not different from business or professional people. They must have an outlet for their energies, ambitions, and hopes of advancement. If this outlet is blocked or denied them in one direction, the natural and helpful direction of advancement in their trade, then another outlet will be sought. This is easily found in trade union and labour agitation activities. An attractive field is open before them.

In place of the difficulties facing them in the struggle for a career in their business, they find that, by espousing the cause of Labour, a welcome career awaits them, with high prizes not depending upon favour or influence, but upon their own powers. Is it any wonder their hesitation disappears ? Before they realise it, they are taking sides against their employer and their trade prospects, and responding to the invitation of the trade unions.

Our young men are, by this method of specialised and narrow training and consequent stoppage of prospects of advancement, being driven from the pursuit of trade ambitions, and ruined as prospective aids in the struggle to connect to man's use the gifts and forces of nature. This educational equipment of the youth has resulted in hundreds of thousands of workpeople being forced into more or less active hostility to their employers. In place of eager joint efforts to expedite production, many in fact seek to retard production, while many are, to say the least, indifferent. Others are imbued with an hostility which develops into antagonism to all authority. Some consolation is no doubt obtained from the thought that, frequent as industrial troubles are, they have so far been surmounted by some means or other, and the hope is possibly entertained that, harassing as the recurring menace is, means will still be found by which the difficulties will continue to be surmounted. The consolation must be small, because the seriousness of the trouble is so steadily increasing that it is obvious a condition of things is growing which, unless rectified, must have a grave effect. No other result can be expected. The knowledge and intelligence possessed by children leaving school is progressive. It is foolish to keep drafting this growing intelligence into industry, and expect it to remain quiescent when the hopelessness of advancement in industry becomes apparent to that intelligence. It is only necessary to meet the young miner, engineer, or factory worker, who has possibly done well at school and science class, to recognise that, if a pace commensurate with his intelligence is not found for him in his trade, he will find a place for himself in the ranks of labour agitation.

There are at least two remedies within reach :

(1) Completing by industrial education the work commenced at school.

(2) A changed method in the workshop handling of labour.

As to completing by industrial education the work commenced at school, if the qualities embodied in children require careful tending during their younger years, it is surely not less desirable that care should be taken when they are just beginning to be aware of the great possibilities of life. The nation, or, if intervention by the nation is to be avoided, associations of employers or individual employers for those within their trade or factory, and trade unions, instead of being satisfied with education and training up to fourteen or fifteen, should aim at completing by industrial education the work commenced at school. The development of our youths is equally the interest of the nation as is the development of the child. Why stop at fourteen or fifteen years of age ? If the education of the child by the nation has proved beneficial, why not go on and see him through part, at least, of his industrial education ? After he is twenty or so, he may safely be left to fight his own battle and specialise if he so wishes ; but until then, guidance, encouragement, and help in the workshop are essential to the broad, general, and varied training which is necessary to his or her full man- or woman-hood. Recent developments of secondary training-schools are only a small beginning.

As to a changed method of workshop handling, the dead level of trade union conditions is not the goal to be aimed at. It is to an upward, not a downward, direction that employers should devote their thought, so that advancement in his trade, not too long delayed and generous, will be possible to the aspiring youth. The ideal to be aimed at is to make every worker act as if the business was his own, and this result can only be reached if an opportunity is given to make the business actually his own in some proportion to his worth to the business.

It may be allowed that the proportion of his worth to the trade may not be an easy question to answer. Is it more than to give to each lad " a fair sporting chance " of getting an opening in life ? I am not saying that every lad can have or obtain a general education, or should learn a whole business or the objects of it. Many lads show no aptitude or ambition whatever for acquiring such knowledge. Their parents, family, sexual inclinations, so fearfully strong and so generally overlooked, laziness or stupidity, may each or all be causes which prevent any desire or attempt to move forward. Those lads will take a back place in the battle of life. They will be in the army of the unskilled or semi-skilled, with no ambition to go farther; but still, it is fair and expedient that they should have had their chance.

Guidance as to vocation may be helpful. Opportunity from the State, the municipality, or the wise employer may afford the opening for those capable of taking it, and the door may advisably never be entirely closed. Nevertheless the fact remains that in modern industry there must be division of work and specialisation. If the opportunity of general education is not taken, or the value of general knowledge of a trade is not recognised or is not sufficiently valuable to an individual, that individual has to select the course that he will or can follow. The most that can be said for him is that he should have had his chance; a chance which under present conditions he seldom gets. The State may do something, but a few hours a week in secondary education do not afford much foothold. Voluntary Associations directing lads in clubs may do much. Employers endeavouring to select the best brains amongst their employees may do more; and if parents are gradually brought to see the importance of lads having their chance and not being hurried, for the sake of present gain at the expense of their future, into minor wage-earning employments, parents can do most. The intention and wider outlook have to be obtained. Then all correlative forces may unite in the same effort. Give the lad or girl the best chance which is possible, up to the age of twenty or twenty-one, and then, as leading-strings cannot be kept indefinitely in being, their place in the body politic and their future must largely depend upon themselves and their own aptitude. Some may become leaders of men, but the majority must follow. They have to follow in the state for which they are fit, according to their merit and ability. Yet those who are leaders must still consider them. The rabbit in the hutch, the fowl in the hen-roost, the cattle in the meadow cannot be healthy or breed or satisfy the conditions of their life if they are not tended. Unhealthy surroundings, insufficient food, close quarters are bad for animals, but how much worse for men, women, and children, beings with powers of reasoning, with standards of comfort below which they will not go, similar in birth and death and many requirements with all other human beings!

At the present day the industrial world moves more speedily than ever. Men and women expect more. They read more, travel more, discuss more than was customary twenty years ago, and in addition, these islands are more crowded. The conditions of life, the standards, amenities, power of movement and amusements have rapidly changed. Better conditions of work are therefore demanded—and each step in better conditions may give rise to a desire for more. It is obvious that they cannot be given unless the means exist to do it. Care, forethought, paternal interest may do something. The end cannot, however, be reached without mutual confidence, without a spur showing men that good work will produce good results to them as well as to others, interesting them in their own career and the success of the business to which they are attached. If so, the business is bound to progress, whereby the means will be obtained for giving better and better conditions. Take the point of view of this example in a big American firm of 6,000 employees and four or five different factories, where it is said that no labour troubles have existed:

"INSTRUCTIONS TO FOREMEN AND MANAGERS

"*Promotions.*—1. Promote employees to operations of higher skill and wage as rapidly as possible.

"2. If you cannot take care of the natural ability of an employee in your own department, see the Superintendent and Employment officer and recommend the man for a better position elsewhere, even when it may mean to you the loss of a good operator.

"*Help every employee to succeed to the best of his ability.*

"3. Any operator wishing promotion or change to another job in the Company open to him shall be transferred, after serving a notice as required. The maximum notice required shall be one week."

I might cite another instance, showing the policy pursued in some large boot and shoe factories employing 13,000 workpeople and producing 86,000 pairs of shoes daily. They announce to their workpeople a notice running:

"SQUARE DEAL FOR WORKERS

"All our better positions filled by promotion.

"All the best jobs in the Factories and Tanneries filled from the ranks.

"No good position filled from the outside, but always from the inside.

"This policy will be followed strictly in future, and be well understood by the workers, so that those in lower positions may confidently expect, in due process of time, to advance into the better positions when open.

"Leaving the experienced man where he is, and hiring a new man for the higher and better positions, is the EASIEST way, but not the best way, and should not be considered for a moment.

"The stability, growth, and future development of this business depend upon the above policy being strictly carried out. The 'goodwill of the workers' can only be secured and maintained through fair treatment, and it is UNFAIR to a working member of our concern to have some-one from outside put in above him. FAVOURITISM should NEVER be POSSIBLE. MERIT ALONE should be the only consideration for promotion."

In the United Kingdom since the war a large number of firms have been aiming in a similar direction. The Government has been taking some steps, by the Welfare Movement, to indicate suggestions and improvements in amenities, though it may be questioned how far Government interference in this matter is desirable. A healthy movement, spreading naturally, is much more lasting than anything imposed by another authority. Amenities alone are not sufficient. Paternal improvements may be accepted, but youth wants power of expression through its own efforts, command of its own money, plans and schemes devised or worked by itself, and a tangible result within a reasonable time.

If the principles suggested by these two notices, and the examples shown by the best firms in the United Kingdom, are adapted to the variations of different businesses, a very remarkable change might be effected in industry, and in the prospects of industrial trouble in these islands. Other results will follow, but a root difficulty is the lack of opportunity and lack of recognition. Sweep that away, engender mutual confidence, commence with the view that every employee should take pride in his prospects, the result of his labours, and the success of his firm; add to it, if you like, by giving a share of surplus profits or by allowing the employees to invest in the shares of the firm, to arrange with the management the method of settling disputes, or to suggest improvements or even the policy—then the position will be strengthened both within and without. There will be no need then for the interference of Government or outsiders, or for discussions over old age, minimum wage, unemployment, hours, demarcations, restrictions, payment by results, piece- or time-work, or any of the thousand and one questions now looming so large over the industrial world. They will be solved because it will be to the mutual interest of everybody in the firm or company, taken in its broadest sense, to have them solved. The wise trade union leaders will leave that firm alone, even if its employees may belong to their union and pay subscriptions for the sake of sympathy, associations, or such benefits as may not have yet been settled within the confines of the firm or trade itself. His energies will still have ample scope. A change is not effected in a day, and there will be the old story of those who lag behind, of those who do not care till a rude awakening comes to them, of those who say, "What was good enough for our fathers is good enough for us."

CHAPTER V

TRAINING AND SERVICE

I MAY be asked what kind of training should be given in order to enable the lad to have his chance; and the answer is not easy to give. Teachers of primary schools alone can adequately depict the feeling of despair which must come over them in considering the long procession of children passing through their hands, from every kind of home, with every type of brain-power and every type of character; some almost hopelessly hampered by bad homes, bad clothes, bad feeding, bad companions, or bad health. And when school life comes to its closing days, there is the desire or necessity of parents for money to be earned, the ignorance of the child as to where to go or what to do, the acceptance of the first opening, however unsuitable, or the idleness induced by a sense of new freedom. Efforts have been made in the past by boys' and girls' Friendly Societies, apprenticeship associations, and many another charitable or philanthropic society. Government has stepped in with schemes for secondary education, notably the recent Fisher Act, taking tentative steps to pass such legislation as will be accepted generally for the time being. My contention is that further efforts must be made, and service of those better able to understand and better fitted by means, knowledge, or position must be given in every possible direction, if the lad is to receive chances, if any unity is to be obtained, if class hatred and industrial strife are to be mitigated. These are in themselves very desirable objects to most men and women, but even if a revolution occurred, if violent methods or a vast succession of strikes were adopted to paralyse or overthrow industrial and social systems, and seemingly succeeded, the same problem would have to be met, and the same necessity would arise. Life has but little value unless use is made of the brain, and unless other aspirations beyond those of a purely material kind have in some measure opportunity of being satisfied.

Are not the stages to be attempted at least three in number ? (1) To get hold of the youth when he leaves or is leaving school, and endeavour to teach or lead him, whether at work or in his spare hours, and the evenings, to some knowledge of the advantages gained by use of brain and hand, service to others, a corporate life, and pride in his association with others and in himself—in fact, to make him a good citizen. (2) To guide and help him to the best career that may be open to him, with such addition of general knowledge and interest or smattering of vocational knowledge as time, ability, and effort will allow, the latter point of vocational training being one which, from the necessities of the case, parents will expect and the lad more and more wish. (3) To give him opportunity, when started on his career, to add knowledge which will improve his interest in life generally, and his trade in particular, and give him a better chance of advancement in his trade, till such time as he is a man, and must fend more or less for himself, and in his turn begin to help those who are growing up around him, " to give our children occupations which will make solitude pleasant, sickness tolerable, life more dignified and more useful, and therefore death less terrible."

Many are the schemes which have been started from time to time, but I may illustrate the first point by the efforts being made by the Y.M.C.A. in their Red Triangle Clubs, with which I am more personally acquainted than with others, to show the class of aid practically within reach. I take them as an example only, with no desire to ignore efforts which have been made by other bodies. The fine work of the Boy Scouts and many another national or local association or club is well known. There is room for all, if care be taken that they do not overlap. I take the Y.M.C.A. because they have clubs of which I know the particulars. The clubs are spreading like wildfire, their enlargement being only limited by means for installation and the supply of the right people to run them. They began as a revival of inchoate work commenced before the War, when in April 1918 I was asked to meet seven district secretaries, and others interested in the work, at Cheltenham, and endeavour to arrange a scheme with a view to coordinated effort. After three days, plans were drafted which were unanimously adopted by all the Committees and the National Council of the Y.M.C.A. A few excerpts may show its intention and method of working. In alluding to " aims and present position," the report said :

" The field for a National Organisation is immense and complex, but if the scheme is sufficiently broad, support should be obtained for it ; its work would strike the imagination and the common sense of the country at large, and the good results which may be obtained are almost incalculable. Seven district secretaries have already been appointed, but four more are requisite immediately to cover the North, the South Coast, the North Midlands, and North Wales. If funds can be granted and the men carefully selected, four paid full-time secretaries should be appointed for these districts as soon as possible.

" The self-respect and discipline resulting from adherence to a recognised body, and the connection of the Y.M.C.A. with all features of the War, will lead lads brought within its influence to be keen to assist in the War and give some preliminary touch of mutual effort which will make training more easy for those who enlist. For those who are engaged, at an earlier age, in any of the trades, any controlling influence is bound to assist in the general production, chiefly, at the present time, that of munitions of war. After the War, such influence will continue and spread, to the advantage of the community at large, in various parts of the country, and particularly in trade.

" Local support, by cities or counties, should, by right tactics, be forthcoming ; and an example is already apparent in the results obtained in the City of Birmingham and its districts, where a minimum of £6,000 a year is assured. Advantage should be taken of the offers or use of suitable premises. Equipment can be gradually acquired if it cannot be provided to an adequate amount in the first instance.

" The country has been mapped out into areas. Those areas may have to be subsequently divided and subdivided again and again, owing to the largeness of the problem and the necessity of not having unwieldy constituencies, and of having close individual influence and control. But for present purposes these areas are suitable for the planning out of the general scheme. This scheme should be either on the basis of—

"(*a*) The City attracting its suburbs and then spreading its influence over districts and areas, such as has been accomplished at Birmingham; or—

"(*b*) By the County absorbing under its general effort such branches as may have been formed, welding them together under County Organisation, and working with the County as the main centre of the interest that may be aroused.

"This latter scheme is, in a sense, the Birmingham Scheme reversed. Either plan is simple to understand, and would depend upon the lines of least resistance.

"The outline of the Birmingham plan is—

"1. The City Board has full control of the Policy, Programme, Finance, and Staff of the whole City. Each Branch Association has its Committee of Management responsible to the City Board. Each Branch Association has its Sub-Committee for Extension Work into outlying villages. Each Branch Association submits an Annual Budget to the Board, which approves or disapproves.

"2. From the City Board are developing strong County Committees which will control Policy, Programme, Finance, and Staff of County. Each Association in the County will have its Committee of Management responsible to the County Committee.

"3. Representatives of the County Committees with the City Board to form the Midland Divisional Committee.

"4. In the City of Birmingham co-operation is established, or working arrangements are made with the Welfare Control Committee, Employment Exchange, Care Committee, Magistrates, Education Committee, etc.

"The efforts hitherto made for boys may be divided into—

"(*a*) Spasmodic and nibbling efforts made by Government Departments and other bodies—or individuals—sometimes religious, sometimes sectional; and generally without organised scheme or cohesion (with the possible exception of the Boys' Brigades and Scouts); and

"(*b*) New efforts, being made chiefly under the pressure of the War, by the Ministry of Munitions, or in connection with the Ministry of Education, the Home Office, and the

Ministry of Labour. It is of the utmost importance that the Y.M.C.A. should not fight against these old and new efforts in any aggressive spirit. Its efforts should be directed in a tactful manner to absorption, co-operation or co-ordination, as local circumstances may dictate. The result at Birmingham shows what can be done, but there should be no disheartening feeling if such wide results are not obtainable in each area. There is no reason to suppose that hostility will be shown by other bodies, and the Y.M.C.A. should not be out to provoke it. After all, the field is wide enough without squabbles and jealousy leading to impairment of work and the waste of valuable time. Strict instructions should be given to all Secretaries as to the value of tact and the absolute importance of working with those whose aim is directed to the same broad object of assisting the boy.

"Internal Organisation

"The National Council of the Y.M.C.A., acting through a Juniors' Committee, will have the supreme directing voice, and also be the ultimate Court of Appeal. For the areas, I emphasise the importance of paid full-time secretaries, whose assistants may ultimately be multiplied to any required extent. It is essential that these secretaries should be capable organisers, and not become too much immersed in detail. They should have power to delegate and delegate again, and if they will not delegate, must be made to delegate. In their Counties or Cities, as the case may be, they will have to deal tactfully with County and also Local Committees, which, though they may sometimes do little work, are a necessary concomitant for obtaining local support and criticism. The secretaries will be responsible for seeing that the right people get upon these Committees; that important types and interests, such as parents, are not left out, and that mere faddists are as far as possible excluded. I would recommend that some women should be members of these Committees. For the staff under the secretary, in Birmingham, it is thought that there should be a centre of training for business staff; where such a centre is obtainable, the gift horse should not be looked in the mouth. Further experience will show whether it is a necessary adjunct in all districts.

The secretaries should have, with the help of the local committees, the discretion of selecting the type of man whom they may choose as their assistants, for forming and managing the Red Triangle Clubs or Branches that may be established, having an eye to the importance of selecting men who like the work and understand boys, and remembering that it is easier to put a man into a post than to get him out. Under the staff the boys themselves should be strongly encouraged in self-government, and for this purpose I am of opinion that the Prefect System should be adopted.

"The Prefect System implies a carefully considered method of Badges as an indication of good attendance, good work, and power of controlling others, and is a method of stimulating competition and merit. All boys joining clubs should make some contribution in money. These contributions will not be adequate to pay for clubs, but where possible should bear some adequate ratio to the expenses of the club. The secretaries may from time to time consider and suggest methods for adding to the income of clubs, with the object of making them, as far as possible, self-supporting.

"SYLLABUS

"I understand that in any work done the objects of the Y.M.C.A.—educational, physical, recreative, or religious—will be kept in view without undue regard to any one of these objects; but considerable discretion should be left to the secretaries in working any schemes.

"Much will depend on the intentions of the New Education Act and other plans now being tentatively put forward by Government Departments; but whatever syllabus is adopted in different districts, trial trips in novel subjects should not be discouraged. After interesting conversations, I think that a general instruction might be given to the secretaries to try to encourage, by small prizes if necessary, those boys who will keep accounts and show accurately how they spend their money, amounting in many cases, at the present time, to pounds a week.

"Very different opinions were forthcoming as to the value of charting boys according to the Canadian System which has recently been adopted in the U.S.A. I would lay down no general rule, but those secretaries who are prepared to try it, and such adaptations as experience may dictate, should be permitted to continue, and should produce their arguments and results at a later Conference.

"MISCELLANEOUS

"Discussion took place on the question of separate clubs for certain definite classes of boys. It is agreed by everyone that there must be grades of clubs varying according to districts, although membership, say, of two clubs, or even of promotion from club to club, might not be outside the possibility of testing. In the same way promotion from the Boys' Clubs to the Men's Clubs should be a subject for careful thought and, in many cases, for personal influence.

"How far, and in what manner, girls should be brought into or have a separate room in clubs should also not be put outside consideration, and trials might be made.

"On the point of separate clubs for very special classes of boys, I think inquiry might be made, and support would be obtainable, say on the Mersey and at Cardiff, for the provision of separate clubs for Riveters' Boys. In connection with these clubs, the problem of men acting as Riveters' Boys, and a separate room for such men, will have to be dealt with. These men cannot be left out. Riveters' Boys are a section especially crying for immediate treatment.

"Clubs in Rural Districts may, in many Counties, involve problems far more easy of solution where the Rural District is pratically semi-suburban. In most parts of counties like Lancashire and Yorkshire, the City would affiliate the semirural district in its immediate vicinity. In other parts of such counties, or in purely rural counties, the County Organisation would have to look after the area, and an assistant secretary might have to inquire and experiment without involving the secretary in minute spade-work of less importance than the main organisation in the big cities. Such assistant secretaries may, in some villages, organise permanent clubs; in others, make use of the perambulating activities of the Y.M.C.A. for weekly lectures, socials, and general encouragement in existing rooms, schoolrooms, or even private houses. Parents should be brought in to some of these functions. In this work, as also in city-work, the great importance of healthy cinema instruction should be a branch for special development.

" London is a problem by itself. I suggest clubs should be established and worked up where suitable premises can be obtained as models, and linked together by degrees. The interest of two or three active Borough Authorities in different districts north and south of the Thames might be invoked, and advice sought from persons having knowledge of such districts as the Dock Districts.

" I would suggest that it be a rule that all the Head Secretaries should meet together at least once in six months, for the purpose of reviving mutual acquaintance, introducing new men, comparing notes, revising and dropping mistakes, and suggesting improvements and developments.

" As a final word, I would only repeat that the Boy Campaign must be broad, boldly supported, and pressed with wisdom and audacity."

Within a few months, the conference met again at Oxford, on November 24, when it was found that nearly all the suggestions made in April had been or were being carried out. About 10,000 boys were being dealt with after these few months' work, and a large amount of spade-work had been accomplished. The Midland System, of which a more detailed account was given, had been practically adopted all round, and found to work. It had become clear that to ask a locality to provide funds before any work was done caused delay and expenditure of effort, which sometimes proved to be fruitless, owing to the difficulty of obtaining subscriptions where no practical proof had already been shown, and where failure of previous attempts by other organisations had created prejudice; but that when work was shown, local assistance speedily followed. Training-schools for club secretaries were advocated, and have since proved invaluable.

The report continued:

" The experience of the last few months entirely endorses the opinion that the Prefect System should be uniformly adopted, and has led to some interesting developments. After hearing a long discussion upon the subject, my opinion is that the first Prefects should be nominated by the Club Secretary, and that after these first Prefects have become established, vacancies should be filled or additions made by the Prefects themselves under a process of co-optation from boys who have earned the Bronze Triangle. The Prefects know the kind of work to be done, and jealously maintain the efficiency and credit of their class. The boys themselves have the competitive objects of gaining first the Bronze Triangle; second, the post of Prefect; and in practice this has proved a better system than the boys choosing their Prefects by election among themselves.

"The second development is that in a large club, under the leadership of their Prefects, the boys can be divided up into boys coming from different areas, the areas, as it were, representing 'Houses' in a Public School. The areas can be named either from a parish or a district, or the name of some popular person. The Prefects look after their own boys, are keen to keep up the number of boys from their area, and to add to their number by new recruits. Further, the area system allows competition within an easy distance in games, gymnastics, or other forms of energy.

"In the District Reports considerable stress was laid upon the almost unexpected interest taken by boys in music. It was stated that the Camp Song-book of the Y.M.C.A. was very popular, but that other classes of singing had also been tried with success, as well as piano-playing. The opinion was that this was an interesting line to follow up, both as giving a mode of expression and developing character. It was felt that a very small assistance by Song-books and Musical Instruments would lead to results which might then be tested by an expert, who would advise whether any and what course of instruction could be suggested for adoption. It must be remembered that most of the boys commence in entire ignorance of music, but seem to be attracted by good-class music, going so far as to take keen interest in competitive singing and choirs.

"Trials, as suggested, have been made in socials, in which both girls and boys join, and also in periodical meetings. It has been found that there was keen objection by the younger boys to these forms of entertainment, but that the older boys and the Prefects did not dislike them, and were desirous of bringing girls to concerts. It is suggested that entertainments of this kind, with boys and girls of all ages, are not very useful, but that there might, from time to time, be an older boys' night, when girls would be admitted and younger boys not be allowed to be present. Such a practice would afford a sort of halfway house to the knowledge, by boys and girls, of one another, without doing any harm. No case of any bad result from these meetings is known.

"Progress has been made with the proposed Clubs for Riveters' Boys, both at Newport and on the Mersey. In Newport the club has been warmly welcomed by all classes. A building near the Ship-repairing Yards and in telephonic communication with them has been secured and adapted. The employers have agreed to recognise it as the Welfare Centre for the boys, and from it the gangs will be called up as required. The officials of the Local Boiler-Makers' Association are in entire sympathy with the development. As the club is situated near to the homes of many of the boys, it will, in addition to the foregoing, form an ordinary Evening Club. A separate room has been provided for the older boys. In this connection it may be well to mention that the belief sometimes expressed that such clubs will afford places for gambling is entirely unfounded and inaccurate. The boys will gamble wherever they can, if there is no club; but where they can be got to attach themselves to a club, the gambling, through the influence of the club secretary, comes to an end.

"I would specially mention the work done by the District Secretary of Wales, in South Wales, among the Workmen's Institutes. About fifty of these Institutes are affiliated to the Y.M.C.A., and boys are admitted as soon as they enter the mines. It has been arranged with the Executive and Representatives of the Institutes to experiment in Boys' Work in certain centres in Glamorganshire and Monmouthshire. The proposal is to assign a room or rooms for boys in the Institutes, and to provide a Boys' Programme, which is being put forward by the District Secretary. I am strongly of opinion that this movement should receive the full support of the National Council.

"It was stated in April that the great importance of healthy cinema instruction should be a branch of special development. An interesting experiment in Bristol tends to show the advantage of this suggestion. Eight hundred boys attended on Saturday evenings, for a whole season, to see a machine showing pictures of travel, sane adventure and educational subjects, at an entrance fee of one penny. It was found that a simple explanation of each picture was received with the utmost attention, and that the show was improved by having intervals for mass singing.

"The suggestion was made that, in London, clubs should be established and worked up, where suitable premises could be obtained as models and linked together by degrees. Some premises have been obtained, and linking-up may in time follow.

"I suggest that the same principle should be continued, when the process of linking-up may gradually develop.

"I am satisfied that the Boy Campaign has come to stay; that it fills a want that other organisations do not cover, and can work in with almost any type of good organisation; that the work done by a small staff has been excellent, and that the Y.M.C.A. may safely and advisedly continue to encourage and support it."

Let me add, too, that such clubs give an opportunity for those who are better educated to give service to those who have had less chance; and to interest and advance them in knowledge of books, games, and a corporate spirit, and develop those qualities which in the War made men so loyal to their comrades, so ready to share with a chum, so generous and chivalrous to those who might be in trouble or unfortunate.

The second stage to which I have alluded in some measure overlaps the first, just as the first may also overlap the second, or continue coincidently with it. There come in it the choice of work, the problem of suitable work, and the education connected with that work.

For use in the Y.M.C.A. Clubs, Mr. S. A. Williams, one of its officers, has prepared a series of admirable charts of the principal trades, by which a lad can see at a glance, when he considers the trade to enter, which line of development he should try to follow, how some branches offer more promotion than others, how important it is to avoid cul-de-sac employment, and how, while working at one section, he may be able to prepare for the next section to which he may have a chance of promotion. Such information as this cannot but be useful and instructive to both employer and lad. A selection of these charts is printed at the end of the chapter, under the heading "Careers for Boys."

There are, however, in addition to choice and advice as to work, the very difficult questions how far education should be general, with a measure of specialised training, or how far general training should be subordinated to that specialised work which may be the lad's lot in life.

Mr. Fisher, in his recent Education Act, has endeavoured to obtain some admixture of the two, recognising that a vast change cannot be made in a day, and that money has to be earned at an early age by the majority of mankind. He has laid a foundation on which much may be nationally built; but apart from the national minimum, it must be recognised that individual care for the individual, and partly by the individual, may and does produce results according to the development of brain and aptitude in individuals, and that industries, trades, firms, as well as societies, may all aid in well-considered advance.

For those lads who can aspire to get through, it is to be noted that the Conjoint Board of Scientific Societies have laid down, for the First School Examination, intended by the Board of Education for pupils of about sixteen and a half years of age, a declaration in favour of the English language and literature as a compulsory subject, with four subsequent groups, history and geography, languages other than English, mathematics, science; and they urge that, in scholarship examinations, credit should be given for general ability, and not alone for excellence in one special department of scholarship or knowledge. Their general opinion has been expressed in important resolutions stating:

"(*a*) In the awarding of scholarship, high importance should be attached to the writing of English, and to General Knowledge, and that these should be tested by an essay paper, and at least one General Knowledge paper.

"(*b*) In examinations for Entrance Scholarships at the Universities, the requirement of minute and detailed knowledge of the main subject or a branch of it, such as is commonly now made, necessitates excessive specialisation at school, and urgently needs to be amended.

"(*c*) In examinations for Entrance Scholarships at the Universities, credit should be given for knowledge of subjects other than that which is the main subject of examination.

"(*d*) Where it is found practicable to do so, consideration should be paid to the school record of candidates, and to other evidence of work which they may offer.

"(*e*) No pressure should be put upon scholars to take their degree in the subject or subjects in which they have gained their scholarship."

As a late Chief Constructor to the Admiralty told me, "After the experience of a lifetime, I find the lads with good general education gradually specialising prove the most apt pupils, advance farther, and have more wide interests, than lads coming forward with high training in one subject. I have tried both systems, and have no doubt as to the best."

The difficulty in practice is the line of demarcation (1) between a general education and vocational training; (2) in vocational training, between general training in everything connected with the industry and the special efficiency required in one section of that industry.

The requirements of modern industry demand, for instance in engineering, not a mechanic with vague bits of theoretical knowledge, and a little knowledge of everything connected with the industry, but an efficient and speedy workman in a particular branch. In training such a workman, it is essential to recognise that it is sheer waste to throw a lad into a large business, and leave him to pick up what he can, as and when he can, with no sequence of training, no understanding that the work he is on is of a useful character, or why it is useful, and no interest in the article he is producing or in the industry to which he belongs.

CAREERS FOR BOYS

CHOOSING A CAREER

This diagram illustrates the two ways of choosing a career. On the left is the " blindfold " way, with its dangers. When the boy leaves school he is anxious to obtain work, and is often sent out to find a job. In the window he sees a card " Lad Wanted," and applies for the post. The left-hand figure shows the probable result of following this course. The chances are at least even that the job holds out no prospects of a career. It is very probable that it is definitely of a blind-alley character which will turn the youth adrift in a few years without a trade or occupation. In many cases he will help to swell the ranks of casual workers exposed to the twin evils of poor pay and frequent unemployment.

On the right is the " explorer's " way.

The schoolboy should follow the method of an explorer, and find out what occupations are open to him, which are suitable to him, and what are the prospects.

The right-hand figure shows what are the probable results of following this course.

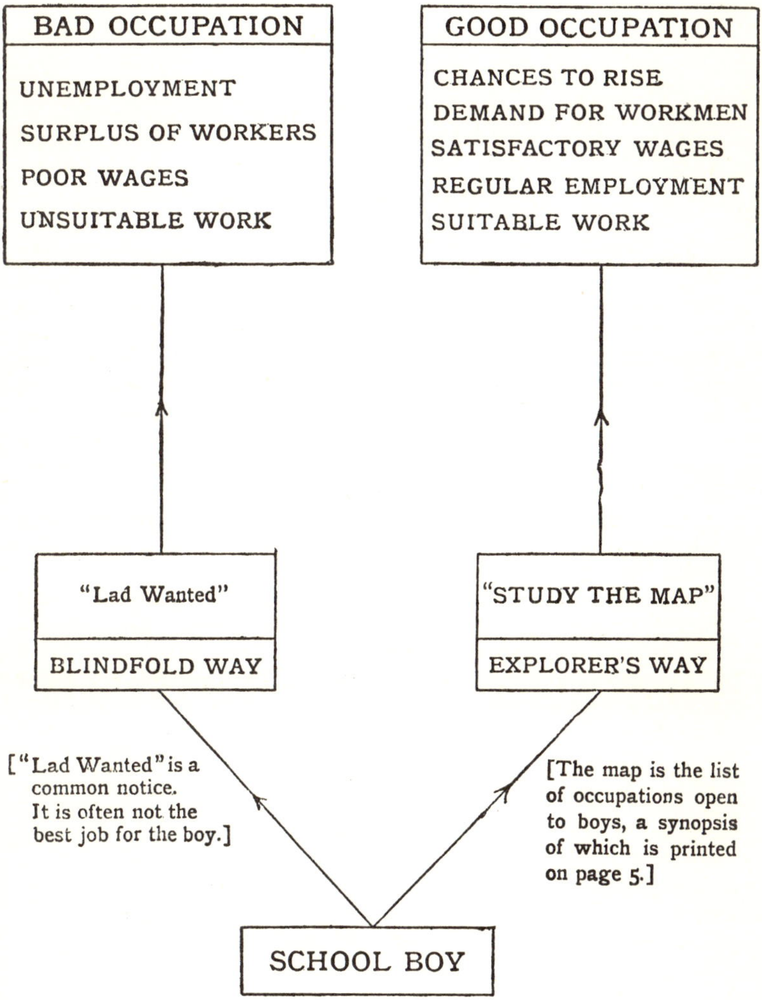
BAD OCCUPATION
UNEMPLOYMENT
SURPLUS OF WORKERS
POOR WAGES
UNSUITABLE WORK
GOOD OCCUPATION
CHANCES TO RISE
DEMAND FOR WORKMEN
SATISFACTORY WAGES
REGULAR EMPLOYMENT
SUITABLE WORK
"Lad Wanted"
BLINDFOLD WAY
"STUDY THE MAP"
EXPLORER'S WAY
["Lad Wanted" is a common notice. It is often not the best job for the boy.]
[The map is the list of occupations open to boys, a synopsis of which is printed on page 5.]
SCHOOL BOY

BOYS IN INDUSTRY

This diagram represents the three courses which are open to a boy when he leaves school.

The right-hand side shows the path of a boy who becomes an apprentice or learner. His training includes instruction in the workshop and attendance at technical classes. At the conclusion of his apprenticeship he becomes an improver, or Young Journeyman, and later a skilled workman, or Journeyman.

The middle section shows the paths which are open to the boy who enters industry as an unskilled worker. During the first portion of his time he may do odd jobs or operate an automatic machine or do other routine and mechanical work.

This period of time is most important, for it probably shapes his future life. If he proves his ability as a worker, and improves his general education and technical knowledge by attendance at classes, he may be promoted to the ranks of the skilled men.

He may, however, simply prove an industrious worker, and thus be of value to the firm, which may retain his services as an adult on semi-skilled or unskilled work.

In many branches of industry, more boys are employed than can be absorbed as adults, and after two or three years' work, many youths are forced to leave the occupation to make room for a new generation of younger workers. This often proves a serious thing for many boys. They are unskilled and without any definite training, and they have not the strength or experience of a man. They often drift aimlessly till they are too old to learn a trade, and are forced to enter the ranks of casual labour.

On the left is shown the path of those boys who enter blind-alley employment—that is, occupations which provide work for boys and youths only. All these young people will be compelled to seek fresh work. It is particularly important that boys in these two sections should realise at an early stage that they will be forced to find fresh employment after a few years. They should prepare for the time of change by considering what they are going to be, and by attending classes to improve their education. Unless they do this the future has few prospects for them.

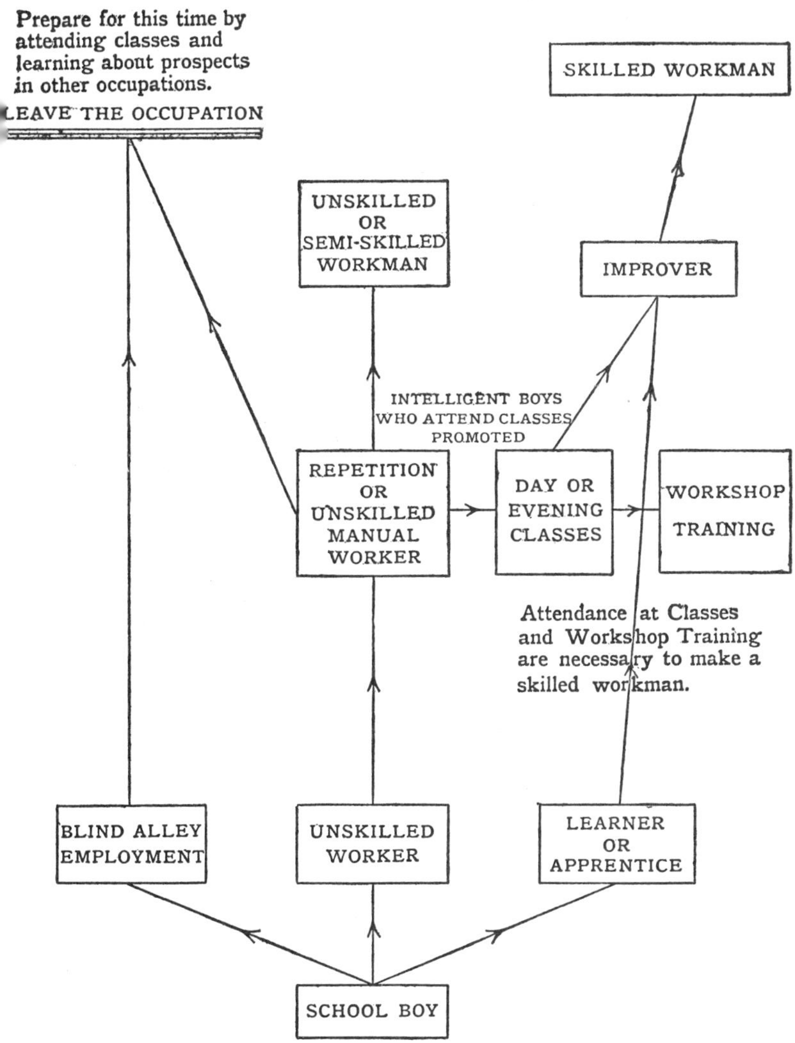
Prepare for this time by attending classes and learning about prospects in other occupations.
LEAVE THE OCCUPATION
SKILLED WORKMAN
UNSKILLED OR SEMI-SKILLED WORKMAN
IMPROVER
INTELLIGENT BOYS WHO ATTEND CLASSES PROMOTED
REPETITION OR UNSKILLED MANUAL WORKER
DAY OR EVENING CLASSES
WORKSHOP TRAINING
Attendance at Classes and Workshop Training are necessary to make a skilled workman.
BLIND ALLEY EMPLOYMENT
UNSKILLED WORKER
LEARNER OR APPRENTICE
SCHOOL BOY

THE BUILDING TRADES

This diagram illustrates the main branches of the building trades and the usual methods of entering the occupation, and the kind of boy who is likely to be successful in the work.

A boy who wishes to enter the building trades can follow one of three methods:

1. He can enter a technical or trade school direct from the elementary school.

2. He can enter a workshop direct from school, and supplement his practical experience by attendance at technical classes.

3. He may enter a workshop and remain content with the instruction he gets there.

The first case is shown on the right hand of the diagram. During the first year the boy will attend a general building course, including workshop training. During this time the boy's tastes and aptitudes are studied so that he can be directed to the branch for which he is best fitted. The remaining time is spent on a special course—building, joinery, bricklaying, plumbing, decorating, etc. At the end of the period he will go as an improver.

The middle section represents the course which is usually followed. A scheme of apprenticeship has been drawn up which follows the method shown in this section.

The boy is apprenticed for five or six years, usually without premium. The pay varies from one-eighth journeyman's rates in the first year, to two-thirds in the sixth year.

He receives training of two kinds :

1. In the workshop and on job.
2. In school.

After he has completed his apprenticeship, the youth becomes an improver.

The left-hand section of the diagram shows the path of the boy who receives practical instruction in the workshop, and does not attend classes to gain technical knowledge. He becomes an improver, but his prospects are not so good as those of the boys who have had a thorough training.

The top line of the diagram shows the various branches of the building trades. It also points out that from carpenter and joiner the position of builder may be attained, and this may include a certain amount of architectural and surveying work.

In the top corners of the diagram the advantages and disadvantages of the building trades are shown.

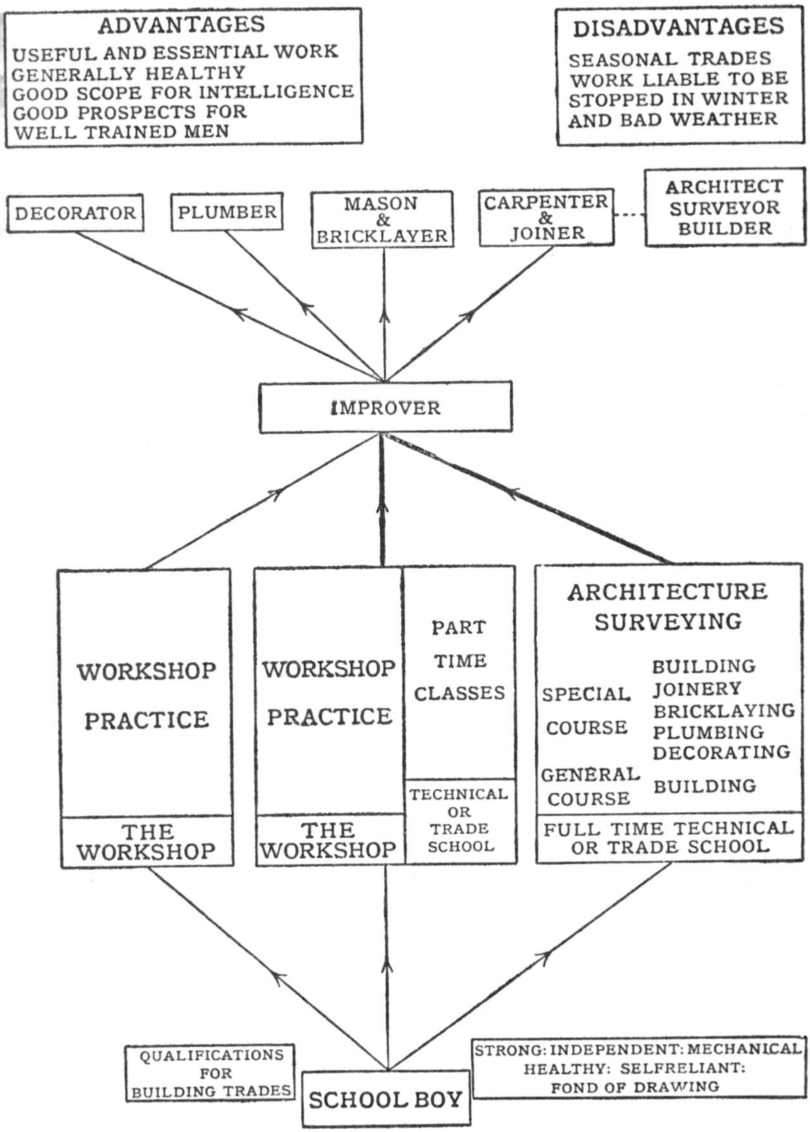
ADVANTAGES
USEFUL AND ESSENTIAL WORK
GENERALLY HEALTHY
GOOD SCOPE FOR INTELLIGENCE
GOOD PROSPECTS FOR
WELL TRAINED MEN
DISADVANTAGES
SEASONAL TRADES
WORK LIABLE TO BE
STOPPED IN WINTER
AND BAD WEATHER
DECORATOR
PLUMBER
MASON & BRICKLAYER
CARPENTER & JOINER
ARCHITECT
SURVEYOR
BUILDER
IMPROVER
WORKSHOP PRACTICE
THE WORKSHOP
WORKSHOP PRACTICE
THE WORKSHOP
PART TIME CLASSES
TECHNICAL OR TRADE SCHOOL
ARCHITECTURE
SURVEYING
SPECIAL COURSE
BUILDING
JOINERY
BRICKLAYING
PLUMBING
DECORATING
GENERAL COURSE
BUILDING
FULL TIME TECHNICAL OR TRADE SCHOOL
QUALIFICATIONS FOR BUILDING TRADES
SCHOOL BOY
STRONG: INDEPENDENT: MECHANICAL
HEALTHY: SELFRELIANT:
FOND OF DRAWING

PRINTING AND BOOKBINDING

This diagram illustrates the main classes of work in the printing and bookbinding trades, the various branches of work in each class, the work which is done by a student or apprentice in learning the trade, and the qualifications which are necessary for success.

In the middle of the diagram the path from a schoolboy through student and apprentice to skilled man is shown. A boy may go direct from school to works as an apprentice, or he may spend some time in a Technical School.

The lower section on the right shows the work which is learnt by a student or apprentice in bookbinding. When he has learnt the general work, he may specialise on one or more branches.

As a skilled man he may either enter the letterpress binding or account-book binding. These are shown in the top right section of the diagram.

The arrows right and left show the work done during the period of training.

On the left are shown the main branches of work in printing: composing, stereo- and electrotyping, and machine managing.

The lower sections on the left show the work which is done by student or apprentice, and the upper sections show the classes of work in which he may specialise as a skilled man.

In top right- and left-hand corners the prospects and scope of the trades are indicated.

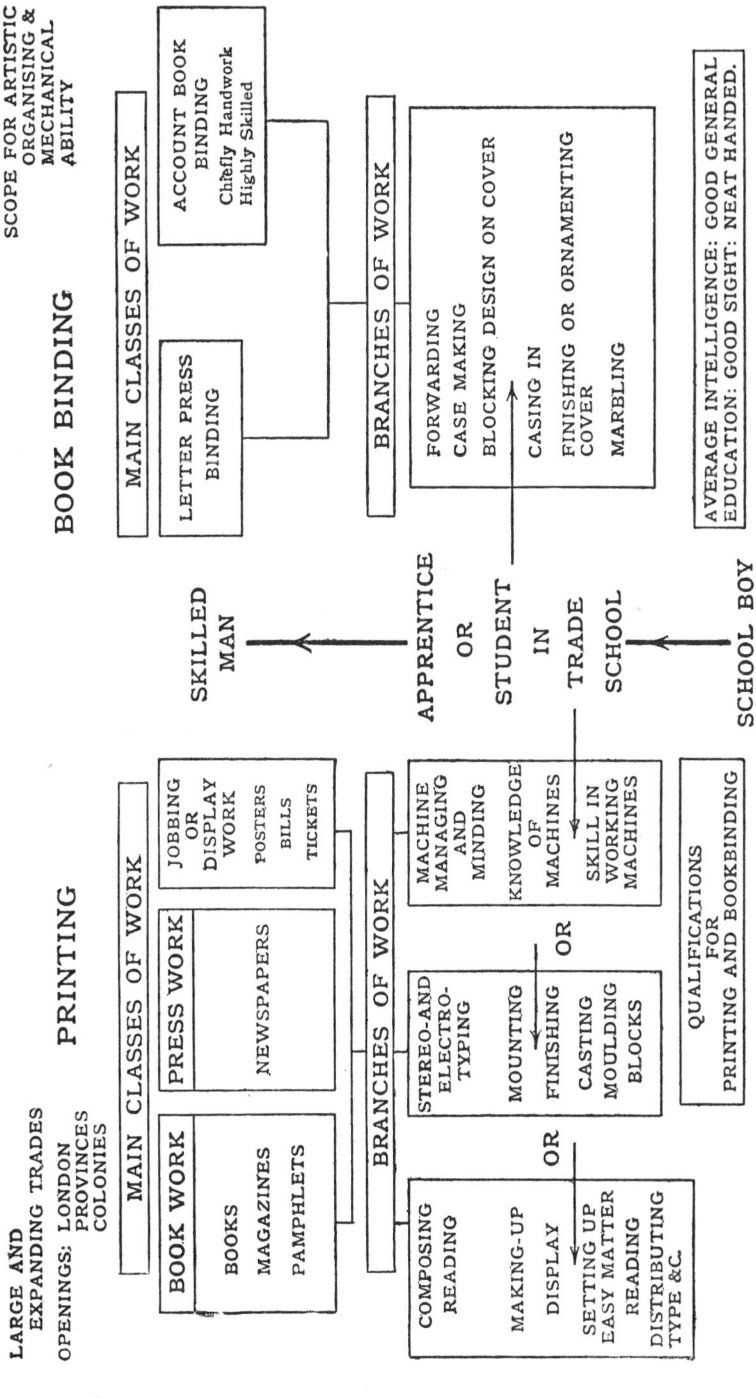
BOOK BINDING
SCOPE FOR ARTISTIC ORGANISING & MECHANICAL ABILITY
MAIN CLASSES OF WORK
LETTER PRESS BINDING
ACCOUNT BOOK BINDING
Chiefly Handwork
Highly Skilled
BRANCHES OF WORK
FORWARDING
CASE MAKING
BLOCKING DESIGN ON COVER
CASING IN
FINISHING OR ORNAMENTING COVER
MARBLING
AVERAGE INTELLIGENCE: GOOD GENERAL EDUCATION: GOOD SIGHT: NEAT HANDED.
SKILLED MAN
APPRENTICE OR STUDENT IN TRADE SCHOOL
SCHOOL BOY
PRINTING
LARGE AND EXPANDING TRADES
OPENINGS: LONDON PROVINCES COLONIES
MAIN CLASSES OF WORK
BOOK WORK
BOOKS
MAGAZINES
PAMPHLETS
PRESS WORK
NEWSPAPERS
JOBBING OR DISPLAY WORK
POSTERS
BILLS
TICKETS
BRANCHES OF WORK
COMPOSING
READING
MAKING-UP
DISPLAY
SETTING UP EASY MATTER
READING
DISTRIBUTING TYPE &C.
OR
STEREO-AND ELECTRO-TYPING
MOUNTING
FINISHING
CASTING
MOULDING
BLOCKS
OR
MACHINE MANAGING AND MINDING
KNOWLEDGE OF MACHINES
SKILL IN WORKING MACHINES
QUALIFICATIONS FOR PRINTING AND BOOKBINDING

SHOP ASSISTANTS

This diagram gives in outline the main branches of the distributive trades. It shows the usual methods of entry, the qualifications of the entrants, and the probable line of developments of the business. In drapery, the Departmental Store will probably be a permanent feature; in grocery, the Multiple Shop System will extend; while in ironmongery there are good prospects for proprietors of small shops.

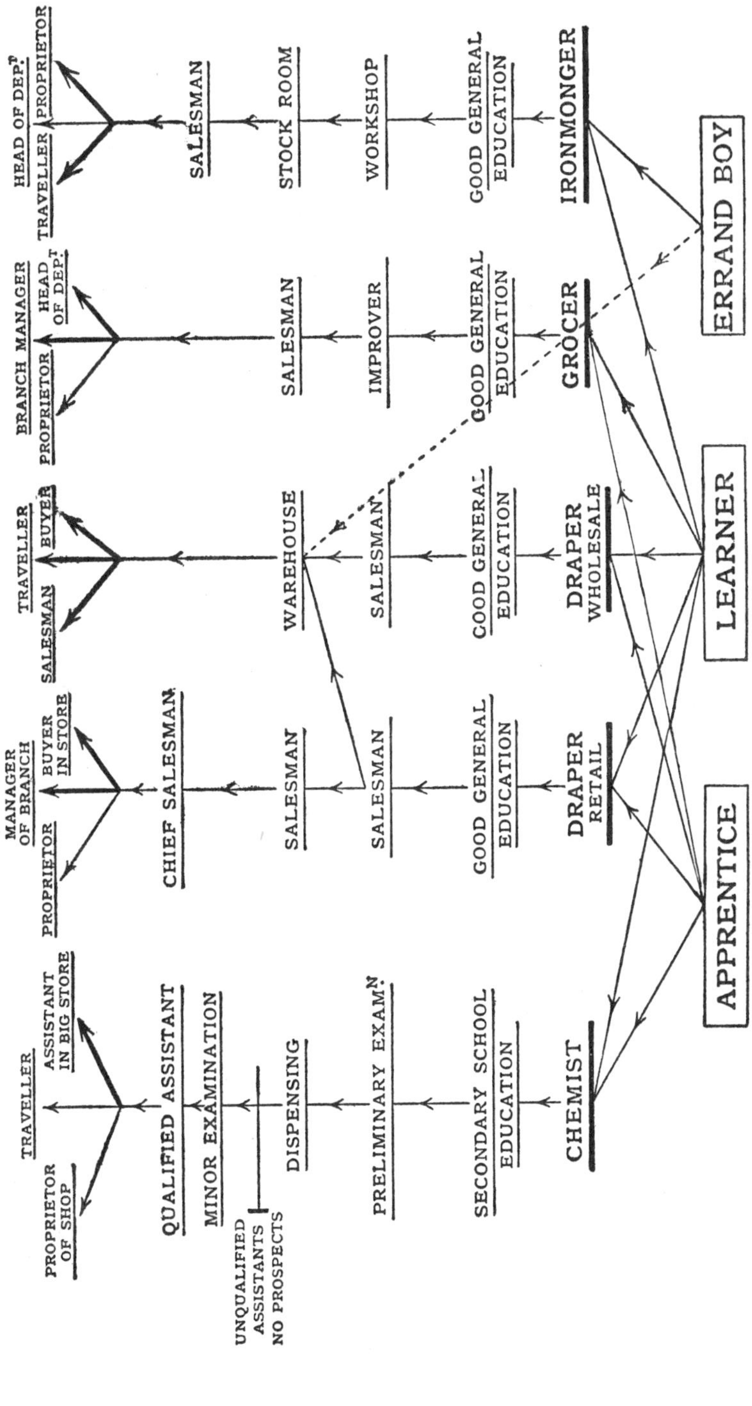
ERRAND BOY
LEARNER
APPRENTICE
IRONMONGER
GOOD GENERAL EDUCATION
WORKSHOP
STOCK ROOM
SALESMAN
TRAVELLER
HEAD OF DEPT
PROPRIETOR
GROCER
GOOD GENERAL EDUCATION
IMPROVER
SALESMAN
PROPRIETOR
BRANCH MANAGER
HEAD OF DEPT
DRAPER WHOLESALE
GOOD GENERAL EDUCATION
SALESMAN
WAREHOUSE
SALESMAN
TRAVELLER
BUYER
DRAPER RETAIL
GOOD GENERAL EDUCATION
SALESMAN
SALESMAN
CHIEF SALESMAN
PROPRIETOR
MANAGER OF BRANCH
BUYER IN STORE
CHEMIST
SECONDARY SCHOOL EDUCATION
PRELIMINARY EXAMN
DISPENSING
MINOR EXAMINATION
UNQUALIFIED ASSISTANTS NO PROSPECTS
QUALIFIED ASSISTANT
PROPRIETOR OF SHOP
TRAVELLER
ASSISTANT IN BIG STORE

THE GROCERY TRADE

This diagram gives in outline the prospects in the grocery trade. It shows that there are two main ways of entering the trade: as an apprentice or as a learner. A boy who starts as an errand boy may enter the business as a learner if he possesses the necessary ability and energy. In many cases, however, errand boys become porters and warehousemen. The articles which are dealt with and the qualities required for success are given as a guide to a boy who is thinking of entering the trade.

The learner or apprentice usually spends the first year in the warehouse, the second year he obtains some experience in the shop, and in the third and fourth years he is promoted to the counter to serve customers. In his last year the apprentice is often regarded as an improver. From this stage the young man becomes a junior assistant and gains further experience. As an assistant he will specialise in provisions or grocery.

During the early years of the trade the young man should get a thorough knowledge of his business and equip himself for higher positions. If he remains as an assistant after he is about thirty-five years old, his chances of employment are not good, and he may be forced to take other work. Many shop assistants in middle life become agents for insurance and sewing-machine companies, bus conductors, etc. Others who have not reached a manager's position and are too old for counter-work become canvassers.

After gaining good experience as an assistant, a man may enter business on his own account, but the number of small proprietors tends to decrease. The multiple shop is taking their place. Under these conditions the able assistant will aim at beginning as manager of a branch shop, or manager or buyer of a department in a large store. From either of these positions he may start business for himself or become traveller for a wholesale firm. The additional experience which he has gained as manager will be a valuable help in building up a business. The next stage will be as director or manager of a firm, which may be the development from his own business, or in an established business to which he comes as an expert.

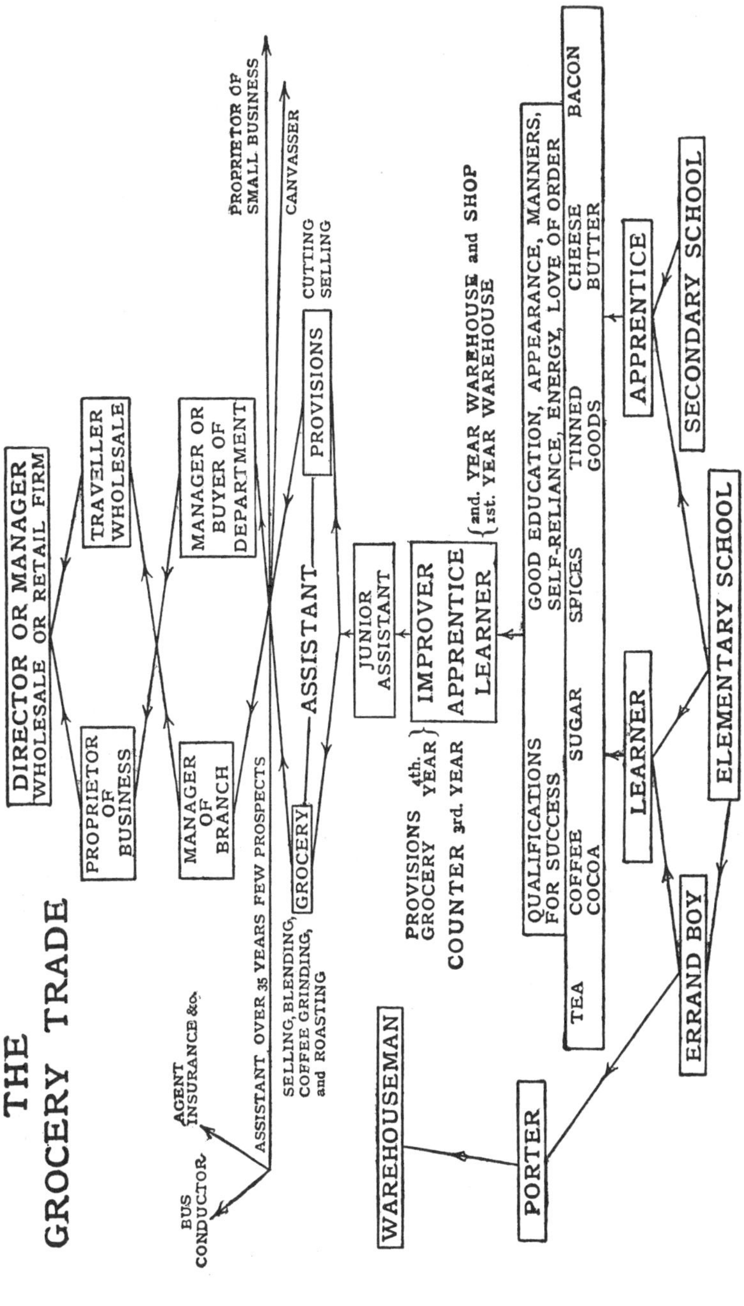
THE GROCERY TRADE
DIRECTOR OR MANAGER WHOLESALE OR RETAIL FIRM
PROPRIETOR OF BUSINESS
TRAVELLER WHOLESALE
MANAGER OF BRANCH
MANAGER OR BUYER OF DEPARTMENT
BUS CONDUCTOR
AGENT INSURANCE &c.
ASSISTANT OVER 35 YEARS FEW PROSPECTS
PROPRIETOR OF SMALL BUSINESS
CANVASSER
SELLING, BLENDING, COFFEE GRINDING, and ROASTING
GROCERY
ASSISTANT
PROVISIONS
CUTTING SELLING
JUNIOR ASSISTANT
PROVISIONS GROCERY 4th. YEAR
COUNTER 3rd. YEAR
IMPROVER
APPRENTICE
LEARNER
2nd. YEAR WAREHOUSE and SHOP
1st. YEAR WAREHOUSE
QUALIFICATIONS FOR SUCCESS
GOOD EDUCATION, APPEARANCE, MANNERS, SELF-RELIANCE, ENERGY, LOVE OF ORDER
TEA
COFFEE COCOA
SUGAR
SPICES
TINNED GOODS
CHEESE BUTTER
BACON
WAREHOUSEMAN
PORTER
LEARNER
APPRENTICE
ERRAND BOY
ELEMENTARY SCHOOL
SECONDARY SCHOOL

A TYPICAL TALK ON AN OCCUPATION

THE GROCERY TRADE

Grocery is the largest of the food trades; wherever there are many people living, there must be a grocer to supply them with provisions. Anyone who is engaged in this trade has the satisfaction of knowing that he is a very useful member of society.

A boy's prospects of promotion depend much upon himself and on the type of shop he enters. At the beginning there is always a good deal of monotonous and hard work, and unless a boy has his heart in his work he will find this to be irksome.

When a boy enters a grocer's shop, his work consists of delivering goods, tidying the shop, wrapping up goods, and work in the store-room and warehouse.

The next stage is that of junior assistant. His work is to cut, weigh, sell, and wrap up goods and make out the bill.

When he becomes a senior assistant, he has to blend tea, roast and grind coffee, judge bacon, butter, and cheese, in addition to the duties of a junior.

From a senior assistant he may go to the position of a buyer or manager, when he will have to buy and store goods, arrange them for sale, apportion the work of the assistants, estimate the cost and selling prices, supervise all accounts and books, and generally extend the business.

To know his business thoroughly, the grocer should study the principles of salesmanship, and the origin, qualities, and prices of the goods he sells. A knowledge of commercial arithmetic, English, and commercial geography will be of great value to him.

The Institute of Certificated Grocers holds examinations in the subjects useful to grocers.

The qualities which are useful for success are industry, thoroughness, punctuality, courtesy, and loyalty.

Useful Books.—*The Practical Grocer*, W. H. Simmonds; *The Grocer's Handbook*, W. H. Simmonds; *The Grocery Trade*, T. Aubrey Rees; Law's *Grocer's Manual*; *Grocery*, W. F. Tupman; *Grocery Business Organisation and Management*, C. L. T. Beeching; *Spices*, H. N. Ridley.

Magazines and Papers.—*The Grocer*, weekly 6*d.*; *The Grocer's Gazette*, weekly 3*d.*; *The Grocer's Journal*, weekly 2*d.*; *Grocery*, monthly 6*d.*, illustrated.

How to Enter.—The parent should write to the firm he wishes his son to enter, and arrange for an interview between the principal and the boy. In the grocery trade, boys begin as errand boys or as apprentices. The apprentices and the best of the errand boys rise to be assistants.

Qualifications.—Boys should be of good general education, good appearance and manners. They should be self-reliant, energetic, and ambitious, for promotion depends very much upon themselves.

Conditions of the Trade.—The work is hard and the hours are long, but in spite of this the trade is a healthy one. The Registrar-General's Report says, " Grocers still continue to be among the healthiest members of the shop-keeping class." Living-in does not exist to any great extent.

Prospects.—Grocery is the largest of the food trades in the country. It is a trade that is necessary to modern conditions of civilisation.

In many shops errand boys with ability and ambition are put to the counter and may rise to be managers or proprietors. In other shops errand boys only rise to be porters and warehousemen. The boy must be careful what kind of shop he enters. As with other distributive trades, if promotion comes at all, it comes early. A man over forty is generally regarded as too old for counter-work. If by that time he has not reached the position of manager, traveller, or canvasser, his prospects are poor.

ENGINEERING

The first diagram is a general sketch of the work. The second diagram illustrates the main ways of entering the occupation of engineering.

On the right is shown the best path to the higher ranks of the profession.

The boy from a secondary school may continue his education at a technical college or university with a view to taking an Honours Degree in Engineering. He then enters an engineering firm as a pupil for two or three years. He may reverse this course by becoming a pupil in the works for three years, and at the end of that period entering a technical college or university. In Scotland and the North of England it is not uncommon for a pupil to attend college during term time and spend the vacations in the workshops.

Without going into detail, the diagram shows that a university or technical college education is required by an engineering pupil who wishes to rise in his profession.

In the middle of the diagram the position of apprentice is shown. This is open to boys from secondary, trade, central, and elementary schools. During his course of apprenticeship the boy should take advantage of all technical classes to which he has access. By this means, if he has the necessary ability, he may enter the drawing office and stand a chance of rising to a high position. In any case, technical knowledge is necessary if the apprentice wishes to become a properly skilled man.

On the left of the diagram are shown the more irregular and uncertain methods of entering the occupation.

The elementary schoolboy may enter a works as a learner, and under proper conditions may have nearly as good a chance of learning the trade as the apprentice. It is most important that he should gain as much technical knowledge as he can by attendance at classes. In this way the best trade positions become open to him, and he may get into the drawing office and the higher positions in the engineering world.

Many boys go as unskilled workers into engineering firms. It is more difficult for them to enter the ranks of the skilled men, but to a youth of energy and ability it is by no means impossible. It depends largely upon the youth himself. He must improve

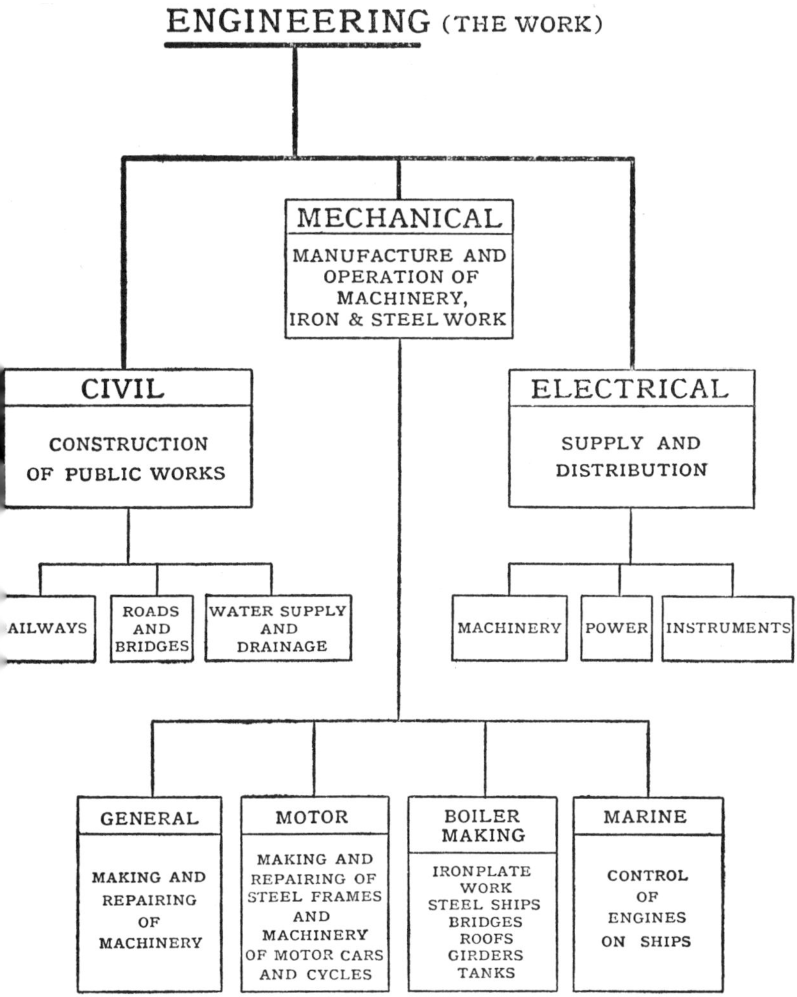

Each Branch of Engineering shown on this Diagram contains many subdivisions

his practical experience in every way he can, and supplement it with technical knowledge by attending classes.

All boys who wish to get on should remember that the lack of a good general education is generally the greatest obstacle to a youth who has to fight his way upwards, and should not neglect to pay early and serious attention to this branch of education.

The extreme left of the diagram shows that many unskilled workers either become semi-skilled or leave the occupation.

ENGINEERING

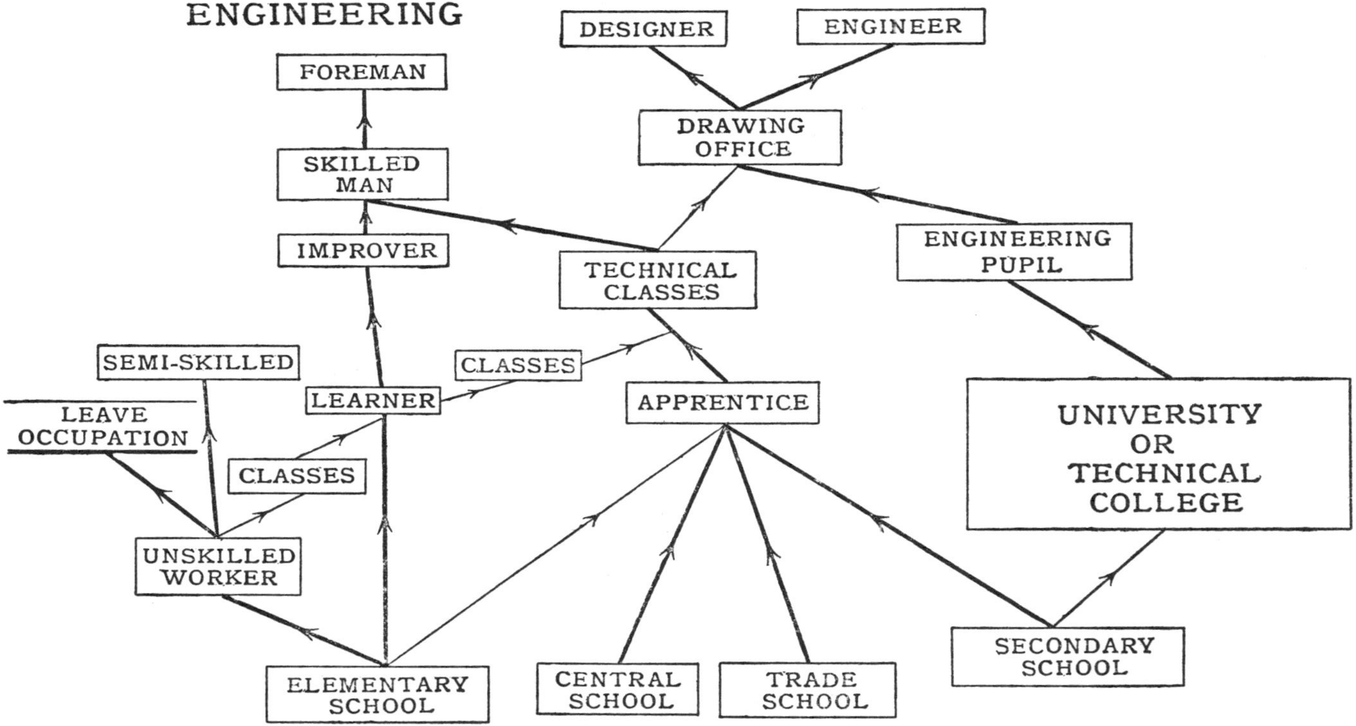

MECHANICAL ENGINEERING

This diagram gives in outline the positions to which a boy may rise.

The figure in the right centre represents the group of trades which probably offer the best chances to the average boy.

A boy usually enters an engineering firm as a learner or apprentice. The first few months are often spent on odd jobs in the store, works, or office. He is then put on to work in one of the shops; it is very likely that he will first go into the machine shop. This includes the work of machine-minding, and should lead to turning, fitting, and erecting; it forms a distinct group within which a boy will find sufficient scope for learning and promotion.

The youth in the machine shop will be put in charge of a simple machine; if he shows ability, and is in a good firm, he may be transferred from machine to machine so as to learn as many processes as possible. In this way he picks up a good deal of fitting, and may be transferred to the fitting shop. Here the youth learns the building-up or erecting of machines. Some fitters become tool-makers. A specially able boy may go from turning and fitting into the drawing office, but as a rule a youth remains in this branch. He has chances of rising to charge hand or leading hand, and chances of becoming foreman. If he possesses the necessary technical knowledge he may rise to be an assistant works manager.

On the extreme left is shown the best course to follow to rise to the higher ranks.

An apprentice may go directly into the drawing office, but as a rule a premium is required for this. Ability to draw is not sufficient: knowledge of mathematics, theoretical knowledge, and workshop experience are necessary if the draughtsman wishes to rise to designer or manager.

To the right of the drawing office comes the pattern-maker. A skilful pattern-maker may be transferred to the drawing office, or he may become foundry foreman or manager.

Founding.—Boys are not as a rule taken for moulding directly. They do odd jobs for the foremen, and are promoted by degrees to moulding.

Smithing.—Boys do not as a rule enter smithing directly. Sometimes they begin as forge boys or odd boys in smithing.

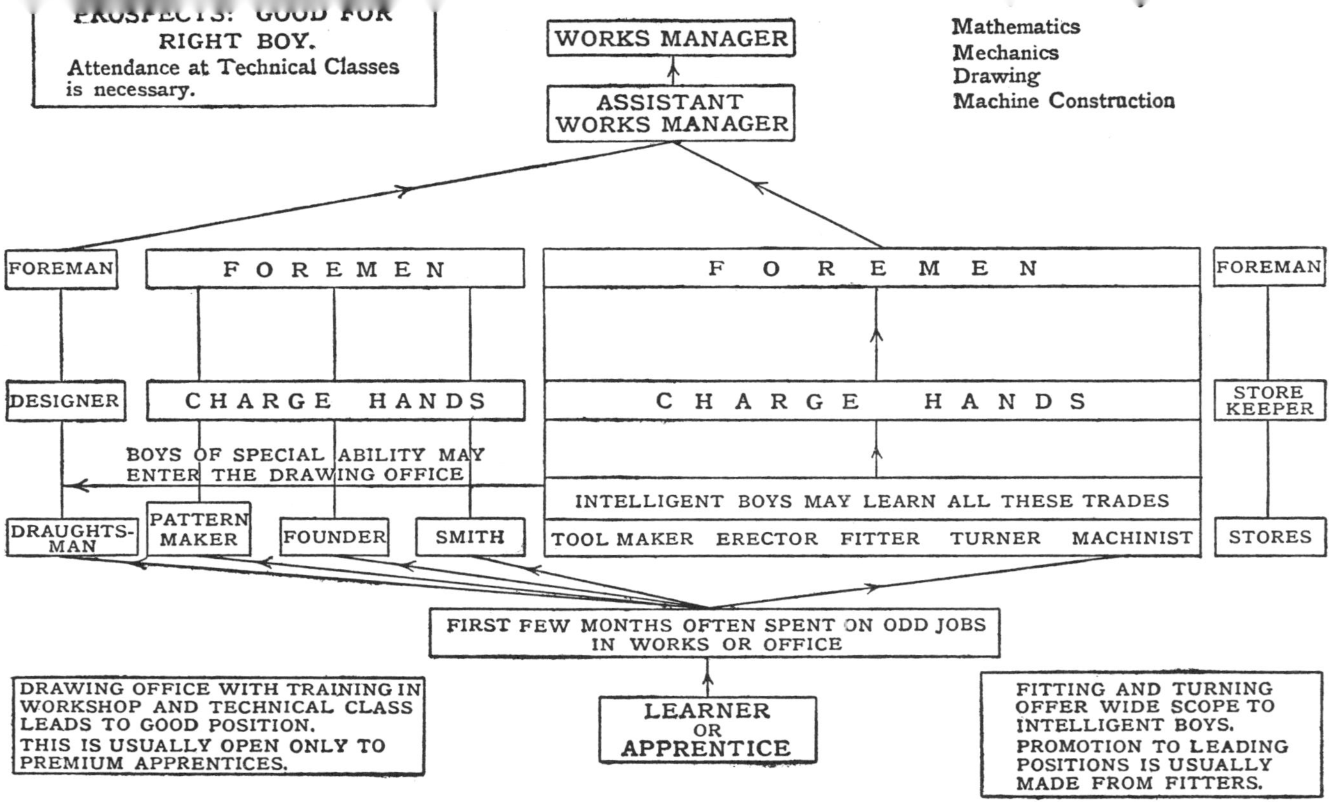
PROSPECTS: GOOD FOR RIGHT BOY.
Attendance at Technical Classes is necessary.
WORKS MANAGER
ASSISTANT WORKS MANAGER
Mathematics
Mechanics
Drawing
Machine Construction
FOREMAN
FOREMEN
FOREMEN
FOREMAN
DESIGNER
CHARGE HANDS
CHARGE HANDS
STORE KEEPER
BOYS OF SPECIAL ABILITY MAY ENTER THE DRAWING OFFICE
INTELLIGENT BOYS MAY LEARN ALL THESE TRADES
DRAUGHTS-MAN
PATTERN MAKER
FOUNDER
SMITH
TOOL MAKER
ERECTOR
FITTER
TURNER
MACHINIST
STORES
FIRST FEW MONTHS OFTEN SPENT ON ODD JOBS IN WORKS OR OFFICE
DRAWING OFFICE WITH TRAINING IN WORKSHOP AND TECHNICAL CLASS LEADS TO GOOD POSITION.
THIS IS USUALLY OPEN ONLY TO PREMIUM APPRENTICES.
LEARNER OR APPRENTICE
FITTING AND TURNING OFFER WIDE SCOPE TO INTELLIGENT BOYS.
PROMOTION TO LEADING POSITIONS IS USUALLY MADE FROM FITTERS.

AN INSURANCE OFFICE

The diagram represents the career of a clerk in an insurance office. It shows that there are two main branches—Life Insurance and other Insurance. It also points out the various grades of clerk in each branch, and the course of examinations which it is advisable for the ambitious man to take.

The youth who wishes to enter an insurance office should have a good secondary school education, and should have passed matriculation or other similar examination. If he decides to enter the actuarial branch in which the statistical work is done, he will become a junior clerk in the head office. His path of progress through actuarial clerk is shown. The arrow on the right shows the examinations which the young clerk should take. On the extreme left is shown the course of the man who becomes inspector or branch manager. To the right of the diagram the path is shown of the youth who enters Fire, Accident, or Marine Insurance. A clerk in these sections should take the examinations of the Chartered Insurance Institute, or if these are impossible, the examinations of the Chamber of Commerce. The insets in the bottom right and left of the diagram show the qualifications and prospects of the career.

Work in an insurance office is divided into two main branches, the actuarial or scientific branch, and the administrative and clerical branch.

The actuarial side is not easy to enter, and a high standard of ability and attainments is required, but on the whole the prospects are good.

The actuary is an official (in a life office) whose duty it is to compile statistical records, estimate the necessary rates of premium, and perform the requisite scientific calculations incidental to the periodical valuation of its assets and liabilities. He may be regarded as an expert in the Laws of Chance as they affect human life and property. It is evident that the work of an actuary requires great skill and accuracy in dealing with figures.

A youth who wishes to become an actuary should pay special attention to arithmetic and algebra, and by his mathematical ability should know that he is fit for the career. Distinct and rapid handwriting is valuable.

How to Enter.—The youth who wishes to become an actuary should obtain a clerkship in the head office (life branch) of an insurance company, or a company transacting life business only. This is often difficult to obtain, and generally requires a nomination from a director or one of the chief officials of the

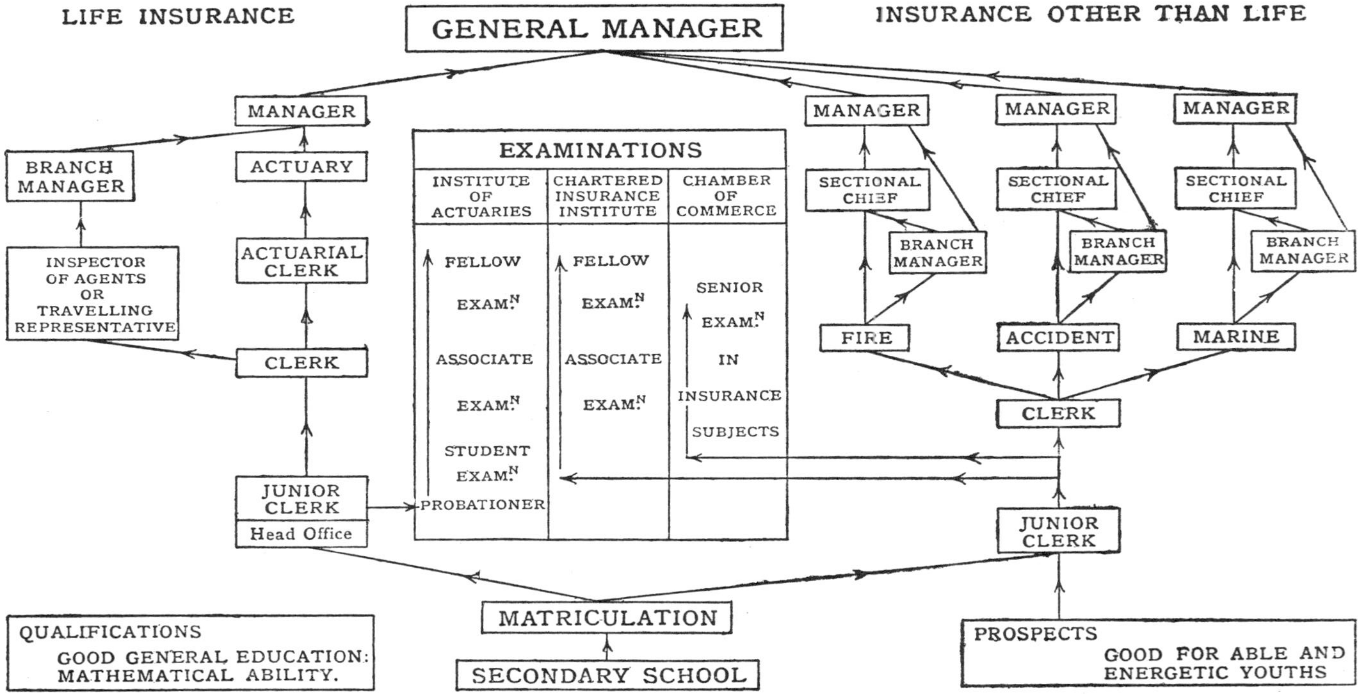
LIFE INSURANCE
GENERAL MANAGER
INSURANCE OTHER THAN LIFE
MANAGER
BRANCH MANAGER
ACTUARY
INSPECTOR OF AGENTS OR TRAVELLING REPRESENTATIVE
ACTUARIAL CLERK
CLERK
JUNIOR CLERK
Head Office
EXAMINATIONS
INSTITUTE OF ACTUARIES
CHARTERED INSURANCE INSTITUTE
CHAMBER OF COMMERCE
FELLOW EXAMN.
ASSOCIATE EXAMN.
STUDENT EXAMN.
PROBATIONER
FELLOW EXAMN.
ASSOCIATE EXAMN.
SENIOR EXAMN. IN INSURANCE SUBJECTS
MANAGER
MANAGER
MANAGER
SECTIONAL CHIEF
SECTIONAL CHIEF
SECTIONAL CHIEF
BRANCH MANAGER
BRANCH MANAGER
BRANCH MANAGER
FIRE
ACCIDENT
MARINE
CLERK
JUNIOR CLERK
MATRICULATION
SECONDARY SCHOOL
QUALIFICATIONS
GOOD GENERAL EDUCATION: MATHEMATICAL ABILITY.
PROSPECTS
GOOD FOR ABLE AND ENERGETIC YOUTHS

company. He should then seek to become a probationer of the Institute of Actuaries. He is then enitled to attend the classes which the Institute has organised for the difficult examinations which have to be passed.

The youth is usually appointed as a junior clerk with a small salary; during this time he acquires experience of the work of his department. In due course he may become an actuarial clerk; and a reputation for exceptional ability in mathematics and calculation may bring him to the post of assistant actuary, and perhaps finally to that of actuary to the company, who is frequently appointed to act as the chief administrative official.

In addition to the practical experience which is obtained in the office, it is essential that the youth, in order to obtain a professional diploma, should pass the examinations which are organised by the Institute of Actuaries; or the kindred Scottish body, the Faculty of Actuaries.

There are three classes of the Institute—Students, Associates, and Fellows—and there are qualifying examinations. Candidates for admission to the first examination must have passed matriculation or other similar examination.

Examination for Admission as Student.—

1. Arithmetic and Algebra; the theory and use of logarithms; the Elements of the Theory of Probabilities.
2. The Elements of the Calculus of Finite Differences, including Interpolation and Summation; Elementary Differential and Integral Calculus.
3. Compound Interest and Annuities-Certain, including the construction and use of Relative Tables.

Examination for Admission as Associate.—This examination is more fully professional; it includes the use of Life Tables, the classification of policies, some knowledge of banking and of Stock Exchange operations and procedure.

Examination for Admission as Fellow.—This examination includes the methods of compiling mortality and similar statistics, the determination of premium rates for various types of assurance, the value of assurance, companies liabilities, the determination of extra premiums for special circumstances, etc.

It also comprises the law relating to assurance companies, life assurance accounts, and administration generally, a considerable knowledge of the money market and of banking finance and foreign exchanges generally, assurance companies' investments, the practical valuation of policies and other kindred subjects.

Full particulars of these examinations can be obtained from the Assistant Secretary, Institute of Actuaries, Staple Inn, Holborn Bars, W.C.

The Administrative and Clerical Branch.—The youth who enters this branch should have similar qualification to a candidate for the actuarial side. He will enter an insurance office as a junior clerk about the age of seventeen years, with a small salary. In time the youth may rise to become head of a small department, and in this way may gradually rise in the office until he is qualified to undertake the more responsible sections of the company's business.

The higher posts of surveyor, superintendent, and branch manager in an office transacting all forms of insurance are open to men of ability who have a thorough knowledge of their profession. This may be obtained by supplementing the practical experience which is gained in the office by taking the examinations organised by the Chartered Insurance Institute.

Candidates for admission to these examinations must have passed matriculation or other similar examination.

Examinations for Admission as Associate and as Fellow.—Particulars of these examinations can be obtained from the Secretary, Chartered Insurance Institute, 11 Queen Street, E.C.

Insurance clerks who do not take the examinations of the Institute should take the senior examinations of the Chamber of Commerce in subjects relating to insurance.

Prospects.—It is generally agreed that work in an insurance office has good prospects for men who have the ability and energy to undertake the long course of study which is required to pass the necessary examinations. The insurance clerk who wishes to rise to a good position should endeavour to qualify as an actuary or as a Fellow of the Insurance Institute. The higher ranks of the profession are not crowded, and during the time that the clerk is qualifying for these positions he is largely supporting himself.

Salary.—The salary to commence is from £50–£80 per annum, with annual increments thereafter, usually on a definite scale.

A fully qualified actuarial clerk will receive from £400–£600 per year.

An actuary will receive from £500–£1,500, while the income of a manager may run into thousands.

The salaries of clerks on the administrative and clerical side are similar in the early stages to those of clerks in the actuarial department.

A routine clerk would probably earn about up to £300 per year, while the head of a department would probably get a minimum of £500 per annum.

CHAPTER VI

TWO CAMPS

The intention in the preceding five chapters has been to indicate that on our youth—for the principle applies to both sexes—depends the future of our country; that far too little attention has been paid to the value and education of youth; the use made of that education, if given; the opportunities of forward progress; the methods applied to giving it; and the methods of enlisting the young in the interest and objects of work.

True it is that, partly as the effect of the War, and as a lesson learnt during the War, steps to better education are being evolved, vocational training is slowly coming under consideration, attention in many a business is being given to amenities, comforts, and recreations never previously considered; the idea of sympathy is published far and wide, and plans for enlisting the workers in joint effort are being tentatively tried. There are developments of the work of conciliation and attempted goodwill, which was slowly coming into being before the War, and had extended a network of boards and associations in the principal trades of the country. There is also a Government dictating from above plans of development remarkable for the number of officials which they entail, and their excessive cost.

All these efforts cannot alter in a day the tendency of several generations; the neglect of youth so spasmodically treated by Governments, employers, and trade unions; the economic movements so generally accepted as intractable, and necessarily leading to unemployment and poverty; or prevent the country being faced with demands for a new order of things or a complete change in the social structure.

It may be said that generalisations are not practicable

about masses of people on both sides; and it is undoubtedly difficult to lay down in brief language propositions applicable to all classes of employers or workpeople. Exceptions may be cited as not supporting a general rule. And yet, the well-known phrase "Capital and Labour" emphasises the view that there are in this country two rival camps or armies, acting sometimes in veiled and sometimes in open opposition to each other, and, according to some prophets, preparing with speed for an open and bitter fight. If such a fight occurred, it would leave behind it as much trouble as the wars of nations; it would ruin the chances of production on which the future depends, it might introduce tyranny far worse than this country has ever known. Hostility has not been abolished by the War, although often turned against new men, many of whom have risen by the War; and if the country is to succeed in repairing the damages of the War and avoid serious trouble in the future, the employing class and the workpeople must unite in a common effort and realise that their interests are identical. Change of mind cannot be very quickly effected, but is generally the result of growth. Traditions, vested interests, class opinion, individual faddism are obstacles, but the rush of opinion has much force in whatever direction it may trend. The question is whether it will trend in the direction of peace or of war; and whether, if great social changes are to be effected, changes will come as the result of an upheaval or after a succession of petty quarrels paralysing the industry of the country, or by peaceful arrangements. Briefly, the proposition is this: that if peaceful arrangement is the best issue for the country and its people as a whole, the two camps or armies now fixed, or getting fixed, in growing hostility, have got to amalgamate and unite in a common purpose: the theory that one side must beat the other has to be thrown out as a bad theory by both sides; and Capital, being unable to beat Labour, as it has tried to do, must more and more recognise that man is not a mere producing-machine, to be worked as a machine, but that human interest and opportunity for the redress of valid grievances and mutual ignorance will do more to enlist men to work together for a common purpose than making the cheapest bargain that can be made with the individual workman or with a trade union.

Men may be contiguous to each other, but yet are isolated

in fact, unless they have a common purpose. If the spirit or the ideal of joint success and of the value of increased production to all concerned can be obtained in any works or undertakings, those undertakings will be the last to have to fear dictation by trade unions, because the trade unions would have no valid ground of complaint. They will also have better opportunity of settling difficulties with their own workmen without the interference of third parties or the Government. They will out-distance or absorb their competitors, who will have from self-interest to follow suit. Any employer who sets himself to develop his business and push forward, carrying his young workmen with him by care for their valid interests, and refusing to be tied down by the level of the most obsolete or badly equipped works in the trade, is bound to find his enterprise and care leading to good results. It may be very difficult, and the hindrances may be great. The application of principle in some industries may be very hard to accomplish. The workers cannot be taught the lesson or be brought to understanding and trust in a day; but they soon know who are good employers and who are the bad. The time has passed when employers can afford to ignore the fact that, unless there is to be continued hostility between two opposing forces, they must show the worker the real objective to which the employer is working; they must consider the comfort and well-being of the worker as a human being; they must have suitable methods of listening to and redressing valid complaints, either by the workmen themselves, or by the workmen with the aid of the management; they must endeavour to ensure to all workmen a direct interest in the result of their work, and enlist their activity in mutual success; and see that the curtailment of advancement or chance of advancement to the youth does not reduce the worker to the position of a machine. A new atmosphere is required in which men can breathe more freely.

The present atmosphere is the issue of a long history. In spite of the theories advanced of the scientific movements of Labour, as if Labour had followed a clearly defined line and supported with inevitable trend the carefully prepared schemes of studious philosophers or the tocsin of inspired and compelling leaders, facts show that no defined line has ever had more than a brief existence.

Strategy has been practically absent. Tactics have been pursued by a few divisional commanders, whose period of office has generally been short, and who, if they are successful, have been hampered by a failure in details which frequently obscures the success. The majority of divisional commanders have failed to have any vision beyond the operations of their own section on which they have concentrated, and of their own men, whom alone they understand.

These remarks may be upsetting to the complacency of historians or writers who wish to make Labour movements fit in with their theories or follow lines which they have mapped out as desirable, but I can only say that Labour has had no great leader, though many have aspired to be leaders; that such leaders as it has had have only been divisional commanders; that it has had no real solidarity, or any ideal views, which it could confidently say must be carried through on every ground of unanimous demand, expediency, and right. If one can say so without offence, class hatred has been helped by the stupidity of the majority of employers, because they have neglected the youths whom they might have assisted, and whose chances in life they might have endeavoured to improve, with a view to the broad issue of better understanding. Class hatred, too, and their own failure as great leaders, have been caused by the action of Labour leaders, who have preached war, and discontent, and theoretical changes, when the advocacy of unity, better understanding, better chances for their flock would have gained more for themselves and for others than anything they have been able to obtain.

Why should Labour leaders have been successful? They have had their own way to fight; their own families to help; a precarious position to maintain; aspirations for their own success entirely inconsistent with any doctrines they might suggest of squeezing "the whole world, visible and invisible, into an imaginary straight line, and in such a manner as to prevent anybody from moving backwards, forwards, to the right or to the left."

They have had vast numbers of men and women to deal with, consisting of individuals wrapped up, so far as industry goes, in their own narrow knowledge of a small section of one industry, and probably looking to the immediate future of their own particular success in that small section, or the interests of that section only ; and also governed, each in a way necessarily unknown to the man who proposes to voice their wants, by mixed motives, varied characters, and desire for one or many of the domestic hopes common to every man : sports, girls, wives, children, home. *They* do not want a strike for a theory or a law, and ought not to be asked to strike for a misunderstanding or some paltry cause which could be settled by a talk ; but they will strike for economic reasons, due to causes which they do not understand, and which are never explained to them, when " the wail of intolerable serfage," as Disraeli called it, meets with no answer, when they realise they have no opportunity for improvement except by a general rise of the grade to which they belong, or when they see signs of prosperity in others and no corresponding or relative improvement in their own. " See that man," said an old Bradford weaver to me, as a motor passed by, with a man and fur-clad woman. " Twelve months ago he hadn't got more than a donkey ; and here am I in the same old clothes. That's why I am on strike, as you know. But you'll see justice done, as far as you can, you will."

Justice is that desirable end which the majority of working men would wish to achieve, and often very different from the political aims which are set forth as their hope by some of their divisional commanders.

CHAPTER VII

THE DOCKERS' DISPUTE OF 1889

On the principle that a question is best understood by examination of facts rather than by argument on theory, an account of some of the chief disputes between employers and employed may serve to throw light upon some of the vexed questions of the present day. Their variations may serve at least to cause some thought on methods of dealing with the youth of the nation, and the subject of unity or enmity beween class and class. Having been concerned in a very large number of these disputes, some account of them may indicate the course of events, and lead the reader either to revise estimates formed only upon theory, or to find fresh material for the support of views which have occurred to his mind. Historical development is always interesting. The trend of events, ideas, political and social movements always are based upon structures existing in the past, which may be rising story by story, or gradually falling into decay.

The present atmosphere is, as I have said, the issue of a long history. Generation overlaps generation, memories remain, ideas develop or are cast aside. It is not my purpose to follow that development through all its ramifications. Historical accounts have been written in many books. It may suffice to say that almost all the Socialism, Syndicalism, and other issues of the present day have in one form or another been discussed during the last century, and some of them have been tried in the course of the building up of the industrial system of Great Britain, and the huge developments which had been reached before the War. The general impression left by the history of these struggles is an impression of confused purposes partly due to the rapidity of economic changes and the development of a vast Empire. The great wave of development coming in the sixties would seem to have arrived at a time when the family or local business still continued as a prevailing system, with close and narrow competition between businesses of comparatively small dimensions. Individual contract at the lowest possible price governed the relation between employer and employed. Any combination among the workpeople was against the law. The union was a secret conspiracy and was not recognised. Arbitration as a means of settling difficulties was refused, even in the most suitable cases. It was regarded as an attempted method of gaining recognition for an illegal society, and had no foothold whatever. Conciliation was almost unknown. There came a period when joint-stock companies began rapidly to take the place of the old class of business, and their relations with their workpeople certainly reduced personal interest between employer and employee, and increased mutual ignorance. In the early seventies the recognition by the law of the legality of combination, and the vast expansion of trade, gave a short period of support for arbitration, when it suited employers to take almost any decision rather than have stoppage of work; and when it also suited the union leaders, who had attempted to obtain its acceptance on the ground that the decision of the arbitrator tended to establish a common rule, which governed the firms within the arbitration, and might be extended to firms not expressly bound by it. About 1874 the wave of prosperity began to lose force, and it was not long before reduction of wages, longer hours, and changes of conditions came in rapidly, in spite of repeated strikes. The unions found themselves far too weak to maintain their position. They were not sufficiently organised, and they had to recognise that fact. Advantages gained in the previous years proved to be illusory. Even in industries generally governed by sliding scales, special reductions were asked for and obtained. There was lack of organisation on the side of Labour, and on the side of the employers little attempt, so it would seem, to carry the goodwill of Labour. Weak organisation fell to pieces. The individual was liable to have piece prices cut if he appeared to be earning too much, while the incentive of production arising from good reward for good results does not appear, in the close competition at a time of depressed trade, to have been recognised as a desirable principle.

The seeds of much ill-will and suspicion, of which the growth has continued to the present day, gained strength in those years. The remembrance has not died away.

It seems to have been felt, by the most able leaders of Labour, that organisation was faulty, and that without organised unions no general advance in the conditions of Labour could be obtained. Beneath the surface great efforts were undoubtedly being made in this direction, but the movement which in fact caused Labour to learn its power did not come from organised labour in the skilled trades, much less from the political aims of Labour leaders. In 1889 the great Dock Strike started with a strike of match-girls and casual labour at the London docks, classes of labour, in the beginning at least, remarkable by their lack of organisation; but it was led, and in a measure headed, after the first outbursts, by two able leaders, Mr. John Burns and Mr. Tom Mann. It was economic, not political, the revolt of the many against the absence of the margin of subsistence, and although in the mind of Mr. John Burns, as he has said, the prevailing purpose was to diminish the evils of casual labour, the minds of the majority of those who struck were centred on the dockers' sixpence for which they struggled.

The skilled trade unions, except the stevedores, had no part or lot in the dockers' strike. They looked on, divorced from the movement, as they have been divorced from many a movement in which unskilled labour has been concerned. It was left for the match-girls to strike the flame which soon flickered up into a fire. So, too, in later years, the outbreaks of 1911 began in the ports with unskilled labour, spreading to those industries where men were graded in large numbers on a fixed and low wage, from which ability, education, or zeal gave them little opportunity to rise; and in 1913 the outbreak, which swept like a prairie fire through the Midlands, commenced with girls at Dudley who said they could no longer live on the wages they received, and would prefer the streets; and in 1915 the strikes of the War began with the dockers on the Clyde, who saw others making profits while they had received an insufficient share.

In 1889 neither the State nor employers nor skilled labour had realised the importance of getting down to the root of the matter, of estimating the pressure of economic circumstances which might be borne in times of scarcity, but with better education and better means of knowledge, and under the influence of widespread propaganda, would not be borne in quiet when prices began to advance and no reciprocal share of improvement kept pace with the rising prices, when the door of advancement was shut and mutual effort was so little practised. Lessons are slowly learnt. The same facts and the same results, in spite of the lessons of conciliation, have been forthcoming to the present day, although skilled labour, by the force of circumstances, has so much altered its tone, and with grievances of its own has attempted to join with those organisations of semi-skilled and unskilled labour which have so vastly and persistently increased since the Dock Strike of 1889. Have they found a common enemy in the employing class or employing companies? And can they unite all trades and all members in a belief that employers are to be changed in favour of State-ownership and State-management, and that industries will so flourish and the workers' status and comfort be generally improved?

The effect of the dockers' strike of 1889 was not limited to the dockers' sixpence. It was from 1889 that many began to think that the power of Labour by collective action sufficiently prolonged and directed against the industry of a great port, particularly if the sympathy and support of the public were enlisted on its side, could be effective, although limited by amount of organisation. It was then, too, that attention was called to the condition of casual labour and unemployment, which led to various experiments, by Acts of Parliament and otherwise, for the purpose of mitigating it. It was then, too, that efforts at conciliation were found not to be without result, a belief fostered by the closing of the long sixteen weeks' coal dispute in the Midlands, under the chairmanship of Lord Rosebery, in 1893; the national agreement established, through the Board of Trade, in the Boot and Shoe trade in 1895; and the reference of the North-Eastern Railway dispute to Sir Henry James in the same year. The dockers' strike, it seems to me, from the various accounts of it, marked a great epoch in the relations of Capital and Labour. It gave a great impulse to the Labour Movement. It revived the waning spirits of trade unions and led to increase in their numbers, particularly in semi-skilled and unskilled trades. It showed efforts which some of their leaders thought would mark out the best method of advance in the future, but it did little or nothing in the way of humanising the relations between employers and employed.

More than a generation has passed away since that great dispute of 1889. In spite of the ferment that it caused throughout the world, a Commission of Inquiry in 1920 has still to report that " the system of casualisation must, if possible, be torn up by the roots. It is wrong," endorsing the very views expressed by Mr. John Burns in the House of Commons in 1910 and on Tower Hill in 1889, and supporting, in line after line, principles on the payment and utilisation of casual labour which in various ports I had from time to time, over a period of years, been able to propose. The root of the matter is still not reached. In spite of the efforts of individual employers in various ports, there has been no general attempt to grapple with the problem, or, whatever the intervening stages may be, to make the dockers' work a stable trade which lads should be glad to enter, and in which they should have opportunities to advance ; and where, I might add, unemployment should be the business of the trade, and not thrown on the community as a whole.

CHAPTER VIII

THE CONCILIATION ACT, 1896

THE years following the dockers' strike provided a period of political strife, and were followed by the Boer War. The condition of the people was not the foremost subject of the day in the eyes of the Legislature. Labour unions gained adhesion of members, and then again lost members in the varying phases of contraction of trade in 1892 and 1893, and agricultural depression in 1894 and 1895, the margin of adherents being, however, very largely in their favour. On the whole, organisation was their obvious ideal, and gradual pressure for such regulation of the conditions of employment as would give to workers a minimum standard of life, that long-standing demand of trade unions. Government had established a Royal Commission on Labour, resulting in a very negative report. In the face of unemployment, it is not easy to meet employers who in answer to demands would close a business without much demur, if it is being run with very small profit or at an absolute loss. Shortening of hours was being pressed in some industries, culminating in the engineering dispute of 1897, but chiefly with a view to better certainty of being maintained in work. Nationalisation was feebly advocated in the belief that the national purse was longer than that of individual employers. A salient fact which did seem to emerge was that conciliation in the coal strike of 1893 and in the boot dispute of 1895 had been deemed to end protracted and obstinate disputes; and in 1896 the Government of the day ventured the introduction of a Bill, which became law under the title of the Conciliation Act, 1896, or "An Act to make better provision for the Prevention and Settlement of Trade Disputes." This Act was practically permissive in its terms. Clause 1 allowed any Board constituted or authorised for the purpose of settling disputes between employers and workmen by conciliation or arbitration to be registered with the Board of Trade; but this clause has been utilised to a very small extent. Clause 2 (1) gave power, where a difference exists or is apprehended, (*a*) to inquire into the causes and circumstances of the difference; (*b*) take such steps as to the Board may seem expedient for the purpose of enabling the parties to the difference to meet together, by themselves or their representatives, under the presidency of a chairman mutually agreed upon or nominated by the Board of Trade, or by some other person or body, with a view to the amicable settlement of the difference; (*c*) on the application of employers or workmen interested, and after taking into consideration the existence and adequacy of means available for conciliation in the district or trade and the circumstances of the case, appoint a person or persons to act as conciliator or as a board of conciliation; (*d*) on the application of both parties to the difference, appoint an arbitrator. A conciliator so appointed was to inquire into the causes and circumstances of the difference and report his proceedings to the Board. By clause 4 the expediency of establishing conciliation boards for a district or trade might be discussed, and by clause 7 three obsolete Acts of 1824, 1867, and 1872 were repealed.

Any success likely to occur under this Act entirely depended on the acceptance by both parties of any aid which an inquiry might give, but it gave no power, without agreement of both sides, for any arbitration to be held, and no power to get one side or the other to accept any suggestions made by a conciliator, either in a report or at a meeting where he might be present. The Act itself gave no indication of the principles to be pursued, or in what direction either an arbitrator or conciliator was to act. Different men might pursue different methods. No system of co-ordination was proposed. At the last moment powers to compel attendance of witnesses or disclosure of documents were omitted. The Act did little more than declare that the Board of Trade could make inquiry or send an appointed officer to see the parties, with the slight protection that officer might have by being able to say that he was acting under a statute, if the right to inquire was challenged. In the course of a generation the Act has become known through the United Kingdom. It was proposed to repeal it in the Bill which has recently led to the Act establishing Industrial Courts, but the Government ultimately decided that it should remain upon the Statute-book. It may be that its practical use will continue when more novel enactments have been scrapped, but it will at least always be remarkable as the very slight legislative base upon which all the conciliation and arbitration work done by the Government, with the wide extension in imitation of it carried out by associations of employers or firms and trade unions, was administered from the year 1896 until the passing of the Munitions of War Acts in 1915. It marked a period, but did nothing by itself to reconcile the growing force of Labour and the resistance of Capital. The idea of united action may perhaps be discerned in the fact that the Act was passed. It was not shown that conciliation was possible, much less that any step could be taken to organise Capital and Labour in any trade as a joint effort. In fact, it was a mere skeleton, and a skeleton so restricted in shape and size as necessarily to affect any life with which it might be endowed.

As this Act was the sole legislative authority under which any efforts at conciliation or arbitration by me, and later under my direction, were authorised during a number of years, it may be permissible to mention how I came into connection with it.

It was in April 1895, when Sir Henry James was requested, by agreement of the parties, in face of a general strike, to arbitrate on the wages, hours, and some of the conditions affecting men on the North-Eastern Railway, that I was for the first time brought into contact with a labour dispute. Each railway company at that date acted by itself, and considerable disapproval and apprehension existed over this consent to arbitration and any recognition of a trade union. It was felt by other companies that decisions, particularly on a connecting railway like the North-Eastern, would react upon their lines. The method pursued, and necessarily pursued, owing to the large number of grades and the interlocking of wage questions and relative positions between grade and grade, so characteristic of every railway company, had to be a friendly discussion by Mr. George Gibb, the general manager, and Mr. Richard Bell for the railway servants, before an umpire who could not possibly know the details, but who had the power to give a final decision, and thus override differences which he could not solve by conciliation. I was only present as an assistant and friend of Sir Henry James, becoming during the proceedings a friend also of the representatives of the parties: but the experience of the many days during which the case lasted showed me that conciliation was much more likely to adjust differences and to be acceptable than arbitration, and that, however different were the interests and characters of the parties concerned, the humanising of the matter, the element of sympathy, could remove difficulties apparently impossible to reconcile when they were first discussed. The difficulty of reconciling the parties outside who were awaiting the result of the decisions which might be reached was a question not so apparent to me at that time as it afterwards became. I could not then try to gauge what they would think, except by the statements of the spokesmen as to their belief of probable effects.

Sir Henry James also asked me to assist him in an inquiry into lead-poisoning in the Potteries; disputes, of which he was umpire, in the boot and shoe trade; and an engineering and shipbuilding dispute on the Clyde. These cases, proved to be useful lessons in different forms of inquiry, but I cite them only to show that cognisance of labour questions cannot be gained in a day, as so many would-be conciliators, especially politicians, appear to think, and in remembrance of a man who received much confidence from both employers and employed, largely owing to his desire to bring them together.

Work on these cases probably led to my selection by the Board of Trade for certain cases under the Conciliation Act, while practising at the Bar and sometimes occupied for a long time in cases, like the Anglo-Venezuelan-Guiana boundary arbitration, which prevented continuity of work. Like other barristers or neutral persons chosen by the Board of Trade for cases of arbitration or conciliation as they might arise, I took cases to which the Board of Trade appointed me. There was no opportunity of a fixed scheme or development of ideas; but only the chance of doing the best that one could in cases not selected by oneself. Mr. Arthur Wilson Fox, who had to deal, under the President for the time being and also under the Comptroller-General of the Commercial Labour and Statistical Department, then a small department, with cases under the Conciliation Act, was an extremely busy man. Departmentally he had tried to work the Act, and in some instances with great success, as in assisting to establish in 1897 the basis of a conference between the parties in the great engineering strike on the subject of an eight-hour day and workshop control. He could not possibly afford the time both for the office work done under the control of others and for uncertain and prolonged absences from Whitehall. Mr. John Burnett, indeed, was attached to the office, but he was not given much opportunity, and had become chiefly interested in the study of various labour questions and writing excellent reports upon strikes and lockouts from a statistical point of view. There was, therefore, an opening for work to any man who could successfully carry out and continue to carry out the delicate work of conciliation.

At first the Conciliation Act had not led to many important cases, and the Board of Trade averred that their policy was caution. There were a few arbitrations, on questions such as the rise or fall of $\frac{1}{2}d.$ an hour in wages of different districts in the building trade, a few hopeless cases where the men were already beaten and interference was resented, a few "tries" at a New Act to see how it worked, but no salient cases are to be found in the reports presented to Parliament, with the exception of the Penrhyn Quarry dispute. While agreeing with some of the proposals of his employees, Lord Penrhyn had refused an advance in wages and the recognition of a quarry committee, with the result that about 2,800 quarrymen left work in September 1896. At the same time they applied to the Board of Trade to take action under the Conciliation Act passed in the previous month. It is unnecessary to enter into the details of this dispute, but it excited great popular interest and led to debates in the House of Commons. Mr. Ritchie, then President of the Board of Trade, dealt with the case himself. Apparently he wrote a strong letter to Lord Penrhyn, which was taken as an order or a threat. Lord Penrhyn replied, rejecting any interference between him and his men, and the strike eventually lasted at least eleven months, without any successful solution by the Board of Trade. This case was a salient example of the inadvisability of interference which was, or might be construed to be, political interference in a trade dispute by a Minister, in place of handing over the dispute to an official or an outside person who would deal with it without any possible political complexion, express or implied. It was for a time a precedent which warned Ministers against political interference. It was a lesson, too, to the trade unions, who, in furtherance of old precedents, again attempted to dabble in industry by buying and setting up rival works in other quarries, where they lamentably failed. The alluring prospect has not, so far as I am aware, been since attempted, though sometimes advocated by newspapers or proposed by employers ignorant of its futility. A definite offer to run the Chepstow shipyards under the control of trade unions was refused quite recently by the unions concerned. Incidentally, however, the strike happened to give me an opportunity and an experience which coloured, and still colours, my views on the relations of Capital and Labour. Mr. Ritchie, much heckled at Croydon, in November 1897, over his action in the Penrhyn strike, was able to cite a telegram that the Board of Trade had successfully settled a long-standing and bitter dispute in Scotland, and claimed that the Board of Trade could and did settle strikes. The telegram arrived in the nick of time. It enabled him to cope with a real difficulty—and probably led to my appointment in a succession of the most difficult cases where action under the Conciliation Act was suggested.

The telegram had been sent by me from Scotland. I had been asked by the Board of Trade whether I would make an effort to settle a strike which had lasted for over four months. From the very first the matter seemed to be almost hopeless. The union, although it was making no headway, did not like to make any move, for fear of showing weakness. Their leaders even asked to see me in another part of the country. There, after a long interview, beginning with some bluff, they told me they would wish the strike to be settled in any possible way, provided the workers could return to their work. Going to Glasgow and then to the place itself, I found the employers as obstinate as men could be—no recognition, no conditions, no return of any person who was supposed to have taken any active part in the dispute, no listening to any complaints. I found the various works situated in the hills, where factories had been built and the people taught by a man obtained from an English trade which certain Scottish merchants hoped to cut out and undersell by means of cheap labour and low rates of wages. They were supposed to have made large profits, and the claim had been for 2*s.* a week advance and reinstatement of some workers alleged to have been dismissed for adhesion to a union. When the dispute, germinating, according to the employers at the dictation of outsiders, according to the workers because they could not stand the wages any longer, resulted in a strike, and then in a general lock-out, free labour was called in. The mills were working night and day with men collected by a well-known "free labour" man from Lancashire. A strong guard of police formed a ring round the works. When I arrived in the evening men were listlessly standing at street-corners, with empty pipes in their mouths, unable to work. There was no other work in the district to which they could turn their hands. Women and children were pale with absolute hunger. Some went on their knees and prayed me to settle the dispute. From that day to this I have loathed the effects of a strike, the continual uselessness of this method of settling differences. I went to those employers next day, determined to get a settlement. I kept them in argument and without food for nine hours on end. I tried every means I could devise, and I think literally wore them down. At last they signed a document even better than what the men had told me they would take; but, foodless as I was, it took me two hours more to persuade those men that they could not possibly get more, when they advanced new points as soon as they saw there was a possibility of a settlement.

The document being signed by both parties, I went under escort of two constables, who insisted on guarding me lest I should be taken in the night for an employer, down to the brilliantly lighted mills, working their night-shift. There the employers, guarded as were the mills, were holding a concert, the free-labour leader, a good singer and comedian, entertaining them. Their astonishment when I suddenly entered and told them the strike was ended, and at meeting in converse the man who had been fighting them all day, remains in my memory. The next day, on leaving the station, I met the free-labour leader. He told me that, though his life was given to breaking strikes, owing to his father being killed by strikers at Pittsburgh, he had got sick of this one—the distress was too great,

He was glad to go, and so were his men. At a later date he gave up this work, and in fact, in a difficult dispute in Lancashire, voluntarily gave me useful information which aided me in settling it. At a later date, too, years after, I met the same firms and their workpeople over a dispute which required the longest consecutive sitting I ever endured—twenty-two hours on end, from 10 a.m. on a Friday to 8 a.m. on a Saturday. They no longer objected to meet the union men. The dispute was not so much between these employers and unionists, but whether both could unite to raise the wages in other new firms in other towns to the same level as existed in their works. The old obstinacy remained, as the length of sitting showed; but the feeling was infinitely better. Could it be that each side had learned a lesson? One employer, at least, said to me, "We took your lessons to heart, and have learned much since then." Both sides hailed me as an old friend; but were curious to learn how I knew or remembered so much about their trade—one of the most intricate in the country. My knowledge had been brought up to date by disputes in the same trade, and in the mills of their rivals in England.

CHAPTER IX

THE TAFF VALE RAILWAY CASE AND THE TRADE DISPUTES ACT, 1906

THE success of Conciliation in indicating a common interest and effecting better understanding between employers and employed does not seem to have made good in 1898, though I cannot claim to have personally followed the movements, owing to engagement in this and the following year on the Guiana Boundary arbitration. In 1898 there appear to have been no important disturbances, except for one great dispute in the South Wales Coal Trade, which lasted 117 days, and involved 100,000 workpeople on claims for an immediate advance of 10 per cent. in wages, higher percentage advances or reductions for every rise or fall of 1*s*. in the average selling-price of coal, a minimum wage, and a joint committee, with an umpire to decide on matters on which the joint committee failed to agree. A strike began in the first week in April, and continued with claims and counter-claims. It was not till June 28th that the men applied to the Board of Trade for the appointment of a conciliator, and when the Board appointed Sir Edward Fry, late Lord Justice of Appeal, " the Associated Employers declined to recognise his position as a conciliator in any way, or to admit of the intervention of any person appointed by the Government or otherwise," a clear indication of the weak effect of the Conciliation Act as an empowering statute.

The year 1899 was " a year of settled good trade; changes of wages were in an upward direction and differences were easily settled. The year is noteworthy for the absence of any dispute of considerable magnitude. Of all the changes of wages and hours in the year, 47 per cent., as measured by the number of persons affected, were arranged by wages boards, sliding scales, or various methods of conciliation and arbitration, while only 3 per cent. of the changes followed strikes." It seemed as if the efficacy of conciliation was slowly growing.

In 1900 disputes were again below the average. "There was no single dispute of such magnitude as to overshadow all others, and 58 per cent. of the changes of wages and hours were arranged by wages boards, sliding scales, or various methods of conciliation and arbitration, while only 5 per cent. followed strikes or lock-outs." Nevertheless there were signs of a change. In the building trades, particularly in the North, employers began to press successfully for reductions in wages; while in other trades, particularly in the mining districts of South Wales, the growing strength of trade unions led to strikes arising from the refusal of unionists to work with non-unionists. This policy was also tried by iron-dressers in the West of Scotland, resulting in a lock-out and failure, while more than a hint that the Amalgamated Society of Railway Servants were trying to get recognition arose on the Taff Vale Railway.

The years 1901 to 1905 passed in comparative calm, although a tendency to reduction of wages led to many small disputes, and in some districts the non-unionist question became from time to time more prominent. The war in South Africa may have had some effect in preventing open disputes. Among the various minor cases to which I was appointed arbitrator or conciliator, a threatened strike of printing compositors in London may be worthy of mention.

There had arisen in the autumn of 1900 a strong demand for an increase of wages, and a reduction of hours from fifty-four to forty-eight hours a week, among the London compositors. The request was met by an absolute refusal; but after some preliminary work by the Board of Trade, both parties at length agreed that the dispute should be referred to an arbitration, to which, in February 1901, I was appointed. It was urgently pressed by the employers that a period of depression in trade was imminent, or existing, and that even through the years of good trade no change had been possible in the "stab" or standard rate of compositors, and ought not be be asked for now. This argument cut both ways, as the men had had no share in better times. It was a difficult arbitration, owing to the great divergency of views of the parties. After a long argument, I decided on a moderate increase of wage and a reduction of hours by one and a half hours per week. The employers were very dissatisfied. Some of the men, who wanted a larger increase of wage rather than a reduction of hours, also complained; but in the result the decision proved right. The award held for many years, and only a few months later several large employers, who had bitterly objected to the reduction of hours, told me that it had brought better time-keeping, better work, and better feeling between the parties. The conciliation board, established by the award as a method of dealing with future disputes, brought the parties together in a manner which had not existed.

The case influenced me to the view that the hours of work in some trades were too long; that the small retrograde firms ought not to govern the standard of the whole of a large trade, even if improvement in wages or conditions made it difficult for small firms to continue; and to an increased belief that better relationship was necessary between the parties for the maintenance of peace in the shop. Owing to the extreme pressure of the employers, and only as an opinion, I appended a footnote indicating that work might be driven to Holland as a result of my decision. This addition was not liked by the Union leaders, though in fact it was harmless; but with better experience I think it was a mistake. It is unnecessary for an arbitrator to prophesy or state pious opinions. No real detriment as suggested occurred in the printing trade, although importations in some classes of the trade may have increased. Constant argument that trade will be driven away if any alteration at all be made, or that some rival will capture it, often proves to be fallacious. Amelioration of conditions is apt to produce better work. If the conditions are improved in some firms, the employees of others are not slow to make demands that the improvements should be copied. The regulations for safety, ventilation, etc., required by the Factory Acts have not driven trade into other lands. Many of them have probably caused better goods to be produced, prolonged the powers of the workers, and obviated the drain of sickness and ill-health. They have tended to make the shop more comfortable, a necessity if the worker is to work with any good heart.

As to opinion about the award, a printers' paper summed it up by saying, "On the face of it, it appears that the men have, if not won all along the line, gained substantial advantages. But we believe there are among their numbers many to whom the award is wholly distasteful, as being too piecemeal. Many would have had the 40*s*. and no reduction in hours; others would have preferred less hours and the same stab rate; yet others, again, think they would have done far better if they had struck; and a few, of the younger ones we need not perhaps add, are for the Society refusing the award altogether. That arbitrator who could give a decision which would wholly satisfy so diversified a body of men—the large majority thinking men—as the London Society of Compositors, would be a veritable archangel; possessed in addition with the diplomacy of an astute politician."

Another type of case may be illustrated by one of a series of small decisions in the tinplate industry, in 1904.

This industry had suffered very heavily from the McKinley Tariff, which had suddenly upset a practical monopoly. The monopoly had led to obsolete machinery and methods, complete lack of uniformity of payment in certain grades, incomplete appreciation of the importance of certain grades in an industry which was bound quickly to reconstitute itself if its trade was to be saved. It did so very well, as the history of the industry in later years has demonstrated; but at that time it had not become so fully organised. A decision given by a third party who had no interest in the trade, after careful hearing of evidence, carried some authority, and was not unwelcome to the trade as a whole, even if nominally it affected only a single firm. Thus a decision as to bar-cutters' rates of wages was thought by a firm to be rather a high rate, but I came to the conclusion that these men were an integral part of the working of the business; they were continually striking; there was no recognised rate of payment, the supply of hefty, strong men being large, however onerous and unpleasant the operation might seem. They were engaged at the cheapest rates such men could be got for, lasted a short time, and were superseded by others. Every time they struck the whole business was held up, numbers of other men losing work. My view was to make them contented, willing to do their part and recognise their position in the success of the undertaking. A few months afterwards, the same employers came to see me, asking to cancel all their remarks ; the result had been good, there had been no further trouble, and the rate had been adopted by their competitors as a rate for South Wales.

The industrial problem which was actually the most important during these years was the protracted discussion over the Taff Vale Railway case, to which allusion has been made ; a case which led up to the Trade Disputes Act of 1906, and largely assisted in establishing the power of the Labour Party in Parliament.

This dispute ostensibly arose over conditions of work and wages, complaints which the directors and general manager, Mr. Beasley, so far met before the actual strike that by themselves they should have become insufficient to cause a stoppage. The feeling engendered by these complaints was aggravated by alleged victimisation of a signalman who did not want to move to a box with higher pay, but not so convenient to his home, and who found that, after an illness, his own box and the proposed box had been filled up. This complaint was so narrowed by the proposals of the Company as to be a bad case, and practically negligible. Underlying these economic complaints there was the great activity of a local delegate and some members of his Committee of the Amalgamated Society of Railway Servants in favour of recognition of the union, which as a matter of principle the Railway Company refused to give. It must be remembered that the policy of the railway companies was to refuse any recognition of unions, and that they were not prepared to follow the example of the North-Eastern Railway in the late nineties. In December 1896 the London and North-Western Railway absolutely refused to " consent to the intervention of third parties in the relations between them and their workmen." The contention was that the Society was weak in numbers and did not represent the men ; that it was inadvisable that one company should pursue a policy entirely inconsistent with the general policy of other companies ; and that, in the interests of public safety on the railways, interference by arbitration or otherwise with the management and regulation of the railways could not be admitted. Mr. Beasley agreed with the opinions of other railway managers,

" that the risk of a strike would be preferable to the settlement of a dispute by outside arbitration."

The head office of the Society had intermittently, for about eight months, during which they had once proposed arbitration, corresponded with South Wales, but although they agreed to give strike pay, they do not seem to have taken much active interest in the situation until after a good dealof whipping-up. A section of men went out on termination of their notices, and others followed without waiting for their notices to expire. Mr. Richard Bell, the General Secretary of the Society, had now arrived at Cardiff, with the support of the President of the Board of Trade and a resolution from his executive. This resolution concluded that the procedure of the men, " by taking action prior to obtaining the consent of the executive committee of the Society, was most condemnatory," that by removal of the signalman the management of the company had acted most arbitrarily, inciting the men to the present act, and that, " having regard to both sides of the issue, we, as administrators of the Society, decide that every effort be made by the general secretary and others we may appoint to bring the dispute to a speedy termination."

Mr. Bell therefore went down to Wales ostensibly on a mission of peace, and it must have been apparent to him that to force the question of recognition on one railway, even if the attempt was successful, would not be very valuable; indeed, he subsequently persuaded the Welshmen not to press this form of representation. He arrived in the midst of turmoil, local agents sending out telegrams about blacklegs, stoppage of trains, warnings to other railwaymen on other lines not to handle Taff Vale goods, pickets, and the usual incidents of an excited strife. He is said to have made a speech, with the words that he came with the determination to fight, but with the additional remark that he did not wish to say anything to irritate the situation, which, as a matter of fact, was not improved by the collieries having to stop and 100,000 sympathetic miners joining in the shouting crowds.

It would be clear to anyone that the introduction of " blacklegs " into such a district, apart from objection to their presence as strike-breakers, must add fuel to the flame. Mr. Bell has told me that his great desire was to stop them from coming in, as worse outrages and riots would certainly ensue, and he would not be able to settle the strike. On August 23 he handed a printed paper to some of them at Cardiff with these words:

"Strike on the Taff Vale Railway. Men's headquarters, Colbourn Street, Cathays. There has been a strike on the Taff Vale Railway since Monday last. The management are using every means to decoy men here whom they employ for the purpose of blacklegging the men on strike. Drivers, firemen, guards, brakesmen, and signalmen are all out. Are you willing to be known as a blackleg? If you accept employment on the Taff Vale, that is what you will be known by. On arriving at Cardiff call at the above address, where you can get information and assistance.—RICHARD BELL, *General Secretary*."

The men observed the hint, or threat, according to opinion, and Mr. Bell paid their fares back to London.

"That is the episode," says Mr. Beasley, "which led to the proceedings being taken against Bell and Holmes and the union. On the previous day the company's solicitor and myself, having regard to the number of outrages which were taking place, were very anxiously considering how we could put a stop to them. He was rather of opinion that there must be some overt act on the part of an official of the union before any proceedings could, with any success, be taken. The material was now supplied, and writs were immediately issued against Mr. Bell and Mr. Holmes and against the Society. That was the foundation of the Taff Vale case which has excited so much interest, and I think I may venture to say that, if it had not been for that episode, there would have been no Taff Vale case at all."

It is unnecessary to follow the details of the strike, which ended after eleven days. The important matter is the litigation which ensued. It will be sufficient to note that Mr. Francis Hopwood (now Lord Southborough) came down on August 24 from the Board of Trade, and suggested certain points which Mr. Bell more or less adopted and endeavoured to impress on a stubborn local executive. He left on the 29th, without effecting a settlement, which subsequently was secured by the intervention of Sir W. T.

Lewis, on terms slightly different. Mr. Hopwood's report on the strike and Mr. Bell's attitude contains this passage :

" Mr. Bell, as is usual in cases in which I have negotiated with him, played his difficult part with admirable firmness. He struggled hard to gain, and did obtain through me, everything which he deemed to be essential to the best interests of the men, and I do not in the least blame him for being unable to induce the Executive Committee to accept terms which he knew to be fair and equitable under all the circumstances of the case. Mr. Bell, taking a wide and generous view of the pros and cons of the whole matter, grasped the fact that the terms would receive the approval of public sentiment. The Executive Committee, influenced by the strong feeling of their constituents, could merely deal with the subject from a narrower point of view."

This opinion of Mr. Bell's action did not, however, appeal to Mr. Beasley, who proceeded with his action, or, having entered it, found it difficult to withdraw, even when the strike had come to an end. Mr. Beasley might have paused if he could have foreseen the future, but he had a passion for litigation. His shelves were filled with rows and rows of reports of the different cases and commissions into which he had brought his Company. He took pride in them, and, I believe, loved litigation for its own sake. He came once to denounce me for some supposed action in hot wrath, which I disarmed by chaffing him upon his success, and suggesting I would not like to lessen it by putting him in a position to bring an action against me. Afterwards he was actually helpful and kindly in giving hints how disputes in South Wales might be brought to an end, and advising me of threatened trouble. If Mr. Bell and he had only met, how different the future might have been !

On August 28 and 30, during the strike, Mr. Justice Farwell granted an interim injunction against Bell and Holmes :

" to restrain the defendants from watching, or besetting, or causing to be watched or beset, the Great Western Railway station at Cardiff, or the works of the plaintiffs, or any of them, or the approaches thereto, or the places of residence, or any places where they might happen to be, of any workman employed, or proposing to work for the plaintiffs, for the purpose of persuading or otherwise preventing persons from working for the plaintiffs, or for any purpose except merely to obtain or communicate information, and from procuring any persons who had or might enter into any contracts with the plaintiffs to commit a breach of contracts."

The Judge took time to consider an application against the Society, who had applied to be struck out. On September 5 he granted an injunction against the Society, from which they immediately appealed. On November 21, the Court of Appeal reversed the decision, holding that a trade union could not be sued in its registered name. The Railway Company appealed to the House of Lords, where the judgment of Mr. Justice Farwell was restored, and it was plainly indicated that a trade union could be sued, whether registered or unregistered. Meanwhile, a further writ had been issued by the Railway Company against Bell, Holmes, and the trustees of the Society for an injunction and damages; and in December 1902 the jury, after a trial of thirteen days, found against the defendants, Mr. Justice Wills asking the jury, after explanation of the law of agency, the payment of strike-pay by the Society, and the picketing, "Have you any doubt as to Mr. Bell's responsibility for the general course of this strike in all its illegalities and excesses?"—though he also paid a tribute to Mr. Bell's personal character.

The Society did not pursue the litigation. They paid £23,000 agreed damages, and with their own costs had to find about £35,000. The sensation was considerable. Anyone who knew Mr. Bell, all his Labour colleagues, found one of the most moderate and good-hearted of men saddled with "illegalities and excesses" when he claimed to have been upon a mission of peace. One strike, with the ordinary incidents of a big strike, had led to lawsuits extending over a year and a half, with a cost of tens of thousands of pounds extracted from the innumerable contributions of working men. Every trade union, every trade union secretary or official, found themselves face to face with the law in a struggle where the law had the whip-hand. Strikes might be legal, but strikes under the restrictions laid down by the law became for all practical purposes absolutely illegal and absurd.

The two points of view may in some measure be illustrated, without too long argument of technical character, by quotations from the Minority Report of the Royal Commission on Labour in 1894, and the judgment of Mr. Justice Farwell in 1900.

The first statement says that the suggestion that it would be desirable to make trade unions liable to be sued by any person who had a grievance against the action of their officers or agents appears to be open to the gravest objection.

"To expose the large amalgamated societies of the country, with their accumulated funds, sometimes reaching a quarter of a million sterling, to be sued for damages by any employer in any part of the country or by any discontented member or non-unionist, for the action of some branch secretary or delegate, would be a great injustice. If every trade union were to be liable to be perpetually harassed by actions at law on account of the doings of individual members, if trade union funds were to be depleted by lawyers' fees and costs, if not even by damages or fines, it would go far to make trade unionism impossible for any but the most prosperous and experienced artisans. The present freedom of trade unions from any interference by the courts of law, anomalous as it may appear to lawyers, was, after prolonged struggle and Parliamentary agitation, conceded in 1871, and finally became law in 1876. Any attempt to revoke this hardly won charter of trade union freedom, or in any way to tamper with the voluntary character of their associations, would in our opinion provoke the most embittered resistance from the whole body of trade unionists, and would, we think, be undesirable from every point of view."

The second statement, by Mr. Justice Farwell, is:

"If the contention of the defendant Society were well founded, the Legislature has authorised the creation of numerous bodies of men capable of owning great wealth and of acting by agents, with absolutely no responsibility for the wrongs that they may do to other persons by the use of that wealth and the employment of those agents."

On the top of these opinions came the judgments of the law lords in 1901 and the summing-up of Mr. Justice Wills in 1902, which, taken together, rendered any attempt at a strike, and also, it may be said, a lock-out, almost certain to bring some of those engaged in the dispute within the purview of the criminal or civil law. The relation of the law to practical facts was intricate, involved, and surrounded with a cloud of uncertainty. The Government took refuge in a Royal Commission (Lord Dunedin, Sir W. T. Lewis, Sir Godfrey Lushington, Mr. Arthur Cohen, and Mr. Sydney Webb, all well-known names), with a view to elucidating this maze of difficulty and considering the shower of Parliamentary Bills, protests, and resolutions which the course of events had excited, while Labour pressed in every constituency pledges from Members that trade unions should not be subject to the crushing powers of the law. The trade unions were asked to take part in the inquiry, but refused, on the curious ground, so I have been told, that the Commission was formed with a view to the establishment of compulsory arbitration, a matter which was not even discussed. I am inclined to think they made a mistake. The difficulties were real difficulties, and an agreed settlement might have avoided much subsequent bitterness.

The Board of Trade asked me to give evidence; and appearing as the first witness, I was examined and cross-examined for nine days on the legal cases which had come before the Courts. The Commissioners, in their report, rewarded me by saying: "We desire to take this opportunity of saying how indebted we have been to Mr. Askwith for the assistance he gave us, and we recommend his evidence to the perusal of anyone who wishes a clear and exhaustive summary of the whole case law on the matters in question"—an unusual compliment, I believe, to a witness before a Royal Commission, but indicating accurately the trend of my statement, a summary of the case law.

That case law had been administered by judges of whom every one had been brought up or practised at the Bar at a time when trade unions were unlawful. "By a combination of causes," to quote the Commissioners, "the presence of Trade Unions or Trade Unionists, as such, in the Common Law Courts, either as plaintiffs or as defendants, either in cases of tort or in cases of contract, was unknown, and to all appearance it was as if they were outside the civil law altogether. Hence the popular notion that Trade Unionists as such were subject to the criminal law alone." I have no hesitation in saying that the result of a summary of the case law showed a mutual shyness, if a mild term may be used, on the part of trade unions to trust tribunals from which they had been excluded, and on the part of judges to realise fresh facts, to keep in touch with the movement of events, and to overcome prejudices, a difficulty not mitigated by an apparent impression that, when some of the great cases came before the House of Lords, political considerations or opinions affected the colour of some of their decisions.

The surprise caused by the Taff Vale case turned into set purpose to change the law, when it was found that a succession of other legal cases involved other unions in heavy law-costs and damages, and retarded movements in big trades. At the general election of January 1906, twenty-nine Labour Members were elected, other Labour officials secured election as ostensible Liberals, and Members all over the country had had to give pledges that the law should be changed. There was a wave of feeling which had a great influence in almost every constituency. The Royal Commission reported in favour of relief to the trade unions from being involved in actions of civil conspiracy—as they were already relieved by Act of Parliament from proceedings from criminal conspiracy—and, with safeguards, from the more stringent effects of judicial interpretation of peaceful persuasion and giving information and the law of tort. Their conclusions, without the safeguards, were accepted, and the far larger step of immunity under practically all conditions from legal liability for torts and from actions at law was pressed upon the Government. For a time the Attorney-General stood his ground, and made a strong speech against trade unions being put outside the laws which affected all other corporations or associated bodies. His Government threw him over, and as a matter of policy, in answer to political pressure and for political reasons, passed the Trade Disputes Act (6 Edward VII, c. 47).

This Act is now regarded as a charter of liberty by some trade unionists, and is denounced as a charter of licence by some employers. It is neither one nor the other, but it has been used to shield some acts by individual officials which, in the interests of the community, might well not be shielded, under the cry of proposed infringement of privileges of a trade union. It has also caused a bitterness of feeling against many actions of trade unions which sensible laws would not have touched, in the belief that, but for the Trade Disputes Act, they ought to have and would have been made amenable to results everyone else had to risk. Class feeling on the part of employers has been increased by suspicion and anger at its supposed effects, often quite irrationally. The people as a whole have a grudge against presumed privileges being accorded to one section of the community. It was passed under pressure, and believed to be passed for the sake of a temporary political advantage. My own opinion is that many of the complaints against it are not based on good grounds, and that it has not been so harmful as many suppose. It would, I think, serve a good purpose and clear away much misunderstanding if an inquiry was instituted into the working of the Act, when, if there were any real cases of gross abuse, safeguards might be devised against their repetition, with advantage to the trade unions themselves; and if there were not, the strong feeling against present alleged privileges and many misunderstandings would be allayed. I have not much belief, however, that such a course will be taken. Privilege, once legalised, is not easily changed; but it will last much longer if it is found not to have been abused.

CHAPTER X

ARMY BOOTS AND NOTTINGHAM LACE

In the spring of 1905 improvement in employment began to cause an upward tendency in demands for advances of wages, and also difficulty in some of the trades which had been specially active during the war, but with its close began to lose Government orders. In March much public interest was caused by a strike of about 700 army-boot makers round Kettering and Raunds in Northamptonshire. The demand for army boots, after the great rush of the Boer War, came to an end. Work grew slack, and there was no disposition, in the absence of contracts, to keep up the high wages. The district got more and more excited, and finally, after some weeks, the men started on a march to London, held meetings, and proposed to besiege the War Office. On May 17, the Secretary of State for War, Mr. Arnold Forster, asked me to make an inquiry whether there was any rate of wages current in Northamptonshire for the making of army boots, and what was the rate in any of the processes. The answer could have easily been given at once. There was no rate; but it was possible to establish a rate and make some arrangement for future rates, and this I determined to attempt, and not only settle the strike, but establish some solid basis for the future. Accordingly I managed to get hold of some of the employers and official leaders of the boot-and-shoe trade, and had it announced that I would make an inquiry next day at Leicester, where I met a mass of unorganised employers, each competing against the other, their competition complicated by the existence of small co-operative firms, and a mass of men quite recently organised under the pressure of common interest in a strike. Recognition was the first point, and after that matters which, in the light of later days, seem almost absurd—a minimum wage, a piecework statement with prices set out in a price-list for existing and future contracts, and a fixed price for the boots most largely required for the army. No two firms had similar piecework prices, and on every single point the discussion was long and warm. I had no power to decide anything, but after two days managed to effect an agreement on all points. Some order was thus evolved out of the chaos; and amendments were made, according to changing circumstances, during the twelve years in which both parties annually elected me as umpire of the Conciliation Board then formed, until this branch of the trade merged with the general arrangements of the boot-and-shoe trade, now one of the best organised trades in the country. The boot-and-shoe trade was not organised then in anything like the measure now reached: and many were the arbitrations and conciliations in which the late Mr. Alderman Thomas Smith, of Leicester, and myself were engaged with respect to it, besides the consultations between us on the subject of policy, particularly in relation to the minimum wage, now firmly established in that industry. I would take this opportunity of saying how much good work Mr. Alderman Smith did up to the last months of his life, in spite of trying illness. He was for many years almost a standing chairman of conferences about price-lists for making boots and shoes, particularly in the Midlands, the great centre of that trade.

To return to army boots, the notorious figure of Councillor or "General" Gribble, who started the march to London, gave way to others less known to the public but none the less keen in argument, met on the other side with equal keenness. Generally I went to Kettering, sometimes, owing to stress of work, I had to bring the members of the Board to London. Discussion raged over every detail of the piecework prices of cavalry boots, Canadian boots, navy and marine boots, Crown Colony boots, Wellington, telegraph, mud, and police boots, and canvas shoes for the navy; but far more seriously over the Army combination boots, for general use by the troops. It may be of some interest to note that this district has an historic past. History and tradition allege that King Burhtred of Mercia, defeated by the Danes, fled from the Midlands and died in poverty in Paris. Certainly he lost his treasure in the Thames, because it was found when a section of Waterloo Bridge was being repaired—new coins with his name upon them. Possibly he tried to avoid the ferry or ford at Lambeth lest His Grace of Canterbury should levy toll, and in the crossing his loaded wherries sank. In any event, he left his relative, King Alfred, to fight the Danes, and it is said King Alfred settled the undesired aliens down in Northamptonshire and its neighbourhood, with certain lands and commission to make boots for the King's armies, without which commodity one of the highest authorities in military matters has indicated no army can exist. From that day to this army boots have come from the Midlands. The descendants of the Danes, it is known, made the boots for Henry VIII for the Field of the Cloth of Gold, for Marlborough, and for Wellington. They have made them, too, for Roberts, Kitchener, and Haig. Leicester and Northampton have been and are the centres of the boot trade of the world. Others have imitated them, with ebb and flow of success, but these great centres hold their own. In face of this, who can talk of lack of tradition and precedent in British life ? I lived for some time near them, at St. Ives in the county of Huntingdon, amongst a race like them but not of them, and they will not take amiss an anecdote concerning them. The fact is, they have a dialect of their own, as have many parts of Great Britain. On one occasion I had to summon them to London, and could give them very little time. They argued on a point referred to me, and would willingly have argued for hours. I managed to bring the discussion to a close, and when they left turned to my secretary, now a distinguished civil servant, with the remark, "That seems quite clear. Draft an award in six lines, and we will get it out at once." To which he replied, "I am very sorry, but I didn't understand a single word they were saying." Such are the minor difficulties of arbitrators, if they or their assistants do not understand the English language as she is spoke ! It is said a difficulty in the American army arose from the men not understanding English in the words of command. Difficulty may arise much nearer than that. I interviewed an eminent peer who had consented to arbitrate in West Yorkshire over a mining dispute. After telling him the exact issue, I remarked that he might have one considerable difficulty, of which he might like to be warned. "What are you suggesting ?" said he, suspiciously, thinking I was going to propose a solution, a course I have never pursued. "Only this," I remarked : "that if you do not understand what the miners' leader says, avoid asking him what his meaning is, or he will think you a fool straight off, and not able to understand plain English: you will not have a chance as a wise arbitrator; but if you wait, the proper issue will become apparent before you have finished." "Oh," he said, "I can follow them." "Reet," I replied. "Tak' t' loomp an' wrastle wi' it!" "What do you say?" he remarked, and I had to tell him he had asked the very question I had been trying to explain he should not ask. It is well to understand good Yorkshire before attempting to settle mining or wool disputes in that county, not to mention the dialects in districts of Scotland, Ireland, or Wales.

If piecework statements on boots and shoes at Raunds, and afterwards, in other cases, at Kettering for army boots, and the East End of London for the civilian trade, were complicated statements, these were child's play in comparison with the fixing of piecework rates in the Nottingham lace trade.

This trade had had at one time a great monopoly, but severe and undercutting competition had arisen from France, Scotland, and elsewhere; and outside the city walls large factories had been erected at Long Eaton to escape the city rates of pay and the city restrictions, and filled with modern machinery. Workers were migrating where full work could be got, while in the city there was heavy unemployment. The trade was subject to continual strikes and petty squabbles over the prices to be paid on different classes of lace, the whole trade being governed by a large number of piece-rate cards, prices being payable according to the card to which the lace was allotted, and the details of the cards, which, often in an anomalous fashion, settled the prices for all the variations in the pattern of the lace when allotted to a particular card. Many employers and more employees did not understand the principles of the cards, and much less were they able to work out clearly the proper amounts to be paid for a given pattern of lace. There were always quarrels as to the cards on which a new lace was to be worked, and still more as to the prices for the details of the patterns. The strange anomalies had been the result of a long series of accretions to the original cards, or additions of fresh cards on the supposition that any new lace required a new card. Further, the majority of the firms were using obsolete, old machinery from which no adequate return could be got by the workman, who was naturally jealous at seeing his colleague, working by the same card, but with new machinery in an up-to-date firm, getting far larger returns than himself. The position is outlined by the following extract on the award from the Board of Trade Report:

" The old price-lists for the Levers section, or Fancy Lace trade, were the gradual product of many years of lace manufacture. A person wishing to calculate wages and cost of manufacture had to know the class of machine, its gauge, width and number of bars, whether top or top and bottom bars. For each variation in gauge, width, and bars a different price was paid. At the present time many bars are generally employed. The old price-list sent the price up by rapid stages when bars were used. In addition to the difficulties arising from bars, some laces could not be made on wider machines, if introduced, as they would be blocked by the price of gauges. The increase in price by progression of amounts for the gauges or quarters or both, and the complicated process of adding points to the width of the machines (now entirely abolished), virtually prohibited their manufacture. Simplification in the use of all extras, and latitude in such processes as flossing, gimping, and using threads traversing gaits, and simplification by the establishment of a wider standard machine on a single rack basis, instead of, on some cards, by estimate on the double rack of 3,840 motions (this complication is now abolished and the standard width raised and made uniform), as well as simplification of gauges and bars, were alleged to be necessary for purposes of competition even with places in the immediate neighbourhood, close to the boundaries of the city."

I concluded there must be a reconstruction from the base. For eight months committees of employers and employed had been negotiating without success, and it took me eight weeks, with interminable discussion over lace curtains, lace nets, and the fancy laces, or " levers " section, the latter being the real crux. The price-lists would be quite unintelligible to the ordinary reader, owing to the mass of detail required in these decisions, but in theresult the cards were cut down from twenty-one to fifteen, and very much simplified. A basis was fixed on which new laces could be adapted to the cards, an inducement given for the employment of modern and bigger machines, and a complete code of working conditions arrived at. Percentages added to the amounts fixed on the cards could be settled if trade was flourishing, the cards still remaining as the basis. There were also arrangements for future trade on these cards. Bickerings there have been, but nothing like the trouble preceding their introduction. They cannot, however, be said to have brought the employers sufficiently to value the importance of new machinery. Trade has been too bright in certain classes of goods, preventing the scrapping of old machines, except with a minority of firms.

This revision of the lace trade continued the policy I had endeavoured to carry out in the boot-and-shoe and other conferences—namely, to make as complete, plain, and solid a basis as possible for a trade in the conditions existing at the time, and by agreement between the parties to establish methods by which the parties could themselves settle future difficulties, and effect revisions made necessary by new processes, new developments, or fluctuations of trade, in such manner that each party might learn the views and position of the other, and govern themselves by mutual knowledge accordingly.

These elaborate Nottingham piece-work statements, covering a large number of factories and many thousands of operatives, as well as the minute statements required in the East End boot trade, proved also to be of practical importance outside the particular trades affected by them, because they formed ocular proof to officials in Government departments and to a Committee of the House of Commons that the most elaborate piecework statements could be worked out by employers and employed mutually set upon the task, with some assistance from an unbiased and patient chairman, even in the most complicated industries, and that statements or calculations were not inconsistent with, and could form the basis for, time rates and minimum rates, even in scattered and underpaid sections of a trade, or in a trade with many grades and classes of workpeople. These facts endorsed the more sentimental aspirations of many supporters of the principle of Trade Boards, when shortly afterwards the establishment of these bodies, now being so widely extended, came into practical prominence and became the subject of legislation.

CHAPTER XI

THEATRES OF VARIETIES

SKIPPING a number of arbitration and conciliation cases in various parts of the country in 1906, a year to which notice for other reasons will be given in the next chapter, I would refer, as an important factor in the promotion of labour troubles, to the outbreak of the variety artistes, musicians, and music hall employees in 1907. It would seem a contradiction that this industry is now one of the most law-abiding, organised, and progressive industries in the United Kingdom. Its initiative has been followed, after some years, by the actors in theatres, and will be, or is being, followed by the cinema trade, the biggest educative force in the world. From the Labour point of view, the serious aspect of the dispute was the notorious and advertised success of a strike in obtaining recognition, order, and a vast improvement in conditions. For years trade union after trade union had been struggling for these results, but their efforts had excited no popular interest, and on the whole there had been, in the great manufacturing trades, a see-saw, with a possible balance in favour of the employers. Then this unexpected strike caused a thrill of interest. Every phase was reported in the newspapers. The reports were followed by the whole of Great Britain with more interest than those of an international football match where the odds were doubtful; and the strike appeared to succeed. Why should not others do likewise?

The public christened the strike "the Music Hall Strike," although those engaged in it adhered to the title "Theatres of Varieties." Few of the public who now frequent the splendid music halls of the Metropolis can remember the conditions existing at the old "Pav" and other music-halls in the early eighties. The room filled with smoke and the smell of drink ; the crowd of noisy men and youths, and women generally of little respectability ; the chairman with his hammer, and the turns frequently characterised by coarseness of every kind. Gradually more and more halls had been built ; gradually able men had seen that the public appreciated good music or singing or dancing, clever turns, and respectability. The industry, however, had grown up without mutual understanding between employers as to any common rules suitable for the industry as a whole, and without guidance or cohesion on any suitable relations between employers and employed. Very low wages for all classes were paid in some halls. The methods and contracts for engagements were remarkably varied in character. They gave rise to continual disputes in the law-courts. Although vast improvement had taken place since 1880, the industry was not in a satisfactory condition, either in London or the Provinces. At the beginning of 1907 a storm broke out over contracts. It created immense excitement in London. All the artistes, musicians, and stage-hands at twenty-two theatres of varieties in London struck. Pickets numbering over 2,500 " peacefully persuaded " both artistes and employees not to act, play, or clean in any theatre. There was no violence, but the sight of the pickets sufficed. The Scala Theatre was taken, and some artistes produced a show of their own, for the benefit of the cause. The " stars " had to join with the lift-boys, and a " National Alliance " between artistes, musicians, and employees was temporarily established, soon breaking up after the strike. After a few weeks of this excitement, which proved to be very expensive, a suggestion was made, I believe by Mr. Somerset Maugham, the well-known author, that a dull arbitration might be useful. The idea was accepted by a so-called Board of Conciliation, which after three days of discussion had failed to agree, and a resolution passed that the declarations and definitions proposed by the Board of Conciliation should be submitted to the parties, and in the event of either not agreeing, " all matters in dispute be referred to Mr. George R. Askwith." As a paper remarked, " All parties to the music hall dispute selected him because they all wanted to make certain of a particular judge."

The Board of Trade, however, for the first time in its life, showed desire to be sensational, and discussed who should be appointed with a view to a sensational appointment. One gentleman at least refused to take it on, and *faute de mieux* I was appointed as the agreed arbitrator on February 14.

My idea was not to be sensational, but to try to establish a solid groundwork for the industry, which I thought the employees, the musicians, half the employers, and half the artistes really desired. The other halves wanted to have nothing done, except to get out of the mess. So I sat down to the work, and ended by being taken off by Mr. Arthur Roberts on the Tivoli stage, in the kindliest manner, but with an exact imitation of gestures and cigarette smoking, and a sketch of the artistes bickering with each other, and standing to attention directly the arbitrator appeared on the scene. Hearing this effort was to be made, I went to see it. Some papers depicted me as surrounded by the stars of the stage, all impressing me by histrionic abilities or comic suggestions ; but though some of them did appear, all were very grave, except Miss Marie Lloyd, who had to be sent for at 11.30, complained of having had no breakfast —though she had time to don a most dainty gown—and thumped her counsel on the back in pleasure at having finished her evidence.

On the day the Board of Trade confirmed my appointment, a brief award was issued dealing with the Scala Theatre, which closed the strike, as far as absence from fulfilment of contracts or work was concerned. Then followed two more interim awards providing for the return to work of the musicians and stage-hands, a very difficult arrangement to negotiate. A return to work was thus effected, but this did not end the matter. It seemed that a temporary settlement could only lead to renewed friction in a short time. I had determined that more ought to be effected, the foundations of goodwill and peace procured, if possible, for the future. It was accepted, though with some demur by some of the managers, that the whole question of wages and hours and all questions of dispute for all the three classes should be dealt with. The result was the Music Hall Award of 1907, settled after hearing more than one hundred witnesses, and holding twenty-three formal sittings and innumerable conferences. The difficulties were much increased by the long time taken by the preliminary cases of the musicians and stage-hands, which were more or less the usual trade cases. The artistes' case was on quite a different footing.

The award contained a complete code for the variety artiste, dealing with existing and future contracts, rules to be observed, a model contract with some compulsory clauses, and rules for settlement of any future disputes.

The award might, in some points of detail and also of principle, have gone farther than it did, but I do not think that at the time, and in view of the various views and conditions which existed, wider terms would have been practicable or found acceptance. In the result it was accepted both for London and the Provinces. The same parties again asked me to deal with its revision when its full term and more had run. A further revision was due during the War, but during the War both managers and artistes decided to postpone a revision, and continue under the terms decided in 1911. Since the War the same methods of settlement have been adopted, and again an arbitrator, after I had left office, has been able to build and revise upon the basis of the previous awards. The award of 1907 was also followed by a decision given between artistes and agents, which completed a gap, settling clearly the principle that artistes should know what their contracts were, their payments and their obligations.

I think both managements and artistes would agree that these awards have had a most lasting and, I hope, salutary effect upon this industry; that mutual good relations between the parties are infinitely better than they were; and that a great amount of useless litigation has been saved.

The award itself covered the whole work and engagements of an artiste, both at one show a night and two shows a night houses. Matinées, transference from theatre to theatre, troupes and sketches, closing of theatres, re-engagements, rehearsals, illness, vulgarities, encores, play-bills, and other details were all provided for; but the chief difficulty arose over "barring" clauses. Was "barring" to be allowed? If allowed, what were to be the terms of "barring"? "Barring" means that an artiste, before or after a certain number of performances at a given place and for a given time, should not contract with any other management to appear at the same place, or within a radius of distance from such place, for a certain time before or after these performances. The radius and the time were matters to be determined, coupled with the problem of the rights of re-engagement of an artiste whose success might be largely due to the discovery, training, or expenditure of a particular management.

It soon became apparent that, in spite of a few enthusiasts urging that the artiste should be entirely free, the majority knew that the industry had been built up by "barring," and that the artiste would really suffer for a possible present gain if there was perfect freedom of sale to the highest bidder; yet at the same time it was most important that unfair terms binding the artiste to unfair restrictions should not be permitted. Other minor points ranged round this difficulty, but the main principles depended upon radius and time, with the addition, in London, of the grades of halls and the geographical position of halls. The great West End music halls paid hundreds of pounds a week for a "star." They had individual contracts settled after weeks of negotiation with those "stars," possibly imported from abroad after much search, exercise of judgment, and heavy outlay. It was useless to import "stars," announce their coming, and find that the "star" had anticipated the date of performance by performing for a rival beforehand; or if the "star" was a success (and there were many failures, all costing money), to find that, at the end of an engagement, that "star" would draw off audiences to a neighbouring rival, to the detriment of the new programme of a hall. There had to be zones within or without which artistes under certain conditions might contract to perform. The zone theory was also invoked for the settlement of the time within which an artiste might again appear without undue disturbance of the new programme of a hall. It was contended that an artiste did not draw from the north to the south of the Thames, that East Ham could not get an audience from Hammersmith, and that a London artiste could appear one day at Woolwich and the next day at Hampstead without affecting either the quantity of audience or derogating from the artiste's own freshness. Fresh artistes, with a reputation, but new in their bloom to a district, were desirable flowers to show. There were managers ready to get them at the expense of other managers; and not caring much if their bloom suffered. There were managers anxious to be sure of their flowers, that they should not be bruised before they had been shown. There were flowers anxious to show themselves at one production and immediately go on to the nearest exhibition, regardless of the fact that, carefully handled, they might bloom for many years, but mauled or too frequently exhibited might soon pass into the limbo of commonplace, fatigue, or lack of novelty. There were a few exotics who could afford to take little note of time and place, and even contracts, secure in the knowledge that, even at enhanced terms, their original exhibitors would only be too glad to show them again.

The problem under the circumstances of 1907 was far more difficult than in 1911, when the matter was again referred to me for revisions which the light of experience and working indicated as feasible. In 1907 the foundations had to be laid and the industry organised at a time of stress and strong feeling. In 1911 the industry was organised, but adjustments were desirable. Since then further adjustments have been made, but the result is as much due to the common sense and mutuality of work which men like Sir Oswald Stoll and Sir Alfred Butt have brought into the music hall world as to any awards upon which they have been able to build, and also to the great energy and wonderful persistence of the late Mr. Clemart, who may be said to have died in the artistes' cause.

Looking back, I feel interested, when visiting these theatres, in the thought that every man, woman, and child appearing on those stages is governed by a contract which I had aided in drafting.

CHAPTER XII

BELFAST, 1907

THE contrast of the next big strike was startling. It was no half-genial dispute, with latest details interesting to the readers of evening newspapers; no orderly arbitration with grave attempt to settle the right lines for future development and peace of an industry; but the city of Belfast held up by a state of civil turmoil, guards at the railway-stations, double sentries with loaded rifles at alternate lamp-posts of the Royal Avenue, a very few lorries, with constabulary sitting on the bales and soldiers on either side, proceeding to guarded, congested, but lifeless docks, and ten thousand soldiers in and about the city. There had been fights in the streets, charges of cavalry, the Riot Act read, shooting to disperse wrecking mobs, a few men and women killed and scores wounded, and the whole business of the city at a standstill. The dockers, headed by Mr. James Larkin, already well known as the leader of many strikes in both hemispheres, and Mr. James Conolly, the brain of the movement, who was wounded, and afterwards shot for the part he played in the Easter troubles at Dublin in 1916, had first gone out with no defined claims. The National Union of Dock Labourers, whose treasurer, Mr. James Sexton, was over in Belfast trying to quiet matters, was practically ignored. At the end of June certain general carters refused to cart goods for ship-owning companies whose dockers were on strike, and claimed an advance of wages. The Belfast Carriers' Association replied by locking out all the carters on July 4. The coal-carters and porters then struck in sympathy, and though for this section a truce had been fixed on July 25 by Mr. Mitchell of the Board of Trade, and Mr. Alderman Gee of the General Federation of Trade Unions, it was only temporary. The sequence of events, so far as regards the carters, seemed to be a sympathetic strike, a sympathetic lock-out, an enlarged sympathetic strike. It was the process so frequently tried in Great Britain at a later date.

In the first week of August 1907 I had entered the Board of Trade as a civil servant, Mr. Lloyd George, the then President, whom I had never previously seen or spoken to, proposing that I should come in as Assistant Secretary in control of the Railway Department. He had in view the coming disputes on the railways: but when pressing telegrams arrived from Sir Anthony MacDonnell, the Permanent Under-Secretary of State, urging the condition of Belfast after the six weeks of strike, and almost demanding that I should be sent to assist him, it was decided that I should go, with Mr. Mitchell, lately secretary of the General Federation of Trade Unions and recently appointed to the Board of Trade, an officer whose loyal and able assistance in many subsequent labour troubles cannot be overrated.

We arrived at Belfast on the morning of August 13, not encouraged by meeting a distinguished Irishman on the boat, who I thought might be a possible arbitrator, if one became necessary. This hope of impartiality was stopped by his remark at breakfast that he knew his countrymen; I had no chance of settling the dispute, even if I was not shot, as I probably should be, and Larkin ought to be hanged. After a brief talk with Sir A. MacDonnell, it appeared that his difficulties were enhanced by the fact that under no circumstances would the employers meet Larkin; that Larkin said he was tired of both employers and Government officers, and would not come to see them; and that nothing could or would be done as regards dockers till they returned to work, but that the carting employers might be willing to settle if a fair tariff could be arranged.

In Irish strikes the strikers frequently begin to strike without saying or knowing what they want, and if they do formulate some demands, and get some part of what they allege is wanted, are apt to change and say they want something else. This strike was no exception.

Mr. Mitchell and I decided we must get hold of Mr. Larkin, and so, after walking to the deserted quays, we found Mr. Larkin's headquarters, where we sat on a table, chatting with some dockers till he returned: a tall, thin man, with long dark hair and blue-grey mobile eyes, at that time wearing a very heavy black and drooping moustache, a large black sombrero hat, and a kind of black toga. In later years he shaved his moustache, cut his hair, and dressed in ordinary clothes. He was very surprised to see us, but after intimating that the British Government and all connected with it might go to hell, launched into long exhortations on the woes of the carters and dockers and denunciation of the bloodthirsty employers, collectively and individually. I said that all this might be true, though, not having been an official for more than ten days, I could scarcely be responsible for the acts of the British Government, and in fact wanted some help myself. Could he tell me what the carters wanted, and put it on paper ? Unless he desired to continue the strike till starvation stopped it, it might be useful to know the claim. For all I knew, the employers might be willing to grant their demands ; but I had not yet seen those gentlemen. I knew that carters are always difficult in a dispute, because of the variety of grades, the strict relative position of grades, and the importance of conditions, such as overtime, distance, care of horses, etc. Mr. Larkin could not tell exactly what the carters wanted, so it was suggested some of them should be got, and we would jointly try to find out. This idea interested him, and it was done. We got chairs from somewhere, and sat down to work it out, sending for some lunch to consume as we worked. So great was Mr. Larkin's zest on this new tack, and so angry did he get at the carters' differences of opinion and changing proposals, that he did most of the talking, with an occasional phrase from me, and gave them lectures which no employer would have dared to utter. Armed at last with a document, Mr. Mitchell and I sought Mr. Alexander McDowell, the solicitor acting for the employers, a most able man, whose death during the War was a great blow to the chances of an Irish political settlement. Mr. McDowell said it was the first definite statement of claim he had seen, and he must consult his clients. When some of them had arrived, another long conference brought suggestions in certain cases better than the men had proposed, but necessary in view of the relation of grades, and in other cases required by the terms on which railway carters were working in the same yards. It was now very late, and we adjourned till the next day. This time

Mr. Larkin with his carters came to see me, the master-carters being in another room of the hotel. The changes were explained, suggestions carried backwards and forwards, and finally a provisional agreement made, subject to ratification. Ratification meant endorsement before signature by the constituents of both parties, dockers and carters being summoned, by a crier with a bell, to St. Mary's Hall. Sir A. MacDonnell proposed that he should explain the terms to the employers, if I would take the men. The employers agreed in ten minutes, but we took an hour and a half, behind locked doors, with the Lord Mayor sending down messengers who could not get in, but reported so much noise that it was seriously discussed whether I ought to be rescued. The body of the huge hall was filled with carters, while the galleries were crammed with dockers, who got nothing, but who might not accept the view that, if the carters were settled, their course was to return to work, when they would certainly get a corresponding rise from employers who would do nothing while they were out on strike. They had had a long wait, and might be hostile. Afterwards we chaffed Mr. Sexton, a small man, for having taken the precaution of putting two revolvers in his breast-pocket. As we entered the hall, Mr. Larkin asked me if I would sit next to him. I said, " Yes. Why ? " " Because," he replied, " I wish you would pull my coat-tails if I say anything wrong." There was no need for that precaution. In two minutes Mr. Larkin had the men throwing up their caps and roaring applause. He ridiculed the employers and ridiculed their own representatives, who, he said, would never have known their own minds if I had not told them what to say, the fact being that he himself had settled these uncertain persons. The men wanted to hear every detail, and hence the noise and passage of time before the agreement was ratified. In this manner Mr. Larkin settled the Belfast strike.

Going out by a side-passage to get to the Town Hall for formal signing, I stopped short on the threshold. The passage was full of women, shawls round their heads. " What is it ? " they cried in unison. " It's all right," I said. " Your boys go back to-morrow morning." Women suffer from strikes. Some of them knelt in the mud to pray, others seized my hands, some kissed me, and others, slapping my back, shot me through into the Royal Avenue, up which I ran so fast, with two or three thousand shouting women, dockers, and carters after me, that I could not answer at first, from lack of breath, the eager inquiries in the Lord Mayor's parlour as to what had happened.

The next day Mr. Larkin took me through the disturbed districts, where the troops had separated two quarters of the city by a cordon down the Albert Road, and showed me the places where the cavalry charged, admitting he had told the crowd not to mind the cavalry, as they could not charge on the cobbles : he had seen it himself on the Continent ; where the infantry fired after having endured filth thrown on them from empty tenement-houses, and stones levered up from the roads by children with old pokers ; and a cul-de-sac into which a Highland regiment inadvertently marched and had to fight their way out, every door and window broken. He was an interesting man. "I don't know how you can talk to that fellow Larkin," said a Dublin employer at a later date. "You can't argue with the prophet Isaiah." It was not an inapt description of a man who came to believe he had a mission upon earth ; and when one reflects, Isaiah must have been rather a difficult person and liable to go off at a tangent. It is not wise to argue with such men, but it is possible to suggest to their minds a different facet of thought.

A paper describing the settlement correctly said :

"The effect of the settlement of the carters' dispute upon the aspect of affairs at the docks was instant—almost magical. By breakfast-time a marvellous change had come over the scene. Lethargy had given place to energy ; furtive activity to open bustle. The strikers, or those of them to whom employment was available, lost not a moment in returning to work. From six o'clock in the morning wagons and lorries moved to and from the docks in ceaseless procession, and the mountains of merchandise, which three months' enforced idleness had accumulated on the quayside, began to crumble away. The soldiers on duty whiled away the time by reading the newspapers. The stalwart constabulary who paraded the adjacent streets preserved an attitude of passive alertness. There was no call for the interference of either military or police —everybody was too busy."

But still, although the back of the strike was broken by the carters' settlement, the work of Sir A. MacDonnell and myself was not yet done. The city was still very disturbed, other outbreaks might occur at any time; it was necessary to watch the dockers' case, and to consolidate, by request of all parties, into a tariff which might be of lasting benefit in the future, the various agreements and anomalies of the coal-porters' and coal-carters' wages and conditions. It was a long tariff, with many details, which was not finally settled till August 24, and is subject to the observation that the prevailing Irish wages of 1907 were on a different scale from the wages of Great Britain, and differed widely from the Irish wages of 1920.

CHAPTER XIII

RAILWAYS, 1907

WHILE the Belfast disputes had been creating turmoil in the north-east of Ireland, there had been slowly gathering on the railways of Great Britain a much more momentous difference, which, unlike the two previous disputes, was concluded for the time being without a strike having been commenced, but heralded a change in the attitude of the State to a great industry in the country. It was of a different type to either of the two disputes which have been just described.

The Taff Vale case and the Trade Disputes Act, coupled with active organising work, had led to an enormous increase in the numbers and strength of the Amalgamated Society of Railway Servants. Freed, too, from the liability to an action such as that which Mr. Beasley had launched against Mr. Richard Bell, the union leaders could advance their programme with greater confidence and less caution in their hints of possible results if their demands were not considered or grievances met. There was a feeling of something more than annoyance that litigation had held up efforts, delayed improvements, and restrained action. On the other hand, there was no cohesion among the railway companies, each acting on its own, but each waiting upon the other before attempting or making any important change in the condition of their servants. At the same time those servants saw large expenditure in competitive races to the North and in various developments, while their wages were unchanged. Although, during periods of unemployment such as had occurred, men had been glad to seek and obtain the safe shelter of continuous work and the subsistence, present and future, which employment on the line gave to an employee of a railway company, the cost of living had been going up, but the payment of grades had not increased proportionately. Wages, generally speaking, were dangerously low. The system of grades, rendered necessary by the great size of the undertakings, grouped men of very varied abilities in one dead level of payment. Although there were instances of men getting through, promotion was slow. Once in a grade, always in a grade, where young men found their chances stopped, and their only chance of increased pay lying in an improved payment for the whole grade, a principle leading to solidarity and support of the Union which gave strength to solidarity. Improved payment of one grade was not easy for a company to achieve, because change of payment of one grade inevitably led to revision or demand for revision of the pay of other grades, in order that relative position and contentment might be attempted. Some companies had endeavoured to meet the difficulty by the creation of a number of small artificial grades which produced confusion and the appearance without the actuality of promotion, or only gave men temporary or acting jobs ; but even then small changes might ultimately lead to heavy expenditure. Heavy expenditure meant decrease of dividends and difficulty in raising capital, or increase of passenger and goods rates, limited by law to statutory maxima. Any increases meant complaints by the general public, growls and perhaps law-suits from merchants and traders, or the diversion of traffic to competing lines which had not moved or expended money, or to sea-borne commerce, ever watchful for freights and unrestricted in their quotations of charges. Hedged round by restrictions and afraid of innumerable complications, the railway companies were rather inclined to let sleeping dogs lie. They were not watching such problems as cost of living, abatement of anomalies, or the rise of wages in other employments. They had no leader and no general governing or co-ordinating body, except such limited opinion as the few managers meeting at the railway clearing house, chiefly upon such subjects as rates, might venture to hazard. The Railway Department of the Board of Trade had little power or authority, and the slightest movement beyond the statutory duties given to it would have been resented, questioned, and refused, as an interference with management and action for which no authority legally existed. As regards recognition of the

Union, the policy of 1896 still held good, when the general manager of the London and North-Western Railway had written:

"The directors are at all times willing to consider the reasonable demands of their employees, addressed to them through the proper channel, and in the usual manner, with which the men are quite familiar; but they could not, having regard to their responsibility for the safe and sufficient conduct of the traffic upon the railway, and for other obvious reasons, consent to the intervention of third parties in the relations between them and their workmen."

The men were beginning to think that their "reasonable demands" were not being considered, and were taking refuge in the Union, which they insisted should act for them in pressing their demands, and should obtain recognition from the companies. The companies shelved the "reasonable demands" and concentrated on refusal of recognition. On this difference of view action was joined and ended in a compromise, which in 1907 did not give recognition, but gave the employees a method by election to Conciliation Boards of obtaining consideration of most of the claims embodied in the Union programme, and some authority for members of the Union, a half-loaf which they seized very quickly. In subsequent years the powers of the Conciliation Boards were further amended and increased, until they broke down under the stress of the War, giving place to the present system of a supreme executive of the men, negotiating with a few general managers acting on behalf of the Government, from whose decisions and attempted settlements the supreme executive proceed to the Minister of Transport, and, if his views do not suit them, periodically proceed to the Prime Minister, who has to choose between a sudden outlay of millions out of the public purse or a general railway strike.

The "All Grades Programme," as it was called, had been embodied in November 1906, and, with slight differences for Scotland and Ireland, made the following demands:

"*Hours.*—(*a*) That eight hours constitute the standard day for all men concerned in the movement of vehicles in traffic, viz. drivers, firemen, guards (goods and passenger), shunters, and signalmen; also for motormen, conductors, and gatemen on electric railways.

"(*b*) That ten hours a day be the maximum working day for all other classes of railwaymen, except platelayers.

"(*c*) That no man be called upon to book on more than once for one day's work.

"*Rest.*—That no man be called out for duty with less than nine hours rest.

"*Overtime.*—(*a*) That each day stand by itself.

"(*b*) That a minimum of rate and a quarter be paid for all time worked over the standard hours.

"*Sunday Duty.*—(*a*) That Sunday duty be regarded as distinct from the ordinary week's work.

"(*b*) That a minimum of rate and a half be paid for all time worked between twelve midnight Saturday and twelve midnight Sunday.

"(*c*) That Christmas Day and Good Friday be regarded as Sundays.

"*Guaranteed Week.*—That, independent of Sunday duty, a week's wages be guaranteed to all men whose conditions of service compel them to devote their whole time to the companies.

"*Wages.*—(*a*) That an immediate advance of 2*s.* per week be given to all grades of railwaymen who do not receive the eight-hour day.

"(*b*) That all grades in the London district be paid a minimum of 3*s.* per week above the wages paid in country districts.

"*One Man in Motor-Cab.*—That the system of working with only one man in motor-cab be abolished on electric railways."

Whether the demands could have been met at that date may be questioned, although almost every point is now fully adopted on all railways; but the Companies, when the programme was presented in January 1907, did not consider the programme. They considered only the request made with it, that "the directors of the companies would arrange to meet a deputation of the men, accompanied by the General Secretary of the Amalgamated Society, to negotiate," and gave a categorical refusal to accede to this request for recognition of the Society's officials. They were again approached with a similar request in February, and again repeated their refusal.

The fat was now in the fire. Meetings began to be held in June and July, particularly at Birmingham, Glasgow, and Dublin. The movement spread, the railwaymen began to talk of force, in face of such a *non possumus* attitude, which seemed to imply neither consideration of demands nor reception of chosen spokesmen from the Society, to which the majority of railwaymen now belonged. It was interpreted as an intention to break the Union, a challenge to every other trade union, which roused the whole of the trade unions to sympathy and at least moral support, particularly as the challenge seemed to come when the trade union was short of funds, owing to prolonged litigation.

But Mr. Richard Bell, the secretary of the Amalgamated Society, was a cautious man. He knew the great strength of the railway companies, the advantage of playing for place, so as not to appear to be aggressive in the eyes of the public; the conservative temper of many railwaymen, proud of their service and accustomed to discipline; and possibly the knowledge that a strike would be very expensive, and difficult with depleted funds and capital locked up, it was said, in mortgages issued by building societies, not the easiest securities for quick liquidation in times of crisis.

Mr. Bell was at the time represented as an agitator and a firebrand. Nothing could have been more remote from the truth. The fact is, in his desire for peace, he did not go fast enough for some of his executive, who did not treat him well some years later, when they ousted him from office, left him without any career, and forgot the great services he had rendered to their cause. I knew him well, and have very high respect and esteem for him. On this occasion he handled his case in a masterly manner, and persuaded his men at the end of July to make a third application to the railway companies. It was refused. The railwaymen now waited till September before taking a ballot whether they were prepared to strike work in order to enforce the programme, including the principle of "recognition." The answer came in October, nearly a year after the programme had been formulated, and was emphatic: 76,825 for a strike, 8,773 against.

It was almost impossible, even if they had wished it, for

the Government to stand by, in a situation like this, and see the country drift into a general railway strike, when the parties were not even attempting to negotiate. Agreements between employers and employed may be the best type of agreements, because they have to work together, know the business on which they are engaged, and can feel that they have settled a difficulty without dictation or suggestion from outside persons. A big industry may agree to formulate within itself certain methods of settlement which the individuals composing it consider so suitable as to make it worth while to adhere and follow in general association the rules laid down by common consent. It is, however, of little use to say that an industrial dispute should be settled within the industry, and to object altogether to any interference of any kind, when that industry is so vital to the whole country and to every other trade in the country as the railway service, and yet, in face of a persistent, growing, and heavily supported demand by the workpeople, does nothing at all to examine, remedy, or deal with the demand.

In my opinion, the railway companies would not examine any or all of the demands for improved conditions of service, and despised the claimants, who, they thought, were not strong enough to carry the railway employees up to or through a strike. There was no group of men controlling or influencing them who could act in common and deal with the whole question in a broad manner, and with fair and statesmanlike considerations of the whole of the facts of the case, the condition of the labour world, and the relations between Capital and Labour, or take stock of the growing power of Labour, or consider its causes. There was no one man big enough to get them together as an industry and say, "Here is this position. We must carefully consider it, and we must meet it with care, not only in the interests of our shareholders, for whom we are trustees, but also in the interests of our workpeople, whose livelihood is subject to our actions, and the community, whose interests are vitally concerned with peace upon the railways." Not even after 1907 did they take any steps in this direction. It was not till 1911, in face of an alleged danger from abroad and an actual strike, that they had to permit a group of able men to act on their behalf and deal with the crisis for the time being, and after that date it was only in 1914, in face of actual and open danger and war abroad, that they were compelled to repeat the process. Foreign affairs have twice reacted upon and controlled the destinies of the British railway companies. On this occasion of 1907 Mr. Lloyd George, the President of the Board of Trade, did it for them, " in view," as the official report says, " of the serious distress and dislocation of trade which would have been caused by a general railway strike." He had no very difficult task. He summoned the chairmen of the six principal railway companies—rather to the annoyance of the general managers, who felt they were more acquainted with the working of railways—and, having arranged they should come with authority from their Boards, gave them a lecture with admirable skill, urging that he should be allowed to complete his statement without interruption, and putting off a well-known Member of Parliament who did interrupt, by calling him " an eminent controversialist, as we well know in the House of Commons," and pleading for his " momentary silence." I think the chairmen must have expected that some such action would be taken, and when Mr. Lloyd George was able to tell them that he would not press, and they would escape, recognition, consent to a proposed scheme of Conciliation Boards was not withheld.

The fact was that I had been able to inform Mr. Lloyd George that Mr. Bell was not going to press for recognition if he obtained a satisfactory method of dealing with grievances, consideration of the programme, and more opportunity for the men to deal with the conditions of their lives, besides the certainty that his union would infallibly be strengthened and could demand more recognition, if it should prove desirable, on another occasion, with greater force and more certainty. " Why," he said, in effect, to me, " should I push myself personally forward and plunge the country into a railway war, because these gentlemen do not desire to meet me ? I cannot deal myself with all these grades, classes, wages, and conditions on all the railways of Great Britain, and I have no clerks at headquarters whom I can send out for the purpose. Union men in localities will be elected, and they can deal with them, and become educated in the process. I will not sacrifice the substance for the shadow, or fight unnecessarily on a false and unpopular issue."

Mr. Bell was, I think, quite right, and many a trade union, when demanding recognition and endeavouring to force a man possibly disliked by employers upon them, might note his attitude, and remember that it is not the acceptance of a particular man, but the position of the Union, which counts.

The agreement was signed in two documents, without "recognition" by any joint document, the first with the signatures of six chairmen:

"The undersigned duly authorised representatives of the Railway Companies named below declare that they are prepared on their behalf to adopt a scheme of Conciliation and Arbitration for the settlement of questions relating to the rates of wages and hours of labour of various classes of their employees, on the general lines of the scheme appended to this Agreement. They will also use their good offices to induce other Railway Companies to adhere to this agreement. Such adherence may be notified at any time within the next three months."

The second, signed by seven railwaymen, stated:

"The undersigned duly authorised representatives of the Amalgamated Society of Railway Servants accept, on behalf of its members, the terms of the Agreement with regard to Conciliation and Arbitration signed this day at the Board of Trade by the representatives of the Railway Companies."

Added to which were two documents accepting, by representatives of the Associated Society of Locomotive Engineers and Firemen, and the General Railway Workers' Union, on behalf of their members, "the arrangements entered into to-day by the Board of Trade." The scheme, largely composed by that admirable draftsman, Sir Hubert Llewellyn Smith, Permanent Secretary of the Board of Trade, began with an outline which explains it, and which stated:

"GENERAL PRINCIPLES

"(*a*) Boards to be formed for each Railway Company which adheres to the Scheme to deal with questions referred to them, either by the Company or its employees, relating to the rates of wages and hours of labour of any class of employees to which the Scheme applies, which cannot be mutually settled through the usual channels.

"(b) The various grades of the employees of the Company who are covered by the Scheme, to be grouped for this purpose in a suitable number of sections, and the area served by the Company to be divided if necessary, for purposes of election, into a number of suitable districts.

"(c) The employees belonging to each section so grouped to choose from among themselves one or more representatives for each district, these representatives to form the employees' side of the Sectional Board, to meet representatives of the Company to deal with rates of wages and hours of labour exclusively affecting grades of employees within that section.

"(d) The first election of representatives to be conducted in the manner set out in the Rules of Procedure. Subsequent elections to be regulated by the Boards themselves.

"(e) Where a Sectional Board fails to arrive at a settlement, the question to be referred on the motion of either side to the Central Conciliation Board, consisting of representatives of the Company and one or more representatives chosen from the employees' side of each Sectional Board.

"(f) In the event of the Conciliation Boards being unable to arrive at an agreement, or the Board of Directors or the men failing to carry out the recommendations, the subject of difference to be referred to Arbitration. The reference shall be to a single Arbitrator appointed by agreement between the two sides of the Board, or in default of agreement to be appointed by the Speaker of the House of Commons and the Master of the Rolls, or in the unavoidable absence or inability of one of them to act, then by the remaining one. The decision of the Arbitrator shall be binding on all parties.

"Duration of the Scheme

"The present Scheme to be in force until twelve months after notice has been given by one side to the other to terminate it. No such notice to be given within six years of the present date.

" INTERPRETATION

" If any question should arise as to the interpretation of this Scheme, it shall be decided by the Board of Trade, or, at the request of either party, by the Master of the Rolls."

The title of the English judge " Master of the Rolls " proved puzzling to some Scots, who asked whether he was a Chief Baker; and for Scotland the President of the Court of the Session was selected to appoint in case of a final arbitrator being necessary. It may be noted that this finality of arbitration was not compulsory arbitration, but agreement under certain circumstances to abide by the finding of an arbitrator.

It fell to my department to conduct the election, receiving nominations of candidates for each of the boards, generally four or six on each of the thirty-three railways in England and Wales, six in Scotland, and seven in Ireland, causing the circulation of voting-papers to each of the thousands of employees on all the railways, receiving and counting the votes, and declaring the result of the polls, no light work, but done without a hitch by a very small number of civil servants.

There followed further proposals from other sources, perhaps as a natural result of the public interest aroused in the railways, for reviewing some of the more important questions affecting the railway companies, traders, and the general public: such questions as the acquisition and holding of land by railway companies, increase of railway rates, owners' risk conditions, the machinery for the settlement of disputes between railway companies and traders, and the desirability of the formation of an Advisory Committee on railway matters. We held many meetings and produced a long Blue Book, but little practical result ensued from the proposals.

There followed, too, some difficult questions of interpretation, and on the inclusion or exclusion of grades in schemes which for some railways, such as the London and North-Western Railway Company, covered over a score of closely-printed pages; and an enormous number of points of detail, explanations to be given, and difficulties to be smoothed, with a view to the oiling of wheels and effective running in such a hastily prepared group of machinery as these Conciliation Boards in effect were. Such questions are, however, connected with the administration of an active Government department, and are not a direct Labour problem.

The broad result, the general effect, of the railway dispute was, I think, that it strengthened the belief of Labour in its power; that it showed the value of organisation; that it intensified bitterness against capitalistic bodies and the alleged pride of Capital, and conveyed the impression that many of them were harshly and callously governed, and ought to be reformed: and that it turned claims, primarily economic, into a more militant channel.

CHAPTER XIV

SCOTTISH MINERS, 1909

MEN are imitative, and the power of suggestion is very great. It may be that these railway schemes were an example, and suggested development on these lines, to other trades. In any event, by the end of 1909, sixty-seven Conciliation Boards in different trades had been added to the number existing in August 1907, in addition to the Railway Boards. In addition, too, to the very large number of cases dealt with by existing and new Boards, cases under the Conciliation Act rapidly increased. In the whole eleven years since 1896 the total cases had amounted to 209, but in the three years 1907–1909 the total came to 156 (39, 60, and 57 in each year respectively). Conciliation was in the air, but while the number of workpeople involved in disputes which were settled in 1908 by conciliation and arbitration was the highest on record, the amount of industrial disturbance caused by trade disputes was greater in 1908 than in any year since 1898, largely due to the disputes in the engineering and shipbuilding industries of the North-East Coast, and in the cotton-spinning industry of Lancashire.

Being immersed in the work of the railway department, and not being concerned in these disputes, I am unable to consider the reasons why the personal intervention of the President of the Board of Trade, Mr. Lloyd George, in the cotton-spinning dispute, was only accepted for the purpose of obtaining an opinion by the law officers on an alleged breach of the Brooklands Agreement, that well-known agreement by which the cotton trade was governed, and why in December both parties would not see him until they had settled the dispute by themselves; though I have heard the refusal was due to the frequently expressed objection to the interference of a Minister of the Crown in a trade dispute, and the use which partisan newspapers made of such interference.

For the same reason I am unaware of the exact causes why he failed to settle the great strike of engineers on the North-East Coast, which began on February 20, in which he intervened, and which did not close till September 24, Mr. Churchill, the then President, getting the parties to meet again in conference on September 9; or the even more important strike of the shipwrights and joiners on the North-East Coast, which began on January 21, in which he intervened in February, and which did not close till June 1, Mr. Churchill following the same course.

Both of these disputes arose over the question of reduction of wages, which the workers were in no mood to accept; and yet the shipbuilding dispute led to conciliation after a series of conferences between the parties, as a result of which machinery was set up early in 1909 for dealing with differences between employers and workpeople; and similar arrangements also began to be considered in engineering and cotton, for the future automatic regulation of wages, though in the cotton industry at least they came to no useful result. Even in the most adverse cases conciliation seemed to be sought.

In order to provide choice of arbitrators for those boards which might require them, and in the endeavour to promote arbitration or conciliation, in September 1908 the Board of Trade, under the presidency of Mr. Churchill, tried the publication of lists or panels—the Chairmen's Panel, the Employers' Panel, and the Labour Panel—from which, on the application of the parties to an industrial dispute, a Court of Arbitration could be nominated. A few courts were established from time to time under this system, but prior to the War no great use was made of them. During the later years of the war, however, the principle of a neutral chairman, a representative employer, and a representative workman, was adopted for the Industrial Courts then established as interim and afterwards permanent courts. The difference lies in the fact of permanence. A tribunal selected from a list of busy men occupied with other affairs inevitably could not be obtained without delay, and the difficulty of fixing convenient dates. Such delay the parties to a dispute did not like, one essential point of settlements being speed at the psychological moment.

The strain and anxiety of dealing with the efforts of Ministers over the engineering and shipbuilding disputes, in addition to the killing work of his department, certainly tended more than anything else to the premature death of Mr. Arthur Wilson Fox in January 1909—a very able man, with a heart of gold, thoroughly overworked by the mass of toil thrown often by Governments on energetic civil servants to whom no sufficient assistance was given. I was appointed by Mr. Churchill to succeed him as Comptroller-General of the Commercial, Labour, and Statistical Departments of the Board of Trade, with its departments scattered all over London, and correspondents all over the country.

So far as Labour matters had been concerned, I had previously had no voice whatever in policy, or indication from any Government of the line which they might desire to follow. In fact, I do not think that the Board of Trade had any policy. It might be said that they waited upon events. They appointed on application arbitrators or conciliators, who gave a decision upon issues of fact after receiving the arguments or evidence adduced in a particular case, or acted as chairmen of conferences where each side gave way a little, but where, after discussion, the differences might become so small that a suggestion or timely hint might avert much trouble and effect a settlement. Some few had gone farther and proposed working rules or arrangements, particularly in the building and boot-and-shoe trades, for the prevention of future disputes. For the first few years after the Conciliation Act had been passed, progress had been very slow. In 1902, indeed, some strong attacks were made in some journals on the inaction of the Board of Trade. By slow degrees the success achieved by conciliators began to make itself felt, without much restraint arising from the personal intervention of the Minister himself during the years following the Penrhyn Quarry dispute. Arbitrators and conciliators, and even officials, began to be regarded as non-political and as having no axe to grind. The attitude of Ministers who have kept aloof has soon become known and has been appreciated industrially, though they have often had credit given to them by the public which, as persons responsible so far as Parliament is concerned, they could scarcely disown. Employers and employed, if they happen to quarrel, however hot their quarrel may be, unite at least on common ground in a mutual dislike that third parties should appear to use their quarrels as a source of self-advantage, or as pawns for real or possible political gain. However disinterested a Minister may be in fact, suspicion is aroused, and suspicion is fatal to the success of advice. Since the War, the principle of non-interference by Ministers has been put aside, and a Minister or a succession of Ministers, pitted against each other, are a court of appeal from arbitrators, conciliators, or agreements, with a final resort to the Prime Minister, and resulting chaos.

For myself, from the influence of the first strike on which I had been engaged, I had determined that wherever possible, in the cases coming to my lot, I would try to end the lock-out or strike, but in all cases where an opening occurred in the course of settling the strike, I would go farther and endeavour to suggest and establish means by agreement between the parties in a firm or an industry for the prevention of future strikes and better relations, more sympathy, between employers and employed, in spite of the hot enmity in which they might have been engaged. With such opportunity as occurred I had consistently followed that policy, and in some cases had an opportunity of carrying it out. Now that official work had come to me—and it was one of the chief reasons which induced me to accept official work—I determined with set purpose to pursue the same policy. I knew perfectly well the difficulties. I had not been deaf to the remarks, formal and informal, made in a long series of arbitrations and conciliations, as to the interference of Ministers, politicians, Bishops, and mayors, unjust though at times those remarks might be; as to the attitude of the courts and lawyers, corroborated, as I knew, by the cheap and jeering remarks made by some County Court and High Court judges as to the incomprehensibility of industrial awards and agreements, though these same documents were, to their credit, invariably upheld and sensibly interpreted by the Court of Appeal in cases reaching them; as to the threats and hatred growing among the young men against Capital, because mere Capital appeared to be the cause why they could not get on in the world and why they could not get more leisure and why they must stay where they were, with a possible halfpenny an hour added to their pay-sheet; as to the obsolete objections to changes possibly endorsed in every surrounding trade, but put forward by firms who failed to recognise facts, and the corresponding warmth of words and sometimes deeds which such opinions evoked; as to the words and views on overthrow of Capital and classes, the political future, the tyranny of all employers, and the coming dawn; and finally, if I may close a long sentence without enumerating more particulars, the solid common sense, the sound views, the real desire to work in general harmony governing the base relations between employers and employed. Whether conciliation might be a mere stopgap or not, I determined to follow the policy of peace and construction I had previously followed, and use the greater power now practicable as far as my strength allowed, in an office where there could be no holidays and an eight-hour day was a short day's work, but where variety at least created interest.

It soon became apparent that the difficulties with Labour were rapidly increasing. In May 1909 it was possible to establish Conciliation Boards for the employees of the tramways department of the London County Council, after a ballot of the employees had adopted the proposal by a large majority. In June a national agreement, supplemental to the terms of settlement of April 1895, was arrived at between representatives of the Federated Associations of Boot and Shoe Manufacturers and the National Union of Boot and Shoe Operatives, providing for reduction of hours to fifty-two and a half per week, the prevention of unauthorised strikes, and the adoption of minimum wages for men and graduated scales of wages for youths. In another industry, however, trouble loomed large. The coal-owners of Scotland, in May 1909, gave notice of a reduction in wages, the effect of which would have been to bring wages below the level of 50 per cent. above the basis of 1888, on which wages were as a base calculated, or, in other words, to make the wages $37\frac{1}{2}$ per cent. above the basis of 1888 instead of 50 per cent. above that basis; and the miners had said they would not have them so reduced; anything below 50 per cent. above this level was too low. The Conciliation Board failed to agree. An offer of arbitration made by the coal-owners was refused. The matter was taken as a question of principle by the men, upon which they were not prepared to risk a possibly adverse decision. In July the owners gave notice that they intended to enforce the reduction; the miners in reply resolved to instruct their men to cease work on July 26. The miners were strengthened by promise of support from the Miners' Federation of Great Britain, who had agreed to back up the decision to secure the minimum of 50 per cent. above basis. A ballot was being organised, the Miners' Federation on July 16 deciding to take a ballot (which ultimately showed a very large majority in favour of a national stoppage) on the question of supporting the action of the Scottish miners, by putting in force Rule 20, under which notices would be given for a stoppage of work at collieries throughout Great Britain.

The position had rapidly become very serious. It was evident that, whatever might have happened in regard to the engineers, shipwrights, and joiners in the preceding year, the miners were not prepared to accept any reduction of wage beyond a certain minimum. It seemed almost certain that a stoppage in Scotland would result, and following that stoppage, a general strike of all the English coal-fields. Mr. Churchill became alarmed. I sounded the ground with various leaders of the parties, but it seemed very unpromising. On July 16 Mr. Churchill summoned the leaders of the miners, including representatives of the English Miners, to the Board of Trade. At the end of a long conference he said that, if nothing else could be done, the Government would have to pass an Act of Parliament in twenty-four hours referring the dispute to compulsory arbitration. As he was leaving the room, Mabon, the famous Welsh leader, turned on him with the remark, in a strong Welsh accent, " Mr Churchill, you cannot put 600,000 men into prison (preeson)." It was a fairly obvious statement, and it was still more fairly obvious that Mr. Smillie, the leader of the Scottish miners, did not intend to give way. Neither did he. He refused all compromise to the very last. To me, as an outsider, equally determined for a settlement as he was for a fight, it seemed a most unreasonable thing that, if a fair compromise without sacrifice of principle could be found, the whole coal industry of the United Kingdom, with incalculable damage to every other interest, should be forced suddenly into a strike.

The first conference at least succeeded in the appointment of a sub-committee, with myself, by request of both parties, as chairman, with the vague reference, " What conditions ought fairly to be attached to the recognition of a new minimum, both as regards the limits and rates of variation of wages above that minimum, and the procedure by which changes in wages should be regulated?" Armed with some power of keeping in touch with the parties, I travelled to and fro between London and Glasgow in pursuit of conferences. Angry and fierce at times they were, the position not being improved by the English ballot showing a very large majority in favour of a national stoppage. The conferences finally centred round proposals I had suggested, the pith of which came to the concession of the principle of 50 per cent. above the 1888 basis as a new minimum, but if prices obtained for coal during the following nine months did not in any month warrant that wage, then an increased percentage in subsequent months should for a like period be diminished, or, in other words, a spread-over of loss and gain. This proviso was to allow adjustments to be made in view of contracts and standing arrangements, while for the future the basis-price for the 50 per cent. minimum was to be fixed by an arbiter, and also the subsequent steps at which on a sliding scale advances were to be made, the new basis-price not to be below the existing basis-price. These clauses meant that the fairness of the existing basis-price, and the subsequent steps of rise, were to be reconsidered and finally determined in a less heated discussion, in view of the principle of 50 per cent. on the 1888 basis as a minimum wage below which wages were not to be reduced being conceded. Mr. Smillie did not sign the agreement. The difficulty of the matter was not lessened by the factor that his own executive had to overrule his view, the acceptance of which actually meant that a national coal strike must ensue. As we went, on July 30, to the place of signature, he stood in Parliament Square, under a lamp-post, a solitary figure wrapped in thought; as we came back he was still there. But after the settlement had been signed, he kept to the agreement and loyally obeyed the wishes of the majority.

I have seen "Bob" Smillie on various occasions since that date. He holds at the present day a post of great responsibility as permanent President of the General Miners' Federation of Great Britain. As a man he has had a hard life, the history of which he would tell anyone who cared to know. He can be a warm-hearted friend, but, brought up and living in a narrow atmosphere, and repeatedly disappointed, he fails to see that views which he supposes to be broad are in fact narrow, and that, schooled as he has been by Monsieur Longuet, Karl Marx's grandson, and other theoretical economists, he exemplifies the doctrine that a little knowledge is a dangerous thing. He should have been a Covenanter as depicted in *Old Mortality*.

A personal anecdote may perhaps be pardoned. In making a short speech on the signature of the agreement, I said that there would be a sigh of relief in many a homestead in Scotland when it was known that the bitter struggle of a strike would not occur; and many a woman and child might look back with gladness to the settlement the parties had effected. Following serious words, I remarked that even I, too, had had a domestic difficulty, owing to the crucial hours coming the day before at the time of the christening of my only daughter, which I had had to forgo. Immediately after, the miners came round me and asked whether it was true. One said, "I don't know what would be said of a father in Scotland who did that." Another said, "Fancy your doing that for our concerns, and never saying anything about it!" Within a month I received a letter stating that the coal-owners and coal-miners of Scotland had united in presenting a silver porringer (a beautiful work of art) to my daughter Betty in remembrance of her christening. A few months later it was given to me at Edinburgh, Mr. Smillie being the chief spokesman for the miners, and Mr. McCosh, a fine man, loved by all parties, chief spokesman for the coal-owners. I told the story to my old friend Sir Henry James. He curtly remarked, with a gulp in his throat, "That is a good thing for a man to hear, and for men to do."

The remaining months of 1909 were only noticeable by the extension of conciliation meetings and machinery, in trades such as trawler-fishermen, trawlers' engineers and firemen, the brass trades, London correctors of the Press, watermen and lightermen on the Thames, and the boot-and-shoe trade, which led to such heavy work in labour matters that the Commercial side had to be separated off from the Labour side of the department in December 1909.

CHAPTER XV

COTTON, BOILERMAKERS, AND COAL, 1910

The year 1910 was a year of improving trade and, says the official report, "marked by considerable industrial disturbance; the number of workpeople involved in disputes commencing during the year was the highest since 1893, while the aggregate duration of all the disputes in progress during the year has been exceeded on only four occasions during the last eighteen years."

Curiously, questions of wages involved only 20 per cent. of the workpeople directly affected by these disputes. A large number were concerned with strikes, particularly in South Wales, where the Miners' Federation was steadily consolidating, on the non-unionist question, but more than half were involved in great disputes in the coal trade of Northumberland and Durham (refusal of certain miners to accept arrangements made between employers and their own executive) and South Wales (refusal to follow the advice of the Conciliation Board, comprising employers and members of the miners' executive), the shipbuilding industry in the North of England and Scotland (alleged breach by the rank and file of an agreement made between the employers' and men's executives), and the cotton-spinning industry of Lancashire and Cheshire (each party accusing the other of breach of the Brooklands Agreement). Besides these five disputes, in all of which I was concerned, more cases came to the department than in any year since the passing of the Conciliation Act of 1896.

Each of these serious disputes conveyed different lessons, but, except the last, were largely due to the action of young men. Coal commenced the year with a dispute in Northumberland. It was one of those cases where sufficient explanation did not seem to have been given to the men, and the leaders did not carry them along the lines to which they themselves had agreed. As in so many cases of these years, the official leaders could not maintain authority, indicating the fact that there is often more difference between the men and their leaders than between the latter and the employers. They had agreed with the coal-owners, after approval by the miners' lodges, on December 31, 1909, as to the general conditions to be observed under the Coal Mines Regulation Act, 1908, which came into operation in Northumberland on January 1, 1910. The miners objected to the arrangements which the owners proposed to make under this agreement; 30,000 struck work, and though some resumed, 11,000 remained out at the end of January, chiefly owing to the methods necessarily arranged for introducing the three-shift system in place of the two-shift system. On February 15 the Miners' Executive called on the miners to resume work, but they declined. A meeting was held at which members of the Miners' Federation of Great Britain were present, and advised the men to resume work and to observe the agreement. The advice was not accepted. In March the Northumberland Miners' Council endorsed the action of their executive and took a ballot on resumption, still without effective result. There was a complete deadlock among the miners themselves, to the detriment of the owners and the public, as well as a refusal to follow the advice given by local and national leaders, with the result that the only chance of a settlement seemed to be an attempt to deal with the matter under the Conciliation Act. I invited the Miners' Executive and representatives of all the districts still on strike to meet me, for the purpose of considering the difficulty. Representatives of the Miners' Federation of Great Britain also came, including Mr. Smillie, who strongly supported the opinion that the miners should adhere to the agreement. After long debate it was arranged that a small committee of the miners' representatives, backed by Mr. Mitchell from my department (who, however, tactfully made no speeches at the meetings), should go round the collieries, explain the terms, and then take a ballot on the question of resumption. The men from the districts on strike did no like it, as they would have to explain that many of their own words had been misconceived; but they went at it loyally, and succeeded, a ballot ending in a vote for resumption. Even then it was some time before work was resumed at all the pits, since, in addition to dislike at giving way, there were such matters as domestic routine interfered with by the change. If a husband and two sons worked in different pits and came home at different hours, the house could never be made or kept clean; if, instead of leaving early, a man wanted breakfast and hung about the house, the babies could not be so well minded or the house-work done, and shopping time was shortened.

Coal in South Wales caused the next difficulty. The owners had given notice to terminate on March 31 a wages agreement made in 1905. A new agreement had to be made, on which the South Wales Conciliation Board could not agree. As all contracts terminated on March 31 unless an agreement was reached, very great disorganisation was certain to be created in the Welsh coal-fields. It was announced that no arrangements had been made for any further meeting of the Conciliation Board. In fact, the parties were drifting into a great dispute without any steps being taken for any further discussion. On March 23 I went to Cardiff, and managed to obtain the consent of the parties to resume talking, and to cement the understanding in London. The parties, separately, met Mr. Buxton, President of the Board of Trade, myself and other officials on March 24, and on March 26 had another meeting at Cardiff, from which a new Conciliation Board agreement was evolved "to determine the general rate of wages to be paid to the workmen, and to deal with disputes of the various collieries of the owners," subject to the conditions which were set out in an agreement extending to twenty-seven clauses, the agreement to continue in force till March 31, 1915, and thenceforth until either party should give three calendar months' notice terminating the same. I waited at Cardiff while this agreement was being settled, but let it be expressly known that I was only there to report results, and not to interfere. The agreement prevented a general strike in South Wales, and perhaps narrowed the serious sectional dispute later in the year.

Cases not dissimilar, in the principle that the parties had got into a deadlock, had ceased negotiation, and were starting on strikes which were bound to spread, or even cause wide disputes, occurred during the summer in Ayrshire coal-mines and with the dock-labourers at Newport,

Monmouthshire. Suggestions were made to the parties after negotiations which occupied much time, but ultimately led to the disputes being referred to Courts of Arbitration. Another dispute, of Huddersfield woollen manufacturers and spinners, yarn-spinners and fine cloth manufacturers with their willeyers and fettlers, promised to have serious developments, as it would have affected so many other sections, but was settled after a long conference I held at Huddersfield. Then in September came serious trouble in the cotton-spinning industry, all through the dismissal of one man, George Howe, who by instruction of the Card and Blowing Room Operatives' Association had refused to " pick " or clean flats, which he declared not to be his work as a grinder, at the Fern Mill, Shaw, in Lancashire. The secretaries of the two Associations got involved in a squabble over the meaning of the Brooklands Agreement, that famous but badly drafted agreement then governing a great part of the cotton trade. It is not surprising that the draft was vague, as it had been signed after an all-night conference at a wayside inn, where some representatives of each party had managed to meet and patch up a settlement after all other negotiations had broken down. The cardroom people asserted that the employers had broken one clause of the agreement; the employers retaliated by asserting that the operatives had infringed another clause.

The 269 mill-hands at the Fern Mill had all struck on June 7. The employers insisted they should return to work, but finally offered arbitration, either by me or the firms of solicitors who represented the organisations at the drawing up of the Brooklands Agreement, on the question as to which side had broken the Brooklands Agreement. Informal conferences of the representatives led to nothing. On September 19 the Federation of Master Cotton-spinners decided on a general lockout, failing an agreement. Meanwhile the delegates of the cardroom operatives had been considering the matter, and almost at the same time agreed to accept me as arbitrator, but they demanded that the Fern Mill should continue to be stopped until the award was given. This proposal the employers refused: they said that, prior to any hearing, work must be resumed without George Howe, whose dismissal was the question in dispute. It was a very delicate matter to intervene or appear to intervene in the cotton trade. That trade had always prided itself on settling its own differences. Mr. Lloyd George had tried to intervene in November 1907, when a strike had been threatened, also on a question of interpretation of the Brooklands Agreement; but though he had gone to Manchester with many assistants, the parties on his second visit would not meet him, but made an agreement by themselves which, out of courtesy, the employers reported to him. It appeared to me, however, that I had been chosen as an arbitrator by both sides, and that as an arbitrator it was proper for me to discuss the procedure of arbitration, possibly whether there was to be an arbitration or not, and on these grounds I managed to arrange a meeting between the parties at Manchester. Both sides were very determined, there was strong and bitter feeling; the question of George Howe was discussed up hill and down dale, the following proposals being exchanged:

Employers—Before arbitration takes place, the Fern Mill must start without George Howe. If you agree to this we will withdraw the lockout notices, and in the event of arbitration going against us, pay George Howe the whole of his wages from the time he was stopped up to the time the arbitrators' award is given. Beyond this we cannot go.

Operatives—Your proposal is practically the same as offered previously. We cannot accept it. Either the mill must stop until the arbitration is over, or George Howe start work with the other workpeople at the Fern Mill. We are agreed that Mr. Askwith be asked to arbitrate on the question as to who has broken the Brooklands Agreement, at once.

The Employers replied: "We have nothing further to add to our previous proposal." This answer closed the conference. The parties separated without any arrangement for further discussion, the notices terminated, and on October 3 the lockout commenced with about 102,000 people, and the certainty that in a few days other sections would have to stop work. The evils of a great cotton stoppage seemed almost inevitable.

I felt that I had no alternative but to attempt to minimise the block caused by the position in which George Howe was placed, and in which both Associations were placed by crystallising on George Howe. My contention was that the real point was to consider the powers each side had under the Brooklands Agreement, and if necessary to amend them, not to assume that one or the other must have broken the agreement. Although the conference had scattered to all parts of Lancashire, there remained in Manchester some of the leaders, and with them I conferred the whole of the following day, when these arguments prevailed. The cardroom workers called a meeting the next day, Sunday, and accepted the suggestion. They proposed to the employers to consider and decide, at a joint conference prior to arbitration, if arbitration should be necessary, under my chairmanship, the respective powers under the Brooklands Agreement with the significant addition, " As by your offer of September 30 it is provided that George Howe shall not suffer if you are found to be in the wrong, and that we on our part shall not allow him to suffer if we are found to be in the wrong, we agree to the starting of the Fern Mill under the conditions of your offer of September 30. As you have stated you have no feeling against George Howe, we take it you will recognise that he was advised by us, and we shall be glad to hear that you would be willing to find him another similar situation as a grinder in the Shaw district."

The secretary of the employers knew, through me, that this message was coming, and that night summoned the employers from various parts of Lancashire to a special meeting the following afternoon. Then the whole plan nearly broke down. The cardroom representatives had managed to send a letter to the employers' secretary, conveying quite a different impression, of which I heard early on Monday morning. This letter, if read, would have roused the employers as a useless renewal of old proposals, made me look foolish, and given colour to suggestions of double-dealing against the men. The employers were in trains and could not be stopped. It was vital to get the matter put in order before they met in the afternoon; but fortunately the position was rectified just in time. The employers replied they would agree to the conference, but that, while they were willing to recommend the employers in the Shaw district to give George Howe the first vacancy that arose, they had no power to find him a situation. On this the cardroom representatives said that, as their proposal was not accepted, they could not accept the suggestions contained in the employers' reply. This did not look very promising. George Howe had again become the stumbling-block; but it was possible to deduce that if George Howe, who was not himself overanxious to remain in the Fern Mill, provided he got an exactly similar berth, could get a suitable situation, both parties would have their points met. Could this be done? As neither side would move, and as there was no vacancy in any mill except at the Fern Mill if George Howe left it, it was necessary to find a mill-owner who would accept him and a man who would fill up the Fern vacancy, and thus create a new vacancy into which George Howe could step. It was eventually done. Another company agreed "to engage George Howe as stripper and grinder to work for them on the same terms and conditions as the men now in their employ"; and the Fern Spinning Company offered "to engage the man who will be displaced by the engaging of George Howe elsewhere, as stripper and grinder to work for them on the same terms and conditions as the men now in their employ."

The preliminary difficulty was closed. Return to work followed, while both parties agreed that an opinion on the original dispute should be deferred till feeling was less acute. It had become practically unnecessary, except for future guidance, but two conferences were held on the matter, and when finally an opinion was given, some months after, I found that there was a gap in the Brooklands Agreement. No provision was made in it, where there was a difference of opinion about a particular change of work, to ensure that it must be dealt with before a stoppage of work, in the spirit of the Brooklands Agreement, by mutual understanding or agreement, and that the secretaries ought to meet, and if they differed on procedure, the matter should come before the Associations for discussion on merits. The suggestion was made that, unless steps were taken in this direction, there was danger of recurrence of similar difficulties, which ought to be obviated. The parties agreed with the suggestion, and provided a clause designed to prevent a recurrence.

In the same autumn, of 1910, another great lockout occurred, in the Federated Shipyards and Ship-repairing yards at all the principal ports. It was alleged the boilermakers were not keeping the agreement of March 9, 1909, at certain ports, but stopping work without following the procedure laid down. The employers were incensed at the number of sporadic strikes, and the absence of control over their men which the executive of the boilermakers appeared to exhibit. The boilermakers' services were dispensed with after Saturday, September 3, with a notification that resumption of work would not be permitted until satisfactory assurances had been given for the due observance of the agreement of March 1909. The boilermakers' executive council were thus put in the big fix of showing the employers that any assurances they gave would be satisfactory and implemented by the men, a position rendered still more difficult when the men, by 10,193 to 5,087, decided against agreeing to support them in any assurances they might wish to give, though they did agree that a representative meeting should be held at Newcastle. Representatives from this meeting conferred for three days with the employers at Edinburgh. No agreement resulted, save the appointment of a small sub-committee of each party to confer further. These sub-committees reached a provisional agreement on October 11, but on a ballot the men turned it down by 10,212 to 9,054. The boilermakers' representatives now tried the effect of getting an explanation of certain clauses of the agreement from the Employers' Federation. They were given, and another ballot taken: 15,563 against the agreement, and only 5,650 for it. The difficulty was becoming worse and worse, more men voting at each ballot, and a huge majority turning down the proposed agreement. I managed to see some of the boilermakers' executive, and put to them a suggestion that the best course might be to get at the heart of the discontent. That procedure had answered earlier in the year with the Northumberland coal trade; and I thought it might be tried in this very obstinate dispute, which the shipbuilders were quietly watching. They agreed, and made arrangements to get specially appointed delegates to come to London. Then, after a preliminary meeting of the emergency committee with Mr. Buxton, I held a conference for three days, at the end of November, with the executive council and, above all, the specially appointed delegates from the districts affected by the dispute. The Boilermakers' Society is a very scattered society, its members being in every port in the country. It is a very difficult society to control from Newcastle. These meetings were probably the first occasion on which many of the delegates had ever met each other. Possibly they did more to weld the society together than any meetings it could usually hold. The discussion was certainly most interesting. Every man had his say, and did not omit to take the opportunity, some very strong remarks being bandied about. After two days it was suggested they should come to business, and a small draft committee prepared a report. It was unanimously accepted ; and the results were forwarded to the employers. On December 7 and 8 the employers again met the boilermakers, including the special delegates ; together with representatives of the other shipyard trade unions, who would naturally be affected by any change in the 1909 agreement. This time the conference was fruitful. The method of settling disputes was revised and expedited. An agreement was reached and signed by everybody, with the following remarkable paragraph :

> "We the undersigned representatives of the Boilermakers' and Iron Shipbuilders' Society, consisting of the Executive Council, the District Delegates, representatives of District Committees and *specially chosen representatives from the various areas affected by the dispute*, unanimously agree that the foregoing is a fair and equitable settlement, and we unanimously pledge ourselves, individually and collectively, to recommend it as such to our members."

The ballot of the members of the Boilermakers' Society resulted in a large majority in favour of the agreement, and work was accordingly resumed on December 15. The Boilermakers' Executive kindly presented me with a souvenir in the shape of a specially bound copy of their Annual Report, containing the new rules.

The third large dispute of 1910 lasted for a whole year, and was the forerunner of the disputes of 1911. Ostensibly it arose over the refusal of Welsh coal-owners to entertain one of the proposals made earlier in the year, when the Conciliation Board was formed, to give payment of a fixed wage to workmen employed in "abnormal places" ; a difficulty not reduced till the passing of the Coal Mines

(Minimum Wage) Act at a later date, but it indicated other symptoms. It showed that South Wales miners would not accept, under certain conditions, either the proposals made by agreement between both sides of the Conciliation Board, or the assurances of the owners or the advice of their own Executive or the Miners' Federation of Great Britain, or the suggestions and efforts made by the Board of Trade. A large section of 10,000 men, when support was withdrawn by their own Association and the National Association to which they belonged, still held out by themselves for months, ultimately accepting, in August, the very terms put before them by me in January, and in the result finding that those terms worked satisfactorily; but resuming work with a feeling of bitterness. It showed that there was serious and growing revolt in South Wales against owners and against their old leaders, a new spirit of disaffection among the younger men, which the events of subsequent years have not dispelled.

As often happens, the dispute had a small beginning. It commenced with a strike of a few men in the employment of the Cambrian Combine in the Rhondda Valley, with differences at one mine called the Ely Pit, Penygraig, over the price-list of a particular seam. The owners, on September 1, closed the pit on the ground that without this price-list the mine could not be worked at a profit. A rumour spread that the men out of work by this closing were being boycotted at other pits, and two other pits struck in sympathy. A price-list was provisionally settled by the chairmen of the two sides of the South Wales Miners' Conciliation Board, a settlement which usually would have been considered final, and at least tried, but on this occasion the Ely men rejected it. The strike now spread farther, about 10,000 men ceasing work. On November 7 serious riots commenced, and police and military were called in. The situation became grave. I determined to try again the policy of getting at the heart of the difficulty, and invited the officials of the miners, together with representative miners from the district where the trouble existed, to meet me in London, in order that the difficulty in acceptance of the price-list might be fully explained. Several conferences ensued, but the various representatives of the men could not come to any agreement among themselves. It seemed that there was sufficient ground, however, for a meeting with the owners. Three were held during December, at Cardiff, but no settlement was arrived at. The suggestion was continually made that the proposed price-list indicated a desire to lower general wages and not give payment for abnormal places, such as were alleged to be likely to occur in this seam. There seemed to be distrust of the faith of the owners, so that I suggested and received an assurance in writing from Mr. D. A. Thomas (afterwards Lord Rhondda) that

> "We have no desire or intention to reduce the general level of wages, while we would readily give our undertaking to supplement low wages by allowances, as is customary throughout the coal-field, when such are caused by difficulties of working places, so as to enable fair wages to be earned."

An assurance had been asked for and an assurance given, but still the men would not accept. The General Miners' Federation now came into the matter, as their members had decided to give financial assistance to the Cambrian men. Messrs. Ashton and W. E. Harvey, their representatives, caught hold of the assurance point, and after a long meeting with the Welshmen and myself, asked me to arrange another meeting with the owners, on the plea of explanations of the assurances. A meeting was held on February 10, and I put down the strongest assurances in writing as given by the manager of the Cambrian combine, Mr. Llewellyn.

Even these did not satisfy the executive council of the South Wales Miners' Federation, who rejected them. The strike dragged on, until a month later I was again asked to arrange another meeting between the parties. This time the owners said they did not consider any good purpose would be served by another meeting. They could not add any further assurances. The miners' executives then decided to take a ballot, with the result that the miners, on March 25, voted by 7,141 to 309 against acceptance. The Miners' Federation of Great Britain once more took the matter up, and resolved that the price-list ought to be referred to arbitration, calling on the Executive Council to give effect to this resolution. The owners would not agree to this, but met representatives of the Miners' Federation, and on May 15 these two parties agreed that the list of October 22, 1910, should be given a twelvemonth's trial, the men having the assurances of the owners, and it being understood that members of the Joint Conciliation Board should deal with any complaints. It was practicable to make such an agreement, which was, in fact, exactly the same as had been suggested at our conferences in the previous January; but it was unanimously rejected by the lodges of the South Wales Miners' Federation. On this result, the Miners' Federation of Great Britain withdrew, on June 13, 1911, and cut off their financial support, but the strike still went on. It lasted till August 31, when the Cambrian men agreed to accept the terms, which they could have had eight months before!

The position at the end of 1910 was so well summed up by Mr. Philip Snowden (then M.P.) that perhaps he will forgive me for quoting and endorsing some of his words. He is the only man, as far as I know, who accurately summed up the position and gave an accurate prophecy. With some shortening, his statement was:

"The year 1910 has been an exceedingly trying time for all who have had any responsibility for the management of trade unions and the direction of the Labour movement. The men connected with a number of important trade unions have shown a good deal of dissatisfaction with the actions of their responsible officials, and this dissatisfaction has expressed itself in some cases in rebellion against the agreements entered into by the Union Executive and in unauthorised strikes. Trouble of this sort has been chiefly active in the North-East of England, on the Clyde, and in South Wales. On the North-Eastern Railway, a matter of the most trivial character was made the excuse for the men in a Newcastle goods yard to stop work, and this immediately led to a general cessation, which for a few days paralysed the railway system. This unauthorised and spontaneous action on the men's part was a way of expressing their general discontent. The company conceded the immediate demands of the men, so that their action in taking matters into their own hands and overriding the authority of the Union Executive may, like the actions of the locked-out boilermakers, be considered to have been justified by its success. But victories of this sort may be bought too dearly. Discipline in trade unionism is too vital a thing to be injured by violation, and, though an occasional irresponsible movement may succeed, such a practice must, if frequently adopted, be destructive of collective bargaining and of trade unionism itself; for no executive could retain office if its authority were not respected. By the side of the success of the North-Eastern strike may be put the complete failure of the unauthorised stoppage of work of the Durham and Aberdare Valley miners.

"The trouble which the trade union leaders have had in dealing with their men has been experienced to some extent by the political Labour movement. A minority in the Independent Labour Party has been actively endeavouring to foment opposition to the Parliamentary Labour Party, but the Labour candidatures at the recent General Election do not appear to have suffered from this internal criticism, which is evidently much more noisy than influential. The trouble with the extreme Socialist critics and the Labour Party is that they want to apply ideal perfection to a very imperfect set of conditions.

"The difficulties of the trade union leaders and of the Labour Party have been increased last year by the legal injunctions which have been granted restraining the unions from using any part of their funds for political purposes. The trade unions made this a test question at the late General Election, and a sufficient number of members pledged to support an amendment of the law as it now stands have been returned to ensure the question being favourably treated in the new Parliament.

"In 1910—a year of record trade—wages remained practically stationary. The cost of living increases, and the working people's desires rightly grow. But with stationary wages, the real condition of the workers is one of diminishing power to satisfy desires. This is one of the causes of the unrest in the Labour world. With the spread of education, with the display of wealth and luxury by the rich, it is certain that the workers will not be content. It is the duty of statesmanship to acknowledge the justice of the desire of the workers for a more human and cultured life, and to satisfy this unrest by concessions of reform. If employers and politicians are so unwise as to ignore the demands of Labour, then what might be done by safe and constitutional methods will, by great suffering and loss, be accomplished by industrial strife, and through social anarchy.

"The increasing activity of the Board of Trade in Labour disputes has been very marked during the past year. Its present legal powers in the way of conciliation are very limited, being confined practically to offering to the respective parties the impartial services of a Government department. Mr. Askwith, K.C., has rendered invaluable services during the past year, and it is a pity that, as the representative of the community which has much at stake in every industrial dispute, he has not more authority to knock a little more common sense into the heads of those responsible for protracted industrial dispute. In spite of the unusual activity of a few persons who have been industriously preaching the new Industrial Unionism—which is the gospel of fighting armed men with fists fed from empty stomachs—the idea of conciliation in industrial disputes has made progress during the past year. If there could be a general recognition of the right of Labour to share to a much greater extent in the national income, the method of conciliation might prove a very acceptable way of securing that end.

"The year upon which we have just entered is likely to be a momentous one for Labour. There is trouble brewing in a number of trades which may break out into open hostilities. Labour has become aggressive, and is not merely opposing attack, but is determined upon advances."

CHAPTER XVI

TRANSPORT WORKERS, 1911

WHILE the Cambrian dispute was still dragging its slow length along, the great outburst of 1911 commenced with a general strike of seamen and firemen at Southampton. The strike rapidly spread to most of the principal ports of the United Kingdom. Dock labourers and other transport workers ceased work in support of the seamen, each branch putting forward its own claims. The strike at Southampton started on June 14, and was based on a national programme, claiming:

1. The constitution of a conciliation board.
2. A minimum rate of wages.
3. Manning scale for stokehold, deck, and galley.
4. Abolition of medical examination by doctors privately appointed by the Shipping Federation.
5. Abolition of payment of seamen in the Shipping Federation offices.
6. Right of seamen to a portion of their wages in a port during a voyage.
7. Right of a seaman to have a representative present when signing on.
8. Hours of labour and rates and overtime to be fixed.
9. Improved forecastle accommodation.

On June 16 Goole also went up, and Goole was followed on June 20 by Hull, the dock labourers striking in support of the seamen and bringing forward claims of their own. The seamen were a more organised union; the dock labourers simply took the opportunity and joined hands with them, without any definite scheme, or organisation of port with port. In fact, it proved difficult in some cases to find out exactly what their claims were, though at the base of all was the economic demand, more money, in view of increased cost of living and rising profits. Although the movement started with the seamen, who had arranged and considered their claims, the real movement came from the dockers and other transport workers, and following them the carters and, later, the railwaymen. One of the leading Labour politicians, so far from knowing of any agreed movement, said to me later, " I don't know what has come over the country. Everyone seems to have lost their heads." Other people talked of the strike fever. *The Times*, in the autumn, suggested the hot weather was largely responsible; to be soon disabused by a serious strike at Dundee in the bitter weather at the end of December. The Midlands complacently talked of the madness of the ports and that all was quiet in Birmingham and its districts, also to be disabused by an upheaval a few months later. The heads of the great shipping lines, much less the dock authorities, did not seem to know. One shipowner came to me and discussed the matter; he spoke of it as a revolution, and so it was. The dockers at Goole and Hull, he said, had new leaders, men unknown before; the employers did not know how to deal with them; the military were close by, but they were Territorials from Hull—what would be their attitude? The shipowners could not recognise the Seamen's Union: the Federation forbade. Metropolitan police had been asked for and were on their way. Fires, looting, riots had started at once. They were thoroughly surprised; and could not understand the cause.

" Well," I said, " what are you going to do?" He did not know. I remarked that the powers of the Board of Trade depended only upon the Conciliation Act; inquiry could be made, but a rebuff might make matters worse. I had been in Hull twice, over disputes with trawlers, and the seamen knew me, or of me. I knew nothing of their present attitude after these settlements, but, if the President agreed, I was willing to come to Hull and see whether it was possible to do anything in the face of this position, provided it could be ascertained that the new leaders of the men would meet me and the employers. This plan was accepted, and I went, with Mr. Mitchell, to Hull, on receipt of a telegram. There was no doubt about the upheaval when one got there, but without dilating upon that, the only definite claims were those of the seamen, and those we proceeded to debate. The others were sympathetic strikes, it was said, and would close with a settlement.

After many hours an agreement was reached. Everybody seemed to be pleased. Though the situation was complicated by a by-election then proceeding, in which Mr. (afterwards Sir Mark) Sykes was standing, and finally got in, few paid any attention to that. A settlement had been achieved. It should be proclaimed to the people; and the men's leaders went out to proclaim it. It was estimated there were 15,000 people there when the leaders began their statement. They announced a settlement; and before my turn came, an angry roar of "No!" rang out; and "Let's fire the docks!" from outskirts where men ran off. The crowd surged against the platform in a space before the hotel; women who had come there to see the show shrieked with alarm.

I hastily told them to keep quiet, and to their credit they did. It was necessary to act at once, and I stood up, with raised arm. There was dead silence. In a windy open-air meeting it was not possible to be heard by all; the sound of a voice could only reach a certain number; but if these were to keep calm, the effect would spread. As clearly as I could I said the meeting was adjourned; the employers and their representatives were going to continue to negotiate. They must go home. With two constables in front, we walked through that crowd back to the hotel, in perfect peace, to find turmoil in its hall. I heard a town councillor remark that he had been in Paris during the Commune and had never seen anything like this: the women were worse than anything he had ever seen, and he had not known there were such people in Hull—women with hair streaming and half nude, reeling through the streets, smashing and destroying.

"Then you ought to have known," said an angry employer; but such bickerings had nothing to do with the question at issue—What was the real cause of the refusal to accept an agreed settlement? I told the leaders of the men very plainly they must find out, though I thought the dockers were the difficulty. I was there to discuss claims, not to put down riots; but as they were anxious to keep men together in order to avoid turmoil in the streets, I agreed, if they would hold several meetings, to speak to them on the value of negotiation in preference to force, and also to speak to the railwaymen, who were threatening to stop the lines, on the points that this dispute was not their dispute, they had their own organisations for dealing with any of their own grievances, and that pending negotiations could only be prejudiced by premature action which would cut off Hull from the rest of the country. These mass meetings took place in halls, to which different sections were directed, and it was arranged that further meetings should take place on the Sunday, when the men could instruct their leaders and also invest them, if they agreed, with full powers, the meetings to be held by themselves; but if they would proceed on these lines and desired me to return, I would come back—otherwise I should not. The rest of the day was spent in interviews with merchants, anxious to get their goods cleared, and insisting that the military should come in and that the goods ought to be unloaded at any cost. Some Bradford consignees were urging delivery of fresh eggs—Bradford had no eggs. The Hull merchants concerned admitted the eggs came from the Baltic, and had been collected over a period of several weeks or months. I suggested Bradford might wait for its "fresh" eggs a few days longer. Another had lost a £40,000 cargo of salmon, and vowed vengeance on the dock authorities. I suggested the salmon was already the food of other fishes and the claim might be deferred. I did not go far from Hull, but late on Sunday heard the meetings had gone off well. Employers and men were summoned for Monday, when exactly the same terms previously agreed to were endorsed, with the addition of a halfpenny per hour increase for the dockers; and this time the agreement was accepted. The dockers had, in fact, been the stumbling-block to earlier acceptance, and the addition of a clause, "The wages of men employed by regular liners, stevedores, lumpers, merchants, wharfingers, in the loading and discharging of ships—ship labour only—be advanced by a halfpenny per hour. The term 'ship-labour' includes men carrying or barrowing direct from ship to quay or from quay to ship," completed the agreement. I have heard it said there is no remembrance of service done or of peace being effected. To that argument I can only reply that during the War, again and again, both parties from Hull brought me questions in dispute, and asked me finally to decide them.

Returning to London, I found the Lord Mayor of Manchester was in telephonic communication with the

President, urging that I should come at once to that city, and so Mr. Mitchell and I dashed back to the North. Disputes had commenced with the seamen. On June 27 the dock labourers at the Ship Canal docks had also ceased work; on July 1 the Lord Mayor had held meetings; on July 3 the carters all struck, both those employed by carting contractors and by railway companies. All transport was stopped. Other trades were following. Police had been drafted from Birmingham into Manchester and other towns, and troops into the neighbouring town of Salford. The Lord Mayor had arranged meetings and suggested I should act as conciliator, which had been accepted. Eighteen or more trade unions had bound themselves by a pledge that none should go back till all were satisfied, a pledge which made settlement by no means an easy matter. In every room in the Town Hall, which the Lord Mayor had put at our disposal, different trades were closeted, employers and employed, debating, discussing, and almost fighting. Hour by hour and day by day, it was only possible to go from one to the other, get a dispute upon apparent lines of possible settlement, and then answer a hurried summons to another room to prevent a conference breaking up. For five days, for all the days and nearly all the nights, these conferences proceeded, until at last, on Sunday night (July 9), all the trades had come to agreements except two, which would require the acceptance by the seamen of an arrangement slightly modified from one which the men had refused but their leaders seemed inclined to accept, and the consent of the Great Northern Railway carters to go back to work without any change. I described what followed, in a speech at Montreal, in these terms:—

"I called the labour leaders into a hall of the Mansion House, and after locking the doors explained to them the situation, and spoke to them in this way: I put before them that they made this pledge one to another that they would not go back to work unless all sections were settled, and that that pledge, being a mutual pledge, ought not to be broken. My arguments had always been directed to the importance of keeping agreements. Feeling that that pledge should not be broken, it was for them, in the interests of Labour and their own interests, either to persuade or somehow obtain the consent of those outstanding sections to fall in with the views of the rest of the labour sections and get a settlement by consent. The dockers' leader got up and made one of the most eloquent speeches that I have ever heard, so much so that when, at the end of it, I said we would now hear what the leader of the railwaymen had to say on the same subject, the seamen's leader said: 'Oh, don't say any more; I am convinced. I will go and tell what has been said to my committee, and to a mass meeting this evening, and I will try to come back at ten or eleven o'clock with our answer.' At ten o'clock he was back, saying he had obtained the consent of the seamen to modify the terms so that an agreement could be made with the employers. There still remained the railway carters—a very difficult set of men, who were very angry and who at that period could not obtain anything. I told the labour leaders that this proposition was up to them, and that I must ask them to go down with me and bring all their influence to bear upon the carters to return to work with the rest of the city. They did so, and for between two and three hours spoke, implored, and almost cursed the carters in urging them to give way. One of the leaders behind me said to me: 'I have been in many meetings, but never in one like this.' He asked me what I was going to do. 'I am going to stay here until ten o'clock to-morrow morning to get a resolution,' I said. About 2.30 a.m. I rose and gave a summing-up of all the speeches that had been made. I put before these men that, because of pledges made by the Great Northern Railway to their colleagues of the other railways, they could not possibly at that time give what the men wanted; that they were under contract and must keep good faith, and that on that ground the men were unable to press the Great Northern Railway to break their agreement. I promised to speak to the General Manager and see whether he could soften some of the difficulties that existed, and also that, in regard to the imprisonment of some of their colleagues, which they said was unfair, I would see the Home Secretary with a view to examination of the cases and possible remission of sentence, but that nothing could be given at that time, and beyond that I would not pledge myself to anything. The moment I sat down, a labour man got up and said: 'By G——, men, give Mr. Askwith a chance. Up with your hands.' Hands went up. 'Those against.' Three hands went up. The resolution was carried.

"'Get away to the Mansion House as fast as you can,' said a friend, and thither we drove. An immense crowd was in the square. 'You can get back to work,' I said; and the words spread like wildfire, a dash being made to the docks.

"That same morning I was awakened by a noise at 7.30. I looked out of the window, and saw one solitary lorry with a detective in plain clothes walking by its side. I thought, 'This thing has failed,' but being too tired to do anything else, I lay down again until 9.30, when a noise like thunder woke me. I went to the window again, and in the large square opposite the Manchester Town Hall, on one side were riding out the Scots Greys, who had been garrisoning Salford, on the other side were the Metropolitan and Birmingham police going to the railway-station to leave the city; and in the main street were mile upon mile of lorries laden with goods coming from the docks to be distributed in the city and to the cotton-mills."

The Manchester disputes had ended. Some of the newspapers expressed a hope that "the strike fever" had closed and that the holiday season would be passed in peace. They had hardly begun to congratulate themselves when, at the beginning of August, transport workers in other parts of the country began to strike. On August 3, a telegram from the Lord Mayor of Leeds asked me to go by the first train to Leeds. The tramway men had all gone out. I went as a conciliator, and after sitting till past two in the morning the parties came to an agreement on a revised code. It was fortunate that this dispute was settled, as its continuance, apart from vast inconvenience to a great city, would undoubtedly have led to much disturbance in Yorkshire. The dispute was scarcely settled when, on August 8, conferences had to begin on a general strike in the London docks. The transport workers had gone out, and were followed by coal-porters, lightermen, and carters. These unions had also bound themselves by a pledge not to return to work till all were satisfied. About 80,000 workpeople had ceased work, the shipping of the Port of London was brought to a standstill, and the supplies of London began to run short. Mr. Buxton intervened with proposals for conferences, when the experience of Manchester was again repeated. For four days I was conciliating in conferences, by which means the most important sections —coal-porters, tanking coal-porters, lightermen, and carters —arrived at agreements, each of them giving a kind of code indicating hours, wages, and general conditions. The strike was then declared to be closed, after lasting eleven days, the other sections consenting to forgo an immediate settlement in view of the detailed examination required for each. In the course of the following fortnight, however, agreements were also reached with shipowners, short sea traders, certain coal lightermen and wharfingers, and three separate lighterage companies, Mr. John Burns presiding over some of the conferences at the Local Government Board.

When, on Friday, August 11, the announcement of the close of the general strike was made, London undoubtedly gave a sigh of relief. The weather was extremely hot, which greatly added to the difficulties of supplies, and also to complications with the owners of perishable cargoes awaiting delivery in the docks. Isolated disturbances had commenced, and as the attitude of the railways was uncertain, the Home and War Offices were considering the bringing of troops to London for the prevention of disorder and protecting the distribution of food. I was obliged to beg for time, with no certainty that a settlement could be effected, but with complete certainty that there would be grave trouble if attempts were made to unload ships and try to convey goods with military aid through the congested streets of the East End. The Home Secretary was much troubled by one merchant, who claimed that his meat must be unloaded and would go bad because there was no available ice. He insisted that the Home Secretary had given him a pledge that the meat should be got to market in time, even if it entailed the use of troops, a statement which the Minister, Mr. Churchill, said was exaggerated, though he admitted that the demand was not easy to answer. As it appeared to me most desirable not to use troops, I asked to see the merchant, and questioned him about the meat. He painted a picture of the present and future condition of that meat, demanding its immediate unloading and convoy by the Guards through nine miles of streets to Smithfield Market. Asked whether this would not be a difficult feat, he said he did not care: the Minister must give him the meat, it was beginning to be musty, and in two or three days might be green. After further questions as to the result of working out the alleged pledge, it appeared that he was aiming at the purchase of the meat by the Government, which alone would obviate his claim for fulfilment. I asked what he suggested the Government should do with the sudden acquisition of £100,000 worth or more of meat, to which he replied unguardedly, "Oh, they can use it for the soldiers." "Indeed?" I remarked. "Musty and nearly green meat to the men risking their lives for your cargo and at your suggestion? Surely you don't wish me to tell that to the country, or the Minister to explain the bargain in Parliament?" It happened that in holding up a hand I had put up my little finger, and he promptly exclaimed with a laugh, "You have got me on the tip of that finger. I'll let him off, and as I see you want time, I won't say a word more for forty-eight hours. Good luck to you!" and thus left the room. He got his meat. Who ate it, and what was its condition, I am unaware, but no claim was made against the Government.

There was no doubt that the very hot weather and the small cold-storage accommodation did hazard the supplies of London. A few paragraphs from newspapers put together illustrate the growing anxiety of the public. Observers said truly:

"As a result of the spread of the strike of transport workers, London finds itself within measurable distance of a meat and butter famine. The docks are at a complete standstill. The strikers have no need to place pickets, because there are no workers to picket. The import and export trade of the greatest city in the world and the most dependent on oversea food is completely paralysed. It is true that some of the claims have been settled, but no section will return to work till the claims of the other sections have been settled. Mr. Askwith's task is a hard one, for as fast as one dispute is ended, another breaks out.

"In London, which depends so largely for its supply of meat on frozen imports from Argentina, the United States, and New Zealand, the price of meat has already advanced 50 per cent. The reserves will not last long, and the outlook is most serious. If the strike continues, the refrigerating ships which are lying in the docks waiting to discharge their cargoes will run short of coal and the meat on board will go bad. As for the butter trade, the Danish butter imported into this country comes in casks and is not refrigerated, so that it will perish in the present hot weather unless it is very promptly discharged. Among the other troubles of the strike is the scarcity of ice, which is being severely felt both by the householder and the provision merchant. The extent of the interests affected by the strike is enormous. Many of the newspapers are face to face with a forcible stoppage within a day or so, through sheer inability to get paper delivered. There is a shortage of petrol, and already the motor-bus services are cut down to about half. The Metropolitan hospitals are very hard pushed to get food and provisions for the inmates. Smithfield Market presents a strange spectacle. Its bustle and activity have entirely ceased. All the big storehouses are completely deserted. Tons of fruit and vegetables lie rotting and neglected on the wharves. The river from London Bridge is a picture of strange quiet. All the big ships are lying up, while the tide in midstream sweeps on, its surface untenanted. The menace of famine becomes more and more imminent."

At the same time sporadic riots or fights were occurring in different districts; troops were held ready at Aldershot and other places; statements were made, with doubtful foundation, that supplies would be assured; every Minister was anxiously wondering and often inquiring whether the use of force would be necessary; newspapers stated facts, but would also, according to their information or policy, urge patience or intervention by physical means. Such is the condition of affairs in a very big strike, and such are the dangers and anxieties which a conciliator, immersed hour after hour and day after day in the manifold details of trade upon trade and in discussion upon every item in each man's work in those trades, has to try to keep out of his mind, with stern concentration on the one problem of effecting a settlement, as clear, effective, and fair as possible, in the business before him. He dares not contemplate or think of the results which may come if he fails to succeed, but the man must be lacking in imagination upon whose mind and body such happenings do not react, or who from time to time is not obliged to force them out of his thoughts with all the strength of will which he can muster.

It was not to be expected that all agreements made under these circumstances of high tension, long hours, and necessary speed could cover all details of large trades or avoid the possibility of subsequent interpretations being required. It proved to be so in several instances, but on the whole the minuteness as well as the wide scope of many of these agreements defined and settled, in a manner that did not before exist, the rights and conditions of work of large classes of workpeople. They formed the basis on which later changes could be made, and did much to establish codes for disorganised classes of men where regulations had been absent or very nebulous. In one or two cases it was possible to effect more, and to put an industry upon a secure basis which could be of lasting value. This result was especially obtained in connection with the men and sailing-barge owners of the Thames, the Medway, Sittingbourne, and Faversham, for work within the port. Owing to the intricacy of the subject, it could not be settled at the time of the general strike, but was deferred for future settlement, with the provision that the new rates should date back to August 21 for all freights. No agreement being reached by the parties in September, a joint conference was called, when a Sub-committee was appointed, with myself as chairman. This Committee did not settle the matter, so it was arranged I should compile a list, in consultation with various interests, putting it before the parties when completed. This proposal was accepted, and a list of rates covering all the principal classes of cargoes carried between various places by sailing barges on the Thames and Medway was prepared, and after some discussion approved. The completed list contained about 600 items, with rates for cement, lime, bricks, clay, coal, coke, corn and grain, ballast, timber, wood-pulp, manure, flints, oil, and a number of miscellaneous items. Rates were quoted for freights of all kinds between various places on the reaches and tributaries of the Thames, Medway, and Lea, and on the adjoining canals. This compilation required great care and laborious work, but it proved, I think, to be worth doing. The list, known from the colour of its cover as the "Pink List," is still the charter of the bargemen.

It stopped bickerings and innumerable squabbles as to the proper rates between barge-owners and men ; it settled the relative rates for different classes of cargo between men and men ; and could be easily added to all round, if there was a general rise of wages, by flat additions or by percentages.

CHAPTER XVII

RAILWAY STRIKE, 1911

Before the transport strike had come to an end, the railways began, so that some of the later transport settlements could only be effected in the hours which could be spared from the pressure of this new difficulty. The first murmur of the storm had commenced with a small strike, on August 5, by railwaymen at Liverpool, who ceased work on the ground that they could not get their grievances dealt with under the Conciliation Boards of 1907, or satisfaction in their demands for increased wages and shorter hours. Other transport workers at Liverpool followed. There was the sequence of disturbance, riot, extra police and the military, to which on August 14 the Liverpool shipowners replied by a general lockout of all men engaged in cargo work; whereupon the workpeople countered by declaring a general strike of the whole of the transport workers. Railwaymen had followed by striking in other centres, just at the time when the London strike was in full progress. The Executives of the Railwaymen's Societies met at the storm centre, and on August 15 suddenly issued an ultimatum, sending copies to all the general managers of railway companies, that they had unanimously agreed "to offer the railway companies twenty-four hours to decide whether they are prepared to immediately meet representatives of these organisations to negotiate a basis of settlement of the matters in dispute affecting the various grades. In the event of this offer being refused, there will be no alternative but to respond to the demand now being made for a national stoppage."

On August 15 the Prime Minister and the President of the Board of Trade, with other officials and myself, had had interviews with seven leading employers of the largest industries and also leaders of the chief Unions, "for the purpose of an informal exchange of views as to the present state of unrest in the labour world, and the possibility of improving the means available for preventing or shortening industrial wars." In particular there was discussion on the principles of a plan proposed at the end of July by Sir Charles W. Macara, Bart., so well known in the cotton world and for his skill in organising and developing schemes, in regard to the establishment of a special business court for dealing with industrial disputes, the court to be composed of leading employers and labour leaders, under a neutral chairman, with no power of compulsory decision, but with authority to review facts and give an opinion on pending or existing disputes.

The Industrial Council was subsequently formed upon the basis of this scheme, but in face of this new crisis from Liverpool and reports from all parts of the country, and with the support of these meetings, it was only natural that Mr. Buxton, with Sir H. Llewellyn Smith, the Permanent Secretary, and me, should see next day, August 16, the representatives of as many railway companies as could be got, and subsequently the secretaries of the railwaymen. It was agreed at these separate interviews that it was desirable to see the executive committees of the railwaymen, with a view to getting at the root of the trouble, and the next day, August 17, they had arrived from Liverpool.

The railway companies had announced that they hoped to give a restricted though effective service; and that they stood by the policy of the Conciliation Boards initiated in 1907, accepted by the men and their societies; while the Home Secretary stated in the House of Commons, "The Government certainly have not promised to support the Railway Companies against the men, nor the men against the Railway Companies. But it would be the duty of the Government, in the event of the paralysis of the great railway lines, on which the life and food of the people depend, to secure that persons engaged in working them shall have full legal protection, and to make sure that no great disaster or catastrophe overwhelms the people owing to the breakdown of the machinery by which we live from day to day."

The promise sounded well, but it was not so easy to keep.

Only 20,000 up to 40,000 soldiers, at most, were available, who could scarcely defend the larger centres, even if collected in the most suitable places. One manager told me he was sure of his drivers, who only wanted to have protection against bottles thrown as engines entered tunnels, and dynamite cartridges in the coal-boxes; but he had formed a wrong estimate. Another relied on the weakness of the union, stating that in any event his line would surely be kept working. Within twenty-four hours I saw on the London terminus a notice: "This station closed till further orders," and not a train was running on the line.

On August 17, when the executives of the men—about forty in number—arrived with their officials, questions were asked and, after a brief discussion, put in writing for their consideration.

The questions and answers were:

"1 and 2. What were the actual causes on which the executive had based their action in issuing their manifesto? and what were the actual grievances in connection with the Conciliation Board Agreement of 1907?

"*Answer.* The failure of the railway companies to behave in the spirit and letter of the Conciliation Board Agreement of 1907, and the utter impossibility of the men's representatives to redress the many grievances of which the men complained.

"3. Were those grievances sufficiently grave to justify the action which the executive had taken?

"*Answer.*—Yes.

"4. Could those grievances not be remedied in a less drastic way?

"*Answer.*—Yes; by the suggestion offered by the committee to the railway companies, requesting them to meet authorised representatives of the men.

"5. Could those grievances be remedied in the way proposed by the men, of a general railway strike?

"*Answer.*—Yes. In our opinion it is the only course.

"We have also considered the possibility of further questions being asked, and we have unanimously come to the conclusion that the only way that will now be an effective method of peace is that the companies consent to meet us."

I went over to Downing Street and sent in this result to the Cabinet, which had been sitting the whole morning, and brought back the Prime Minister with the reply.

He stated that the men's answer to the first two questions was that the ground of their action was the failure of the railway companies to behave in the spirit and letter of the Conciliation Board Agreement of 1907 and the difficulty of redress; their other answers were based upon and assumed the correctness of those statements;

"and it is of first and most essential importance to establish or disprove by impartial investigation the soundness of your statements. For this purpose His Majesty's Government are prepared to appoint immediately a Royal Commission to investigate the working of the Conciliation Agreement, and to report what amendments, if any, are desirable in the scheme, with a view to promote a satisfactory settlement of the grievances.

"I hope to announce without delay the names of the Commissioners, who will meet at the earliest possible moment.

"I may further add that I confidently hope we may rely on your assistance in giving the Commission the fullest possible help and information."

The Prime Minister added that the Government were completely impartial as regards the merits of the various points of dispute which have arisen between the companies and their employees. The Government had to regard exclusively the interests of the public, and, having regard to those interests, they could not allow a general paralysis of the railway system of the country, and would have to take the necessary steps to prevent it. They had therefore put forward a proposal which would ensure prompt investigation, by a perfectly independent tribunal, of the complaints formulated in answer to Mr. Buxton's questions. It was for the representatives of the employees now to consider whether they would fall in with that proposal. Their refusal would, in his opinion, impose upon them heavy responsibility, and, quite apart from the merits of the case, would put them in the wrong in the court of public opinion. He had not employed, and had no wish to employ, the language of menace, or even of warning, but he earnestly desired them to weigh carefully what he had said on behalf of the Government before they came to a decision.

Immediately afterwards a similar statement was made to the general managers.

The latter part of the Prime Minister's speech was put to the men with lucid clearness, but, to say the least, in no conciliatory tone, and in stronger terms than I have indicated. The Prime Minister, it seemed to me, was rather nervous, and, sitting next to him, I longed to pull his coat-tail, as Mr. Larkin, in 1907, had suggested I should pull his if he said anything wrong. As the speech went on I saw the jaws of the Northerners stiffen. They took his words as a threat and his tone as " take it or leave it." The exact form of the Royal Commission and its intended speedy inquiry was not explained. It was easy to see the result would be a refusal, and it was. At three o'clock they came back and told him curtly that they were not prepared to accept his proposal. Matters were not improved when he muttered, " Then your blood be on your own head," as he left the room, the members at once going off to call out the railwaymen all over the country. Their manifesto spoke of an " unwarrantable threat," and " with the full sense of the grave step we are taking, we feel satisfied that our duty to those we represent compels us to refuse the offer of His Majesty's Government, and reluctantly revert to the decision of this body on Tuesday last."

In addition 2,000 telegrams went out to the branches, with the words, " Your liberty is at stake. All railwaymen must strike at once. The loyalty of each means victory for all."

That evening Mr. Lloyd George made a statement to the House of Commons following questions by Mr. Ramsay Macdonald, and intimated that the proposals had not been fully understood : it was not a shelving Commission : the Commission was to be a Commission of three, to work at once and quickly, " with a view to administrative, and if necessary legislative, action being taken by the Government in order to see a fair state of things established " ; and added that negotiations were not entirely broken off ; " the parties are giving full consideration to the interpretation which I now place upon the proposal of the Government." The men's executive were, in fact, sitting nearly all the night, but even after this speech issued, at 1 a.m., another manifesto calling upon "every railwayman to join his fellows and so strike a united blow for deliverance from petty tyranny."

It will be observed that the men had not given, in their answer to the first question put to them on Thursday, except in a very general way, any details of the grievances which they suffered; and also that nothing whatever was said by the Government or the companies on the question of recognition. The companies stood to the Conciliation Boards as an agreement; they maintained the policy which they always maintained, of not recognising the unions as representing all the men, both union and non-union men being eligible for the Conciliation Boards; and they were not prepared to face large concessions unless they had some power given to them to increase rates for the purpose of covering general expenses. The men had chiefly dwelt in their manifestoes on the grievances of the men and the difficulty and delay in getting them settled, and also appealed to sympathetic action in favour of railway workers locked out at Liverpool. They had not said much about recognition, except that grievances could have been dealt with more easily if union representatives had been met. They hoped to attract men who were not members of the union to join in the strike on the subject of grievances, but the executives kept firm in their minds the aim of obtaining recognition, if that could be got.

The directors and managers were seen by us at an early hour on Friday, and agreed to delegate powers to a smaller committee, with whom we sat the whole day, preparing a draft basis of negotiations on the lines of Mr. Lloyd George's speech, and hearing through Mr. Ramsay Macdonald the views of the men. Both parties easily agreed that there should be speedy meetings of the Conciliation Boards to get rid of petty differences. The arrangement for the future Royal Commission was more difficult. Amendment and counter-amendment passed backwards and forwards, emphasising the great difficulty of settling terms without a meeting round a table, but by Saturday morning an arrangement was practically complete. Meanwhile railways had stopped almost everywhere, and some violent acts occurred in a few places. Parliament, instead of adjourning to the end of October, adjourned to the following Tuesday. Rumours of promises of assistance were coming in from different trades. A circular from the Home Office, issued without conference with other departments, giving particulars of the progress of protection, and speaking of "defections" from the ranks of the men, stiffened the views of the men's executives. They absolutely refused to sign unless the railway companies' and men's representatives met. The crisis was certainly acute. The Chancellor of the Exchequer then played his last ace, and used an argument which he has, on later occasions, brought into play when other arguments failed—the national danger. It was the time of the Morocco crisis, when Germany had sent the *Panther* to uphold her alleged interests in Morocco. Whether the fact of a railway strike would have furthered her interests or not, or paralysed any efforts we were making, it is not easy to say. The argument necessarily prevailed with the railway authorities when put by the Government; and on this August 19, after debates lasting the whole morning, a joint conference was held at 3 p.m., of which the official notice stated that, "acting on representations made to the railway companies by the Government, they to-day empowered Mr. Claughton (general manager of the London and North-Western Railway) and Sir Guy Granet (general manager of the Midland Railway) to confer on their behalf with representatives selected by the Joint Executives of the Trade Unions of Railway Employees, with a view to discuss with them the suggested terms of settlement drafted by the Board of Trade"; and it went on: "During the course of the conference Mr. Claughton stated that, upon certain representations of the Government, Sir Guy Granet and himself had authority from the companies to meet the representatives, under the special circumstances, and with a view to discussing the suggested terms of agreement." So recognition, or an attitude which could be claimed to be recognition, was gained—not by argument of a domestic character or by consent, but by the foreign political situation. The same weapon was used during the War in connection with the Welsh coal dispute—French opinion being the reason given in that case. Personally I am in favour of hearing disputants and meeting both sides at the table, but I make no comment upon this method of obtaining such a result, except that the weapon used is a dangerous weapon to employ for the sake of settling domestic difficulties. I also make no comment as to whether it was justifiable or not in this case, except that a few days after I was expressly told to use the same weapon, if necessary, in connection with the Liverpool strikes.

An agreement was not reached without much difficulty—reinstatement; speedy discussion of outstanding questions in dispute by Conciliation Boards, with retrospective decisions; speedy discussion by each company with employees not covered by conciliation, and, failing agreement, arbitration; and both parties to give every assistance to the Special Commission of Inquiry, the immediate appointment of which the Government had announced. All these terms amounted to nothing in themselves beyond what the companies would have given or the Government would have imposed, without much demur by the parties, except the fact that the two parties had met "under the special circumstances." This result may have seemed at the time a great achievement to have been obtained from a strike which convulsed the country and required the coercion of a plea of national danger before it could be closed, but it is difficult to say that the sense of proportion on both sides was fairly considered. There was far too much evidence of a desire by each side to get the upper hand. That this was the case was at once shown by the fact that the North-Eastern Railwaymen, where recognition had been granted years before, did not see any tangible result in the settlement. The men there had a conciliation scheme of their own. The company proposed reinstatement as in the other companies, but there was nothing else which they could gain. The men rejected the offer. It required a visit to York by the railwaymen's executives, and some pressure, before the men consented to return to work, some days after the other companies had resumed. Beyond this, the rank and file were disappointed.

The Royal Commission was established and produced a scheme, reporting on October 18. It failed to give satisfaction. The Executive Committees of the railwaymen, having carefully considered the report of the Royal Commission with the suggested scheme, expressed "our sincere regret that we cannot accept the scheme in its present form," and added, "unless the scheme can be amended so as to become more acceptable to us and to the men we represent, we shall have no alternative but to reject it in its entirety and to report to our men accordingly." They suggested an

12

immediate meeting between the companies' representatives and the signatories to the recent settlement. This letter, worded in a tone which diplomats will recognise as the tone which certain Governments have used traditionally in their despatches, and which seems to have been not unpopular with the railway unions, again seemed to threaten a crisis. On receiving it, the Prime Minister saw the representatives of the companies, who took a very strong view on the matter. They said it was a breach of the agreement, and their opinion was given in the reply. "The companies consider," said the Prime Minister's secretary, "that it was an integral part of the agreement of August last which led to the appointment of the Royal Commission, that both they and the representatives of the railway employees bound themselves to accept and act upon the findings," and that, in their opinion, any points of difficulty were susceptible of adjustment by the various companies so soon as the scheme as a whole has been put into operation." The men made no reply, but proceeded to a ballot returnable on December 5, asking—(1) Are you prepared to accept the findings of the Royal Commission? (2) Are you prepared to withdraw your labour *in favour of the recognition* of the trade unions and a programme for all railwaymen to be agreed upon by the members of the Joint Executives? It was quite certain that a large majority would vote in favour of the second question.

In comment upon this situation, in which, if the questions and the refusal were carried to a finish, no account whatever was taken by the parties as to the broad issue of the public interest, and the troubles of a struggle on the railways in December, I think that both parties had a great deal to say for the positions taken up. The railway managements were very strong in the contention that there was an agreement, that they would adhere to that agreement, and would be no parties to any breach or connivance at a breach. They also treated the previous meetings as special, and were not without desire to retain their own autonomies. The railwaymen, on the other hand, as the second question shows, deemed that the recognition of the unions was not accepted and was being side-tracked, after they thought and had said they had gained it: if it was in fact gained, why not discuss a long technical document, the details of which must require adjustment, if satisfactory working was to be achieved, at a meeting between the parties, including the Government representatives, by whom the questions had been referred ? Neither party was prepared to yield, but, as I have said, neither party was consulting the public. In this very serious crisis, with very little time for action, it was suggested that the public might be supposed to have their say, by means of their representatives, the members of the House of Commons. I think it would be generally admitted that the House would not be a very suitable body to decide the intricacies of a strike ; nor, if an industry was nationalised, could well take action on their own behalf, being one of the parties to the issue. But here the question was to meet or not to meet, under the peculiar circumstances of the principles held by the parties, in a matter upon which the country was vitally interested. On this issue the House of Commons had a clear point of principle before them, and on November 22 a debate was held, after which the House unanimously adopted a resolution :

"That in the opinion of this House a meeting should take place between representatives of the parties on whose behalf the agreement of August 1911 was signed, to discuss the best mode of giving effect to the report of the Royal Commission, and this House asks the Government to use its good offices to bring both sides into conference without delay."

This expression of opinion was accepted by the parties : a meeting was held on December 7. I was elected to be chairman, and held further meetings on December 8 and 11, when more or less amicable discussions resulted in the maintenance of the Report of the Royal Commission, and in an agreement on points of detail connected with the scheme, and especially permission for the secretaries of Conciliation Boards to be present at deputations with the men. In practice this permission enabled the union officials to advise and speak for the men, and while express confession of recognition was not put down in black-and-white, the resulting effect was that no railway company subsequently raised the point of non-recognition as an answer to claims of grievances. For good or evil, practical recognition of the unions, and the principle of negotiations with the railway companies as a body, were the chief results of the railway strike of 1911.

CHAPTER XVIII

JUTE, 1911

DURING the early days of the railway strike it had been quite impossible for me to leave London in order to deal with the aftermath of the settlement at Manchester; but as the railway strike gained ground, trouble had begun to show again in that city through large numbers of carters ceasing work in sympathy with the railwaymen. It became imperative to try to close the carters' dispute, which was holding up the business of the city, and threatened trouble in other directions. The comparatively hasty settlement between the team-owners and the carters, while settling many points, had included a clause stating "that the other questions contained in the men's demands should be referred to a joint conference of the parties, and in the event of no agreement within a month, the matter to be referred to the Board of Trade." All questions relating to carters are very difficult, and this was no exception. The parties had discussed and discussed without any semblance of an agreement.

The railway strike closed at midnight on Saturday, August 19; on Monday morning the Lord Mayor urged me by telephone to come down at once, and, taking a train, I began conferences on the Monday evening which lasted from 7 p.m. to 8 a.m. It took the whole of the next day to arrange a carters' code, an agreement being reached at midnight. On August 23 the agreements were signed, and as I returned to London on that afternoon I received a telegram in the train to expect a messenger at the London station on an urgent matter. It was to the effect that the tramway dispute at Liverpool was not ended, because the Corporation refused to reinstate certain tramwaymen; that Mr. Tom Mann was in another section of the train, on his way to see the executive of the Transport Federation, with the object of demanding national support, and a general strike of all railwaymen and transport workers together; that the Executive might defer such action if it was stated that I had gone to Liverpool on this question. There was a train back to Lancashire in two hours—time occupied in rushing to the Board of Trade, where, under the express fiat of the Prime Minister, I was authorised to pursue the same line as the Chancellor had followed five days earlier with the railwaymen, if it became absolutely necessary—viz. to tell the Lord Mayor that the Government in the national interest must require this dispute to be closed, owing to the position of foreign affairs. This notification settled the question of going North that night, though I did not reach Liverpool till about 3 a.m. Meanwhile, the Joint Committee of Railwaymen requested from Liverpool, the Board of Trade, and the Premier, an answer as to "whether the tramwaymen now on strike or locked out in Liverpool will be reinstated before noon to-morrow," and adjourned till 10 a.m. to await a reply.

Liverpool had been in a very serious state of turmoil. Military had been called in. There had been riots and attacks on the soldiers. A Commission from the Home Office, consisting of Mr. T. P. O'Connor, M.P., and two colleagues, had been there for some time, inquiring into the food-supply and the general position. They had been active in settling many disputes, Mr. O'Connor especially managing the Irishmen with great skill. I only came in at the end, to help in smoothing out matters and especially this tramway dispute. The dockers, sailors, carters, and others, numbering 70,000, would not go back until this dispute, involving 250 uniformed tramwaymen, had also been settled. As is often the case with government by committees, the Corporation Tramways Committee were divided in opinion; while the powerful influence of the shipowners was directed against any concession. They issued a long document, speaking of "a monstrous threat of a general strike on an extended scale," and "an anarchical campaign against the public," statements which did not make more easy the task of the Tramways Committee. Later events have largely modified the attitude of shipowners, even of the very men who issued this document, but at the time they appeared to be opposed to any concessions by themselves or anybody else.

So far as my part was concerned, a slight hint as to the

possible Government situation brought no response, and I dropped any pursuit of that line, but did emphasise that it was hard to say men had broken their contracts without notice, when the tramway drivers and conductors had had to convey military along part of a route, and then were supposed to continue their journey without defence to the suburbs, to which strikers had taken a short-cut with a view to pulling them off the trams; and that discrimination between those actually coerced and those voluntarily ceasing work would be more than difficult. In the final result the committee, after three hours' debate, finally resolved unanimously on a compromise of reinstatement of the uniformed men "as and when required and satisfactory to the general manager," which, in fact, meant that they got back, though some questions of delay were bound to occur. The main strike was called off in the evening.

There remained a strike at Garston and difficulties over the carters, which were settled the next day, the carters being able to follow the code established at Manchester and to take its principles as a precedent. Dock-workers at Cardiff and Grangemouth, confectionery-workers in London, and other minor disputes, were subsidiary strikes going on during this hot month of August, but the importance of these disputes was minimised by the great strike to which allusion has been made.

Punch had the following skit on strike news:

"LATEST STRIKE NEWS

"MR. ASKWITH OUT

"NATIONAL CONSTERNATION

"Commercial England was thrilled this morning by the announcement that Mr. Askwith, the famous arbitrator, the keystone of the business arch, had himself come out on strike. The Government decided at once that every effort must be made to induce him to return to his duties. A regiment of cavalry was wired for from Aldershot, and the Chancellor of the Exchequer motored round to his residence.

"Mr. Askwith sternly declined the employers' terms—£20,000 a year plus time and a half for overtime and double time for Bank Holidays and Sundays. He made no objection to the pecuniary terms, but he insisted on a maximum of sixteen arbitrations and two thousand miles railway travelling per week, and that no working-day should exceed eighteen hours. The Chancellor was compelled to refuse the terms, as the Board of Trade has already 124 arbitrations in hand, and fresh ones are coming in at the rate of three a day.

"*Later*

"A Cabinet Meeting has been called to consider the crisis. It is felt by Ministers that, if Mr. Askwith does not return to work, no strike in England will ever end. The Cabinet is at present considering the possibility of nominating Mr. Askwith as arbitrator in his own strike. The difficulty is that Mr. Askwith cannot arbitrate without constituting himself a blackleg."

Punch was quite right in suggesting that it had been a strenuous time. It was a welcome rest when His Majesty, who has invariably taken very keen interest in all questions affecting Labour, summoned me to Balmoral for a few days and was graciously pleased to invest me with the insignia of a Knight Commander of the Order of the Bath.

During the autumn of 1911 various settlements arising out of the August strikes had to be made, the usual number of small disputes occurred, and the Industrial Council was established; but the comparative calm was so marked that some newspapers put the movements down to such causes as the hot weather! A disproof of this contention occurred at the very end of December, in the middle of a frost, when Dundee carters and dockers went out with a closing-down of jute-mills and factories owing to shortage of coal and material. The Lord Provost opened negotiations, but the strike continued, with some disturbance which led to the presence of extra police and the Black Watch.

A personal story illustrating the stress of disputes and the necessity of speed may possibly be permissible in recording the strange settlement of this dispute.

The Lord Provost had intimated that matters were assuming so serious an aspect that he might desire aid, but that any message to that effect would arrive in London in the morning of December 22. No message came, so I left for my country house at St. Ives, in Huntingdonshire, for the Christmas holidays, craving for a rest. That evening, at 9 p.m., the postmaster, after hours, personally brought up a telegram, saying that against all rule he thought I should have it. The wire was to the effect that a meeting had been arranged for next morning at 9.30, my presence was promised, and to come without fail; the position was most serious, and all Dundee out. Then there followed a hustle. The chauffeur had to be found; there was no petrol, but St. Ives gallantly turned out to get it; we rushed to Peterborough at top speed; the right station had to be found, with all the inhabitants asleep, and those who know Peterborough know the puzzle of its stations. The train had gone; but an active and cheering set of railwaymen stopped another, hustled me on board, had wires sent to retard the mail train at Grantham; another set pushed me into the mail at that junction; and next morning I emerged at Dundee to meet a smiling Lord Provost and walk through a crowd to the Town Hall. When I returned, unannounced, at early morn of Christmas Day, once more at Peterborough, after a settlement, I was greeted with: "Well, sir, you've done it, and we did not think you could. We should all have been out this Christmas if you hadn't." A taxicab was produced from nowhere. The man would only take his fare on pressure as a Christmas-box for his children. "We might have been starving in a fortnight," he said, "and I would like to do my bit." And so I got my Christmas.

These may be petty incidents, but they serve to illustrate that men do not want these quarrels, interfering with their homes, prospects, and lives, at unknown and unexpected moments, and coming from unexpected quarters. Great is the responsibility of those who cause them or who thoughtlessly disregard complaints; though an intermediary must, so far as I can judge, most sternly keep sentiment subservient to justice, lest he fall into a quagmire of difficulty, and soon be despised for his action. Such incidents occur over and over again in disputes, but I have ventured to cite these personal matters in this dispute as a type.

On arrival at Dundee, we sat for seventeen hours, well into the morning of December 24, when an agreement was reached. Experience of carters at Manchester and Liverpool helped much towards the quick settlement of this dispute, which seemed at first to be very threatening, and likely to spread to other places. The difficulties consisted in the divergent views of two sets of carting employers, the railway managers, who were not prepared to hazard changes likely to affect other districts and other companies, and the general carting employers. These were adjusted by the afternoon, but the settlement of the claims of the dockers, with their work interlocking with the work of the carters, proved to be a long business. The shipowners of Dundee would not act without the consent of shipowners at Leith, who had interests in the port and feared extension of any change to Leith ; and they also shrank from possible reproof by the all-powerful Shipping Federation, if they consented to any change. Restrictive orders by absent persons or associations are an unreasonable and almost unfair clog to efforts at agreement or conciliation, but in this case were overcome by telephonic conversations carried on till a late hour of the night and up to 3 a.m. on the Sunday morning, without any question being raised about work on the Scottish Sabbath.

What is to be said about these disputes ? My own strong opinion is that they were economic. Trade had been improving, but employers thought too much of making up for some lean years in the past, and of making money, without sufficient regard to the importance of considering the position of their workpeople at a time of improvement of trade. Prices had been rising, but no sufficient increase of wages, and certainly no general increase, had followed the rise. It may be said that employers had waited too much upon each other.

I endeavoured to express this opinion at the Cutlers' Feast at Sheffield, on October 17, in remarks which at the time were said to be bold, but which I think have been proved to be correct. On that occasion I said :

" If it is, as I think, true that the cost of living in the great towns has risen in a proportion out of the proportion to which wages have risen, and if, as is also true, that with large numbers of men earning, say, between 19*s*. and 25*s*. a week, 60 per cent. of those earnings goes in food ; and if the cost of living rises, and the other 40 per cent., which goes in clothes, rent, rates, and any little luxuries that the man may be able to afford, is changed and altered so that the 40 per cent. is largely infringed upon at a time when men are desiring greater comfort, are listening to active propaganda, are having instilled into them upon every platform in the country their economic position and the comparison with their colleagues in Germany and America, it is scarcely to be wondered at that some disturbance and desire to obtain more should arise.

"On the other hand, when the complex equipment for the improvement of the harnessing of the natural forces of the world in the service of mankind is going forward throughout the world, and when the demand for capital in its largest sense is increasing, no doubt those who hold gilt-edged securities cannot obtain such a price as they would when the loanable value of capital elsewhere is so much greater, and the attractions for the use of capital elsewhere are possibly greater than in the United Kingdom. There is an adjustment to be made, which may be difficult to arrange, and which cannot be arranged at a moment's notice.

"Further, if at such a time, in the course of the adjustment, you have various disorganised industries united for the first time and feeling their strength, you may have not only those industries, but others allied to them, getting into a state of turmoil. The effects of war and of earthquakes, of shipwrecks and of disturbances of that kind, are palpable to all. From the view that I take of it, industrial war is equally disastrous to both Capital and Labour.

"If you think that in August last there were on actual strike 373,000 persons, and also hundreds of thousands of persons thrown out of work by the strikes, you will find that the wage of the people concerned runs in one month into millions; that the spending power runs into more millions, and that the resulting waste in this complex machinery runs into a loss which can scarcely be estimated. If anything can be done to prevent that in a city of this kind, it must, without doubt, be valuable, and it may be hoped that Sheffield may be able so to examine matters that the pride and common sense of her citizens may prevent these disturbances occurring."

The first grave disputes arose in the sea-ports, where

there was, speaking generally, extraordinary alienation and lack of sympathy between employers and their men. The pools of casual labour allowed the employers always to obtain labour. There was no cohesion among employers, and no section of employers who dared to come forward and give a lead. Employers and trades were so interlocked and dependent on each other that no section could move without affecting other sections, and there was no consideration by anyone in any port of the proper course to be pursued or the best advice to be given. Labour was there, and Labour had not complained in any forceful way, or combined. If a man disliked work, he need not take it. Another man would step into his place. The unions had in some places been organising; but in other places they had little cohesion. The cumulative effect, however, of increasing prices and no increase in wages bound together men as soon as a move was made. In almost every port the movement started with unorganised men, generally young men. The labour leaders were taken by surprise. Some quickly headed the movement and tried to regain lost authority. Others frankly expressed astonishment, and could not understand the outbreak and determination. With the magnitude of the outbreaks, a large number of the new men came to the front, many without experience of leadership, a clear knowledge of the real wishes of the workpeople, or much skill in ascertaining them. Interspersed with these new leaders there were a few who had had experience of labour troubles in the United States, also a few who were said to be members of the Independent Workers of the World. But these were not well known, and their violence did not appeal much to the majority of workers, who were not out for talk but for practical results. Some of them hampered the more moderate leaders badly by watching them and endeavouring to suggest suspicion about them. One who had been particularly difficult had the coolness to write to me a year afterwards, asking me to recommend him for a post, on the ground of his assistance in settling the Manchester strikes!

I would repeat that in my opinion these strikes were economic strikes; but that they showed to the workers the value of organisation, and that organisation has been improved and continued during succeeding years.

CHAPTER XIX

THE INDUSTRIAL COUNCIL, 1911

In view of the serious disputes which had burst out during the summer, many suggestions were made with the idea that Labour and Capital might be brought more closely together. Although throughout the country there were so many voluntary arrangements for conciliation and arbitration, with which nobody desired to interfere, a number of trades were not organised, or, in spite of organisation, had found their arrangements very defective. The interlocking of trade, and the effects which a stoppage in one trade or section of a trade might have upon another, were very insufficiently realised. There were also constant recriminations alleging breach of agreement, so that there was much talk about the necessity of enforcing agreements or establishing some methods for avoiding breaches of agreements. The public had, as usual, no use for strikes or lockouts, and through the Press urgently asked, "Cannot something be done to stop these upheavals?" Among those who had especially promulgated opinions, Sir Charles Macara, chairman for many years of the Masters' Federation in the cotton industry, had been the most emphatic. In July and August 1911, after the Manchester strikes, he had proposed the establishment of a business court for dealing with industrial disputes, and secured considerable support. "Before work is stopped," he said, "either by employers or employees, the facts of the dispute would have to be reviewed by the members of the arbitration court, with a trained chairman such as Mr. Askwith presiding over the deliberations. The court would be composed of leading employers and labour leaders, selected from the half-dozen chief industries in the country. Their decision would not be compulsory, but it would, I am convinced, be the deliberate judgment of men anxious to arrive at the truth of the case, and would be of such a character as would in most cases make any trade, whether employer or operative, hesitate before setting its verdict on one side.

" There is nothing revolutionary in such a scheme. It is a business proposition put before business people, and, I am glad to see, is being considered as much. With the growing feeling of unrest that is around us, the establishment of some such body as I have indicated, bringing a calm, judicial mind to the case, would be of inestimable service."

Sir Charles Macara, at least, even if other men did not realise the fact and its supplements, understood the interlocking of trade. The cotton industry, his special trade, had necessarily been much inconvenienced by the difficulties at the ports, and indeed had suffered considerably. He had a great belief in organisation, and was continually citing the Brooklands Agreement, and his confidence, not as yet affected by the non-union quarrel, that in organisation, particularly if it was assisted by the opinion of other trades which must be influenced by sectional disputes, lay the possibility of a reasonable method of avoiding internecine war. His advocacy largely led to the establishment of the Industrial Council in 1911.

At the same time, the excessive work and travelling over labour matters had made it quite impossible for me and my immediate officers to carry on the proper control of other branches of the Board of Trade, such as Exhibitions, Trade Boards, Standard Weights and Measures, certain departments of the Labour Exchanges and of Patents and Designs, Copyright, Statistics, a Gazette, and other matters. I advocated strongly the importance of whole-time service being devoted to the subject of Labour.

The Government, through Mr. Buxton, the President of the Board of Trade, took up both these subjects. An Industrial Council was established, of which I was appointed chairman; and also a special department for Labour, the other branches being separated from it, came into existence, new premises being assigned to it and the title of Chief Industrial Commissioner being given to me as its chief, with the rank of a Permanent Secretary. The two offices of Chief Industrial Commissioner and Chairman of the Industrial Council had evidently to be worked as far as possible in unison.

The Industrial Council was established after a great time of stress. It was obvious that, if organisations had been asked to elect, they would have deliberated about the whole idea, and possibly sent an ordinary committeeman to serve on it, even if it had not been deliberated out of existence. Time was also against deliberation. At any moment it was possible that new outbreaks might arise. The public were clamouring for action. There was no one organisation which could come forward and take the lead. It was, therefore, decided to nominate for a period of one year the leading men of each principal organisation on both sides, with the addition of certain others whose names were known as leading men in the past, or who had taken and shown great interest in industrial matters. The leading men had been appointed Presidents by their own Associations, and therefore it could not be argued that, in naming them, there was any preference on the grounds of politics, complacency, or favouritism. The response was good. The list was a remarkable one, if only for the position occupied by each individual, as may be gathered from the names and positions of the representatives given at the end of this chapter. Then why did the Council not succeed in achieving more power and influence than it did ?

The answers, I think, are many, and cumulative in their effect :

1. The idea was quite new, and a little too early. The British people take a long time to absorb a new idea. After practical illustration in a smaller form by the efforts of the Committee on Production, the Arbitration Tribunals, and the Industrial Courts, the idea of a tribunal to which parties can voluntarily go for a decision without a preliminary fight has become more acceptable, but it is open to doubt how far the strength of such tribunals will continue in times of depression.

2. The Council had no power to bring disputants before it, and none to enforce any decision. "Will labour leaders, too," said one paper, "who, when merely labour leaders, are unable to control their followers, be more likely to have success when surrounded with the official aura of joint membership with capitalists of an Industrial Council?" "From its size alone," said another critic, "it must be cumbrous and slow-moving, and nowadays these labour wars blaze out almost in an hour."

3. The Council was imposed as an act of the Government, and not by the growth of an idea among the parties principally concerned. All those who were opposed to Government interference looked askance at it. All those trades who could not be represented on it, because size was necessarily a matter of importance, were rather doubtful of making use of it. Some large industries, such as the cotton trade, except for one section, would not accept it. It was considered by others to be a political move, and therefore to be discountenanced.

4. Although the Council was established by the Government, when it made an elaborate report after much hard work and at least one unanimous recommendation, the Government did not take the report as the last word and as the best recommendation which the most important leaders of Capital and Labour had ever jointly evolved. They tried to get the opinion of another body, the Trade Unions Conference, on the report, by the help of the representative of a small union which had had no seat on the Council. Anyone who knows the machinery of the Trade Unions Conference, the pressure upon its time, the method by which its agenda are prepared, the authorities given to its members, and the form of its debates, would have realised how futile such a proceeding would be. The proposals were hardly discussed, and finally brushed aside on the suggestion by the cotton trade and the miners that it might be a step towards compulsory arbitration, a system which probably not a single member of the Council would have intended, supported, or deemed to be practical. Acceptance of the report and a Government Bill would have caught no votes, with the result that the Government took no interest in it any more than they did in the Industrial Council itself, which they appeared to consider to be a kind of debating society. When the crisis of acute strikes had passed, they quietly dropped it, without referring any more questions to its judgment, or maintaining its existence for possible emergencies.

5. The Council did not succeed with strike settlement. It must be admitted that the first strike coming to it, the refusal of certain dock-workers at Newport, Mon., to work to an award of an arbitration court, and a sympathetic strike of other cargo workers in that port, was an extremely difficult case; but a committee of the Council failed to

settle it. The strike spread to Swansea, and threatened trouble throughout the Bristol Channel ports. In order to relieve the Council from its position, I had to see the parties interested by themselves, and eventually persuade them to meet in local conference, with some suggestions for settlement, which were accepted. Soon afterwards the cotton lockout came into being, and here again a large trade would not make use of the services of the Council, Sir Charles Macara himself being chairman of the employers who decided upon a lockout. No application was made to the Council in the Dundee dispute, though so urgent a matter could scarcely have been dealt with by a committee travelling on the eve of Christmas to a Northern port, particularly as committees necessarily take time to assemble.

In fact, intervention or settlement of labour disputes requires selection of an exact moment for action, complete and speedy grasp of the real causes of the dispute and the technicalities of the points at issue, speed and experience in judging the characters, sayings, and real views of the individuals on either side, both in and out of the conference room. Committees are singularly inapt bodies for these purposes. They may be suitable as arbitration courts, but very seldom as conciliation courts. The judgment of the trades was, I think, generally sound in not caring to use the Industrial Council as a conciliatory body, and this opinion, so far as conciliation is concerned, is now accepted by the new Arbitration Courts, who never attempt conciliation or interference to prevent outbreaks before they occur, but only decide on issues put before them for determination.

Mr. Buxton, the President of the Board of Trade, was quite right when he said :

"The more I have seen of them the more I am convinced, first, that the best and most satisfactory method of settling disputes between employers and workmen is for the parties directly concerned to come to an agreement among themselves. Secondly, that when the parties are unable themselves to come to terms, and a stoppage of work is imminent, or after a stoppage of work has taken place, assistance from outside is very often effective in preventing, shortening, or ending a dispute. Thirdly, that this method of action, if and where it takes place, must be done at the right moment, in the right way, and by the right person."

He was also quite right when he denounced political interference, the bane of Government methods at the present time, by saying:

"One disadvantage of the existing system is undoubtedly that it brings into action and prominence the Parliamentary Head of the Board of Trade, who is necessarily a politician . . . and a member of the Government, in disputes and conciliations which ought to be purely industrial. It has been my policy, and, I hope, my action, during my two years at the Board of Trade to efface as far as possible my personality as a political President, and I believe my department has won the confidence of the public and of the two industrial sides to a remarkable degree. At the same time, I realise that, if the action of the department in these matters could be still further removed from the sphere of politics or the suspicion of politics, it would give even greater confidence, and there would be greater willingness by the parties to a dispute to seek the assistance of the Board of Trade. The President cannot, of course, dissociate himself from all responsibility, and in certain circumstances the Government may have to intervene as a last resort. But such cases would be few and far between."

But experience proved that he was developing a wrong path of practical work, when he said that the Council should be a National Conciliation Board, and laid stress upon its action before rather than after a stoppage of work. His words were these:

"The other reason for the creation of the Industrial Council is that we believe that the powers and position of the Board of Trade, its good offices, could be advantageously strengthened in the direction of what may be called a national industrial body of weight and of repute, consisting of representatives of the two great sides of the industry of the country . . . a body that would bring to bear on these problems a great range of advice, great weight, and a greater likelihood, therefore, of useful and acceptable action, especially—and I lay stress on this—before, rather than after, stoppage of work. Such a body would also enable an appeal to be made to it by one or other of the combatants, without loss of dignity.

"I would point out further that of late years, both on the side of the employers and on the side of the workmen, considerable steps have been taken towards what I may call federated effort—combinations of trade unions on the one hand and of federations of employers' associations on the other—and that, from the point of view of trade disputes, trade and industry are far more interdependent than they used to be. While, therefore, a few years ago the creation of a National Conciliation Council, representing all the great industries, might have been thought to be premature, its existence is really now essential, so that these matters can be considered as a whole."

These remarks are interesting because the practical rock of the difficulty of conciliation by a committee is a rock which the League of Nations is very likely to find an obstruction in its way. Unless its members are very careful, and can be ensured the support of public opinion of all Governments and their peoples throughout the world, insisting that the League shall be the Conciliation Board of the world, their functions as a Conciliation Board, although outlined as part of their work, may derogate from their usefulness as an Arbitration Board, and possibly conduce to an isolated and barren position. Advice not desired, sought, or taken, and decisions without sanction of possible force, would, after a few failures, have little or no value. Usefulness can only be acquired by success.

It must not be supposed from the foregoing that the Industrial Council was idle or did no good work, both directly and indirectly. Indirectly in numerous sittings, it brought together the leading men who had the official positions of headship of the great industries of the country. Many of these men had never met each other, much less heard the difficulties or details of each other's industries. The sittings of the Council from first to last were conducted with the greatest harmony. The members of the Council became friends, and on many occasions later on acquaintance and friendship led to better understandings. Directly, the main work of the Council was an inquiry requested by the Government upon the subject of Industrial Agreements, to which later reference will be made.

INDUSTRIAL COUNCIL

Employers' Representatives

Mr. George Ainsworth (Consett), Chairman of the Steel Ingot Makers' Association.

Sir Hugh Bell (Middlesbrough), President of the Iron, Steel, and Allied Trades Federation, and Chairman of the Cleveland Mine Owners' Association.

Mr. G. H. Claughton (London), Chairman of the London and North-Western Railway Company.

Mr. W. A. Clowes (London), Chairman of the London Master Printers' Association.

Mr. J. H. C. Crockett (Northampton), President of the Incorporated Federated Association of Boot and Shoe Manufacturers of Great Britain and Ireland.

Mr. F. L. Davis (South Wales), Chairman of the South Wales Coal Conciliation Board.

Mr. T. L. Devitt (London), Chairman of the Shipping Federation, Limited.

Sir T. Ratcliffe Ellis (Wigan), Secretary of the Lancashire and Cheshire Coal Owners' Association, and Joint Secretary of the Board of Conciliation of the Coal Trade of the Federated Districts, etc.

Mr. F. W. Gibbins (South Wales), Chairman of the Welsh Plate and Sheet Manufacturers' Association.

Sir Charles Macara (Manchester), President of the Federation of Master Cotton Spinners' Associations.

Mr. Robert Thompson, M.P. (Belfast), Past-President of the Ulster Flax Spinners' Association.

Mr. Alexander Siemens (Woolwich), Chairman of the Executive Board of the Engineering Employers' Federation.

Mr. J. W. White (Sunderland), President of the National Building Trades Employers' Federation.

Workmen's Representatives

Rt. Hon. Thomas Burt, M.P. (Newcastle), General Secretary of the Northumberland Miners' Mutual Confident Association.

Mr. T. Ashton (Manchester), Secretary of the Miners' Federation of Great Britain, and General Secretary of the Lancashire and Cheshire Miners' Federation.

Mr. C. W. Bowerman, M.P. (London), Secretary of the Parliamentary Committee of the Trade Unions Congress, and President of the Printing and Kindred Trades Federation of the United Kingdom.

Mr. F. Chandler (Manchester), General Secretary of the Amalgamated Society of Carpenters and Joiners.

Mr. J. R. Clynes, M.P. (Manchester), Organising Secretary of the National Union of Gas Workers and General Labourers of Great Britain and Ireland.

Mr. H. Gosling (London), President of the National Transport Workers' Federation, and General Secretary of the Amalgamated Society of Watermen, Lightermen, and Watchmen of River Thames.

Mr. Arthur Henderson, M.P. (Newcastle), Friendly Society of Ironfounders.

Mr. John Hodge, M.P. (London), General Secretary of the British Steel Smelters', Mill, Iron, and Tinplate Workers' Amalgamated Association.

Mr. W. Mosses (Manchester), General Secretary of the Federation of Engineering and Shipbuilding Trades and of the United Pattern-makers' Association.

Mr. W. Mullin, J.P. (Manchester), President of the United Textile Factory Workers' Association, and General Secretary of the Amalgamated Association of Card and Blowing Room Operatives.

Mr. E. L. Poulton (Leicester), General Secretary of the National Union of Boot and Shoe Operatives.

Mr. Alexander Wilkie, M.P. (Newcastle), Secretary of the Shipyard Standing Committee under the National Agreement of 1909, and General Secretary of the Ship Constructive and Shipwrights' Society.

Mr. J. E. Williams (London), General Secretary of the Amalgamated Society of Railway Servants.

Additions may be made to the above list.

The members of the Council will in the first instance hold office for one year.

Sir George Askwith, the present Comptroller-General of the Labour Department of the Board of Trade, has been appointed to be Chairman of the Industrial Council with the title of Chief Industrial Commissioner, and Mr. H. J. Wilson, of the Board of Trade, to be Registrar of the Council.

CHAPTER XX

LANCASHIRE COTTON AND CLYDE DOCKERS, 1912

DUNDEE was not to be the only winter dispute. With the new year of 1912 very serious trouble arose in the cotton trade in North-East Lancashire—not on a wage question, but on a question of principle, of union or non-union labour.

At the end of December there flamed out into action the ever-present dislike of union workpeople against non-union workpeople, believed by the employers to be an attempt on the part of the Weavers' Associations to force the North and North-East Lancashire Cotton Spinners' and Manufacturers' Association by striking mill after mill. Notices had been handed in at various mills to cease working with non-unionists. The intention was announced by the operatives' representatives to take similar action at all mills where union members objected to working with non-unionists. This proposal went much farther than any leaders of the operatives had previously gone. There were union, non-union, and mixed mills. Many employers and many individual workpeople were in opposition to any forced membership of the union. If union leaders had desired it, they had not been strong enough to press such an issue. They had been content to rely on the influence of the union and quiet efforts to ensure membership wherever they could. The employers resented force because they pronounced themselves to be impartial between unionists and non-unionists, and desired to employ good labour without taking into account whether the operatives belonged to the union or not. They objected to an attack upon them one by one, without knowledge which mill would be next stopped, and to embroilment in disputes between operatives, or any onus of ascertaining an operative's membership. They considered they would be used as the tools for doing the work which the union secretaries had failed by persuasion to effect. Accordingly they decided to be free, and posted notices to determine all existing contracts, so that at any time a general lockout could be ordered if any mills were stopped for this cause. The union retaliated by striking two mills on December 21, because non-unionist weavers refused to join the local Weavers' Association. Then the employers acted. Association followed Association, the Hard Waste Manufacturers came in, a general lockout commenced, with 160,000 workpeople directly involved, and another 150,000 soon following with short time.

It was an extraordinarily difficult dispute. Apart from the difficulty of an intervention in the cotton trade, the looming dispute had rapidly been brought to a head in the Christmas week, though not fully realised till after the "play days" of the New Year; both parties were fighting for alleged principles, and strong feeling existed. I think it was only because the Howe dispute had been settled without political interference, and because neither side saw any way out of the impasse, that on January 2 the employers consented to meet me next day "with a view of stating clearly the Associations' attitude on the non-unionist question, and the fixed determination to adhere to the position they have taken up"—not a very promising beginning for conciliation.

Long conferences, held separately with each party, took place on January 3, 4, and 5, at the end of which some suggestions were made, and an adjournment was taken until Monday, January 8, so that the parties might consult their constituents. Meanwhile other difficulties came in. The employers stated that they could not consider, during the present state of unrest, an application for a 5 per cent. increase of wages, which many persons had looked forward to as a possible compromise, in the belief that any settlement on the principle of unionism and non-unionism was impracticable. The reply did not improve the feeling between the parties, and this impression was reflected in the public Press, where the most gloomy prognostications were prevalent.

The card and blowing room operatives also came forward, saying they had nothing to do with the weavers' actions, but the employers had locked them out too, and had thereby broken an agreement with them. This complication did not soften feelings. After three conferences with the employers, no result had been obtained, but both parties then asked me to decide the matter. I met them on January 6, when an amicable settlement cleared away this difficulty. The other remained. Long conferences on January 8 and 9, at which the parties came jointly together, brought no result, and the prospect looked black. The general opinion seemed to be that there was nothing to be done but to fight it out. There had now been five days of conference, in addition to many conversations, but no solution appeared to be within sight. The Press of the whole country kept discussing the matter, but although every suggestion was examined, not one practical hint emerged for a settlement or even a renewal of work, in face of the very difficult problem, involving questions of individual liberty, rights of contract, the limitations of the use of force, the right to management of the mills, and any number of clashing principles. One could only rely on the fact that the community wanted a settlement. Every paper, every caricature emphasised that fact. There was also the fact that both parties, as time went on, or so I thought, must want a settlement. The one did not want to lose their place in the world competition for trade, the other did not want to lose their present and possibly their future livelihood. It was necessary to play for time and to keep cool—not an easy matter when hotheads were urging a fight, and in some districts seemed to be elated by the apparent failure of the conferences; thousands, nay, tens of thousands of workpeople were being stopped from work every day in the allied trades, by absence of supplies; no issue was suggested by any political economist, employer, or workman; and some individuals of the parties were breaking down, and did afterwards break down, under the strain and responsibility. I felt that, however difficult the case might be, a solution might not be impossible so long as the parties were meeting face to face instead of denouncing each other from a distance. It was with some difficulty that they could be induced to meet again, but at last they consented to another conference on the following Monday, and I purposely put the adjournment at a week, in view of the high tide of passionate feeling. January 15 failed to bring any settlement; January 16 was the last chance. I knew perfectly well that after seven days of negotiation, however spread over, practical men would negotiate no more. Everything that could be said would have been said. I also knew, or guessed, that Lancashire, except for some very good reason, would not cut its own throat, but, although it was gashed, would think twice before severing the jugular vein. My plan was to give further time for reflection, if under the surrounding circumstances the parties would agree to reflect. If a generalisation may be allowed, it seems to me that, on the assumption that a settlement must be effected, say at 12 o'clock, with the alternative of a fight, generally perfectly useless, Scotland will settle at five minutes before the hour and make quite sure; Lancashire will settle one minute before that hour; Yorkshire will debate so long that they may by inadvertence pass the hour and have trouble; Wales will take no note of the hour and sometimes settle and sometimes not; and Ireland say that the clock is wrong, and that if it is right they will settle or not without any regard to it. Personally I prefer the Scottish method.

My plan succeeded. During the week more conciliatory expressions of opinion had been published both by employers' and operatives' representatives. The public Press began to assume a more hopeful mood, after being in the depths of despair, but again relapsed when no settlement was reached on January 15, after a sitting of ten hours. On the following day their views again brightened when at last an agreement was effected. The agreement was based upon the principle of time. It said this:

"As each side claims a principle—the operatives that the workpeople have a right to refuse to work with non-unionists at any shed or mill; the employers that they must maintain their established practice of strict impartiality as regards unionists and non-unionists—and as both parties attach great importance to maintaining such rights, it be now agreed by the employers' and operatives' representatives that, with a view to provide means whereby the dispute may be settled by reason and in a friendly manner, work shall be resumed on Monday next, January 22, under the old conditions of employment, on the understanding that at the end of the period of six months, during which no action shall be taken in tendering notices or striking mills on the non-unionist question, Sir George Askwith, who has been chairman of the conferences, and has heard the views which have been expressed by both sides, will, if requested, submit to the parties his suggestions upon the matter, containing, if possible, a means by which both sides can maintain their principles without injury to the rights of each other.

"If such suggestions are requested, the parties shall meet within twenty-one days after receiving them for the consideration of the subject.

"In the event of the foregoing procedure not providing a solution of the question, neither side shall be entitled to take any action on the non-unionist question involving a stoppage of the machinery unless six months' notice in writing has been previously given by one side to the other."

There was some doubt, even after the agreement, whether it would be endorsed by the districts, as the operatives' leaders, although they had full power, desired to ascertain the opinions of their associations; but on the following Friday the agreement was accepted, in spite of protests from some militant districts. Although no suggestion for settlement had been produced anywhere, criticism, coupled with sighs of relief, indicated that some superhuman intelligence should have evolved a clean-cut settlement. The critics failed to see that neither party could accept such a settlement, which must mean complete defeat for one or the other, and that sheer tenacity could only succeed in averting an unnecessary, inconclusive, and ruinous struggle.

It might be correct to say that this agreement did not settle the question, but it gave time, and it also gave opportunity for withdrawing from an untenable position if, after exercise of calm judgment, it was so considered by either side. In order to revive the question, I had to be asked to give an opinion, but not before the end of six months. Further, if that opinion was obtained, the parties had to meet to consider it, and finally, whether it was satisfactory or not, neither side was after that to take any action involving a stoppage of machinery without six months' previous notice in writing. Thus plenty of time for consideration and discussion was afforded before any drastic step could be taken. Peace was established for a year at least. No principles were sacrificed, but ample time for reflection was given to consider whether the fervour of organisation was sufficient excuse for entering again upon such serious strife.

Several months afterwards my opinion was asked, and on these lines it was given. No general rule could be laid down, and the parties recognised that fact by not reviving discussion. In my letter I said :

" I have given very careful consideration to the subject, and have had the advantage of the views of many of the most prominent employers and trade union officials in other industries. I have also examined the past history of the subject.

" This consideration leads me to the conclusion that it is not possible, at the present period of industrial development, to appraise the value of the contending opinions of each party respectively, nor the modifications which time may render it possible for either party to accept on this question.

" In theory both parties must desire and will maintain their liberty of opinion and action. In the common interests of the maintenance and security of business, neither party may desire to use that liberty to the full measure. Practical common sense, rather than any written rule, will define the measure in which it can be used, and lead to efforts for preventing any difficulty that may arise from becoming acute. Under all circumstances, I think that no written rule can advisably now be made."

The annual report of the Lancashire Weavers' Amalgamation recognised the situation by saying :

" The letter gives no suggestions, which brings us to the conclusion that none could be made, because if the unrivalled experience and knowledge of Sir George Askwith cannot find a solution for the non-member question, then we don't know who can."

Some statistics of the dispute were :

Looms stopped	450,000
Spindles stopped	3,000,000
Spindles on short time	45,000,000
Weavers and allied workers idle	160,000
Spinners on short time	100,000
Total cost to trade of Lancashire	£7,000,000
Cost to the trade unions	250,000
Weavers' and allied workers' loss in wages	725,000
Operative spinners' loss in wages	160,000
Cardroom operatives' loss in wages	115,000
Total loss in wages	1,000,000

The very day that the proposed agreement in the cotton dispute was completed, I had to leave for Glasgow over some disputes in that city in which I had been asked to attend conferences. Although Mr. Mitchell and I had come on other business, the visit was interpreted as an attempted intervention in a threatened dockers' dispute. As a matter of fact, I had previously suggested, when a stoppage was threatened in December, that the parties should endeavour to settle the pending dispute by themselves. They had had several meetings, and reached agreement on some points. The employers had suggested reference of the remaining points to me, but the men resolved that the time had not arrived for intervention. I had no anxiety to interfere, and left them to themselves.

On January 19 the executives of the employers and the principal Dockers' Union had managed to reach an agreement, but three factors prevented its acceptance: the existence of another union with whom the employers were not prepared to deal, the objections of stevedores, who said they had not been consulted, and complete refusal of the rank and file to consent to the proposed terms. The leaders of the dockers were new men, and again the old story came up: they did not know what the men really wanted, and they could not control the men so far as to induce them to accept an agreement which they did not like.

It was put before the men, and they rejected it. The employers were in a complete quandary. Under these circumstances they posted notices that on January 29 they would put into operation the terms and conditions as adjusted at the conferences. They did not know what else to do, or could not ascertain what were the real difficulties. On that day about 7,000 men replied by ceasing work, bringing the whole of the shipping of the port to a standstill. The situation had become very complex. A dispute which might not have been difficult in December had now become mazed with conferences and proposals, while the executive of the men did not seem to know what the real complaints were. My presence in Glasgow was required for three other disputes, partly in completion of arrangements made in the middle of January; but going there on Sunday, February 4, it was impossible not to take notice of the state of affairs existing at the docks, even though neither side had definitely requested intervention. Accordingly the employers were seen informally, with a view to ascertaining their opinion. They agreed at once to a conference. It was a sequence to their expressed views, as they had proposed a month before that outstanding points should be left to me. The men were much more difficult. Some strong speeches had been made to the effect that they should fight it out, particularly by persons from other ports, who had nothing to lose by inflaming the Glasgow dockers. Mr. Mitchell, however, explained that there was no intention of an arbitration, such as they seemed to think the employers meant, but of a joint meeting, at which the chairman would not act as an arbiter. Then they readily agreed, and the first phase was completed when the parties met before me at 10 a.m. on Tuesday morning.

Even after a tangled skein of misapprehension and confused councils has been unravelled, it is not easy to make clear the different chances of long discussions, but it is still more difficult at the time when angry recriminations may be bursting out and when different persons on the same side may have very different views of the points which they may wish to have decided or which they consider to be most important. The position was clearly this; an agreement had been made to which the executives on both sides had given their adhesion, but the rank and file outside, who had not heard the arguments, would have none of it. What was their reason? After two hours' discussion, the men's executive said that they wished for an interpretation and explanation of the full meaning of some of the clauses. We adjourned for these queries to be drafted. They were put before the employers, who in their turn drafted their replies. Conferring with each side separately, the queries and replies were made still more precise, and lastly a joint conference sat till midnight, when everyone was too tired to debate any longer. The only point made clear during the day was that the supposed contention that the men were insisting on the elimination of non-union labour was wrong. Some sections of the men had been putting this question forward as *the* point on which issue was being joined, but the employers showed that they did not mind whether a man belonged to a union or not; they would retain the right to employ a man, unionist or non-unionist; but in practice some sections were all union men, in others not. There would be no interference with custom. The union leaders, on the other side, knew this fact, and knew they were not sufficiently strong to insist that every man working in the docks should belong to their union. In some sections there was another union claiming the right to have men within their ranks. The analogy of the recent cotton dispute proved a useful argument against unwise pressure for a principle which could not possibly be enforced. The employers were exceptionally strong, and all united, whatever their mercantile competition might be, in solid opposition to such alleged interference with management. A second phase of the trouble had been passed.

On the next day conferences lasted from 11 to 7.30, and then broke off. There appeared to be an absolute deadlock. The agreement had been accepted. The union leaders, if they desired to retain authority as negotiators or as interpreters of the wishes of the rank and file, could not wisely denounce it as absurd. The employers insisted upon the agreement being implemented. The answers to the request for explanations were clear, and had practically been arranged in conference. Why was there no final agreement ? The answer entirely depended on one question : the terms of resumption of work. The employers in the previous year, under extreme pressure on individual firms, had given concessions which involved chaos in the port. They were not prepared to continue these concessions. They had consented to a joint committee, with power to call in a neutral chairman for the settlement of any disputes, including revision of rates of pay or hours of work and the conditions of employment for any particular class of work, and also any question concerning the mutual welfare of the employers and the dock labourers. They demanded that work should be resumed, without notice of intervening concessions, on the same terms as had existed a year before, and if any complaint was made, appeal should be lodged before this committee. The union leaders said no resumption of work was possible on these terms. Work could only be resumed if the conditions existing immediately before the dispute were to be accepted, when the employers could appeal to the joint committee and attempt to get the conditions changed. It took a long time to make the men see that their proposal would not be accepted. The difficulty surged round the conditions at the port, which both sides admitted would not work, and the fact that, if existing conditions were renewed, any subsequent change would be fought by each section affected by it, involve the whole port, and be considered a concession by the workers. The workers would be out for loss and nothing else. The whole dispute turned on revision of the conditions. Without revision, the employers would be supposed to be beaten. They would not consent to accept that position under the present circumstances, with an agreement in their pockets. Both sides were claiming return to a *status quo*, but the *status quo* was fixed at different dates. So I argued to myself, and partly to both sides, as the anxious hours sped by; until the conviction came that a *status quo* was impossible, and the idea that a new line must be taken. Why not anticipate the joint committee, settle the best terms on which work could be conducted, as both sides were agreed the existing terms were wrong, and then allow either side to appeal to the joint committee? It seems a very simple deduction on paper, but in practice deductions are not so easy to impress on excited partisans, with a proportion of "die-hards" in the committees of either side, and many more "die-hards" in the constituents outside. The difficulty was that the union leaders at that time had no real knowledge of the actual wishes of each section of their men. They could not say what were their claims in detail. They were not tabulated. I suggested they must be tabulated; it would have to be done sooner or later; and meanwhile I would deal with other disputes—lace, turkey-red workers, and ironmoulders—on which my mission to Glasgow had been based, and assist by seeing any sections of dock-workers they might wish. This policy appeared to some employers to be a policy of delay, to which they objected, desiring to attempt employment of new labour. If it had not been for the moderating influence of Sir Joseph Maclay, subsequently Shipping Controller during the War, negotiations might have come to an end. Some firms did try to deal with urgent cargoes of fruit. The leaders of the men also issued a manifesto, saying:

"After negotiations lasting two days, the Dockers' Committee has unanimously decided that they cannot possibly accept the proposals of the joint owners, and whilst regretting the failure of Sir George Askwith to bring about a settlement, they feel that the proposals of the owners are too preposterous for the men to contemplate, in that they propose to ask the men to go back to work under the abominable conditions prevalent for twenty years up to June last. The owners' interpretation of Clause 6, the principal clause in contention, leaves no other conclusion possible, and taking all the circumstances into consideration, we have unanimously agreed that the owners have not, and never really had, any intention of settling the dispute, but have rather played a game of bluff, apparently with a view of throwing the onus of the dispute upon ourselves. We feel, therefore, our only course is to accept the owners' challenge and get on with the fight."

Another manifesto read :

"Dockers, carters, sailors, firemen, cooks, stewards, cranemen, riggers, and all sympathetic to the cause are requested, in their own interests, to resist the latest efforts of the shipowners. They must be beaten, and we must fight !"

In addition, messengers went to London with the view of pressing the National Federation of Transport Workers to call a general strike. That association wisely took nothing upon trust, but sent delegates down to Glasgow, with the result that they agreed with the steps suggested by me, and advised consent to another meeting with duly prepared claims. The meeting was almost stopped by serious riots on the river-banks, extra police having to be called in. The Corporation met to consider whether soldiers should not be summoned, and only decided to wait till Saturday morning and the chance of an agreement being reached on the Friday. I had arranged that a smaller committee should meet me to discuss the technical details of conditions of work. This conference met at 2 p.m. on Friday and sat till 4 a.m. on Saturday morning. The agreement then signed was adopted in the course of the day by the associations on both sides. The original agreement was confirmed, the questions and explanatory replies were confirmed, but there were also now fixed the conditions to be followed on resumption of work, that vague field which had previously been left open for the joint committee to arrange. It was a tremendous tussle, and, as the hours drifted by, it seemed as if no issue could be effected. At last patience, tenacity, and will sifted out the difficulties and the dispute was officially closed. The dockers' leaders courteously came to give me good-bye at the station. One of them said, " I wouldn't have your job for thirty thousand a year."

It was inevitable, with feeling so very high as it had been and after such a bitter dispute, that there should be an aftermath of difficulty which nearly caused a renewal of the dispute in the next week, but the leaders had now a stronger position; real grievances had been rectified, the terms were down in clear black-and-white. The hotheads failed to get adequate support. It was alleged, indeed, that certain employers had wrongfully reduced shore-gangs, and the men of two steamship lines refused to work. Conferences between the parties did not settle the matter, and on February 15 the employers locked out about 6,000 men employed in connection with seagoing vessels. I had again to see the representatives of the Dockers' Unions and communicate with the shipowners, with the result that both sides agreed to an arbiter appointed by me giving a decision. Lord Mersey decided the employers were quite right, under the terms of the agreement.

So long an account of this one dispute may seem to be out of proportion, but I have given it in detail in order to show that part of the plan, just as in the cotton dispute, was due to the growing aim at improved organisation, and an attempt, which failed, to use that organisation in favour of the principle of unionism, which the organisation was not strong enough to enforce, and which employers were not prepared to assist or put in practice. As Mr. Arthur Henderson, ex-chairman of the Labour Party, said of the cotton dispute:

" 'Sold again!' is the language with which the temporary settlement in the cotton trade is received by some of the operatives. One can easily understand the disappointment which must be associated with the truce which Sir George Askwith has succeeded in achieving.

Ardent trade unionists were out for a great victory on a principle, vital, as they thought, to the union position. They have failed in this object. This, however, is no justification for the wild talk about being sold. The position was an exceedingly difficult one for the officials of the union, and they did their best. The fact is that some of the rank and file expect too much in these days. They believe all too readily that the strike weapon is omnipotent, and when it fails they conclude that they have been 'sold' or 'given away.' In my opinion the result would have been the same no matter how long the fight had lasted, and even if the end had come through a process of exhaustion of the union resources; the strength of trade union opinion against their non-union fellow-workmen is the measure of the employers' determination to be free to employ whom they please."

The other part of the plan was economic—a desire to know exactly the conditions under which men were to work, and to have some share in fixing the amount of work or assistance which each man would have to expect. There was also the strong desire not to increase the chances of unemployment by large or uncertain reduction of the number of men employed on a job. Those were the reasons, in addition to amount of pay, for such terms as the following in the conditions for resumption of work:

"General cargo liners and ocean steamers loading general cargo, eight men to be in hold; discharging general cargo, six men to be in hold.

"When oil is to be discharged from lower holds in lots of 100 tons or over, eight men to be employed.

"Slings to be regulated by the stevedore with due regard to safety and economy of working.

"ORE TRADE

"Unloading of vessels to start with two tubs and swinging tub till bottom is reached, after which four tubs to be used.

"Men's committee to consider if they will agree to the fourth tub when twelve feet from the coamings.

"NUMBER OF MEN IN GANGS

" Sixteen men in holds of boats from foreign ports—Spain, Portugal, etc.—as at present.

" Special consideration to be given to men at special boats, such as the *Glenmore* and *Behera* type.

" Boats of coasting type, wherever from, up to 150 tons, 9 men in gang; boats 150 to 350 tons, 13 men in gang; 350 to 1,000 tons, 15 men in gang; over 1,000 tons, 19 men in gang."

Each section of men desired to know where they were. Each section desired to have as good terms as their neighbours, or to maintain a relative position. Employers, on the other hand, desired to maintain control and management, not to pay unnecessary men, and to support the authority and technical judgment of their stevedores. There was no principle of overthrowing society, or establishing new theories for the conduct of industry. Possibly it may be said that the next strike proved the first great struggle which led up to some of the views now being so much talked of. In Disraeli's *Sibyl* Chaffing Jack remarks: " I fancy from what you say it's a cotton squall. It will pass, sir. Let me see the miners out, and then I will talk to you." " Stranger things than that have happened," said Devilsdust. " Then things get serious," said Chaffing Jack. " Them miners is very stubborn, and when they gets excited, aren't it a bear at play, that's all ? " The miners were coming out.

CHAPTER XXI

COAL, 1912

MINERS are not averse to striking on slight pretext. They like to "play" at intervals, and then return to scrabble harder in the pits, whence they can direct their thoughts with some contempt to the people who have to pass all their hours on the surface. The public takes no notice of these small disputes. They are not even reported in the papers, except by some short paragraph stating that 2,000 men have stopped work because a non-unionist has been discovered, or a foreman is disliked or the appointment of a check weighman is questioned. The man in the street wonders why such a storm in a teacup should upset so many people, and possibly deems the stoppage to be the work of an "agitator" or an unnecessary exhibition of strength. He trusts it will not affect his own supply of plentiful and cheap coal, but otherwise thinks of it only as an affair of the coal-owners and the miners. A national strike had never occurred. Although in 1909 a national strike, owing to the pledge of England to the Scottish miners, had been within an ace of happening, it had not happened, and the British public went to sleep again. Now it was to happen, and proved the forerunner of similar effort in future years, and an example which railwaymen and transport workers have followed, or are in process of organising so as to be able to follow, either separately or in union with the miners.

Immediately upon return from Glasgow on February 11, 1912, the closest attention had to be devoted to the serious position in the coal trade. The miners were demanding the acceptance of the principle of an individual minimum wage for all men and boys employed underground at certain fixed rates formulated by them. Their demands had been refused. Notices were being put up all over the country to cease work at the end of February, and no negotiations were being continued between the Mining Association of Great Britain, representing the coal-owners, and the Miners' Federation. These bodies had separated on February 7 without making any arrangement for resumption of negotiations, and on February 13 and 14 the Miners' Federation adjourned, " to be called together again when the officials of the Executive Committee find it advisable." There was still a possibility that negotiations in the Federated Area, covering North Wales and the whole of England except Northumberland and Durham, might result in an agreement, and as long as the parties, or any of them, were still negotiating, any interference from outside was contrary to the policy I have always endeavoured to follow. It was possible that, if the Federated Area could settle, a precedent might be set for other districts; but there was so much doubt and time was running so short that, having ascertained the latest date up to which the parties could reasonably negotiate, I felt that, unless there was a settlement, speedy action would be necessary, or the country would drift into a coal strike without an attempt at prevention. Even if there was a settlement in one area, some effort at inducement to the other parties to get together again might be necessary. The difficulty was to decide on the best method to apply, when there were two bodies with many leaders, and no one responsible head who could say, " We will agree to meet." There was no indication that representative leaders of the employers, as a whole, would respond to any invitation from the Industrial Council, and on the other hand there was clear indication that some of the miners' leaders would not accept its invitation, if invitation was sent. Under these circumstances it appeared that the Government must be the collecting authority, and on the very day (February 20) upon which I heard that the miners had finally refused the proposals of the owners in the Federated Area, I suggested to the Industrial Council, specially convened for that day, that in the interests of the community they should consider whether the position should not be clearly put before the Government. 445,800 miners had voted for a national strike, and only 115,721 against it. No negotiations were being continued. The prolonged effort in the Federated Area had broken down, South Wales was particularly active in pressing for a national strike.

If an invitation was sent by the Government, the parties could not well refuse to accept, when it could be proposed that they should resume conferences, or that they should consider the questions with expert business men, representative of employers and employed.

The Industrial Council concurred, and agreed to the letter which the Prime Minister signed the same day, and sent to the representatives of the coal-owners and of the miners. It ran as follows:

" *February* 20, 1912.

" SIR,

" His Majesty's Government have watched with close attention and growing anxiety the development of the present crisis in the coal trade. Up to the present they have entertained some hope that means would be found by direct negotiation among the parties concerned to avert the disaster of a national stoppage. As, however, the date approaches when the miners' notices for cessation of work will mature, His Majesty's Government cannot conceal from themselves that the prospect is gradually lessening that amicable arrangements, covering the whole of the coal-fields of the country, will be arrived at before that date.

" There is no need for me in this letter to enlarge upon the very serious consequences, both to the industries of the country and to all classes of coal consumers, which would inevitably follow a general stoppage of industry, and His Majesty's Government feel that they could not allow such a calamity to ensue without making every endeavour to aid in preventing it.

" In this connection I have received a communication from the Industrial Council, which, as you will be aware, was appointed last year with the object of dealing with the prevention and settlement of labour disputes, in which they advise that, in view of the critical position which has arisen, immediate steps should be taken by His Majesty's Government to convene a meeting of the representatives of the coal industry, with a view to discussing the grave situation which has arisen, and the possibility of arriving at some means of averting the disaster of a national stoppage.

" His Majesty's Government have given their earnest consideration to this communication, and to the circumstances of the case, and I desire accordingly to invite representatives of the coal-owners of the country to meet me and some of my colleagues at the Foreign Office on Thursday next, February 22, at three o'clock.

"I am, etc.,
H. H. ASQUITH."

A similar letter was sent to the Secretary of the Miners' Federation.

The Ministers met the representatives of the parties, and there followed the longest series of declamatory speeches and explanations, without any business being done, I have ever heard. The Ministers had no particular plan, and evolved no particular policy. They did not propose that the parties should resume conferences or consider the questions with expert business men, representative of employers and employed, but seemed to be very interested in hearing for the first time some of the difficulties of the miners' lives and their proposals. Days were consumed in talk, and meanwhile the strike grew more and more near, while the nation waited.

In order to estimate what this crisis was all about, it is necessary to refer to the scars of the past, such as those left by the Cambrian disputes, when, as already stated, the men had kept out and in the event found themselves in the wrong. Whether right or wrong, the result was that there were elements ready to retaliate, rather than to reciprocate. In addition, for years past there had been in different districts frequent disputes—varying in number and intensity according to the seams of coal, the action of foremen, or the position of trade—over payment for abnormal places. The miner working on piece might be in a position where for some time he received little ready cash, and when the abnormal place was passed did not like the deduction due to pay for any advances he might have received to keep him going. He wanted a minimum wage. The employer, on the other hand, said that if there was a minimum wage, and a high minimum wage, the miner had not the incentive to get through the abnormal place, where no coal or less than the average amount of coal could be got, and get out the coal from which both parties could get profit.

The trouble had existed for many years. It came to a head in a very quiet way in September 1911, soon after the

Cambrian miners had resumed work. Both parties met, and memoranda were exchanged over the rate of payment for working in "abnormal" places. The Miners' Federation had decided to demand payment of a minimum rate of wages to miners working in such places. The men proposed

"that this joint conference of coal-owners and miners' representatives recognises the right of a miner working at the coal face at fixed tonnage rates to receive full wages; if employed at an abnormal place, the rate to be the average rate of wages previously earned by the workman under normal conditions, which shall not be less than the recognised minimum or average rate paid in each district. Further, machinery should be set up in the different districts for the purpose of deciding on the question as to whether the place in dispute is abnormal. Pending the settlement of the dispute as to whether a place is abnormal or not, the men to be paid the district rate."

The owners replied:

"(1) The owners recognise the right of workmen who are engaged in places which are abnormal to receive wages commensurate with the work performed. (2) The customs and circumstances of the different districts vary so much that it is, in the opinion of the coal-owners, impossible to deal with the question collectively as applied to the whole country, and, therefore, the method of dealing with it can only be satisfactorily settled locally in the different districts. (3) The collective meeting of coal-owners, therefore, recommends the coal-owners in the various districts of the country to meet the representatives of the men in their respective districts when requested to do so. (4) It must be understood that in coming to the foregoing conclusion the meeting must not be assumed to have done anything to abrogate existing agreements."

On the next day, September 29, the miners met and resolved

"that, in view of the employers having admitted the right of men working in abnormal places to be paid fair wages, and having recommended that the owners in each district should enter into an arrangement to carry this out, we hereby recommend that the owners in each district should be now met on the subject, and a National Conference be held at the earliest possible date to consider the result of the negotiations."

On October 6 the Miners' Federation met at Southport and went a step farther. They proposed to get rid of the abnormal place question, which meant a bargain with the individual collier on his work in a particular place, by the comprehensive demand for an individual district minimum wage for all men and boys working in mines without any reference to the working places being abnormal.

Pursuing a method which has been very usual in later cases, the Miners' Federation followed up this demand with a brusque intimation to the coal-owners that, if there was no assent, there would be action; and they amended their rules in order to make action feasible. They said: "In the event of the employers refusing to agree to this, then the 21st rule to be put into operation to demand assent"; and made that rule to read that, "whenever a federation or district with the approval of a conference specially called has tendered notices . . . a conference shall be called to consider the advisability of *joint* action being taken." Each district was instructed to meet the employers and come back to a special conference on November 14.

There can be little doubt that the coal-owners did not realise the strength of this united movement by the miners. They had been accustomed to deal by districts, and there was no leader of sufficient weight to bring them together in united counteraction. They put forward and continuously adhered to the principle of the maintenance of existing agreements, which would preclude a national change. The miners, on the other hand, were seizing hold of the ideal of a national settlement, with equality for all districts and persons, irrespective of any district agreements. National settlements and an equality of treatment are all the vogue now, but in 1912 were an aspiration, deemed generally to be unsuitable in practice and liable to create greater anomalies than settlements which took account of geographical or historical conditions. The owners met the miners by districts, but no settlement was reached in any district, much less by the districts as a whole. The conference of November 14 was held, and to it the complete lack of success was reported. Scotland relied on an existing agreement which would not expire till 1915, South Wales on an agreement which would not expire till July 1912, although they were willing to discuss the question of abnormal places, " upon condition that the men would be willing to give an undertaking to loyally carry out the existing agreement; but only on that condition"; and the Federated Area or the English Conciliation Board, while accepting the principle of the minimum wage, came to no settlement on the amount.

This conference of November 14 was very important. It resolved that the conference was glad to learn that the English Conciliation Board had obtained the principle of a minimum for all men and boys working underground, and considered that their discussion should be adjourned to a future date, "so that further efforts may be made to bring about a satisfactory settlement." Then it further resolved that the best course to pursue with a view to obtaining an individual district minimum wage with the least delay was to negotiate nationally, instructed their Executive Committee to formulate claims for each district, and meet the coal-owners of Great Britain; and added, " but this resolution shall not prevent or interfere in any way with the negotiations now being carried on in the various districts."

It must be confessed that the coal-owners were not put in a position in which they could proceed to any negotiation with much chance of success. What was the good of conducting negotiations in various districts, if there was to be a national demand which might purport to overthrow any local settlements, in the same way as the miners were asserting that a national claim overrode and was outside any existing agreements in Scotland and South Wales? And, further, the demands for each district which the executive were to formulate were not ready, or before the owners, and indeed were not ready until the following February.

In any event the owners adopted a passive attitude, and no settlement was reached or apparently attempted. The Miners' Conference, on their part, took the line of activity. They met again on December 20 and 21, and decided to ascertain the feeling of their constituents on a ballot: "Are you in favour of giving notice to establish the principle of a minimum wage for every man and boy working underground in the mines of Great Britain?" There could be no doubt, particularly in view of the way in which miners' ballots are usually conducted, as to the result. It was declared at Birmingham on January 18: 445,800 in favour to 115,271 against. Thereupon the conference agreed that notices be tendered in every district so as to terminate at the end of February, though an intimation was to be made to the owners that they were prepared to meet them to continue negotiations in districts and nationally.

Although the sword, in the shape of the tendering of notices for the end of February, was kept hanging over their heads, the owners only received the formulated claims after a meeting of the Miners' Federation held in London on February 2. The claims included: (1) Individual minimum wages, varying in each district, for pieceworkers at the face of the coal; and added: (2) No underground adult worker shall receive a rate of wages less than five shillings per shift (changed later to five and sixpence); (3) arrangements for boys' wages to be left to the districts, but to be not less than present wages nor in any case less than two shillings per day. Individual minimum wages for pieceworkers other than colliers were to be arranged by districts, as near as possible to present wages, and day-workers underground also by districts, with instructions that an endeavour be made to arrange minimum rates for each class or grade locally in each district. It will be seen that the complexity of the subject was great, and required in some grades minute care, but the general claim became known as the "five and two": five shillings at least for all underground workers per shift, and two shillings at least for all boys per day.

The full claim was now out, and the employers met the miners in national conference on February 7. Both sides passed resolutions. The owners stated:

"The owners are prepared to assent to the proposition that each person in their employment should receive a fair day's wage for a fair day's work, but are convinced that the principle of payment in proportion to the amount of work performed is the only one which can be applied successfully in the case of coal-getters. They are aware that there are cases in which, owing to difficulties arising in consequence of exceptional conditions in the working-place, a man, while doing his best, is unable to earn what he would under ordinary circumstances. In such cases the owners recognise the necessity for special consideration, and are willing to discuss with the workmen the means by which this shall be ascertained. In assenting to the above, those districts which are now under agreement reserve their rights thereunder, and the districts comprised in the English Conciliation Board area reserve their rights to continue their negotiations."

To which the miners replied

"that we express our regret that the coal-owners have refused to accept the principle of an individual minimum wage for all men and boys employed underground, as we know there can be no settlement of the present dispute until this principle is agreed to. In view of the fact, however, that we have no desire for a serious rupture in the coal trade of the country, we are willing to meet the coal-owners at any time to further discuss the matter if the coal-owners desire to do so."

The owners in effect refused the demand for a minimum wage. They went back to the original demand made by the miners in September, and said they would discuss abnormal places, ignoring all that had occurred since that date. In fact, it seemed to me that many of them were extraordinarily ignorant of all that had been happening in the miners' movement, and how strong the feeling had now become. Some of them in conversation did not appear to understand the difference in the demands, and that the mere discussion of abnormal places had long since receded into the background. As before mentioned, the parties left each other with no arrangement for further discussion; the Federated Area continued local discussion till February 20, and when the discussion broke down, the Government asked the parties to meet them.

Four Cabinet Ministers—the Prime Minister, Sir Edward Grey, Mr. Lloyd George, and Mr. Sydney Buxton—sat to hear the case. The miners said they could do nothing without leave of the National Conference called for February 27, so their statement had to be adjourned till the 27th, and meanwhile ninety coal-owners at first, and afterwards a committee, met Ministers in three sittings. On the 27th both parties were seen. All these conferences were interesting, but most clearly exemplified the futility of conciliation by a committee. There was no plan, only a renewed statement of points which everyone except the four Ministers had heard over and over again. Any one of them by himself would probably have got down to the kernel of the case, but the four together never worked it out, Mr. Lloyd George keeping conspicuously quiet, and possibly keeping himself in reserve for a crisis. Time was running fast, and it was decided a pronouncement must be made. It took the form of saying that the Government were satisfied, after careful consideration, that there were cases in which underground employees cannot earn a reasonable minimum, from causes over which they have no control, and were further satisfied that the power to earn such a wage should be secured by arrangements suitable to the special circumstances of each district, with adequate safeguards to protect employers against abuse. Then it was proposed to have district conferences with a Government representative present, and if no settlement was soon reached in any district, the Government representatives were to decide jointly the outstanding points in that dispute.

This pronouncement was not altogether unfavourable to the owners, and possibly, if they had had an outstanding leader, or there had been longer time and opportunity for talking to them by districts, or if the policy of a national settlement, with the waiver of local agreements in favour of a national settlement, had been adopted, they might have seen that it would have been a wise course to accept the pronouncement. But none of these elements came into being. The parties spent February 28 in considering the proposals, and the owners came back with an acceptance by the Federated Districts, Durham and Cumberland, but a refusal by Scotland, South Wales, Northumberland, and the smaller districts (Forest of Dean, Somerset and Bristol). The miners returned with a resolution that there could be no settlement unless the principle of an individual minimum wage for all underground workers was agreed to by the coal-owners, adding: "We are still willing to meet the coal-owners to discuss the minimum rates of each district as passed at special conferences of this Federation." Asked what they meant by the minimum rates, they said: "Our definition is the minimum referred to in the Schedule of Wages already laid before the coal-owners and His Majesty's Government."

These propositions sounded reasonable. The Government and many districts had already in effect agreed to the principle, and the miners appeared to be willing to discuss the amounts in each district, although they had said nothing about safeguards against abuse, on which the employers laid great stress. The Prime Minister proceeded to inquire about safeguards and the procedure which might be adopted. Then there emerged the fact that the miners were not concerned with this kind of discussion: they wanted the money, and at once. "You are out for the money, Mr. Barker?" said the Prime Minister in an imperturbable manner, and Mr. Barker, a member of the Welsh Miners' executive, agreed that he was, and would not go back without it.

The Prime Minister had been more than conciliatory to the miners' representatives, and seemed to be a little irritated by the strict adherence of the Welsh coal-owners to a position which prevented any settlement by agreement, but as an observer I can only say that this new contention, and the statement that the miners could only enter into such conferences on the understanding that the minimum wage to be fixed in each district must be at the rate revised and finally adopted by the Federation on February 2, and nothing else, was too much for him, and also that the miners made a mistake. It appeared as if they thought the Government was on the run, and that they could coerce coal-owners, Government, and nation. It seemed to be a demand sprung at the last moment. After saying they would discuss, they presented an ultimatum. What was the use of conferences to discuss an irreducible minimum, arbitrarily fixed by the Miners' Executive and first promulgated on February 2? The whole scheme of discussion became a farce. Possibly the Government had made a mistake by Cabinet Ministers involving themselves in an industrial dispute and listening to long platitudes from both sides, instead of making use of their own creation, the Industrial Council, or a non-political, unbiased tribunal, and insisting that industry must settle the disputes of industry; possibly the owners had made a mistake by lack of cohesion, knowledge, weighing of consequences, and generally a short-sighted policy; but the mistake of the miners by reaching out too far and attempting dictation was, if I may say so, an alienating movement. Mr. Asquith decided to put the matter before Parliament.

It was most important to know what the real views of the coal-owners were. There were only two hours available in which they could be seen. The days which had passed in instruction of Ministers could not be retrieved. On the morning of February 29 I saw as many representatives of districts as time allowed. The great district of Northumberland had been divided in opinion, and after debate passed a resolution in the terms:

"After hearing suggestions of Sir George Askwith on the present position of the coal dispute, the coal-owners of Northumberland are prepared to state that they do not dissent from the clauses 1 and 2 of the proposals of the Government [which amounted to settlement by districts, with adequate safeguards]. In assenting to the above resolution, the owners do not retire from the position they have taken up, that they cannot consent to pay an individual minimum wage to underground workers irrespective of their ability or disposition to earn such wage."

The smaller districts seemed inclined to follow this decision, and possibly, with further time for explanation, Scotland might have agreed, but finally decided to abide events. The meeting in the Cabinet room at Downing Street, where the owners were to express their views, was not without interest and even humour. No districts were quite sure of the opinion of other districts, and when Scotland declared that they must wait and see, the chairman of South Wales jumped up and, waving a paper containing an unequivocal refusal, sang out: "Stands Scotland where she did?"

Mr. Asquith stuck to his guns. He told the miners that, if the Government were to undertake responsibility, it was essential they should discuss with both sides the reasonableness of the particular rates for various districts, or, in effect, he would not accept without discussion the miners' ultimatum. He told the House of Commons that, with the exception of South Wales and Scotland, who objected on the grounds of existing agreements, the coal-owners in practically the whole of England and North Wales had accepted the proposals, but that the miners would not negotiate rates for coal-getters, and that under these circumstances conferences were at an end.

This position was not very hopeful. The official report states:

"Meanwhile the men's notices to cease work had expired; a number of men in Derbyshire and other districts had ceased work already between February 26 and 29, and on March 1 the whole industry was virtually at a standstill. It is estimated that altogether about a million workers engaged in the coal-mining industry ceased work as a result of the dispute."

It was necessary to find an issue from this impasse—and so, on March 4, the Industrial Council again met, and decided to hold meetings every day. They appointed a committee which met the Prime Minister, and urged that there should again be an attempt at discussion. Neither of the parties were in the least likely to give an impression of weakness by coming forward to propose further conferences. Under the circumstances the Government alone could make such a proposition, they having elected to be concerned with the meetings and to preside over them. It was with some reluctance that the Government did decide to make another attempt, as another failure would not be very pleasant; but it was informally ascertained that the parties would accept an invitation, and on March 8 the invitation was sent.

"His Majesty's Government," it said, "consider that the proposals which they have already placed before the representatives of both parties offer the fairest means of arriving at a satisfactory settlement of the dispute. In view, however, of the difficulty of making any progress towards a settlement without mutual discussion, His Majesty's Government invite both parties to meet them jointly in conference, without prejudice, with a view to the free discussion of the whole situation."

Conferences continued on March 12, 13, and 14. It was not till the 15th that the Prime Minister had to say that no agreement had been arrived at, and they had come to the conclusion, with great regret, that though they had done all in their power to arrive at a settlement by agreement, "that was impossible; other measures must therefore be taken."

"The Prime Minister then stated that the Government would ask from Parliament a legislative declaration that a reasonable *minimum* wage, accompanied by adequate safeguards for the protection of the employer, should be a statutory term of the contract of employment of people who are engaged underground in coal-mining. As regards the important question of how such a *minimum* was to be ascertained for any particular area, the Prime Minister, without pledging the Government to any precise form of machinery, indicated that the district *minimum* should be locally fixed by a joint board in each district, consisting of representatives of employers and employed with a neutral and independent chairman, who might be selected by the parties themselves, or if necessary by the Government. Such a body would, in the opinion of the Government, afford what they have always regarded as all-important—a means of securing finality. The proposals of the Government would include provisions to secure promptitude in point of time in the presentation of the cases of the parties and in the adjudication thereon."

After all these long days of talk, the statement that a settlement by agreement was impossible certainly exhibited a confession of failure. It was an example at least to show that conciliation by a committee, however powerful, was not a very effective method. The method was not sufficiently elastic. Opposition crystallised more and more. The same points were discussed round and round, while the country was expectantly waiting—and beginning seriously to suffer.

On March 19 a Bill was introduced "to provide a minimum wage in the case of workers employed underground in coal-mines (including mines of stratified ironstone) and for purposes incidental thereto" ; and its second reading was carried on March 22, by 348 votes to 225. Even at this late stage an amendment was proposed to fix in the Bill the general minimum of five shillings for adults and two shillings for boys as demanded by the miners. Sir Edward Grey shelved the question for the moment by suggesting another conference, and for two more days Ministers conferred with the parties, without success. The Prime Minister was very firm on the principle that Parliament should not make a guess at the proper figure, and that such legislative enactment of wages would be a bad precedent. No agreement was reached ; the Bill proceeded, 326 to 83 voting against the inclusion of the "five and two" in the Bill, and the Bill became an Act on March 29. It is said that Keir Hardie jumped with joy at the result, not because he agreed with all the terms of the Bill, but because legislative enactment had recognised the minimum wage.

Under the Act, minimum wages were to be "an implied term of every contract for the employment of a workman underground in a coal-mine," unless the workman was excluded by the provisions of district rules. These rules were to lay down conditions in regard to aged, infirm, or partially disabled workmen, emergency interruptions, and the regularity or efficiency of work ; and the persons and modes for determination of various questions likely to arise through the existence of a minimum rate. Joint district boards of workmen and employers with an independent chairman were to settle minimum rates of wages and district rules in twenty-three separate districts, and in settling any minimum rate "shall have regard to the average daily rate of wages paid to the workmen of the class for which the minimum rate is to be settled." Groups or classes of coal-mines in a district might have special minimum rates or special district rules. There might be subdivision or combination of districts. Minimum rates might be varied by agreement or on notice after expiry of a year since the last settlement. If the joint district board failed to settle minimum rates and district rules within a specified time, the chairman had to settle them. The office of chairman might be held by one person, or committed to three persons, of whom a majority was to be deemed to be the chairman for the purposes of the Act. The Act was initially to continue in force for three years and no longer, unless Parliament otherwise determined.

There had, however, been a crisis. There were two questions—the attitude of the miners and owners, and the attitude of the Opposition; and an unwonted scene in the House of Commons, where both those difficulties came to the front. A contemporary journalist wrote to this effect, in a description which I can endorse:

"The Prime Minister spoke with growing slowness, until he was scarcely audible. He mourned the fact that the expectations the Government had of obtaining peace had been disappointed. 'But,' he exclaimed, 'we laboured hard.' Yet—and his voice sank back—he pleaded that those who had the deciding word would stay the havoc to the community with which the country was confronted. He narrated all that had been done to obtain a settlement, how hopes had risen and hopes had been shattered. He would not apportion blame, but he was filled with sorrow that, when the issue had been narrowed down to the matter of five shillings and two shillings a day, agreement could not be reached. The one thing the Government could do was to pass the Minimum Wage Bill, and provide machinery for a reasonable wage to be decided.

"But when it was passed, would the strikers accept it, and would they go back to their work? That was the question in men's minds. It was deeply embedded in Mr. Asquith's brain, for he knew that the strike leaders had proclaimed that they would not recognise the Bill unless in plain print there was inserted the five shillings and two shillings minimum. He turned toward the tight-wedged Labour benches. If their case for five shillings and two shillings was strong, could they not rely on the district boards giving those rates? The law would be changed, and yet would they continue to subject the community to increasing hardship?

"Then the awful strain got too much for Mr. Asquith. 'I speak under the stress of very strong feeling,' he said, with an effort. Hesitating between his words, he asked Parliament to pass the Bill as the only possible solution in a great emergency. 'We have exhausted all our powers of persuasion and argument and negotiation,' he added swiftly, as though he would deliver the words before agitation checked him. He struggled to control himself. Tears were in his eyes. Then he said, in thick, low, halting tones : ' But we claim we have done our best in the public interest—with perfect fairness and impartiality.' The House was profoundly impressed. Asquith, the cold, unemotional Prime Minister, showing the soft side of his nature before Parliament—that was a spectacle which will ever be remembered.

" The crisis was acute. The Opposition was gallant. Mr. Bonar Law appreciated the straits in which the Government were. The Opposition did not think the Ministry had adopted the best method, but it was the Government's method, ' and so no obstacle will be put by us in the way of the Bill passing '—a remark which was frankly appreciated by Ministerialists. But with his eye on eventualities, the Leader of the Opposition gave advice. ' The members of the Miners' Federation,' said he, ' are not merely members of the federation ; they are citizens of this country, and whatever may be their view, we rely upon them to obey the law. But unless society is to fall to pieces, the Government will be expected to use all the resources of this country to protect from molestation any man in any part of the country who desires to obey the law.' A tornado of cheers swept from the Opposition benches ; Unionists would back the Government so long as the Government saved the genuine worker from tyranny."

The owners recommended their colleagues to adopt the Act. The miners held a ballot, 244,011 voting against resumption of work and 201,013 for resumption. There was, therefore, a majority against return to work, but as there was no exact precedent as to the majority necessary to support such a decision, the Executive recommended that the principle of a resolution of December 21, 1911, requiring a two-thirds majority for a national strike, should be applied, and that the same majority should be required to continue the strike. They advised a resumption of work. This advice was accepted at a National Conference on April 6, and gradually, by the middle of April, practically all the men had resumed work.

What was the effect of the strike? I quote from the official report, which said:

"It is estimated that the aggregate duration of the dispute amounted to 30,800,000 working days. The almost complete cessation of the coal-mining industry very seriously affected employment in other industries. The industries most affected were those engaged in the manufacture of pig-iron, iron and steel, tin-plates and sheet steel, pottery, bricks, and glass. The pig-iron industry came practically to a standstill early in March; 10 per cent. of the blast furnaces were stopped by March 2, and nearly two-thirds by the end of the following week, while by the end of March only 13 per cent. were still working. Employment at iron and steel works suffered a heavy decline in the week ending March 9, which was further accentuated in the following weeks, nearly 60 per cent. of the men being unemployed by March 23. More than half the tin-plate mills had ceased working by March 9, and by the end of the month only 76 mills at 13 works were still working, as compared with 489 mills at 80 works at the end of February. The sheet-steel works in connection with the tin-plate trade were practically at a standstill by March 9. In the pottery trade of North Staffordshire the majority of the workpeople were out of employment in the middle of March, and in the brick trade nearly one-quarter of the workpeople were idle by March 23, and many more were on short time. The glass-bottle industry, especially in Yorkshire, was the branch of the glass trades principally affected, and was brought almost to a standstill by the end of March.

"Owing to the great curtailment of railway services, railway servants were considerably affected; many of the regular employees were put on short time or were required to take their annual leave, while large numbers of men in the lower grades were thrown entirely out of employment. This was particularly the case with men employed in the coal exporting ports; and for similar reasons large numbers of seamen, coal-trimmers and teemers, dock and waterside workers and coal-porters were unemployed. The fishing industry was greatly affected, especially at Grimsby and Hull, where most of the trawlers were laid up, thus throwing large numbers of labourers, in addition to the crews, out of work. Generally it may be said that casual labour, in its various forms, was severely affected throughout the country."

This account does not estimate the hardship to every household in the country, the loss of trade, the expense to the nation, and the loss to the miners themselves. Was the strike worth all this trouble and turmoil ? and was the result adequate for the trial of strength ? I think not. Minimum wages had become usual in many industries in the country. I had myself continuously established them. The principle may be contested, but they prevent much hardship and abuse, and do not as a rule prevent the exercise of individual ability or the incentive to effort in the majority of men. Some there are who will be content to earn the minimum only, if the margin between the minimum and the amount obtainable by piecework is narrow, but not the majority. In most trades such rates do not become the standard rate, as is commonly asserted. The Federated Area were prepared to accept the principle, and if the miners had not pressed for so high a rate at first, the principle could have been adopted in that area, and the increase of the rate, if it was insufficient, obtained at a later date. If by agreement in that area it had been started, other districts, some of whom were not averse to it, would have been bound to follow, and very possibly Scotland and even South Wales might have been willing to waive their contention as to breach of agreements. They would at least have had to give way as soon as those agreements terminated.

A certain section of the miners, however, were determined to fight, the rest speedily got their backs up, and the owners entirely failed to realise the seriousness of the position. The intervention of the Government and Parliament followed, a situation which led to subsequent Government action from time to time when disputes arose in coal, culminating in the present demand for nationalisation by means of the State, though some at least of the miners would desire to press the State by direct action as they tried to press the owners in 1912.

CHAPTER XXII

TRANSPORT WORKERS, 1912

THE coal strike of the spring was to be followed by a transport strike of the summer involving about 100,000 workpeople, and a duration of about 2,700,000 working days; chiefly confined to the Port of London.

It was a dispute varied by extraordinary changes in the demands made, in the allegations of breaches of faith put forward by both sides, and in the attempted methods of settlement. It exhibited proofs of astounding obstinacy on both sides, and, as it would seem, an intention to misunderstand each other, with strong objection, particularly by the employers, to the action taken by the Government. It was a dispute with which I had little to do until the close of it, although I had to be present at some conferences, and was supposed by the employers to be the "devil" behind the scenes.

The initial cause was based on the old question of non-unionism, where the employers maintained a passive attitude, refusing an undertaking to restrict themselves to union labour; and the unions found that, though in effect they might enjoy in practice a preference for union labour, they could not force by agreement the employment of union labour only. Behind this cause was the perennial irritation existing in the London docks, and the policy of some labour leaders at that time to get the most they could out of an arbitration or an agreement, and then to raise questions of interpretation or breaches of agreement, heading and turning the irritation and the men's demands into a claim which bore the aspect of legality. Their excuse might be that they averted worse trouble by showing that they were doing something, and certainly some unions had difficult constituents. Their condemnation by the employers was that they could not control their men, that they were fomenting trouble, and that it was of no use making agreements with them—the last point being of importance, as this was the main cause of a general reference to the Industrial Council on the subject of breaches of agreement.

The strike was too variegated for detail of all its features, but some of its incidents are not without some interest. The question of the Federation ticket, to be worn by all dockers as proof that they were members of the National Transport Workers' Federation, had not been really fought out or settled in 1911. It was revived in 1912, and the attempt showed the lack of organisation and weakness of that union, a lack which they have been working studiously to remedy ever since. The trouble began with the Watermen, Lightermen, and Bargemen, where some employers and some employed for years failed to get on with each other. A watchman, who seemed to have been a foreman and continued to belong to the Society of Foremen Lightermen, did not want to join the Society of Watermen, Lightermen, and Bargemen. The lighterage company by whom he was employed said they had nothing to do with the dispute, on the ground it was a dispute between two unions, whereupon, on May 16, the lightermen were called out on strike. The Association of Master Lightermen and Barge Owners had resolved to stick together, under the belief that their heads were to be chopped off one by one, and decided to do the lighterage company's work for them. They told their men to do this work; the union men refused, and were discharged for not obeying orders. This lockout at once enlarged the dispute, and the fire quickly spread. On May 18 the executive of the watermen passed a long resolution saying the master lightermen had broken an agreement of August 19, 1911, that by this agreement only foremen were exempt from a Federation card, and they had locked out men who were under the agreement for refusing to work for a firm employing union and non-union men. On May 20 the master lightermen issued a statement that they had never agreed to anything of the kind or to employ only Federation members. On May 21 the watermen and lightermen's time expired; they came out, and the dockers began to strike in sympathy. The Executive of the National Transport Workers' Federation held a meeting, and on May 23 called upon "all the transport workers to cease work to-night." This drastic command succeeded in London and on the Medway, work gradually ceasing in the course of the next few days. The London transport trade was stopped.

I went on a Sunday to Trafalgar Square, where Mr. Ben Tillett and other speakers were addressing a mass-meeting, and heard the end of his address, closing with a bow and the words, "Good luck to you, boys." There was little enthusiasm; the prospect was rather grim. I heard a man say, "I hope Sir George can stop this."

As I was one of those who countersigned the agreement of August 11, and as there was nothing in it about the Federation Ticket being obligatory, I saw the parties separately, since they would not meet, with a view to seeing whether the agreement was really the only issue: if that was the trouble, as alleged, it was a matter of interpretation; if there was another issue, could they meet and discuss the difference? Frankly, I do not know how Ministers started in to deal with the dispute. The Prime Minister had left London for a Whitsun rest in the Mediterranean, and some of them may have thought they should deal with so serious a matter as a stoppage of the London transport trade, or were "rattled" by a fresh disturbance in his absence. First one and then another had informal interviews with representatives of the parties, and finally it was announced in the House of Commons that the Government had decided to cause an inquiry and report to be made "on the facts and circumstances of the present dispute affecting transport workers in the Port of London and on the Medway."

One of the Ministers (Mr. Haldane) asked me to take this inquiry, but I pointed out that I had been immersed in negotiations with both sides, that both sides knew I was aware of every point, and that nothing could be gained by a fresh inquiry by me, so that I proposed a new mind might be brought to bear upon it, if this inquiry was desired, suggesting a list of two or three names, from which Sir Edward Clarke was selected.

Sir Edward, with his usual ability, heard the parties, and produced a report recording what had been said many times before. He found that, according to the agreements, recourse should have been had and should now be had to the decision of the Board of Trade in the event of difference between the Associations; and that the extension of an agreement to parties such as shipowners or traders not belonging to the contracting parties, so as to make it binding upon them, could only be dealt with by legislation.

This report did not settle the dispute. The employers definitely refused to accept it as an award on the points dealt with by Sir Edward. The men concentrated on the fact that it had not settled a question now put forward as their main contention in place of the compulsory union ticket which had been the initial reason for the dispute. This contention was that a man named Bissell, who employed two carters, and had been a member of the London Master Carmen and Cartage Contractors' Association, had broken the agreement of August 11, 1911, by paying less than the award. Bissell had resigned his membership and refused to renew it or to appear at any proceedings; there was no power exercisable by the Carters' Association, or under any Act of Parliament, as Sir Edward pointed out, to compel him to appear or to pay; and his own carters stuck by him. In fact, the dispute was shifted off upon this issue, but it was used as a lever to press denunciations of the employers for alleged breaches of agreement, the employers on their side being equally persistent in urging breach of agreement by the men in striking upon the matter of the union ticket.

The Report was handed to the Government on May 27, but the dispute continued till well into July, and work was not resumed till the first week in August. Public opinion may have a certain effect in shortening a strike, but the contention that there has only to be an open inquiry for the public to take cognisance of a dispute, and settle it by public opinion, is a fallacy. The public cares little or nothing about disputes which do not immediately affect them; the newspapers never publish, and cannot publish, for the simple reason that they cannot afford the space, full reports of disputes, inquiries, or even very important awards; a sensational murder trial will oust industrial disputes entirely out of the papers; and the most sensational dispute of recent years, the Music Hall dispute, was certainly not settled by the Press or public opinion. It may almost be said that it was kept alive by the sensation created by it.

After Sir Edward Clarke's report, five Ministers again

began interviewing both sides, or, rather, different sections of both sides, but without the slightest effect. The employers took up an attitude of passive resistance. At a conference with Mr. Lloyd George, the shipowners said they had nothing to do with a dispute about a master-carter; the dockers had left work and injured them in a dispute over which they had no control, and an agreement with which they were not concerned: if they chose to hold up the whole port, the shipowners were not going to be involved; if they recognised this dispute, they would have to look after every contract made by any association or any single employer; the dispute had commenced over the claim for the union ticket, which they absolutely refused to recognise, and that claim had not been withdrawn; they could not form, and objected to forming, a federation of employers; and one of them bluntly said they were not going to listen to "the cajolery of Mr. Lloyd George."

The impracticability of proper settlement of a dispute by a Committee of Ministers was abundantly apparent, and was emphasised still more strongly in my mind when I heard a politician tell a Minister that it was inadvisable the dispute should close too early, as a London election then proceeding might not go in the desired direction if it did. Although the Minister may not have been influenced by the tale, yet it illustrates the objection to politics or the suspicion of politics coming into or being allowed to affect the settlement of industrial disputes.

In reply to the suggestions for a federation of employers, the employers finally sent a formal answer:

"That His Majesty's Ministers be informed that their suggestion with regard to the formation of a federation of employers has been most carefully considered, and it is the unanimous opinion of those employers who have this day discussed the question that under existing conditions such a scheme is impracticable.

"Moreover, the employers desire that it should be distinctly understood that, whilst they are willing to discuss with His Majesty's Ministers at all times any suggestion made by them, no such suggestion, however acceptable in other respects, will be adopted until work has been resumed throughout the Port. Further, that they will not under any circumstances consent to any recognition of the Union or Transport Workers' Federation ticket, or to any discussion for such recognition."

Then, accepting the meagre statement that the employers would deign to discuss with His Majesty's Ministers any of their suggestions, further proposals were put forward on behalf of the Government, with a query whether there was any reason why the lines of the Brooklands and similar agreements should not be followed, with elaborate suggestions for a joint board consisting (1) of representatives nominated by groups of employers, and (2) of representatives of the men, as an Appeal Court with power to inflict penalties for breach of agreement. The men accepted this scheme, which would have been a very possible basis of sound settlement earlier in the course of debate, but now appeared too late. They madc thc mistakc, in my vicw, of adding to their acceptance that they intended to declare a national strike if a reply was not given by the employers on the next day. This challenge was met by a refusal to accept the principle underlying the Government's proposals, the real reason being objection to the threat. Their answer was conveyed to the men, when the National Transport Workers' Federation found themselves in the position of having to fulfil a threat or confess to an impotent threat. They sent telegrams to all ports saying, "Employers point-blank refuse to accept proposal for settlement. National Executive recommend general stoppage at once." Satisfactory answers did not come. Unions affiliated to the National Transport Workers took a ballot, and although about 20,000 men in various ports came out for a few days, the results in each case showed a majority against a stoppage. The other ports had had their struggle the year before, and were not prepared to support a lost cause. Meanwhile in London the employers began to fill up with new labour, very inefficient, but supplying in number at least some proof that work was going to be carried on. There were about 5,000 new men in the Port of London early in June, and about 13,000 by the end of the month.

It was obvious that, when Ministers were dealing with the problem, the Industrial Council could not cut across any action they might be taking, but at their meeting on June 12 they took note of the repeated charges of breach of agreement made by both sides in London, and also in general terms throughout the country. They unanimously adopted this resolution :

" The question of the maintenance of industrial agreements having come before the Industrial Council, that Council are of the opinion that this subject is of the highest importance to employers and trade unions and workpeople generally, and would welcome an immediate inquiry into the matter. "

The Government, by this time in a fix, at once seized hold of this proposal, and the next day the Prime Minister, who had now returned, stated that the Council would be requested to make an inquiry and report.

" It seems essential," he said, " to ascertain :

" 1. What is the best method of securing the due fulfilment of industrial agreements ; and

" 2. How far industrial agreements which are made between representative bodies of employers and of workmen should be enforced throughout the particular trade or district.

" The Government are anxious to have inquiry made into the matter, and to receive advice from those best qualified to give it. In these circumstances, they propose to refer the above question to the Industrial Council, which is representative of the employers and of the men in the great industries of the country ; to request the Council carefully to consider that matter ; to take such evidence as they may think fit ; and to report to the Government any conclusions to which they may come."

Although Ministers were in fact quietly dropping away from intervention in a dispute which they had failed to settle, there was no opening for the Industrial Council to step in and attempt to pick up the threads. The employers had issued a statement that

" schemes for dealing with labour questions in the Port of London as between and affecting individual trades and their workmen must, in view of the vast and conflicting interests involved, be complicated and require exhaustive discussion if the settlement is to be of a permanent character, and in the opinion of the Conference this discussion can only take place after work has been resumed."

Their theory of passive resistance was, however, pushed so far that, in answer to the query whether it could be said that a discussion could take place after work had been resumed, they replied curtly that " it would not be in accordance with the resolution to inform the men that after work had been resumed discussion would take place between the respective associations of employers and the representatives of the men." They were apparently determined to give no opening whatever for return to work with hope of future amelioration, but to insist on confession of error by unconditional surrender. Opinions may differ as to the value and sense of these tactics, but everyone will, I think, agree that they would not conduce to cessation of an industrial dispute. The dockers' leaders said, " We are going to tell the men frankly that there is nothing else to do but to fight."

Even in reply to a formal letter intimating the reference to the Industrial Council, and asking whether the Port of London Authority would nominate one or more representatives to give evidence before the Council " in regard to any, or all, of the Industrial Agreements to which the Authority has been a party, or with which it is concerned, or any other matter which it may deem material to the terms of reference," that body replied that

" the Authority has been a party to one agreement only—that known as the Devonport Agreement, signed by the parties thereto on July 27, 1911. The history of that agreement is set out in the Authority's communication handed to His Majesty's Government on the 10th instant, and as the Authority has nothing to add on the subject, it does not propose to be represented at the inquiry before the Industrial Council."

A Labour Member brought up a proposal on July 1 in the House of Commons, and got a resolution accepted " that, in the opinion of this House, it is expedient that the representatives of the employers' and the workmen's organisations should meet with a view to arriving at a settlement"; to which the employers, on July 4, only announced that "they adhere to their decision conveyed to the Members of the Cabinet Committee on the several occasions when meetings have taken place, viz. that they agree to no conditions precedent to the men returning to work," and that "in the future as in the past the freest submission of grievances will be allowed to employees, and just and generous consideration promptly accorded to them." This reply was unanimously confirmed on July 11 by another meeting.

Meanwhile, as the weeks went by, there was beginning to be serious distress in the East and South of London. One Bishop opened a relief fund, and three Bishops, possibly with the best intention or aiming at following the precedent of Cardinal Manning, butted in with a summing-up of their own as to the points of difference, and the futile and despairing suggestion, "Cannot some arbitrator having the confidence of both sides suggest a formula which may bring employer and employed together, and thus close a dispute which is causing untold misery and injuring the whole country?"

It was about this date that the Prime Minister asked me to see him privately. He requested me to explain the full position. I told him the whole history in an unvarnished tale, without any comment, although the obvious deduction was the absolute failure of Ministerial interference by a Committee of Ministers in an industrial dispute, and the bad effect upon Government prestige, particularly in the event of a failure. He walked up and down the Cabinet room in Downing Street, with his hands in his pockets, and, turning to me, said, "Every word you have spoken endorses the opinion I have formed. It is a degradation of Government. Can you suggest *anything*?" I said that the only chance I saw of a settlement which did not leave great bitterness behind it, and a determination for reprisals on a suitable occasion, would be a formal announcement by the employers that they intended to keep and maintain agreements, which must be their policy and which they had always said had been their policy; that such a declaration could only come from Lord Devonport, as Chairman of the Port of London Authority; that it would not be believed unless the transport workers' leaders saw Lord Devonport and had it from him personally; and that, if an interview took place, Lord Devonport would be well advised to say nothing about the union ticket, which was dead, and not now a live claim: otherwise the strike would continue and would revive on the very first opportunity. Mr. Buxton was called in, and agreed. The Prime Minister saw Lord Devonport alone. I was told that he had said he would be at his private house between certain hours the next morning, and if two of the transport leaders (who were both members of the Port of London Authority) called, he would see them and say to them that he was prepared to denounce breaches of agreements by any employer. The Prime Minister asked whether this could possibly be done, to which I said the attempt should be made. I asked two of them to breakfast on urgent business, one coming back especially from Manchester; explained matters, and took them to Lord Devonport's door, waiting to see that they were admitted. He gave them the assurance, published his assurance in the Press on July 18, and a few days after they called off the strike. The intervening days were interesting. The two leaders had no mandate. They could only wait to ascertain whether Lord Devonport's statements in the Press, that he had explained to them how far existing agreements would remain in force, what variation would be made, and the reason for such variation, would be accepted by the transport workers. Meanwhile they worked with quiet hints that the promises were sufficient to end the strike. When the time was ripe, the Strike Committee issued a manifesto on Saturday, July 27, recommending an immediate resumption of work: "Strike declared off. All men to return to work Monday." Even then the men, on Sunday, July 28, unanimously resolved not to resume work, but on the Monday some of the dockers and stevedores resumed. I was able, after certain interviews, to state that sailing-barge owners would continue to pay the "pink-list," and all their men returned to work. Others quickly followed. Finally, after some disturbances between the returning trade unionists and the non-unionists who had worked during the strike, a general return to work had come by August 6.

This long strike had been most ineffective. It was initiated, not for improvement of wages and hours, but in the belief that by force the employers could be induced to employ men of the Transport Workers' Federation only. When the force proved insufficient, the claims were shifted on to alleged breaches of agreement, including a case where a small master-carter had resigned from an association bound by an agreement, and of which he was a member when the agreement was made. He had then paid wages lower than the agreed rates. There was no power to oblige him to remain a member or to continue as an individual to be bound. Into this varied tangle five or more Cabinet Ministers threw themselves, though many of them in their respective offices had nothing whatever to do with the matter, and could only have interfered because they considered their influence to be large or because they thought their action would serve political purposes. Their efforts completely failed.

The Prime Minister was so annoyed that he gave strict orders that Ministers, even the President of the Board of Trade, who, if any Minister should intervene, was the proper Minister to intervene, were to leave industrial disputes alone and not mix themselves up with them. This request was almost unnecessary in the case of Mr. Buxton, the then President, whose policy it endorsed. It was scrupulously followed by his successor, Mr. Burns. Mr. Runciman, until the War came and he had to tilt by advice a few cases on to the arbitration tribunals, also followed it. Mr. Harcourt, who was Acting President for some months, rigidly maintained the same policy. It was left for Mr. Lloyd George, by his personal action, to reverse this policy, during the War, in the case of the Welsh coal strike, and to make it impracticable by handing over to the vast number of new Ministries, and even the new Departments, established during the War, the authority and power to deal with every kind of dispute which in the least affected their Departments, a policy which led to conflicting decisions, a maze of authorities, and a large number of disputes which ought never to have occurred, and would never have occurred but for this change.

Some bitter remarks were printed in various papers on the action of Ministers, which might well have been taken to heart. As one paper remarked:

"In many respects the strike that has just ended has been the most remarkable for many years. There was no question of non-payment of reasonable wages, but only alleged small causes of friction and pressure to compel the employers to make themselves agents to force non-unionists to become unionists.

"The first and foremost lesson of the struggle is that a strike, if it is prolonged, is the worst weapon for getting real advantages, and that, although it may be used as a warning, it is unwise to treat it as a battle to the end. Some opinions to the contrary were expressed on both sides last year, particularly when the efforts at conciliation had proved successful, and when such efforts did not prevent strikes breaking out in other quarters. It was even said that strikes were induced because it was thought conciliation would be used. . . . People forget that last year conciliation in towns where it had been used had been effective in causing a cessation of strife in those towns, subject to small cases of aftermath. A proof of its value and of the settlements made has been evident in the fact that, in the provincial towns where settlements were made, hardly any disturbance occurred when these towns failed to follow the lead of London.

"Another lesson from the strike is that the less the Government and political persons interfere with trade disputes the better. There is no intention to propose special legislation in this trade, and yet a Committee of six members of the Cabinet, supposed to be sitting to inquire into the general causes of unrest, chose to interfere in an individual case, and buoy up the minds of the strikers with belief in legislation and the interference of Parliament. This created a notion that there was a court of appeal above the officials who had acted with success in previous strikes, not necessarily preventing them, but bringing them to a close within reasonable time.

"Mr. Sydney Buxton, the President of the Board of Trade, last year earned general praise for keeping out of the strikes himself, although, being Member for Poplar, he had great temptation to interfere. He held up the conciliation part of his Department as independent of politics, and as separated from the Board of Trade in all respects except so far as it was necessary to have a Minister who could answer questions in Parliament on matters of fact. The conciliation department of the Board had kept upon those lines, and the Government had themselves established an Industrial Council with the object of emphasising the lines on which policy should be directed. But in the absence of the Prime Minister other members of the Cabinet thought that there was a good opportunity of advertising themselves, and interfered, with the most disastrous results. The Prime Minister at least deserves credit for having endeavoured to bring matters back to the more normal condition, and it is to be hoped that the action of the rest of the Government will not have interfered with the successful efforts of the Industrial Commissioner's Department."

The most disastrous disputes are not without humorous incidents, of which one perhaps may be mentioned.

In the middle of the strike there came out Mr. Ben Tillett's *History of the Transport Strike*, 1911, in which he indulged in a pen-sketch of me :

" Sir George Askwith, the patient, plodding man, with pigeon-holes in his brains ; who listened without sign of being bored or absorbed, who concealed his mind like a Chinaman. Emotionless, excepting that he would peer through his glasses at someone making a statement of moment, never raising his diplomatic voice, or appearing to hurry over anything ; guiding without falter or apparent effort the disputants, however heated they may be, himself the inscrutable, patient listener.

" And such patience ! It was more than dour in its persistence and calmness ; it compelled by its coldness, and saved us from bickerings on occasions when the wisest become puny and spiteful.

" He is the most dangerous man in the country. His diplomacy is and will be worse than war. Unless it absolutely succeeds in forcing industrial combatants to appreciate the human oneness of the community, it will be a danger, inasmuch as it will make with its great genius for a peace that, after all, will be artificial."

Let me be allowed to reciprocate with a few words on Mr. Tillett. He could almost deprecatingly wish the boys good luck in Trafalgar Square, or utter wild words on Tower Hill, but in the council-chamber he was not always so effective. " Where is Mr. Tillett ? " I asked. " I want to see him." "Oh, we have put him out of the way, to write manifestos *in your room*, so that he won't interrupt us," was the reply. There I found him, with his coat off, his shirt-sleeves rolled up (it was very hot), his long hair ruffled, scribbling for all he was worth, on sheets and sheets of *Government* notepaper. I watered down that manifesto for him, just as he consented to go back by the next train from Manchester at a crucial moment, when he could only have upset things. Ben Tillett is a far more sensible man than some people think, and, be it said, with a very kindly heart.

CHAPTER XXIII

INDUSTRIAL AGREEMENTS, 1912

WHILE the London transport dispute was pursuing its unhappy course, many suggestions from many quarters were put forward with a view to anticipation or mitigation of strikes. Of these the Government, dimly aware that they were in a mess and that they had no policy, seized hold of two stopgaps, which could at least allow them to answer that inquiry was being made. The first stopgap was upon the subject of the breach and maintenance of industrial agreements, a suggestion made by the Industrial Council; the second an inquiry into the working of Canadian law, proposed by a deputation from the Association of Chambers of Commerce to the Prime Minister on June 21.

The members of the Industrial Council were requested on June 14 to inquire and report (1) what is the best method of securing the due fulfilment of industrial agreements; and (2) how far and in what manner industrial agreements which are made between representative bodies of employers and of workmen should be enforced through a particular trade or district.

The reference stated that "the Government will give the most earnest attention to any recommendations that the Council may be able to make."

On July 24 Mr. Lloyd George in the House of Commons followed the same line.

"The Executive," he said, "had no power to go beyond inquiry and conciliation. There was no other power vested in the Executive for cases of this kind—none. Up to the present public opinion was opposed to any fresh powers. If they proceeded beyond conciliation, the next step was compulsion, and if there was to be compulsion, it must be compulsion on both sides.

" But, after all, it was impossible to legislate for each particular case. Problems of this kind ought to be dealt with generally, and his own opinion was that the public were beginning to feel very strongly that there ought to be some means of determining disputes without on the one hand driving one party to starvation, or on the other ruining the industry.

" He was perfectly convinced that the time had come for a reconsideration of the whole problem of settling trade disputes.

" The Government had set up an inquiry into the subject, and the Industrial Council were considering the best means of dealing with matters of this kind. He did not think it would be possible to deal with them without some form of legislative sanction, but before legislation could be carried it necessarily involved that there should be a guarantee on both sides that decisions could be enforced.

" The Government had come to the conclusion that it would be necessary to deal with this problem. It was not merely this particular dispute. Other disputes were constantly cropping up, and therefore the Government had come to the conclusion that it was necessary to deal with the whole problem, and that in the immediate future."

But in spite of these pledges, when the report of the Industrial Council was presented, and also the report on Canada, the Government did nothing. The crisis was passed, opportunist policy no longer made it important to fulfil promises, nothing was done except shelving the report by reference to the Trade Union Congress, and the Government went forward with no labour policy at all.

With regard to Industrial Agreements, no observation is more often heard than the statement that it is of little use making agreements with workmen or their representatives, because no sooner are they made than they are broken. Many also have been the proposals for enforcing the maintenance of agreements or the awards of arbitrators by such expedients as penalties, imprisonments, blacklisting, expulsion from associations or unions, etc. It is certainly as a rule more easy to oblige employers to keep agreements. There is damage to their trade and credit if they are marked as failing to fulfil agreements made with their workpeople. They are fewer in number ; the bad opinion of their fellows is more easily applied. They are liable to have more force brought to bear upon them, both by their fellows and by their own workpeople. On the other hand, even if some workpeople have not equal education or moral sense to see the importance of keeping agreements, or will down tools without the slightest regard to their own or their union undertakings, most unions have rules by which they endeavour to lay down standards of conduct or punishments, such as suspension, refusal of out-of-work pay, or, in some cases, expulsion for offending members. The complaint of employers is that those rules may exist, but are not adequately enforced, or are not sufficiently deterrent. The subject is a difficult one, particularly as in a trade dispute there are generally charges and countercharges of bad faith by both sides.

I have found that allegations of breach of agreement are very often due either to misinterpretation or to misunderstandings. Industrial agreements are not always worded with great clearness or legal precision. Even if they were, who has not known cases where statutes or wills, apparently drafted with the utmost precision, have been construed in different ways or formed the subject of action in the courts ? Employers or workmen who have not been present at conferences read these documents, and possibly read them in different ways. Even if the employer desires to follow out the terms of the agreement, his methods of payment or the rules at his works may make the application extremely difficult, and the application selected may not appeal to his workmen as being correct. A very little divergence of view serves to give rise to charges of breach of faith. It is the same story of suspicion which might often be obviated if there was a recognised system, well matured in many works, of bringing the question before the management, and failing agreement referring it to the association or union. In the case of an arbitrator's award the arbitrator should always be asked to say what he meant, by consent of both parties ; or the document, if the parties are legally bound, may be capable of being brought into the courts. Sad difficulties, however, have from time to time arisen, when arbitrators have been so lax in their wording or understood the intricacies of a trade so slightly as to be unable to say what they meant ; and others have been known to be so foolish as to give an interpretation without notice to the other side and ascertainment whether they agreed to the reference or whether they had anything to say. An agreement, too, is only binding on the parties to it, just as an award only covers the parties named in it. It is only too common for this plain fact not to be realised, with the result that accusations of bad faith may be made against those who are expected to follow it by analogy or by being in business in the same trade, even in cases where their methods may be quite different, or where special circumstances have not been dealt with or heard, or where those accused may be genuinely ignorant of the existence or the terms of an agreement or award. A fertile source of trouble is the fact that only a synopsis or part of an agreement is generally published in the Press, and may be taken by workmen as the real agreement, when it may give a complete travesty of the proper effect.

As regards personal experience, I can only recall a few instances where my awards have not been carried out, and few instances where agreements effected or drafted by me have been broken. In the first category a case arose at Grimsby, but the cause was found to be the nefarious work of bribing middlemen. In the second, cases of complaint have arisen, but almost invariably I have been asked to rule on the point or to settle some subsidiary point of application or of the course to be followed in special circumstances not specifically brought forward at the conference. This procedure should be invariably followed. It would prevent many strikes.

It is true that small sections of workmen do break away from agreements, very often in ignorance. In other cases I have known employers put up notices giving their own interpretation and in their own language, hopelessly wrong; instead of putting up the whole and actual terms of the agreement. An abbreviation always gives rise to the belief that something is being concealed. The actual agreement should be published in full; each workman should know of it and be able to see it; and the simple announcement made that the terms will be carried out in the works, with a notification by what method any complaint concerning its mode of fulfilment can be brought forward.

On the whole, therefore, I endorse now the view of the Industrial Council given in 1913, and think the statements as regards breaches of agreement so commonly bandied about contain a great deal of exaggeration on both sides. A better method of dealing with the charges would diminish bad feeling; and with better feeling the charges would be less likely to arise.

The Industrial Council held thirty-eight meetings, heard ninety-two witnesses from the principal trades, and in their report dated July 24, 1913, said:

"Notwithstanding the difficulties inherent in dealing with large numbers of workpeople, we find from the evidence that agreements in most cases are well kept. Although a number of instances of alleged breaches of agreements have been referred to in the course of the Inquiry, the evidence of a considerable majority of the witnesses is to the effect that agreements have, viewed generally, been duly fulfilled by both parties. The breaches that have been mentioned were, with a few exceptions, the result of the action of comparatively few men, or due to exceptional circumstances or to differences and misunderstandings in regard to points of interpretation, and are not, as a rule, countenanced by the respective organisations.

"It is recognised by both sides that they are under a strong moral obligation to observe agreements which have been entered into by them or by their representatives on their behalf. The principal exceptions appear to be in trades which are unorganised, or in which on one side or the other the organisation is incomplete or is of recent origin; but we find that where agreements are the outcome of properly organised machinery for dealing with disputes they are, with very few exceptions, loyally observed by both sides. Where agreements have been broken it is frequently found that they were made at times when, owing to the abnormal conditions, great difficulty must have been experienced in arriving at a fair adjustment."

After considering the merits of monetary penalties for breach or an obligation imposed by law not to assist in any manner persons in breach, the Council reported:

"Our view is that voluntary organisation and collective bargaining cannot successfully proceed upon a basis of broken faith, and that breach of faith should be discouraged by all voluntary action that can be taken by associations on either side. In many associations rules for the punishment of persons committing a breach already exist, and we recommend that other associations should follow the lead which has thus been taken, and consider whether it is not advisable that similar rules should be adopted in their organisations.

"While we are convinced that it is to the interests of both employers and workpeople that industrial agreements should be duly fulfilled, we think that in the long-run this object is more likely to be secured by an increased regard for the moral obligation and by reliance upon the principles of mutual consent, rather than by the establishment of a system of monetary penalties or by the legal prohibition of assistance to persons in breach.

"The suggestion that no support should be given by either employers' associations or trade unions to their respective members acting in breach of an agreement (e.g. that the union should give no strike pay in case of breach, and the association should also render no assistance to a defaulting member) has, as a principle, received general support from almost every witness who considered the matter in the course of the evidence.

"We think there can be little doubt that the fact that financial or other assistance could not be given to persons acting in breach of agreement would be an aid to discipline and would tend to assist in the maintenance of agreements, and we are of the opinion that, where it has been decided by an impartial tribunal (or by mutual consent of the parties to an agreement) that a breach of an agreement has been committed by any person who is a member of an association represented by the signatories to the agreement, no assistance, financial or otherwise, should be given to that person by any of the other members of the associations who were parties to the agreement.

"It appears to be the case that many industrial agreements contain no clause providing for cases of disagreement regarding the interpretation of the document, and we are of opinion that such a clause—an 'interpretation clause' —is an essential part of an industrial agreement and should form part of every such agreement. We consider that a model clause of this character would be one which provided that, in the event of a dispute arising as to the interpretation of an agreement, the point in dispute should be referred to an independent chairman, or to arbitrators, or a Court of Arbitration, agreed upon in each case by the parties. In the event of the parties failing to agree upon the person or persons to whom the matter is to be referred, it should be referred to a chairman or a Court of Arbitration appointed in accordance with the provisions of the Conciliation Act, 1896. Such a chairman or Court should have a casting vote, or at least be able to recommend a solution should the parties fail to agree."

So far the Industrial Council did not specifically indicate legislation, though the circulation and development of their unanimous opinion might well have been undertaken.

As regards the second portion of the reference (as to how far, and in what manner, industrial agreements which are made between representative bodies of employers and of workmen should be enforced throughout a particular trade or district) there was some difference of opinion, but the majority of the Council said :

"We have come to the conclusion that, subject to an inquiry made by an authority appointed by the Board of Trade, an agreement entered into between associations of employers and of workmen representing a substantial body of those in the trade or district should, on the application of the parties to the agreement, be made applicable to the whole of the trade or district concerned, provided that the agreement contains conditions to secure—

"(*a*) That at least . . . days' notice shall be given by either party of an intended change affecting conditions as to wages or hours ; and

"(*b*) That there shall be no stoppage of work or alteration of the conditions of employment until the dispute has been investigated by some agreed tribunal, and a pronouncement made upon it."

To which one member suggested the addition of the words—

"(*c*) That it should be illegal for any financial assistance to be given by either the Employers' Association or the

Workmen's Association in support of any person who, having been a member of an association represented by the signatories to an agreement, has been declared by an impartial tribunal or by mutual consent of the parties to the agreement to have contravened the terms of the agreement."

The point of the Report was that industries desiring extension of agreements could obtain that boon, under due safeguards for those to whom it was proposed to extend the agreement, if they were prepared to undertake to give notice of any change affecting conditions as to wages or hours, and not to strike until the dispute had been investigated by some agreed tribunal and a pronouncement made upon it. It was not compulsory arbitration, it was not an interference with the right to strike, but a voluntary restriction which many industries desired and were prepared to accept. No industry need have come into the scheme unless they so desired. The Government, however, as I have said, only shelved the question. Six or more years afterwards, when the Whitley Committee endorsed the report, and also the Canadian report, the Ministry of Labour did take some steps in the direction of extension of agreements by order, but left out the important part, that agreements might be extended only in those trades which agreed not to engage in a strike unless notice had been given and the dispute had been investigated and a pronouncement made upon it. Without this compensatory bargain, extension would be entirely one-sided and unfair to small firms, to whom the application of the agreement might be onerous, largely inapplicable, or strangling.

CHAPTER XXIV

CANADA, 1912

An inquiry into Canadian labour legislation, especially the working of the Act known in the Dominion as the Lemieux Act, was in a sense supplementary to the reference to the Industrial Council—an interesting sidelight promised in the middle of the transport strike on June 21, 1912. The Prime Minister then said :

"The Canadian Act does not provide for compulsory arbitration by an impartial authority before either masters, on the one hand, lock out their men, or the men, on the other hand, strike. . . . I should be sorry to pronounce an opinion, and I do not know how far the social conditions of Canada make it easier to work a scheme of this kind there as compared with this country. I think we ought to inquire very deeply into the matter without delay. We propose to do so—to make a very careful inquiry as to how this machinery is working in Canada, with a view to seeing whether it is not possible to adapt it to the conditions of this country. That will require prosecuting with promptitude."

On July 31 I gave notice to the Industrial Council that the Government had requested me to make the inquiry, and on August 23 sailed from Liverpool, with my wife and Mr. Mitchell. Our journey extended from Quebec to Montreal, Toronto, London, the Trade Union Congress at Guelph, Ottawa, Winnipeg, Calgary, Vancouver, Victoria, Nelson, Cranbrook, Frank, and again to Ottawa, and then for a few days to Washington and New York. Although inquiry in the United States had also been mentioned, time and the requirements of work in Great Britain prevented any opportunity for more than official calls. One could only express hope, never fulfilled, that another visit would facilitate some examination of conditions in the United States. In both countries the welcome from every class of the community was such as one can feel but not adequately express. In Canada we saw everyone we could, from H.R.H. the Governor-General, Ministers, ex-Ministers, and high officials, to minor clerks in remote Government offices; from employers like Lord Shaughnessy, settling with a wave of his hand a large grant to telegraphists on the Canadian Pacific Railway (on the eve of the Trade Union Congress), to representatives of the coal industry of Nova Scotia and the small owner in Victoria, exercised over the restrictions of trade unions which hindered him from painting his garden gate; and from the French workpeople in Quebec, through telegraphists endorsing the Lemieux Act (at the Trade Union Congress), to recently arrived Independent Workers of the World in the building trades of Vancouver and the mines of Vancouver Island, who paid little attention to it. In Washington the Commissioner told us the troubles of a railway crisis, and Mr. Gompers took three hours of his valuable time in showing the Temple of Labour, and introducing me to his officers, with a final bestowal of a badge of the Trade Unions of the United States.

The most interesting features were the Trade Union Congress held at Guelph, a town in Ontario, and some interviews at the Labour Temple in Vancouver. At Guelph there was a special debate on the Lemieux Act. The opinions of unions which were not governed by it, and irritation at a recent legal decision given by a judge, in an exceptional case, as to its supposed effect, caused a vote to be given that the Act should be repealed. If the word "amended" had been substituted for "repealed" the effect would have been better, as the principle of the Act was warmly defended by some of the unions chiefly affected by it. The real point was that the railwaymen had come under it by consent, while it had been imposed upon the miners at a time of great crisis in Alberta. The miners, therefore, looked upon it with suspicion, and in that vast country any enforcement in Alberta or Vancouver from so distant a city as Ottawa was more than difficult to achieve.

In Vancouver the building trade is the governing trade. Both the city and the island are subject to invasions of Independent Workers of the World and other associations, from Washington State and other districts of the U.S.A.

There are some interesting men to be met there. At one interview they started off with long remarks about social regeneration, the destruction of everything, and the new world, when Mr. Mitchell quietly remarked that I had heard these arguments nearly every day during the last few years and knew them by heart, but he believed I wanted to know the facts about Canada and what they were practically doing in Canada. I had maintained silence, but was then asked to put a few questions, when we soon commenced to discuss business points. Hour by hour flew by, and since then I have from time to time received letters from Vancouver, including an appeal to see that their men should be drafted to this country to take part in munitions work during the War.

The Lemieux Act, named from the Postmaster-General of the day, and passed in March 1907, with an amending Act in 1911, was chiefly due to the work of Mr. W. L. Mackenzie King, now leader of the Liberal Party in Canada; and is expressed to deal with "the prevention and settlement of strikes and lockouts in mines and industries connected with Public Utilities." It defines "strike" as "a cessation of work by a body of employees acting in combination, or a concerted refusal or a refusal under a common understanding of any number of employees to continue to work for an employer, in consequence of a dispute, done as a means of compelling their employer, or to aid other employees in compelling their employer, to accept terms of employment"—a definition which includes the direct strike and the sympathetic strike. Its scope is indicated by the definition of "employer," which is given as meaning "any person, company, or corporation employing ten or more persons, and owning or operating any mining property, agency of transportation or communication, steamships, telegraph and telephone lines, gas, electric light, water- and power-works," or, in a brief word, public utilities.

Upon my return from Canada, and after a few weeks of rest in Algiers, my report came out in February 1913. The rest was necessary, since, as one paper remarked, "We have often wondered how the peacemaker got through his strike work last year, because it was enough to kill anybody made of iron or adamant."

Of this report the salient principle was this: that there

should not be read into and expected from the Act features which were never intended by those responsible for its becoming law and were not included in it, but that

"the simple purpose of the Act is to ensure the recognition of the interests of the public, as a third party, in trade disputes, and the insistence that that third party, through the Government, shall have a voice in regard to a dispute affecting their interests, and, according to the Act, before a stoppage of work takes place."

That simple purpose, the right of the public, was the principle of the Act and the principle to which all the explanations in the report were directed. After considering the points of objection, as well as the favourable features of the Act, I stated:

"that it might be feasible in the United Kingdom, with advantage both to employers and employed, to give opportunity for such investigation and recommendation as would bring into light the real causes of difficulties, and create in the public mind and in the minds of employers and employed the opinion that, when opportunity exists by law, such opportunity should be taken advantage of, and that strikes and lockouts ought not to be commenced, and certainly not supported by 'sympathetic' strikes, while such investigation and recommendation are pending."

Finally, the end of the report again emphasised the value of conciliation being legally authorised, in cases where the public were likely to be seriously affected, even if the proposals for delaying stoppage of work were not inserted in a statute or were not compulsory. In spite of the Act, inquiry after stoppage had in fact necessarily to be employed in certain cases in Canada; but that did not take away the value of an inquiry being allowed, authorised, and, in fact, required under the ægis of the law in cases where the public were interested, possibly in even greater degree than the contending parties.

The report ended with these words:

"I consider that the forwarding of the spirit and intent

of conciliation is the more valuable portion of the Canadian Act, and that an Act on these lines, even if the restrictive features which aim at delaying stoppage until after inquiry were omitted, would be suitable and practicable in this country. Such an Act need not necessarily be applied in all cases, but neither need it be confined to services of public utility. It could be generally available in cases where the public were likely to be seriously affected. Without the restrictive features, it would give the *right* not only to conciliate but fully to investigate the matters in dispute, with similar powers in regard to witnesses, production of documents and inspection, as are vested in a Court of Record in civil cases, with a view, if conciliation fails, to recommendations being made as to what are believed to be fair terms. Such an Act, while not ensuring complete absence of strikes and lockouts, would be valuable, in my opinion, alike to the country and to employers and employed."

This proposal did not suggest such stringent conditions as the Lemieux Act enjoined. That Act requires that any dispute arising in connection with the class of industries named—mining, railways, shipping, and other public utilities—shall be submitted to a board of conciliation and investigation, with a view to arriving at a settlement before a strike or lockout can be legally brought about. It also stipulates that at least thirty days' notice of an intended change affecting conditions of employment with respect to wages or hours shall be given, and that pending the proceedings before the Board, in the event of such intended change resulting in a dispute, the relations to each other of the parties to the dispute shall remain unchanged, and neither party shall do anything in the nature of a lockout or a strike.

It has been said that the Lemieux Act is compulsory arbitration in disguise, but such a criticism could only be made by persons who have not read the Act or examined the practice under it. The Act differs essentially from compulsory arbitration. It only endeavours to postpone a stoppage of work in certain industries for a brief period and for a specific purpose. It does not destroy the right of employers or workpeople to terminate contracts. It does not attempt to regulate details of administration of business by employers, or interfere with organisation of associations of employers or of trade unions. It legalises the community's right to intervene in a trade dispute by enacting that a stoppage, either by strike or lockout, shall not take place until the community, through a Government Department, has investigated the difference with the object of ascertaining if a recommendation cannot be made to the parties which both can accept as a settlement of the difference. It presupposes that industrial differences are adjustable, and that the best method of securing adjustment is by discussion and negotiation. It stipulates that, before a stoppage takes place, the possibilities of settlement by discussion and negotiation shall have been exhausted; but, and here it differs from Compulsory Arbitration, it does not prohibit a stoppage either by lockout or strike if it is found that no recommendation can be made which is acceptable to both sides. If no way out of the difficulty can be found acceptable to both parties, there is no arbitrary insistence upon a continuance of either employment or labour, but both sides are left to take such action as they may think fit. As a result it does not force unsuitable regulations on industries by compulsory and legal insistence, but leaves an opportunity for modification by the parties. It permits elasticity and revision, and, if it does not effect a settlement, indicates a basis on which one can be made.

My argument was that both parties might well be, as it were, educated, or become accustomed in due course of time, to see that discussion was necessary, and should be exhausted before strikes or lockouts hurtful to the community as a whole should be suddenly forced upon it, without any knowledge of the facts by the community, and in a manner wholly detrimental to it.

It is contended that the owners of commodities can sell or withhold them without any restrictions whatever, and why should workmen, who have only their labour to sell, be prevented from disposing of it or withholding it at the moment most favourable to them? The answer seems to be that, if wheat, coal, iron, or any other commodities were to be held up in such a way as to endanger society, and active steps taken to hinder all importation from any other source, society would take steps to protect itself. It was the danger of society being held up by a cessation of labour which apparently induced the Canadian Government to pass the Industrial Disputes Investigation Act. Carried to its logical conclusion, the claim to cease work at a moment's notice, if acted upon, would make business impossible. In a civilised community business must be made possible. Therefore, it is not very unreasonable for a community to say both to employers and workmen: "If you desire to engage in this or that business under the protection of our laws, you can only do so under certain conditions, one of which is that before bringing about a cessation of work which may seriously jeopardise the public well-being, certain notice must be given." This principle of notice has long been recognised both by the Government in dealing with labour, and in everyday business contracts. The policy of well-established trade unions, both in this country and America, is in the direction, not of the sudden attack, but of obtaining discussion, and exhaustive discussion, before a stoppage is resorted to.

The Canadian Act is an extension of this principle of exhaustive discussion. In effect it stipulates that not only shall the principals themselves exhaust their own efforts at securing agreement, but the community must also have full knowledge of the matter, with a view to seeing if a tribunal free from the prejudices of both parties cannot suggest some way out of the difficulty. With a view to obtaining this result, the Act gives a right of obligatory discussion, and enforces the production of witnesses and books for the purpose of proving whether contentions are right or wrong.

It is surely true to say that the public have no use for strikes or lockouts. While the public might often have much difficulty in bringing opinion to bear in favour of acceptance or rejection of technical suggestions, which in many trades it would be impossible for persons who had not examined the questions to understand, their support to the principle that the ordeal of battle should give place to reasonable judgment would probably be emphatic and frequently effective. From the point of view of the employers, examination need not interfere with the administrative details of business or discipline, but should give better opportunity for regular and consecutive business by reducing the number of strikes, by bringing strikes to an earlier conclusion, and by the powerful effect which would result in the direction of rendering unnecessary and ineffective the progress of sympathetic strikes by which employers having no quarrel with their own workmen are so frequently disturbed.

At the present day, when business is becoming so huge and complicated, the redress of grievances becomes more and more difficult by reason of the absence of the " personal touch " in the conduct of many businesses. In the interest of such businesses, as well as in the interest of other trades which are closely affected by a disturbance in any connected trade, or even in trades in the same town or district, it becomes more and more necessary to clear the issues and to ascertain the actual source from which trouble has arisen. From the point of view of the employees, such a course would enable them to bring forward valid grievances with some opportunity of their being heard. Discussion, or opening the way towards discussion, is often found by the workpeople to be impracticable either in fact or in belief. Everyone who has had any experience of strikes or lockouts knows how very often a main difficulty consists in bringing the parties together, or even, if the parties do not meet, in examining the case of each party.

If there was an express and legal power of making recommendations or of informing the public on the rights and wrongs of a dispute, a large number of trade unions should be quite willing voluntarily in many cases to afford time for investigation and recommendation, and so an atmosphere would be created in which the voluntary granting of time would be deemed to be a proper course to pursue. Workpeople themselves, now frequently coming out in sympathetic strike over disputes in which they have no primary concern, would understand that such action was unnecessary prior to examination of the initial dispute. Workpeople forced to cease work because some allied section, necessary to the conduct of the business, was not continuing work would be likely to exercise their influence in favour of examination before a cessation of work involving innocent persons should take place.

Criticism of the Canadian Act in Canada has not been wanting.

" The Department of Labour," to quote one paper, " has magnified its office and given a good deal of advertising abroad to the Industrial Disputes Investigation Act, sometimes called the Lemieux Bill. But seen closely, it is found that strikes often occur in public utilities before investigation, though the Act forbids it; and that since this Act came into operation, Canada has suffered far more from coal-mining strikes than Great Britain in proportion to the number of men employed. Strikes of this kind have been more frequent and have continued longer in Canada than in Great Britain. The prohibitory clause of the Act has been violated scores of times. No attempt has been made to punish the offence. The Act provides no machinery for enforcement, no penalty for disobedience, nor does it appear possible to add to it any of these effective sanctions."

There were also strong complaints of delay from the western states, so distant as they were from Ottawa.

Such criticisms as these would either have not applied, or were met, in the suggestion outlined in the report upon the principle of the Act; but whether such an atmosphere as has been outlined in the preceding sentences could have been, or could now be, created in this country, it is not possible to say. The Government had no labour policy and did nothing at all. No attempt was made to do anything, although some of the leading papers urged that action should be taken. A Bill drafted by Lord Buckmaster met with little support. Six years afterwards, the Whitley Committee endorsed the report, but Committees of Inquiry which were from time to time appointed since the War have been apt to be *ad hoc* committees, controlled by men who are partisans or reputed to be biased in view, a form of tribunal generally found in past years to be unsuitable, both in this country and in Canada.

Recently, during this year, an Act giving statutory power has at last been passed. The appointment of a Commission with legal powers of requiring attendance of witnesses and production of documents had at least the indirect effect of influencing the settlement of an awkward dispute in the electrical industry. But for many years an opportunity, and a good opportunity, was lost owing to the absolute lack of any Governmental policy except that of drift.

Canada, as compared with the United Kingdom, has many different factors to consider. Some of the characteristics most striking to a traveller from these islands are the great distances between place and place ; the difficulty of quick communication with Ottawa ; the influence of the United States and the connection of unions with organisations in the States ; the vast tracts of agricultural, prairie, forest, and mountain land ; the French-speaking provinces ; the numerous emigrants from all countries ; and the enterprise and opportunity of individual effort. But the factor that struck Mr. Mitchell and myself more than any other was the power, grit, and success of the educated Scot, particularly in the West, coupled with his keen interest in everything connected with the mother-country. The spirit shown by so many of these men and women irresistibly recalled the fine lines :

> "From the lone shieling of the Misty Island
>   Mountains divide us, and the waste of seas,
> Yet still the blood is strong, the heart is Highland,
>   And we in dreams behold the Hebrides."

CHAPTER XXV

THE MIDLANDS, 1913

THERE seemed to be a lull after recent storms in the early months of 1913. Acting on a suggestion which I had been able to make in the previous year, the Boilermakers' Society were negotiating with the Federated Shipyard Employers on the terms of an agreement for preventing stoppages in the shipyards; and the Variety Artistes brought before me claims for amendment of the Music Hall Award of 1907. A strike involving 12,000 operatives in the "Morley trade," where cloth is manufactured from a mixture of cotton and shoddy or mungo, on a claim for increased wages by willeyers, who blend the cotton and mungo, and fettlers, who clean the machines which mix the materials, was settled after many hours of mediation. A building dispute in the Garden City of Letchworth and a plasterers' strike in London were also composed by conference.

Then suddenly there occurred a flare in the Midlands, which spread rapidly through Birmingham and the Black Country, directly involving about 50,000 operatives in boiler and bridge works, metal-rolling works, tube works, railway carriage and wagon works, nut and bolt works, and other allied trades, and thousands of workpeople indirectly in various industries. The principal claim was for a minimum wage of twenty-three shillings a week in Birmingham and the Black Country, but the strike commenced with the small beginning of some girls at Dudley saying that they could not live any longer on the wages paid to them. Just as years ago the London match-girls had started the London dock strike, so these girls lit the torch which fired the Midlands. The men followed suit in factory after factory. The year before a Midland employer had said to me that at Birmingham they could not understand what had come over the sea-port towns; things were managed much better in the Midlands, where all was quiet. The present movement did not seem to show that the employers had correctly estimated the position of their own works or taken any notice of the growing improvement in trade, the rise in the cost of living, and the probable effect upon their workpeople. In any event the employers were taken completely by surprise. There was no cohesion amongst them. As the strike went on, slowly various groups began to federate under the title of the Midland Employers' Federation, but in some sections there was a strong objection to recognition of the Workers' Union, no account being taken of the fact that the Workers' Union had been organising until it had become a very powerful body. Other employers were yielding, or inclined to yield, the problems being to them comparatively simple. Others employed large numbers of women and youths and were not united on any scale of payment. An additional strike of the firebrick makers at Stourbridge added to the confusion. The whole position, with varying classes of firms, workpeople, and claims, was complicated, and exactly fulfilled the conditions under which a legally authorised inquiry, as suggested in the Canadian report, might well have unravelled the skein and brought forward lines of agreement. Instead of that, nothing had been done by the Government on the lines of the report, but a Bishop had come forward with unacceptable proposals, to be followed by a peer quite inexperienced in industrial disputes, both of whom the employers emphatically ignored. On May 29, and again in June, tentative inquiry was made by Mr. Cummings of my Department, when it appeared that some meetings were to take place between the Employers' Federation and the Birmingham and Allied Trades Societies' Federation; but it was not until July, after a ballot of thousands to 99 against acceptance of the employers' proposals by the workpeople, that it became plain that the parties would be glad to receive suggestions of settlement.

On my arrival at Birmingham I found that the parties were assembled in different hotels. There did not appear to be any desire to meet. The employers had stated their terms, simply announced that they were final, and proposed to await a reply, which they seemed to think I should induce the men to give in the affirmative. The men stated that some of the terms were so vague that explanations were necessary. This answer annoyed some of the employers, who said it was mere equivocation; the terms were perfectly clear, and could be taken or left. "Well," I said, "that may be so, but as I have to explain to the men, will you tell me for my own information, what do these clauses mean?"—citing three clauses. One employer gave his explanation, and was promptly contradicted from the other side of the table. "You see the difficulty," I remarked. "You are not agreed on the meaning of your own clauses. I can convey no unanimous explanation. If I give my own, you may not agree with it. These men have got to explain to the rank and file. They may give different explanations which one or other of you may disown. Nothing but a clear statement heard from yourselves can be satisfactory, with amendments, if necessary, to your document, in order that the statement may be clear both by word of mouth and in writing." I suggested a meeting, where, if they liked, I would be present, but take no part except by request; and at last they met. That document required several amendments and long discussions, lasting for three days.

In the intervals of the second day the firebrick trade was separately induced to come to a settlement, which got one difficulty out of the way. As was remarked:

"The dispute has extended over a month, and it took the peacemaker rather more than three hours to adjust the terms upon which 1,200 workers will return to their occupations on Monday. Why should not such a conference have been called in the early stages of the dispute, or even before open warfare commenced? It does seem a pity that a month should have been wasted before the possibilities of discussion were quite exhausted. Perhaps some day we shall be wiser, and adopt some system making it impossible for a strike or a lockout to occur before the art of conciliation has been tried and has failed. This success with the Stourbridge trouble encourages an optimistic view, but can Sir George succeed in ending the whole of the industrial turmoil in the Black Country?

"Save as evidence of the widespread demand among various classes of workers for improved conditions, the strike of brickmakers in the Stourbridge district was unconnected with the strike of unskilled and semi-skilled labourers in the metal, tube, and allied trades. But the fact that an agreement for the settlement of the brickmakers' dispute has been drawn up is surely an excellent omen for the success of mediation with employers and workmen concerned in the bigger trouble. The terms approved by the brickmakers' representatives have yet to be ratified by the unions interested; but since the men and women employed in the brickmaking industry gain an advance of 10 per cent. on piecework and day rates, and the women have secured a minimum wage of ten shillings a week, there is unlikely to be any general indisposition to resume work. Furthermore, a wages board is to be established for the trade, and pending its formation disputes are to be settled either by negotiation or by reference to an independent umpire of the Board of Trade. Obviously in the new conditions they have been able to obtain the brickmakers have substantial cause for satisfaction."

The larger dispute was a much more serious matter. It was being fought with very great determination.

"In some parts of the strike area men have been idle for nearly three months; in others large numbers of workpeople have been voluntarily unemployed for periods varying from four to eight weeks, while other workers have experienced the serious and depressing effects on general trade that a large disturbance of staple industry invariably produces. The actual loss in wages suffered by the men on strike and locked out now exceeds a quarter of a million sterling, but large as that figure may be, it represents neither the whole of the material loss brought upon the affected districts nor upon the workmen themselves. The semi-skilled and even the skilled labourers in the Midlands have been called out in support of the upheaval. These are the men, aggregating some 37,000, who have dispatched three marching contingents to London with set determination on their faces. Every day added to the duration of the strikes intensifies the suffering and loss: in spite of the activities of relief agencies, distress among the families of the strikers becomes increasingly acute, and no one who appreciates the realities of the struggle will suggest that the intervention of the Board of Trade has come a moment too soon."

The discussion of this embittered dispute soon resolved itself into conciliation, lasting a full Thursday and Friday, and finally the whole of the following Monday, when an agreement was reached. This agreement, besides dealing with reinstatement, certain existing agreements, and the minimum wage, and the wages of women, girls, and youths, all of which were raised, was remarkable for the success of its provisions for avoiding disputes, whether on general rates, piecework, and sectional rates, or sympathetic strikes. It created quite a new spirit in the Midlands, and months afterwards both employers and workmen informed me how successful it had been. It created order out of a very chaotic condition; the strike perhaps proving a blessing in disguise, because it provided methods of dealing with difficulties which proved of service during the War.

These provisions stated that:

"With a view to avoiding disputes, deputations of workmen shall be received by their employers by appointment for mutual discussion of any question in the settlement of which both parties are directly concerned, or it shall be competent for an official of any trade union to aproach the secretary of the trade committee of the federation involved, or vice versa, with regard to any such question, or it shall be competent for either party to bring the question before a conference to be held between the trade committee and the trade union. In the event of a trade committee or trade union desiring to raise any question, a sectional conference for this purpose may be arranged by application to the secretary of the trade committee or of the trade union as the case may be. Sectional conferences shall be held within twelve working-days from the receipt of the application by the secretary of the trade committee or of the trade union concerned. Failing settlement at sectional conference of any question brought before it, it shall be competent for either party to refer the matter to the Executive Board of the federation and the central authority of the trade union or trade unions concerned. Central conferences shall be held at the earliest date which can be conveniently arranged by the secretaries of the federation and of the trade unions. There shall be no stoppage of work either of a partial or a general character, but work shall proceed under the current conditions until the procedure provided for above has been carried through.

"(2) This agreement is entered into on the understanding (which the federation are informed to be the case) that the rules of the various unions involved efficiently deal with breaches of agreement by their members and that the rules in such cases will be enforced.

"(3) No notices to stop or suspend work to be given in on account of any dispute in any works outside the membership of the federation. The trade unions agree to abstain from giving notice for the workmen in the employ of members of the federation in the case of an outside dispute, and the federation will not support any firms who are not members of the federation.

"(4) This agreement shall remain in force for a period of at least twelve months from the signing of this agreement, and within fourteen days of the end of the term of this agreement notice to terminate may be given by either party. Work, however, shall not be suspended pending any negotiations which may be proceeding. Should the negotiations fall through, work shall not be stopped until seven days from the termination of such negotiations."

The scheme involved stages of exhaustive discussion, speedy examination of claims, and no stoppage of work while negotiations were pending, together with avoidance of stoppage or suspension of work on account of outside disputes, while at the same time the right to strike or lockout was maintained.

The dispute in the Midlands was a sequel to the economic disputes of 1911 and 1912, but it must not be supposed that any of these disputes failed to leave a mark. They indicated to Labour the value of organisation, which was being actively pressed throughout the country, and the value of propaganda, which more and more made its force felt; they increased the cohesion of labour, particularly among semi-skilled and unskilled workers; they educated both leaders and the rank and file on things to be done and things to be avoided in the course of a strike.

After the close of this trouble the month of August

passed, with conferences over a dockers' dispute at Leith and a china-clay workers' strike in Cornwall; the issue of the report of the Industrial Council, dealt with by the Government in the futile manner already described; and a telegram from General Botha asking that I might be permitted to go to South Africa to deal with the strikes on the Rand. The Government refused the request on the ground that a long absence from the United Kingdom was not feasible.

CHAPTER XXVI

LARKIN, 1913

It was a very different disturbance to which attention had to be given in September 1913. If the disputes in the ports and inland cities of Great Britain had been chiefly based upon economic causes, the serious riots in Dublin, although founded upon poverty, low wages, and bad conditions, included determination to establish the transport workers' union as the "one big union" in Ireland, and to put into practice the doctrines of syndicalism. Mingled with these ideas the prejudices of politics and religion affected the minds of individuals, amongst both employers and employed. Mr. Larkin was determined to win, to hit the employer whenever and wherever he could, while on the other hand there were employers, especially Mr. William Murphy, who were out at the cost of any expenditure to smash Mr. Larkin, if they could. The influences of "ca' canny" propaganda, the overthrow of Capitalism, and revolution against existing authority, were all present. The Irish riots of 1913 were the precursor of many things which are alleged to be features in recent industrial differences, and to be the methods now inculcated by social writers, extreme socialists, and syndicalists; and practised by some trade unionists and workpeople in recent strikes.

On August 1 *The Times* remarked:

"The report of the Industrial Council on industrial agreements which was issued yesterday is not likely to attract the attention it deserves. . . ." The perturbation which prevailed fourteen months ago had passed; "the public have reassured themselves and general interest in the subject has died away. Strikes are no longer of interest except in so far as languid attention may be given to events 6,000 miles away on the Rand."

A month later, on September 2, Great Britain was startled from this dangerous apathy by the brief announcement:

"Dublin, September 1. Killed 1; injured 460; arrested 210. Of the injured, 60 are policemen.

"The rioting of the past two days has been desperate, but it will appear like a playful skirmish compared with what may be expected during the present week.

"Dublin is now practically in a state of civil war between Labour and Capital."

The dispute was more serious even than either of the policies of trade unions, which were well described at the time by Mr. Snowden in a morning paper, when he said:

"The old policy of the trade unions was to build up strong reserves; to refrain from exasperating the public and the employers by never-ceasing threats of strikes; to exhaust every possible means of conciliation before calling out the men, and then not to do so unless there was a reasonable chance of victory. By this policy the unions entered upon the strike with the most useful of all assets—namely, a public sympathy which had been won over by the willingness of the men to adopt every possible means to avert a strike. The new policy is to enter upon a strike without any effort to obtain a settlement of the grievances by negotiation; to exasperate the employers by every possible means; to indulge in wild and sanguinary language, which makes it impossible for a self-respecting employer to meet such leaders of the men; to never pay any attention to the rather important matter of preparing some means of support during the strike; and to endeavour to cause as much public inconvenience as possible, by involving the services upon which the public needs and convenience depend. These are the two trade union policies which are now in conflict."

One of the largest firms in the city, Messrs. Jacobs & Co., the biscuit manufacturers, who had made many efforts for the welfare of the employees, locked out their employees, chiefly girls, on the ground of the "intolerable tyranny and injustice" of Mr. Larkin's transport union. Mr. William

Murphy, chief man in the Dublin tramways, took a similar line, stating that the dispute was forced upon him, and that it was impossible to carry on business under the dictatorship which was attempted to be imposed.

On the other hand, Mr. Larkin attacked everyone right and left, but was adored in Dublin, as he had been in Belfast in 1907, and had about 10,000 members of the union behind him, and at least 20,000 other supporters of both sexes and all ages. In a brief time the whole number was estimated at 80,000. It required but small observation to see that the conditions of Dublin were the chief source of his power.

With the continuance of disturbance, the question of "tainted goods" began to arise in Great Britain, about 7,000 railwaymen going out at Crewe, Sheffield, Derby, Liverpool, and Birmingham. The railway trade union leaders composed this difficulty, inquiry showing that many of the "tainted goods" had not come from Ireland, and that the Irish goods arriving in Birmingham were barrels of stout loaded by trade union labour. Individual railwaymen could not possibly judge the source of goods, or pick and choose what goods a railway should carry, if a railway was to be run according to law or as a business concern. With a view to general sympathy for fellow-workers, however, the Trade Union Congress, sitting in September, voted the supply of a ship filled with food for the hungry in Dublin, and sent over a mission of inquiry. They made no headway. The Lord Mayor of Dublin came forward with some proposals for a board of employers and transport workers, which, as the employers would have nothing to do with the transport workers as constituted, met with no acceptance. The National Transport Federation also proposed to take over the strike, but though their efforts were nominally accepted, Mr. Larkin showed them scant courtesy.

I was very busily engaged in a successful attempt to avert an omnibus strike in London, which would infallibly have spread, if it had not been composed, to the tramways and tubes, when the Irish Government, after long consideration, and many suggestions from the Press, asked that my Department should endeavour to deal with the difficulty. It was with considerable hesitation that I approached the task, but proposed a Court of Inquiry as preferable to an attempt by a single Englishman to intervene in the welter of a revolution. Sir Thomas Ratcliffe Ellis, secretary of the Mining Association of Great Britain and of the Conciliation Board of the coal trade of the Federated Area, and also a member of the Industrial Council, and Mr. J. R. Clynes, M.P., Chairman of the Executive Committee of the Gas Workers' and General Labourers' Union, were appointed to join me in the effort, " an absolutely impossible effort," as Mr. Clynes subsequently wrote me. Mr. Mitchell and Mr. H. F. Wilson came with us to Dublin from my Department. Although neither party refused to come before the Court of Inquiry and make statements, we soon found that no settlement was meant. Mr. Murphy was out for a fight to the finish ; his counsel, Mr. Timothy Healy, did not cross-examine Mr. Larkin ; Mr. Larkin abused his best friends in Ireland, descending to personalities which were at least unwise if he desired a settlement ; and even during the sittings of the Court sympathetic strikes continued to occur. The situation was not assisted, as I afterwards heard, by secret advices from Great Britain not to listen to the proposals of the Court, and by rumours that "blackleg" dockers were going to be imported.

The only parties who would have liked to negotiate were the English transport leaders, but the employers would not listen to them, unless they could show more power of control over the Irish workers than the Irish workers would accept or they could promise ; and more guarantee that any agreement effected would be adequately maintained. Hence a conference or negotiation between the parties, though pressed by the English leaders, proved to be impracticable. " If the Transport Workers' Federation," it was said, " is not more fertile in resource and does not possess sanctions hitherto unsuspected, the inquiry must leave the position no better, if no worse, than it found it." The inquiry was open to the Press, and held at the Castle in public, but neither side would meet separately with the Court or carry on methods of conciliation or ascertainment of the real points at issue in a manner which had been found to be useful in other cases. The Court could only listen for four days to a tale of sympathetic strikes, on very flimsy grounds ; lack of control or attempts at control by labour leaders ; recriminatory accusations of breaches of agreement on both sides ; and a deplorable picture of Dublin as it was. Mr. Larkin in one speech managed faithfully to pronounce equal criticism on the Government, the Catholic Church, Ulster, the Pope, and the Salvation Army. No institution or person seemed to be safe from denunciation.

The Court came to a unanimous report in which it was pointed out that proposals for conciliation or avoidance of disputes had been fixed by agreement or arbitration or conferences time after time since 1908, without any effect being given to them. Nothing had been done. Although we agreed that events indicated that "grievances of considerable importance have existed," the Court spoke on the subject of the sympathetic strike in the following terms:

"The sympathetic strike may be described as a refusal on the part of men who may have no complaint against their own conditions of employment to continue work, because in the ordinary course of their work they come in contact with goods in some way connected with firms whose employees have been locked out or are on strike. This practice has far-reaching results, as, for example, the refusal of porters at Kingstown to handle parcels of publications consigned from England to a firm of newsagents in Dublin, who had declined the request of the union that they should refuse to distribute newspapers printed by another firm whose dispatch hands were involved in a dispute.

"In actual practice the ramifications of this method of industrial warfare have been shown to involve loss and suffering to large numbers of both employers and work-people who not only have no voice in the original dispute, but have no means of influencing those concerned in the original cause of difference. Even collective agreements, signed on behalf of employers and men's organisations, a provision of which was that no stoppage of work should take place without discussion and due notice, were entirely disregarded under the influence of this ever-widening method of conducting disputes. The distinction between strike and lockout became obscured, attacks on one side being met with reprisals on the other side in such rapid succession as completely to confuse the real issues.

"No community could exist if resort to the 'sympathetic' strike became the general policy of trade unionism, as, owing to the interdependence of different branches of industry, disputes affecting even a single individual would

18

spread indefinitely. If this should be the policy of trade unionism, it is easy to understand that it does not commend itself to the employers, but in our experience of the better-organised employers and workmen, the sympathetic strike or the sympathetic lockout is not a method which is recognised as a reasonable way of dealing with disputes."

There followed a very adverse criticism of a document, which some firms had asked their employees to sign, with reference to obeying all the orders of the employers and not becoming members of the Irish Transport and General Workers' Union, as contrary to individual liberty and likely to create a maximum of ill-feeling; and a statement of the imperative necessity for a truce.

"We have given," the report said, "very careful consideration to the contention put forward that the labour conditions obtaining in Dublin required on the part of the workpeople action of the drastic character which seems to have been taken during the past few years, and, without attributing undue blame to those who considered that these conditions necessitated a resort to the methods which they adopted to remedy them, we think that the time has now come when a continuance of the same methods will be fraught with disastrous results to all concerned. Thousands of workers have now become associated with the Transport Workers' Union, and the workpeople in many of the industries of the city have shown, during the past few years, a determination to organise themselves under its officials. If this struggle is not adjusted by consent, rather than by resort to the extremes of force, the industries of Dublin will not, we think, be free from further serious troubles. Even if, after many weeks of suffering and loss of business, the resort to force should seem to be successful and result in a resumption of work, resentment and bitterness would remain, with a very probable recurrence of the disputes. On the other hand, it cannot be expected that employers, many of whom have no grievance whatever with their employees, can continue their business if they are to be subjected, no matter what conciliatory steps they may themselves take to prevent it, to consent interruptions through the effects of the sympathetic and sudden strike.

"All the great industries of every civilised country have long recognised that trade and manufacture can only be conducted by the practical acceptance on the part of both employers and employed of the fact that there is a mutual interest, and that such interest can only be adjusted satisfactorily by friendly discussion. Irish employers and Irish workers will find they can be no exception to this modern development.

"We think, therefore, that this position should be frankly accepted by both sides; and while we recognise that a uniform method of settling differences is impracticable, owing to the varying circumstances in different trades, we think that a method of settling differences that exist or may arise hereafter might well be accepted as a basis for discussion."

The method proposed by the Court, a scheme founded upon the Canadian plan, was set forth at length; and its value indicated as a means "to remove the necessity for the sudden strike and for the sympathetic strike or lockout." There was also laid down a method, as proposed by the Industrial Council, for deciding, and dealing with, questions of breach of agreement; and in view of the personal feelings and hostility engendered by the strike, a recommendation on the personal element.

"We recognise that personal objections to individuals have entered into the disinclination on the part of some of those interested to negotiate, and difficult as this subject may be, we think it necessary to deal with it.

"In ordinary business dealings, as well as in private matters, men have the right to decline to associate with people whom for one reason or another they prefer not to meet, but in a community such as the city of Dublin, with its interdependent interests, this right is necessarily subject to great limitation. This matter is, however, one for individual consideration and determination, and should not, in our opinion, influence any decision to discuss the proposals which we have made."

The whole report, while expressing a clear opinion against the sympathetic strike and going beyond the final opinion of the Industrial Council, after an exhaustive inquiry, as to the feasible methods for preventing or penalising breaches of agreement, indicated a method for avoidance of disputes in the future as a "basis of discussion." Discussion was necessary, since amendments suitable to varying conditions might be necessary; goodwill had to be, if possible, resuscitated; the difficult and delicate question of reinstatement, which might vary in different trades and different firms, required negotiation; guarantees, if any could be suggested and accepted beyond the proposed terms, would also require negotiation. The English transport leaders accepted the report as a basis for discussion. The employers, through Mr. Healy, made a long statement that their evidence had not been disproved or proof offered to justify the strikes and intimidation by means of witnesses who could be cross-examined; that Mr. Larkin failed in spite of his undertaking to go into the witness-box; that he had made new imputations in a speech which was only listened to "on the basis that his allegations could be sifted by cross-examination" (a request which Mr. Healy could have made and did not make) "or would be substantiated by evidence." The statement concluded with the words:

"On the whole, therefore, we feel it would be unwise for our committee, without an opportunity of consultation with the general body of the employers, to proceed to the discussion of the details of the report. The elaborate machinery it provides will doubtless be submitted to careful examination on both sides; but in our view it offers no effectual solution of the existing trouble. The employers are much more concerned to put an end to present difficulties than to consider problems relating to future unrest. Accordingly we feel that the failure of the report to touch on the question of guarantees for preventing further outbreaks affords proof that the Court has found itself unable to devise a remedy for the difficulty which led to the breakdown of the recent negotiations with the members of the English Trades Congress. This, we need hardly say, is to us a matter of deep regret."

To this statement the Court made the announcement:

"As there appears to be no immediate prospect of a

meeting of the parties as invited by our report, the proceedings of the Court of Inquiry are now concluded. If, subsequently, a different opinion should prevail, the services of the Board of Trade will, of course, be at the disposal of the parties, should they desire to avail themselves of them."

The fact was that the employers did not want discussion, and definitely, though politely, refused the invitation to follow the only method by which a settlement could be arrived at, both in the existing dispute and in future disputes. Although they spoke of guarantees, none of them suggested what guarantee they wanted or proposed. The guarantee they desired in actual fact was to show that they could beat both Larkin and "Larkinism." The feeling at the time was very bitter.

"The task set the Court," it was remarked, "was almost impossible. It had to intervene in a dispute of long standing, a dispute of wide scope, a dispute that had reached almost its fiercest point. Sir George Askwith received very little help from the parties concerned. Almost from the outset there was felt to be an atmosphere of rancour and bitterness. Consciously or unconsciously, those present seemed to allow personal animosity and the memory of ancient wrongs to unbalance their judgment and colour their assertions. The spirit was the spirit of the law court and not of the council chamber, the methods were those of partisan warfare and not of cool conference. Personalities were common, the issues were confused and shifting, evidence was too obviously biased, eloquence too obviously heated. In such circumstances it would have been almost a miracle if Sir George Askwith's diplomacy had succeeded."

The strike continued, the hungry of Dublin receiving considerable aid both in food and money from the English unions, Mr. Larkin speaking in England of the leaders of the Labour Party being as "useful as mummies in a museum," and making the remark, "To hell with contracts!" Taking up these speeches and the report of the Commission, the employers issued a long statement in the form of legal pleadings controverting the report, and after stating that they were in favour of trade unionism, said :

"While it is in no way the province of employers to interfere with the internal management of Trade Unions, and whilst not desiring to appear to dictate, they, in face of conclusions come to by the Court, regarding sympathetic strikes, broken agreements, and, further, the statements made since in public by the Secretary of the Irish Transport Union, including the declaration in London: 'To hell with contracts!' are compelled again to refuse to recognise this Union until—

"(*a*) The Union be reorganised on proper lines.

"(*b*) With new officials who have met with the approval of the British Joint Labour Board.

"When this has been done the Executive Committee will recommend the employers to withdraw the ban on the Irish Transport Union, and to re-employ their workers as far as vacancies and conditions permit; but until then they regret that existing circumstances compel them to continue to insist on the undertaking referred to being signed.

"Apart from any settlement that may be arrived at now, the different stages of the dispute have made it very clear that the difficulty in arriving at any form of guarantees for the keeping of agreements must be the subject of legislation, as it has become of universal importance to the whole trading community."

The employers thus jointly adhered to the document condemned by the Commission, for the time being at least, and shelved their claims for guarantees upon the legislature, while the attitude of individual employers was expressed in a statement by one of them, who remarked:

"Look how difficult Mr. Larkin makes it for both of us. The Askwith Report, which the men's representatives as a whole agreed to, was dead against the sympathetic strike. Yet Mr. Larkin, who was one of that body, makes a speech in London repudiating the whole thing. Had we agreed there and then to settle the strike on the basis of the Askwith Report, where would we be now? My own opinion is that, whatever chance there was of a peaceable settlement, Larkin's last speech has now made it impossible. As long as the workers are content to have him to represent them nothing can be done."

Mr. Larkin continued his orations, and at the end of October was sentenced in Dublin to seven months' imprisonment for seditious speaking, but acquitted on counts for incitement to revolt and incitement to larceny. On the ground of his acquittal on these two counts he was released in the middle of November, and meanwhile a war of argument went on in the Press, and a more active war by transport workers holding up the shipping in Dublin, responded to by importation of "free" labour. A Dublin Industrial Committee and the Archbishop of Dublin made no headway in proposals for a truce. Mr. Larkin started a "fiery cross" in England, appealing to the rank and file, calling the trade union leaders "fools who mask as leaders," and saying, "I never trust leaders, and I don't want you to trust leaders. Trust yourselves." On this the secretary of the Miners' Federation issued a statement, concluding:

"A leader of men should be at the seat of war, and if Mr. Larkin would only consider the position from a common-sense point of view he would cease his 'fiery cross' mission, which appears to be the trying to create strife and enmity between the trade unionists of Great Britain and their leaders, and will go back to Dublin and use his energy and influence in trying to get a fair and honourable settlement of the dispute."

Mr. W. Murphy also issued a pronouncement, which did nothing to assist the cause of peace. At last a special trade union congress was summoned, committees were appointed, "representatives of the whole might of British trade unionism proceeded to Dublin" and took up the threads of negotiation. For three days they conferred with employers, who seemed willing to withdraw the document which the Court of Inquiry had so criticised, saying that it had not been used by all the employers. It appeared at first to be possible that the principle of the report would be adopted, but the dispute by its very length was the cause of a breakdown, on the point of reinstatement. So many other workpeople had gone out that it was impracticable to reinstate all who had been either on strike or locked out, at least within a short time. The old opinion that the employers would fail to reinstate those men who had been active in the strike came up. No form or method of getting over this difficulty was devised. No provisional agreement was accepted by the employers or by the local trade unionists. The committee had to report failure.

The congress began with some very moderate speeches. The speakers desired to maintain the principles of trade unionism, to continue aid to the women and children, and to avoid " petty personalities." The scene changed when one of the speakers brought forward a telegram sent by Mr. Larkin, in which he had denounced " the tactics of our false friends in the trade union movement," and Mr. Larkin replied in a long, rambling speech, hurling attacks right and left. Uproar and disorder followed; Mr. Larkin hurt his own cause. In the afternoon the storm had passed. Renewed negotiations were proposed, an amendment for a general sympathetic strike was lost by a huge majority. The railwaymen would have none of it; the miners, through Mr. Smillie, condemned it on the issue before them, and without reference to their constituents, in no sparing terms:

> " They had not come there that day with a mandate on the question of the extension of this fight to other trades. Neither were they in a position to vote on the question of a general stoppage. There might be a difference of opinion as to how best to fight the capitalists, whether by localising a strike or by extending it. That was a matter which would have to be seriously discussed in the future. It did not arise here and now, but when the time came either to face a general strike or to take action which the miners' organisation was tending in the direction of, that was the knitting together of the miners, the railwaymen, and the transport workers for common action, it would not require to be done in a slipshod fashion. It would require to be done after full discussion and negotiation between the representatives and the rank and file of those organisations. So that, if such a step was taken, it would have to be the final step by which they would win."

The delegates from the congress again reopened negotiations, but any chance of agreed terms once more broke down on the question of reinstatement. No aid was given to agreement when Mr. Larkin published a manifesto before the meeting, commencing, " Comrades, a foul and black conspiracy is afoot here." The fact was that Mr. Larkin had promised so often that every man should regain his former place, and had buoyed up his followers with this hope through so many weeks, that he could not face a settlement. He preferred that there should be no settlement, and that he should be recognised as the man who would not yield, the *intransigeant* ever ready to lead the extreme left wing. The report and the conferences had, however, produced their effect. Everyone was weary of the dispute. The Catholic Bishops issued a pronouncement against it. The ban on trade unionism was practically withdrawn by the employers. Those who could be taken back were gradually absorbed; and the strength of any united effort ceased. By the end of February 1914 the interest and present influence of this dispute melted away, but it must not be supposed that the aftermath of bitterness and resentment was not without effect during the War.

Mr. Larkin had attempted more than he could achieve. On one occasion he called himself an Ishmael, popular and powerful owing to conditions which anyone who knows Dublin must recognise as a ripe field of work for a man who promised better things. The fervour of his nature probably led to some results, though at very heavy cost of suffering, but his scheme of organisation was not perfected, and connoted not only organisation of his own men, but counter-organisation of employers. In his own words when a witness before the Industrial Council, he advocated the Big Union: "All workers should be in one union, controlled by elected representatives from each section, and there should be no strike without the consent of all units to that affiliated body or organised body." "Whenever we find one of our friends attacked anywhere, we take up the fight, too." An experiment should be made in Ireland immediately. "The workers should elect those they have confidence in, and they might meet employers elected by the employers and try to come to a common understanding, and for those who break that agreement the punishment should be either to put them outside the country or put them inside a place where they would be quiet."

Mr. Larkin had to leave the country at the beginning of the War. He has not since returned.

CHAPTER XXVII

LABOUR EXCHANGES

THE three disputes just described were the principal overt and cohesive acts prior to 1914, but before giving any estimate of the position immediately before the War, I would make allusion to some administrative institutions, some practices and theories, some economical factors, all of which had greater or less influence upon the industrial situation at the outbreak of war and at a later date. The list cannot be called exhaustive. Space alone forbids essays upon all points, but I have endeavoured to choose the most important subjects. It is not possible to confine the statements entirely to the period before 1914, since all the factors exist now, and frequently with increased influence and force. Consecutive narrative necessarily carries them through to the present time.

The first administrative institution which perhaps is worthy of some mention is the system of Labour exchanges, now called Employment exchanges.

On his advent to the office of President of the Board in 1908, Mr. Churchill is reported to have said, " There is nothing to do here. Lloyd George has taken all the plums " ; but there awaited him the scheme for labour exchanges, which at least afforded a subject for a legislative Bill. The presence of Labour Members in the House of Commons rendered their adhesion to any schemes a desirable factor. The adhesion, too, of the leaders of the principal trade unions could not be ignored. Discussion with these representatives was carried out with considerable skill, and in the result the Labour Exchange Bill passed through both Houses without division or amendment.

It must be allowed that the Bill rested on high recommendation. The majority report of the Poor Law Commission had stated : " In the forefront of our proposals we place labour exchanges." The minority report used these words: "This national exchange, though in itself not an adequate remedy, is the foundation of all our proposals. It is in our view an indispensable condition of real reform." Acting upon this, Parliament passed the measure, and in 1909 and 1910 ninety exchanges were started in Great Britain. Five or six Irish exchanges were opened a month afterwards.

The Bill itself was largely the work of Mr. W. H. (now Sir William) Beveridge, who had studied the unemployed question, chiefly in London. It was based partly upon his theories and practice, and the temporary work of the Central (Unemployed) Body in London, and partly on the systems used in Germany.

Labour "registries" had been tried for some years in Belgium, Germany, Francc, and Switzerland, but had had their chief growth in Germany. A public registry had been established as long before as 1865 in Stuttgart, as 1874 in Cologne, and as 1883 in Berlin. In 1902 there were 136 German labour registries of various types. The earliest types seem to have started with the labour organisations, whose object was at first to keep the provision of labour in their own hands. Organisation of registries by the commune or by any public authority was opposed by labour organisations on principle. This position was gradually given up, "because for large masses of workmen the Trade Union Registry remained ineffective, and more than all because the employers converted the supply of labour into a monopoly." The employers, in fact, had produced a corresponding movement on their own side, under which registries were introduced as a means of controlling the labour market. One of their objects was to prevent the employment of workmen on their "black list," and the members of the masters' unions agreed together to use their own registries to supply their own wants, particularly in the metal trades, where the system was specially developed. Under these circumstances the State and municipalities stepped in with public registries, controlled by employers and representatives of employees, with some outside persons and officials representing the public authority.

"In Germany," reported Mr. David Schloss in 1904, "where the systematic organisation of labour registries has been carried to the highest pitch of perfection, we find arrangements which enable every workman, even if he be living in a remote village, as soon as he falls out of work, to ascertain the situations then open for men of his trade in the whole of an extensive section of the country, and, in case he is unable to obtain immediate employment in this manner, to put himself in communication with a labour registry in the nearest important town, through whose agency he may hope before long to hear of employment available for him, either in that town or in some other place. For the operations of each of the public registries are not confined to the city in which the registry is established, but, by means of a carefully planned organisation of clearing houses—central registries, by which a great number of different local registries are linked up—cover a very large district, and in some cases extend to a still wider area, not alone with the German Empire, but even beyond its confines."

It was this system, so suited to the German ideas of organisation and so useful to a nation which wanted to know where every man was and what every man could do, which was hastily imposed upon this country. It was received with some doubt, but at least without opposition, since it was advertised as a free gift from the State and as the basis on which further social reforms were to be built. Its suitability to the United Kingdom and the effects which it might have upon the relations of employers and employed were not thought out. The example of German organisation cannot truthfully be said to have had no effect.

After the passing of the Act and a hurried visit of officials to Germany (on which I went) in 1909, the new department was established in the course of the year 1910 and attached to my division of the Board of Trade, until, owing to pressure of work, it had to be separated off at the time when the Industrial Council was formed. In the first year of its existence more money had to be got from the Treasury, owing to wrong estimates of its cost. Since then, its cost has been increasing annually by leaps and bounds, until it is one of the expensive luxuries of the country.

In 1910 I visited Ireland, going to Belfast, Dublin, Cork, and Waterford, with a view to explanation of the hopes and aims of the institution. The scheme was explained to be that the whole of the United Kingdom was now marked out in ten divisions, over each of which there was a divisional officer, with so many exchanges of the first, second, or third class, according to the number of big cities in the division. Those exchanges had managers, and sub-offices existed in minor towns, whilst there were waiting-rooms in the smaller towns, forming a network over the whole kingdom. The divisional officers were in close touch with the national clearing-houses in London, and from the central office directions and regulations were issued for the guidance of the officers all over the country. It was the intention of the Board of Trade to set up advisory committees centred around the great areas, both with regard to the management of the labour exchanges and also with regard to juveniles. These committees would be composed half of employers and half of employees, the chairman, failing agreement, to be nominated by the Board of Trade. They would have certain functions handed over to them, but still more important would be the junior advisory committees. The country was getting more and more annoyed at the use which was being made of the juvenile, and it desired more and more that the children should not be put into " blind alley employments," but that capable children should have an opportunity of advancement or of getting into positions from which they might be able to rise. Without the assistance and the advice of people who knew business, it was scarcely possible to suppose that most children could do so, but with that assistance and care which many voluntary workers were willing to give, it might be possible, largely through the medium of the exchanges, to organise the juvenile industry of the country so as to give the best chance to the children and the best advantage to the employer. For with all the vast sums spent on technical education, it was more a case of children trying to find employment than of employers who knew exactly where to find them. Any locality that wished to tackle a subject so important to future generations could from its own people find those who were best able to deal with the subject. It was a thorny and difficult subject, but unless it was tackled by localities, it was hard to see how it was to be dealt with.

That hope has not been too well fulfilled. The exchanges have assisted the pool of casual labour by encouraging the supply of juvenile labour rather than the training and right placing of the young. Other points were that the exchanges would be national, " a national market for dealing with labour " ; they would be free, " worked at the national expense, with no expenditure either by employer or employee " ; they should be impartial, " neither side should consider they were in the least favoured " ; they should be voluntary, as they aimed at bringing together employer and employee ; their object should be to send the best men on their lists, sift out the best, and, where possible, afford a selection ; there should be absence of delay, which was one of the most important factors with regard to these exchanges.

" If there was delay in finding the right sort of men that were wanted, or if there was delay on behalf of the unemployed in finding the work that was being sought for, that delay must necessarily mean a wastage in the production of the goods or articles that were being made, or in the carrying out of the work that was in hand. Speed was what was wanted, and anything that caused an absence of waste between the bringing together of the employer and the unemployed must necessarily be of value to production. In big works that was of the utmost moment. It might in time become as natural and as usual for an employer to go to the exchange as it was for an ordinary householder to go to the servants' registry in order to obtain a domestic servant. In all ordinary commodities hawking had practically gone to the wall, and there were regular places where a commodity was bought and sold. It seemed curious that in this country up to so late a date the most important necessity of all—labour—should have remained without a definite place where it might be obtained. Other countries had for years had systems of labour exchanges—Belgium, France, Switzerland, Germany. In establishing the labour exchanges as a national system in England, the endeavour had been made to see upon what points the Continental labour exchanges had achieved success, and upon what points they had been failures ; and so build up the system in these countries with the idea that successes might be followed, and failures as far as possible avoided. It might be said, and was said by some employers, that it was much more easy for them to get their labour at their own gates than to get their supply from the labour exchange. It was so very often, but a large number of employers in Great Britain had already found a choice, and a much easier choice, in the labour exchange than they formerly had by going outside their gates and picking up Tom, Dick, and Harry, who were waiting there. From the working of the labour exchanges there would be prepared statistics which would help in dealing with other problems that may arise in the future, such as the decasualisation of labour."

With the beginning of the work under the new Act a fair start was made, although the civil servants were new to their work. The head officers had all been personally selected by Mr. Churchill with great care; the minor officers were chosen by a committee, which endeavoured to judge the applicants upon their merits. A trial of the new system was made: some of the civil servants have worked hard, some employers and some employees have made use of the facilities given by the Government. In some cases a good advisory Committee has attempted developments, in some ports partial decasualisation has been effected by methods to which the exchanges were useful adjuncts, at some crises work has been found from other districts to meet the needs of employers, or men requiring work have been able to migrate. Nevertheless by 1911 and 1912 murmurs began to arise that the labour exchanges were not coming up to expectations. The trade unions, especially in the skilled trades, kept or reverted to former methods of dealing with their unemployed members. In spite of the requirements of the Insurance Act, which made it necessary for the insured to use the exchanges, they became more and more unpopular, particularly in Scotland and the North. During the War they were used for the transfer of labour, sometimes with ludicrous or lamentable results, sometimes with moderate success achieved at enormous cost. After the War they have been used for demobilisation purposes, practically with similar results. Though the name was changed to Employment Exchanges, as if a name would change the character, there is now a growing feeling against them, strongly developed in that great hive of industry, the North of England. The Ministry of Labour has had to appoint a Committee to inquire into their value, and, it may be hoped, their cost—the cost per man and per woman and per child placed and kept in work in comparison with the cost of an army of officials, of a vast number of buildings, of a proposed huge expenditure upon new buildings, and the loss of the life-work of the officials if their efforts are directed to an unfruitful channel. Some members, at least, of the Committee will doubtless say all that can be said in their favour. Personally I feel that their cost is out of all proportion to their value. The test of results has not proved to be sufficient. The high hopes with which they were started, the possibilities which seemed to be feasible, have not ended, and do not show sign of ending, in practical and useful tendencies or a solution of any industrial difficulties. They were an interference by the State between employer and employed at the cost of the community, when the cost should have been borne by employers and employed in the industries concerned with the production of the required goods. Many of the general propositions mentioned in 1910 have not been developed or have not been reached. If they could be said to be opinions which should preclude any remarks against labour exchanges, I have changed my opinions. The course of events has proved different to wishes or expectations. The system, particularly in the North of England, does not bear the test of results, and by that test its ultimate continuance or failure must be settled.

My main objection is not to the working of the exchanges or to the efforts of the staff, but to the result. The exchanges have been a disintegrating force. Instead of bringing classes together, they have served to emphasise the distinction of classes. As the employer in Germany tried to use exchanges to maintain his own monopolies and keep up his "black-lists," so the employer in England can use them for the purpose of discarding his men in times of scarcity, sending them to the exchanges, and taking men on from the exchanges when again he desires more labour. They tend against sympathy, fellow-feeling, and responsibility. They place upon others the cost of unemployment. They afford no incentive for such regulation of production, time, and contracts as may mitigate the chances or the amount of unemployment. They tend to assist the division of classes into two camps, they form a prop to class war. In comparison with the number of applicants, real success from application has been the exception, not the rule. Those exceptions may be used as a defence to any criticism, but are they worth the cost which they have entailed ? The general result is that the working-classes dislike them, the trade unions are becoming more and more hostile, even though their expenses may have been lessened by their existence. The efforts of the trade unions over many years to assist and serve their members have been curtailed and impeded. The incentive to clear the books of the unemployed, and to work with the employers to reduce unemployment in a firm or in a trade, has been lessened. Division in place of co-operation has been the principle which the system has aided. The Labour Exchange Act heralded a policy of State interference and expenditure with incommensurate results. The policy of allowing industry to solve its own problems gave place to a policy whereby the workers were encouraged by lavish expenditure to look to the State to find employment for them, and discouraged from reliance upon their own efforts.

The principle should be recognised and supported that employers must accept some responsibility for their unemployed; that every industry ought to regulate its business so as to reduce unemployment to a minimum, and that the cost of maintenance of those for whom no employment could be found should be a charge upon the industry. Adjustments should be made between industries for those workpeople changing from one to another industry, men on the border-line, and as in the case of trade boards special arrangements might be necessary for women.

As I stated in *The Times* of October 28, 1919 :

" Encouragement, even strong pressure, along the lines that employers should join with trade unionists to carry out this work—a work backed by an ideal and by incentive to all—might have had great results. Joint Industrial Councils might well have grown naturally in every trade, with mutual determination to regulate employment, solve unemployment, and assist those for whom employment could not be found. The problem would have been in the hands of those best fitted to deal with it. By extension of the principle of the necessity of united action and of the burden being carried by the industry concerned, the country would not only have been freed from the weight of these costly labour exchanges, but the vast sums now expended on unemployment would have been placed where the weight should be borne. The amount would have been minimised by organisation on the part of those vitally interested in solving the problem and knowing the business; not left to the discretion and efforts of officials who know little of industry and labour, and the direction of a Minister who generally knows less.

"The working of the present system is in the result contrary not only to development and recognition of the duties of industry, but a direct incentive to unemployment. Employers are encouraged by the very system of labour exchanges to accept no responsibility for continuance of employment by the workmen in their industry. Labour exchanges encourage employers to come to them for workmen. As soon as it suits the employers' interests, the workers are thrown back upon the State, and the State maintains them until another employer finds it to his interest to seek their services. There is no collective responsibility by employers in a trade that every workman in that trade should have his share of employment, no arrangement of business so that exchange of workmen could easily take place as demand varied between one employer and another. Many are the cases in which, if a central exchange had existed in a district, managed by employers and the unions, and to which all employers and men, through their associations, were attached, it would not have been difficult to transfer workmen from one employer who was slack to another who was busy; and if work generally dropped below the normal, to reduce hours, so that all workmen could secure a share of the possible work. The joint effort, besides having a high aim, would be mutually helpful and lead to appreciation of views and difficulties in other matters.

"Even now the necessity for lightening the ship of State makes it imperative that each industry, by its associations, trade unions, and councils, should take hold of this problem, establish the necessary simple organisations, and face such cost as may ensue. Let employers and workpeople get out of the hands of officials, of whom they are always complaining. The joint effort would tend to co-operation, not the array of class against class which, in spite of the War and the soft words of those who do not know, is now so harmful and embittering. It would unite both in a great object, with incentives to efficient results, and tend seriously to lay the spectre of unemployment, which so continuously haunts the minds of an actual majority of workers."

CHAPTER XXVIII

TRADE BOARDS

If the principle of the intervention of the State in industry was pressed upon industry in the case of labour exchanges for political purposes, and was copied partly from Germany by men who admired German organisation, with the idea that it would be suitable to this country, no similar causes operated to produce trade boards. They arose in this country from the energy of those who felt for poor workers. By persistent effort and proof of evils the Government were reluctantly induced to face the issue, and accept the argument that organisation of sweated trades could be effected and administratively worked with success, at small cost and with great advantage to persons unable to take action by themselves. With a few notable exceptions, the leaders of the large trade unions did not trouble much about the subject. The establishment of Trade Boards was not a plan pressed by the political power of the Labour Party in Parliament, although it endorsed the principle of a minimum wage, both for time- and piece-workers. In fact, there was necessity for a great deal of hard spade-work and some more or less sensational exhibitions and meetings before the Government or the public began to understand that something should be done.

As long ago as 1890 a Select Committee of the House of Lords had reported that the evils of sweating could ' hardly be exaggerated." The Labour Commission of 1894 mentioned the subject and practically left it alone. They said :

" The natural difficulty, in not highly skilled occupations, of organising persons who work at home, or are dispersed through numerous small workshops, even if it can be overcome in the case of men, would seem almost insuperable in that of women. In the absence of organisation, and in the face of the unlimited competition for the cheaper and less skilled kind of sempstress and similar work, there seems to be little to prevent wages from sinking to the point at which, in the words of one witness, 'it is easier to starve without the work.' So long as there is abundance of cheap labour, without any minimum wage affixed by the action of trade organisations or otherwise, it seems to be beyond the power of small employers and contractors, wholly unorganised themselves, and keenly competing with each other for the custom of wholesale houses, and for small profits, to give women more for their work than the lowest pay at which it can be obtained."

The minimum wage was indicated in this report as a possible remedy, but nothing had been done until *The Daily News*, Miss Gertrude Tuckwell, her uncle, Sir Charles Dilke, and a small band of keen persons, amongst whom Miss Mary Macarthur was noticeable, pressed for action.

Some of the arguments used by their supporters may be indicated by passages from a magazine article I wrote upon the question, in which I said :

" The subject seems at last to have struck the imagination of the whole community, claimed its interest, and raised the desire to cure by close investigation and practical means. It is recognised that sweating hurts the trade of Great Britain. It hurts the people of Great Britain. It hurts the race, their happiness, their health, their progeny, so that effective steps should, if practicable, be taken speedily to restrict its dire influence.

" The investigators have only needed encouragement to come forward and tell their tale. Those working amongst the poor in great towns, in slums and cottages, in the purlieus of docks and arsenals, knew many an instance of women and men living at the mercy of the sweater, if living it could reasonably be called. Charity societies, ministers, sanitary inspectors, poor law officials, and many others, can tell of localities and trades where no fair wage for fair work is paid, where it is a case of 'take it or leave it' at the sole dictation of the 'master.' That 'master' may have no regard to the condition of the workers, or no object save undercutting another tradesman, who would, if he dared, pay sufficient wage for reasonable subsistence. Yet neither the 'master's' competitors nor his workpeople have redress. The competitors cannot leave their shops or study social conditions. The workers are not organised, they have no spare time, they cannot tilt alone at a system, or hazard their work by complaint, or reproof, or even remark. They have to bear the load without being able to move, and without much hope of help, when hope is confined to little else than the chance of earning enough to keep body and soul together.

"The social reformer who desires to deal with this system is at once met with an initial criticism—that, if the wages are raised, work will be driven from the country, foreign goods will come in, British trade will be injured, and the Empire will be ruined. It is not, indeed, a very strong argument that the British Empire's strength has been based upon the exploitation of slaves, but even if the criticism is not meant to go so far, it does seem to ignore certain historical and mercantile facts. Was the trade of the country seriously and irremediably injured by raising the age of child-labour in the factories, or by regulating the work of women, or by insisting on sanitary requirements? Are we to have the same howl if there be any interference with child-labour in button-making or with the making of clothes in fever-stricken dens? Or, to take minor industries: has the pottery trade left the country because regulations were made as to the use of lead in glazing? Has there been a fresh invasion of American boots because the minimum wages of clickers have been raised to thirty shillings a week? Or has the tin-plate industry gone rapidly downhill because bar-cutters received at one time a heavy increase in their minimum wages? Has the music hall industry ceased because some classes of scene-shifters or stage employees received a rise in wages and a minimum wage? If this be the case, some arbitrators have a very serious indictment to answer, and many conferences of employers and employed in all parts of the country have a still heavier one to meet.

"Persons who make these criticisms in good faith cannot have any real grasp of the huge size and extent of the mercantile interests of this country, or of the infinitesimal portion of goods which is made by the sweated in relation to the real trade of the United Kingdom.

" When future difficulties are considered, are they great ? Take the employer. My experience is that the fair-minded employer is willing to pay a fair wage, if he can ; but if he is undercut by sweating employers, and does not know what his neighbour is doing, he is naturally suspicious, and obliged to take his tone or make his price by what he thinks his competitor is doing. If somebody else was not paying, or thought to be paying, a less price, many employers would be ready to pay higher wages. Get these men together, let them fight the sweater themselves and insist upon reasonable equalisation of minimum rates, and they will be able to fix a price for their locality and possibly for the kingdom. Produce them from their shops, put them together, hear the prices, and then, in conjunction with the employees or representatives of the employees, let them consider whether it is fair and reasonable, and can be taken at least as a foundation on which payments can be based, without immediate and undue injury to the industrial conditions of the trade or locality.

" The question will arise, whether by regulation of wages the price of articles would be materially raised to the community as a whole. I believe not. As one factor, it must always be remembered that sweating may only affect one part of a garment. The rich man's trousers may be cut by the most expensive tailor, the buttons on those trousers may be made by sweated industry. Higher payment for those buttons would be a minute part of the cost of the whole article. As another factor, though the poor man's trousers might be imported from Germany, if there was a serious rise in their cost, does not experience show that the saving of freight, transhipment, middlemen, packing, and many other incidents, give some margin in favour of the industry on the spot ? And would they not be better made by better-paid workpeople ? And would the influx of foreign goods be easy when it is considered that Great Britain exported in 1906 nearly £5,500,000 in value of garments alone ?

" Yet, though the movement on behalf of sweated industries is a movement partly on account of the whole community, it is chiefly on behalf of the employee. Will it better the condition of the employee ?

" It may possibly be that some persons at first will be hurt. I am not prepared to urge that this result is impossible. Those desiring work at any cost and unable to get it, or too unskilful to do it, may be hampered, but the argument that hurt may result in some instances, and in some places, has always been an argument against every interference with the casual opportunities of the casual individual. It was advanced against every improvement in the Factory Acts, and every restriction upon the employment of men, women, or children. It is the argument of the powerful individual against the right of less powerful individuals to combine, and to obtain greater strength by united effort. It is the argument which was put forward to stop, or at least to hinder, the trade unions. It proceeds upon the fallacy that all regulation is an interference with freedom of exchange. When it is advanced as a solid argument against those incapable of standing up alone, and notoriously incapable of organising, or ensuring real freedom of exchange, by lack of time, opportunity, knowledge, money, or any ordinary attribute of strength, it is an argument which primâ facie must excite suspicion, and cannot be accepted as conclusive by the mere statement of it. In answer to it, I would not prophesy the result of wages boards. I would prefer to say I admit the argument, but that since it has so often been proved to be specious and bad, I would like to try this humble experiment, and see whether the argument can hold good in relation to those few industries, those weak people, this particular sore. The sore may yield only partially to the action of wages boards. Their action may require to be reinforced. In some trades, licensing, inspection, cleansing, etc., may have to be added to effect a cure, but that is no sufficient reason why the most adequate remedy as yet suggested should not be first applied.

"Another important question will be this: Are you not going to swell the ranks of the unemployed by preventing people from getting work? I think the answer to that is that the more labour and wages are reasonably organised, the better chance there is of the genuine unemployed getting work and of fair distribution of work, of not being sweated by oppression from above or by the undercutting of casual labour and uncertain influx of work, and of receiving more work and more regular work by better organisation of the so-called seasonal trades. The unemployed will be better known and better defined.

The method of dealing with them will be brought more clearly into view. The limits of the assistance of the State, charity, and local authorities to the individual will be more easily determined. At present the State, charity, and rates are continually taxed to produce cheap goods, and in a manner and in directions unequal in incidence, unfair as between individual employers and workers, and harassing to the whole community.

"Further, the more labour and wages are reasonably organised, the more chance there is that the worker gets fair pay, and, with fair pay, his standard of comfort and self-respect is raised. He becomes one of the community, anxious to work with and for the community, not against it, nor in continuous enmity to all that is and to all that have. Employers brought together on a wages board will go outside the narrow compass of one shop, one detail of trade; employees brought together will learn each other's difficulties; employers and employees brought together will better judge the capacity and possibilities of their joint enterprise.

"One of the objects of the boards is to bring employers and employed together, to permit discussion over mutual interests, just as organised trades have formed voluntary boards and discussed disputes, wages, hours, etc., at those voluntary boards. True it is that direction is necessary, and official or voluntary aid must be given to effect a result which these workers themselves certainly cannot, and the employers probably would not, be able to accomplish by themselves. Hence legislation is necessary, because without legislation the proper machinery could not be set up, and when the machinery is set up, administration will be required to make it work.

"It may be said that in such trades as tailoring, shirt-making, buttons, cardboard-box making, fur-pulling, and other trades, piecework statements cannot be made; that the processes are too minute, the fashions change too rapidly. I can only say that piecework statements have been made in the Colonies for such trades, and in very complicated trades here, and that 'particulars lists' already exist for some of those very trades in many districts in the country.

"I am not afraid of the complexity of piecework statements. They may take a long time to make, and must be susceptible to variation, particularly in trades where fashion changes rapidly. But district copies from district, trade from trade, with variations suitable to district or trade. And in the same way as this process occurs, so an employer should be able to judge by analogy, without any infringement of the minimum wage principle, what prices should be generally paid on the production of a new fashion or a new variation. He need not run risk of disclosing his invention or his market to competitors; and if the change is one which is to be adopted by the trade generally, the wages board will be in existence to deal with it. The board will be a body meeting from time to time and dealing with changes in the same way as is now done in organised trades when new fashions and designs are continually being introduced.

"In the boot trade, the lace trade, and many other trades, of which I have had personal experience—such as printing, tinplates, flax, coal, paper-making, building—questions of a minimum wage have come up over and over again. I have settled scores of minimum wages, without, as far as I am aware, having ruined any person or any industry, or ever seriously hampered any industry. If this has been the case within the experience of a single individual doing similar work to that which other individuals have done or are now doing, how can it be said that the fixing of a minimum wage is such a serious matter that it must endanger the trade of Great Britain and the organisation of society? The fear must surely be founded upon some popular fallacy of which it is difficult to judge the exact cause, and also upon ignorance of facts. Theoretical difficulties seem to become less potent an objection to all minimum wages, when one knows that they exist on all sides, and in some measure in nearly every trade, not only in experimenting colonies, but here, in England, Scotland, Ireland, Wales.

"I am aware that Mr. Ramsay Macdonald, M.P., in an argument directed to show that a socialistic distribution of wealth is the only panacea for social ills, has cited New Zealand and Australia as examples of countries where arbitration courts and wages boards have not, in his opinion, produced the result he desires. Personally, I see small analogy between the present proposals and the compulsory arbitration courts of New Zealand, or experiments in a continent where the whole population is about equal to that of Glasgow and its suburbs. But, even in his article, he indicates that opinions flatly contradictory to his own are held by persons who have passed their lives in Australasia. He omits to mention the general benefit to the community which industrial peace, even for a few years, must have effected; he gives scant credit to the facts that wages boards are not meant to be a sovereign remedy for all ills, or to exclude the use of other remedies; and he seems to lament that sweating had not wholly disappeared in ten years.

"Ten years! It seems to me that Mr. Ramsay Macdonald is not unlike those early Christians who believed that the end of the world must come within their lifetime, and took steps for the disposal of their days and goods in a manner which later generations have regarded as a marvellous example of the power of faith. A more cautious philanthropist might feel less confident of the power of any generation to obliterate so deep-seated an evil, but none the less would not lose heart in the opinion that each generation should do what it could to effect tangible results, within the limits of practical power, from which their successors could proceed to such better conditions as the course of time and experience might indicate. Wages or trade boards may not be, as a principle, wholly ideal, but I think they are possible, practicable, and likely to be advantageous to the people of this country."

In preference to wages boards there were many people who supported a system of licensing employers or contractors. When the Government appointed a Committee of the House of Commons, in 1908, under the chairmanship of Sir Thomas Whittaker, the two systems were considered, the Committee finding in favour of the minimum wage. This Committee said:

"If 'sweating' is understood to mean that work is paid for at a rate which, in the conditions under which many of the workers do it, yields to them an income which is quite insufficient to enable an adult person to obtain anything like proper food, clothing, and house accommodation, there is no doubt that sweating does prevail extensively. We have had quite sufficient evidence to convince us (indeed, it is almost common knowledge) that the earnings of a large number of people—mostly women who work in their homes

—are so small as alone to be insufficient to sustain life in the most meagre manner, even when they toil hard for extremely long hours. The consequence is that, when those earnings are their sole source of income, the conditions under which they live are often not only crowded and insanitary, but altogether pitiable and distressing; and we have evidence that many are compelled to have recourse to Poor Law or charitable 'relief.' Lord Dunraven's Committee, after hearing evidence from as many as 291 witnesses, drawn from many different trades and localities, recorded their opinion in 1890 that the evils of sweating 'can hardly be exaggerated.' In the almost complete absence of statistics on the subject, it is impossible for your Committee to decide whether the volume of sweating is at the present time more or less than in 1890, either actually or relatively to population, but sufficient evidence has been put before them to show that sweating still exists in such a degree as to call urgently for the interference of Parliament. While it is impossible to measure the number of sweated individuals, there is, unfortunately, no doubt whatever that it is very large, and that it is still true that the evils of sweating are very great. While our evidence has been chiefly concerned with home workers, it has been shown that very low rates of remuneration are by no means confined to them, but are not infrequently the lot of factory workers also in the trades in which home work is prevalent."

Trade boards have had to deal with both home and factory work, but initially the Committee said little or nothing about the factories; and, in fact, confined their recommendation to wages boards for home workers. After discussing the difficulties of licensing, they stated:

"In the opinion of your Committee, the second proposal —for the establishment of wages boards—goes to the root of the matter, in so far as the object aimed at is an increase in the wages of home workers. No proposals which fail to increase the income of these people can have any appreciable effect in ameliorating their condition. Improved sanitary conditions are important and necessary; greater personal and domestic cleanliness in many cases is very desirable; but the poverty, the miserably inadequate income, of so many of the home workers is the great difficulty of the situation. With the increase in their earnings many of the other undesirable conditions which intensify and in turn are aggravated by the ever-present burden of grinding poverty would be very appreciably modified and improved."

This Committee, by condemning the policy of licensing, which would have established an inquisition, onerous to employers and still more so to employees, and an army of officials, rendered a great service. For my part, so far as I had influence in the movement, by speaking at the Mansion House, at Glasgow, and at the Albert Hall, writing the magazine article, and giving evidence before the Committee, I endorsed the wages board proposal. My opinion was that the minimum wages should be worked out by employers and employed, who knew the trades, with such aid from officials as might be actually necessary in view of the class of workpeople with whom it was intended to deal. I thought also that the chief difficulty of business men was to see how the principle could be applied to piece-work, and particularly concentrated on examples from the Nottingham lace trade and the boot and shoe trade, with the view of showing how it could be done.

Nevertheless, the report of the Committee was very carefully guarded. The scheme was treated as an experiment, the result of which could scarcely be foreseen.

"Your Committee are of the opinion," they said, "that, unless Parliament steps in and gives these workers the protection and support which legislation alone can supply, the prospects of any real and substantial improvement in their position and condition being brought about are very small and remote. We are further of opinion that carefully considered legislation would aid them materially; and, that being so, we cannot doubt that it is desirable that an attempt should be made, and an experiment be tried. At the same time we recognise that legislation which will affect the well-being and may interfere to some extent with the livelihood of a number of extremely poor and helpless persons must be considered with the utmost care, and be entered upon with great caution.

"Your Committee attach importance to the experience and opinion of Mr. Askwith, of the Board of Trade, who for many years has, from time to time, rendered most valuable service by acting as arbitrator and conciliator in trade disputes of various kinds. He has settled piecework rates in industries where the complication and diversity of patterns, etc., is great, and the results have been arrived at without excessive difficulty, and afterwards have worked satisfactorily. He is of opinion that 'wages boards are workable and practicable, and would be beneficial, and ought to be tried.' After making full allowance for the fact that these settlements have been made in trades where the employees were organised and had trained members of their trade unions to represent them, and where the whole of the conditions were much more favourable than would be the case when piecework rates for home workers had to be fixed, your Committee agree that the experiment ought to be tried.

"In view of the fact that this proposal represents a very considerable new departure in industrial legislation, and fully realising the many difficulties that surround it, your Committee are of opinion that it is desirable that Parliament should proceed at first somewhat experimentally, and apply the general principles to one or two trades, in which the necessity for some legislation is great, and where experience could be gained without running any serious risk of dislocating an important industry.

"The conclusions at which your Committee have arrived are that it is desirable—

"(1) That there should be legislation with regard to the rates of payment made to home workers who are employed in the production or preparation of articles for sale by other persons.

"(2) That such legislation should at first be tentative and experimental, and be limited in its scope to home workers engaged in the tailoring, shirtmaking, underclothing, and baby-linen trades, and in the finishing processes of machine-made lace. The Home Secretary should be empowered, after inquiry made, to establish wages boards for any other trades.

"(3) That wages boards should be established in selected trades to fix minimum time and piece-rates of payment for home workers in those trades," etc.

The resulting Bill became an Act, scheduling at first

industries such as chainmaking at Cradley Heath, cardboard boxes, finishing in the lace trade, and wholesale tailoring. The administration was attached to my Department, and slowly made its way. As I remarked to Sir Charles Dilke, to whom the Parliamentary success of the Bill was almost wholly due, "This is a very delicate plant. It appears to offend the canons of many political economists. If it is to be allowed to live, its roots should get firm hold of the soil before many experiments are made." Sir Charles Dilke absolutely agreed, curbing enthusiasts who could not understand the saying, "More haste, less speed."

What has been the result of this Act? It has been extended, and is likely to be still more extended. Home workers and factory workers come within its scope. An Amending Act, giving large powers to the Ministry of Labour, was passed in 1918. If these Acts are used for the purposes for which they were intended, and not for purposes of unreasonable or transient advantages, their effects may be far-reaching. At present the tide runs in their favour. On May 19, 1920, the Minister of Labour stated in the House of Commons:

"Steps are being taken to apply the Trade Boards Acts to a great number of trades in which it is desirable that legal minimum rates of wages should be fixed. Since the Amending Act of 1918 there have been established thirty-seven new trade boards, affecting 1,500,000 workers, and it is estimated that 2,000,000 workers are now covered by trade boards. I hope that during the next twelve months 2,500,000 more workers will be brought under the operation of the Acts."

CHAPTER XXIX

PROPAGANDA AND CA' CANNY

Of all the causes of division of classes, it is possible that the employment of active propaganda has been the most important.

Methods of propaganda are necessarily very varied in their form. The only unsuccessful method up to the beginning of the War which had been adopted by Labour in this country was a dominant Labour newspaper. Though many efforts were made, no newspaper achieved lasting success or commanded a wide number of readers. Since the War, one newspaper at least has gained a more powerful influence. But although ordinary daily newspapers often quote portions of speeches or arguments which may have some influence, there are other methods besides newspapers by which views may be communicated. In organised trades pamphlets or reports of union secretaries are circulated among the members. In these trades, too, the meetings of lodges or branches give opportunity for speechifying as well as for more sober debate and discussion, for the budding orator and the skilled and trained lecturer. In unorganised trades and in time of disturbances in all trades, speeches outside, varying from wild tub-thumping to reasoned argument, command the attention of audiences. All have their influence, and there is very little answer or argument adduced on the other side of the case. Catchwords may have their effect, just as "liberty, equality, and fraternity" had a vogue during the French Revolution and often since.

The capitalist; the associations of shareholders, many with tiny holdings, who by union formed a capital aggregation; the wage-payers generally, large and small, can be all compared together and equally denounced as capitalist profit-makers, sucking the blood of the wage-earners.

Everyone in a motor-car, every woman in a new dress, can be jumbled up in the generic term "the idle rich"; jealousy, not co-operation, can be placed in the forefront. Appeal is made to those who have an interest in accepting the propositions, whether the methods of attainment be right or wrong. The case of objectors goes by default.

Peaceful persuasion in all its forms, from the mildest type of information to the giving of information which may verge so close to coercion as practically to be indistinguishable from it, is available under the express protection of the law.

I heard a delegate, on one occasion, go up to a train full of labourers for the purpose of giving information. He said, "You ——, you ought to know there are between this station and the docks hundreds of men with stones and iron nuts. If that's not enough, the docks are pretty deep and not easy to get out of. The last lot didn't get to work. That's all I've got to say." Not a man left that train. In a court of law the delegate might reasonably have argued he had saved their lives by giving information, or, as a solitary individual, had peacefully suggested to them not to run the risk. "Stick to your union," or "your colleagues," or the cry of "No blacklegs!" are quite enough for most men.

Beyond this, at street corners, in parks, on market-places or the seashore, there is a vast amount of speechmaking, apart from processions or organised assemblies in any open places and along streets and roads. Very little attempt at counteracting influence seems to be sought by employers, or by any of those denounced without their knowledge in season and out of season; and yet the doctrines and the leaflets command a large amount of belief. It may be true that Marx died in obscurity, and that his works were not generally known for many years; but now Marxian doctrines in various forms, some of which Marx would not have recognised as his own, are preached from end to end of the country, with more fervour than the doctrines of Henry George were preached to the last generation.

The speeches and the literature are wont to bear a common stamp, that Capitalism is the enemy and that the present system must go. Bolshevism goes farther in saying that the system and everyone connected with it must be destroyed before the new era of reconstruction can even be entered. " Buy up and change the ownership," " Divide up and change the ownership," " Destroy and start again with a new form of ownership," " Take the ownership for the State," and many another shade of colour may be selected according to the taste of each listener and the amount of thought which each man can devote to his choice. New waves of opinion are natural to the human mind, and in times of quick change and great events and strain of body and nerves the waves gain movement and force, particularly when there has existed a feeling of discontent and possibly of injustice.

That was the position of affairs before the War, when big movements were pending. Education and self-education had been going on more and more rapidly for years before. More and more young people were being turned out into the world with better knowledge of books and wider aspirations than their grandfathers had, but with no equal speed had a right start or opportunities for advancement or any system giving them a return for their efforts been opened up. Can anyone be surprised that the various forms of propaganda find adherents ? The seeds fall upon fertile soil in the sense that people are thirsty for endorsement of half-baked opinions or preconceived ideas. It says much for the general effect of our education and standards of right and wrong that so little violence follows from wild statements. Remarks in the heat of an oration on Tower Hill that So-and-So should be shot lead to no result, while a similar suggestion, if only insinuated, has been known in Ireland to be taken as a hint upon which action will follow. So far as such incidents are connected with the actual work of conciliation, I have almost always had to treat any threats or acts of physical violence as matters outside the attempt to settle a dispute by argument or agreement. It is of no use to hold men who are debating in the council chamber responsible for speeches made outside without their knowledge or authority, or for acts which can only hamper and retard the consent of the other side to negotiate, or which may even cause the breaking off of negotiations. There are occasions when attention may be called in public or in private to sheaves of expostulation or serious breaches of the peace, but as a rule for practical purposes it is useless. Sometimes, too, the complaints verge on the ludicrous. A high official once strongly complained to me that an agitator had called his wife an "idle, well-fed woman," with the remark that at any rate she was not idle, and asked me to stop him. In nine cases out of ten the messages are only an indication of the spread of a dispute or the commencement of sympathetic strikes. They may worry politicians, and if forwarded from a Minister may worry a negotiator, but the maintenance of the peace and acts of violence can as a rule only be left to the efforts of the police, except so far as quiet advice may be given. Such advice, as far as my experience goes, has generally, within their powers, been taken by the leaders to whom it has been given.

An exception may be made in two classes of cases, both in South Wales. One was where, on the advice of leaders, subordinate leaders had agreed to accept and arranged to advise a provisional settlement to their followers, and next day, to the open disgust of the leaders, repudiated any agreement ever having been made by them, and produced a hostile meeting. The other was where an undertaking had been given by leaders to ballot on the terms of a provisional settlement, and perforated cards were printed with "Yes" in one half and "No" in the other. Any man who came out without the "Yes" fixed in his hat or pinned to his clothes, so as to show he had voted "No," was received with hostile demonstration as soon as he appeared. That was not a free ballot.

How is the word passed round? There is no doubt that there is often warm debate among the members of an executive or in the inside of a lodge. But even there the more enthusiastic and aggressive men have far more weight than their numbers justify. A cautious leader may sometimes hold them in hand or advise tactics of delay, with a view to renewed debate after he has tried methods of his own with the employers. Yet if there is money to be drawn from the union purse, a grievance which can be magnified and exploited, the presence of a few hot-heads, then disputes may be brought about where no dispute ought reasonably to have been incurred. It is then that the mettle of a leader is put to the test. He may curb the trouble, if he knows it to be unwise, before it is too late, but if he cannot and will not do so, or if he serves but does not lead, he knows well that, when once a decision has been sent out by an executive or leaders, there is little chance of the movement being stopped. Any apparent reference to a ballot is coloured with a particular view in the form of the questions or the method of taking the ballot: and sometimes a storm may be created far larger than its originators may have intended or even desired. There is a great responsibility in reality attaching to men who launch a strike, and change or interfere with the lives and hopes of many a man, perhaps at a crisis in his career. It is the fate of almost every working man to have to learn that, whether he wills it or not, he is liable several times in his life, perhaps at moments which he, as an individual, might least choose, to be obliged to leave his work and his means of livelihood for an unknown period of time. At least the issue and the ballot should be fairly placed before him, and many men may well feel that a fair ballot, properly conducted and by secret and unbiased voting, would be the most reasonable method of obtaining the real opinion of the majority before so serious a step was taken.

During the War the art of propaganda became very intensive. Literature could not be safely disseminated. Speeches of the kind which had been made before the War would not only have been dangerous from the point of infringement of the laws, but also from the temper of the audience. Some at least of those who had been wont to speak strong words occupied themselves, to my knowledge, in doing all they could to aid our men and our cause. There were others who did not. An emissary, generally a young man, could drop into a shop and get taken on, skilled or semi-skilled, stay a few weeks, grumble that it was no place for a decent workman, sow discontent, and move on to another factory. A few days later another similar man would appear. Apparently unconnected with the first, he would say the same things, or worse; possibly a third or a fourth would follow. The seed thus sown was bound to bring forth some fruit. A strike; a movement with intention to go to another place; a circuit of factories on the suggestion that a rival paid more wages, would easily ensue. The Munitions of War Act did not act as a deterrent, when managers and foremen were anxious to let men go who would not work properly and were known or suspected to be causing trouble. "These are the devils of my works," said a manager to me, as we watched twenty or thirty young men dashing into their coats and rushing away on the stroke of the hour. "Where are they going ?" I said. "To hold a meeting and prepare an ultimatum," he replied. "Why don't you give them a football ?" I remarked. "They would make two teams and fight each other." Since the War, although the cessation of censorship does not require the use of swift cycle-riders to carry messages from Lancashire to Sheffield, or analogous subterfuges, plenty of discontent can be more openly promulgated. It may be well worth consideration whether facts, apart from arguments, the truth which it must be in the interest of man to know, cannot wisely be given in some form or other, so as to give a chance to young men for the exercise of judgment and brain upon the problems of their life and future welfare. Propaganda at the present time is apt to be too one-sided.

Following on the propaganda, that demoralising doctrine, so harmful to the State, the employer, and the man himself, commonly called by the name "Ca' canny," or "Go slow," to limit work to the level of the slowest man, to restrict production when the world is crying out for goods, has before, during, and after the War been a great influence in setting class against class. The interests of employer and employed become entirely adverse, when the employer is craving for production and the man will produce as little as he possibly can without losing his job.

This disease, originating possibly in the innate pleasure of man in laziness, has also a certain measure of scientific interest as a practical method of protection by the man against exhaustion, the desire to retain a reserve of force against the continuously wearing effect of long hours, dull work, low wages or driving. Each factor might exist as a stimulant to a man's conscious or semiconscious objection to work. A man would not give more work than he could help for a very low wage, or he would not respond to continual commands to speed up, or he got frankly bored with his work, or felt tired or unwell. No good example was set when employers might be seen to be slowing down with the object of lessening production and keeping up the prices of goods, or discharging men so that by scarcity the prices might be maintained and existing stocks got rid of. That policy was ca' canny by the employers. It often came to grief, because, even if groups of employers might decide to slow down, other employers or foreign countries might take a different view of the shortage, foresee a future demand, be able more cheaply to carry stocks, and get the orders in advance which the others could not fulfil. As an example, those firms in the cotton trade who, in spite of gloomy prophecies, bought material, carried stocks, and ran their mills in the winter of 1918–19 reaped a golden harvest. They, and the employees in their demand for better wages, which the employers would not give without the undesired dictation of the Prime Minister, had the imagination to foresee the world's shortage and the huge demand for goods which must arise from the fact that the War could not be renewed.

In answer to the difficulty of overproduction where lessening of supply might occasionally be necessary, or even actually justifiable, the cotton trade and also the woollen trade have from time to time, by joint arrangement between employers and employed, successfully provided by temporary systems of short time. Discharge of operatives could thus be avoided. But in other trades short time has not been often attempted, or could not easily be applied, particularly when the use of machinery made it difficult. Discharge and unemployment were accepted as the general practice of firms who, even if they retained a nucleus of skilled men, a commodity difficult to replace, ruthlessly dismissed semi-skilled or unskilled men with little or no compunction. It was against this system, this horror of unemployment at short notice for reasons over which they had no control, that men banded together and had their unemployment funds, their out-of-work donations, their insurance systems, until the State itself came in with compulsory insurance schemes and State contributions in the case of specified trades. These benefit systems have been of the essence of trade union policy ever since trade unions began, but they took time to organise, were imperfect, and only applied to a minority of workpeople. The schemes did not cover the ground. Seeing this, workmen argued that, if production meant ultimately unemployment or the risk of discharge, they would minimise that risk by taking care that they would produce as little as possible. It would be the same type of thought which led the workmen in the early days of the nineteenth century to resent so strongly the introduction of machinery, on the ground that fewer men would be employed and that too much production would ensue from the use of machines. The argument might apply in certain cases to the single workman or to groups of workmen or to a whole trade union. It could be speciously defended by the plea that they wanted the work to go round and last longer, that there should be jobs for more men, that their comrades should have work to do, and, from the point of view of trade union secretaries, that the funds of the union should not be depleted by providing out-of-work pay. Instead of pressing the employers to unite with them in fixing joint schemes of insurance suitable for emergencies of trade, instead of the employers having the sense to see that spells of unemployment deteriorated the workers and the produce of their work, and that men required for an industry should be supported by that industry in good times and in bad, each went their own way, with disastrous results. The policy of the ports relying upon pools of casual and ineffective labour, or of getting semi-skilled or unskilled labour as and when wanted, was followed in almost every industry in the country in the same or minor degree. It was this policy which led certain unions to restrict their members and to demand that no non-union labour should be employed. As men, too, by the extension of the franchise, realised more political consciousness and power, and by extension of education widened their thoughts, it was this policy which led to increased embitterment between Capital and Labour.

Labour followed its own plans for dealing with an accepted evil; Capital never united to plan out a joint method of dealing with it; the State crept in with its ineffectual and expensive labour exchanges, which could not cope with it and only led to worse estrangement. Meanwhile the canker of ca' canny spread, mitigated by the earnest desire of individuals to succeed, to get advancement in life, to have outlet for enterprise. Its evils are manifest in such trades as the moulders, who even during the War would not give up their methods of slow-time work lest the struggles of their unions in past years should be endangered: and now amongst the builders, who will not break away from the restricted amount of bricks to be laid within a given time. It was only the common purpose of the War which hindered its influence in many works, and showed what its absence might produce. It would be useless to calculate how much talent and how many rising hopes have been dashed down in the atmosphere of insistence on time-work with its watchword, "Keep your time by the slowest," or in the absolute command of foremen or colleagues that the number of rivets, the tale of bricks, the lasting of boots, the cuts of clothes, or the output of articles of every kind must be kept within or below the rule of the shop.

As late as January 1918 Sir Lynden Macassey, who did arbitration work during the War, and became head of the shipyard Labour Department, published a few uncontradicted instances which will serve as illustrations. He said:

"A discharged soldier who returned to work for a motor-car firm at Birmingham found that in turning cylinders he could do a job in forty-three minutes, and he maintained this speed for three weeks. The man was warned that the official time was seventy minutes. The warning being ignored, on November 4 last the union stopped the shop until the man was moved to other work. The same kind of intervention seems to take place on most engineering work on which piece-rates are paid.

"In the collieries the restriction is exercised indirectly. If a miner exceeds a certain output per day, varying from four to seven tons, he finds himself delayed by the 'shunt' men, who cut down his supply of tubs and props. In South Wales and Lanarkshire the output laid down is a fixed number of tubs per day, called a 'stint,' and if this were regularly exceeded the pit would be stopped to enforce it. The same applies to the docks. Recently a ship discharging grain in bulk in Birkenhead was stopped because the union considered that 150 tons a day was an excessive rate, though the rate was laid down both in the ship's charter-party and the sale contract; the result is that the elevators are now running at 23 per cent. below full speed. In Cardiff and elsewhere carters are not now allowed to load more than one tier on team wagons. On November 10 last a team-lorry was stopped in Bute Street, Cardiff, by the union delegate, and the carter made to unload eight bags which were in a second tier. At Immingham a motor-lorry was stopped because it had a full six-ton load.

The driver asked the delegate what the limit was, and he said: 'I don't know, but you have got too much on there, anyhow.'

"Sometimes the restriction appears to be applied by the men more than by the unions. At the Cardiff coal-tips the men are turning over one truck every seven minutes, compared with two minutes before the War; they will not keep their machines running at full speed. The ships' painters in Liverpool and Birkenhead are working 16 per cent. per hour below the pre-war rate. In leather-stamping at Leicester the men refuse to cut more than a certain number of pieces at a time, and this amounts to a loss of effort by the machine of 4 per cent. In bushelling wheat at Barrow, the men will not allow any more than two bushels to be made up every three minutes, and the unions have adopted this agreement among the men as a definite rule. In shipbuilding on the Clyde an attempt was made to limit the output of riveters by keeping the boy rivet-heaters to a set number.

"The restriction is of special moment when we find it applied to house-building. At Huddersfield, during the building of an extension, four men were stopped by their union for three days because they laid 480 bricks in a day of eight hours. A slater was warned at the same place because he fixed a gutter—a plumber's job—in order that he might get on with his own work. Instances might be multiplied indefinitely."

The few instances alone serve to show an amazing restriction on personal liberty, but no Acts of Parliament can cope with it.

Even in the War the express provisions of the Munitions of War Acts enacting that "any rule, practice, or custom not having the force of law which tends to restrict production or employment shall be suspended, and if any person induces or attempts to induce any other person (whether any particular person or generally) to comply or continue to comply with such a rule, practice, or custom, that person shall be guilty of an offence under this Act" were flouted or set at naught. Arbitrators tried to enforce the enactment, but with little effect. The doctrine that it was not to be done for the employers' benefit fell in with the view that old custom or so-called privileges should continue, and counteracted the principle that a fair day's work should be given for a fair day's wage.

Now, with the rise of wages and the reduction of hours, there is far less pith in the contentions which have been advanced in favour of ca' canny, but the preaching of slackness still continues, its practice is grievously general, and once again, unless a common purpose and better feeling can be and is obtained, with direct interest of a man in the result of his work, the blows which ca' canny has received will have no more effect upon its strength than the flip of a boxer's glove.

CHAPTER XXX

UNEMPLOYMENT

It has been said that one defence of " ca' canny " is that it is a preventive of unemployment, by prolongation of the time taken on the work and delay in permitting supply to overtake demand. The general result must be that the cost of production is largely increased, and if the article is a necessary of life, or one of the articles known as an amenity of life, the increased cost affects the workpeople concerned as well as the majority of the community.

Besides this drawback, no account is taken that, if production is increased, goods can be sold at a cheaper rate, demand is stimulated, articles become more and more required for the maintenance of a better standard, and far greater employment is apt to result than if goods are maintained as expensive luxuries for the few. The cycle, motor, sewing-machines, gas-stoves and fires, and soap trades might be cited as instances. If " ca' canny " could have held its own against new inventions or foreign competition, the hand-loom would be attempting to supply garments to the nation. Unemployment for a time might not have existed among hand-loom weavers, but the greater employment, if " ca' canny " could have won, would have been absent. There would have been no huge textile industries employing hundreds of thousands of people; clothing millions at a reasonable price; increasing the demand almost always in advance of an increased supply; and leading to the introduction or vast development of innumerable other industries—machine-making, building, agriculture, and all the industries concerned with the provision of wool, cotton, and every kind of textile.

It seems sometimes to be assumed that unemployment can be stopped by Act of Parliament. Strikes and lockouts cannot be stopped by Act of Parliament. The most that an

Act of Parliament could do would be to give privileges to persons who voluntarily agreed to defer the rights of freedom connoted by the power to lockout or strike, in return for delay in the exercise of the rights. So, too, unemployment cannot be stopped by Act of Parliament. The right of a person to live may be doubted, though in a civilised community it is not desirable in the interests of the community that a person should starve. The right of a person to work may also be open to question. What work ? The special work which alone the individual can do. Is Parliament to keep on providing hand-looms and insisting that hand-loom weavers must be provided with hand-loom work ? In the United States, if a man cannot earn enough at one trade, his wife will tell him to seek elsewhere, that there is plenty of work to be found if he will use his brains or his hands. He can come back to his own trade when there is work available there. In this country the tendency is for a man to say he can do nothing else and will know nothing else than the particular trade he has chosen and of which he knows a little; say, for example, joinery. Unless there is joinery to be got, he will remain idle, and suppose that somebody must provide joinery for him to do. Joinery may not be wanted by anyone. Scientific arrangement might have spread the joinery required in a district over a longer period, but it might have been extremely difficult for any person to judge the exact time or the exact amount of work required before the joinery demand of that district was entirely satisfied. He may seek joinery work elsewhere, possibly breaking up his home for that purpose; he may rely on unemployment insurance, which at least will tide over a period; but he cannot gain much by sitting still and expecting that somebody will invent joinery work for him to do.

Is it not the fact that in every trade, from time to time, there is slackness, not enough work for all who desire to do it ? or not enough to supply all the skilled or all the unskilled workpeople who in times of great demand might be engaged in that trade ? Even the best and most scientific schemes could not accurately settle the exact amount of goods required, or the hour when supply begins to exceed the existing demand. Foresight in obtaining new markets, division of work by temporary short time, unemployment insurance, emigration to new fields of work, may all assist to meet the difficulty, but the difficulty must remain unless the individual himself has brains to meet the emergency, education to turn his powers to another and, for the time being, more suitable method of earning a livelihood. The barrister without briefs and no resources will turn to writing or journalism, the clerk adds typewriting or stenography to his qualifications, the shopkeeper tries another line of business. The unskilled men have not the brain or the initiative. In earlier chapters I have pointed out the urgency of training youths, so that brains may be brought out, and that if possible they should learn as much as practicable of several lines or divisions of business at which they would be capable of working, even if at times they had to take a lower place than that to which they had advanced. The fact remains that in any event and from time to time there will be seasons or periods when unemployment looms up, unemployment which, if continued, demoralises men and tends rapidly to make them as unemployable as those whom physical disability or mental tendency have brought to the same position.

The number has been diminished, and should be diminished by effort. Even in the London docks it was calculated that in 1889 there were only 16 per cent. permanently employed, but that in 1911 the number had risen to 72 per cent. In times of bad trade and in seasonal trades, such as building, the unskilled and casuals are the first to be unemployed, and have nothing else, through lack of brains, to which they can turn their hands. When, in 1908, the unemployed were registered for relief, 53 per cent. were casuals and 19 per cent. in the building trade, that trade which now, for years and years, does not seem likely to cope with even the ordinary demands of the population for better housing. Labour colonies were tried, and found to be disastrous failures. The unemployed and unemployable could not work together. The colonies destroyed the self-respect of the honest worker, they were laughed at by the tramp who did not wish to work. As Mr. Burns truly said, in February 1911, relief works are like opiates, and the more you take the more you want. He added, "I know no more serious danger, morally, physically, and economically," Mr. Burns being a man who knew what he was saying and had headed the London dock strike on the principle of reducing casual labour. "You have no right to break the proud spirit of the poor. You have no right to undermine the sense of industry . . . a disaster to the nation."

The Reports of the Central Unemployed Body showed very clearly (1) that the vast majority of those applying had been casual labourers, and certainly not those for whom the Unemployed Workmen Act was intended; (2) that the work provided had done nothing to permanently improve the position of those who had received it; (3) that it had been impossible to provide work for more than a small proportion of those who applied. Surely this is a very apt description of the work and tendency of labour exchanges, to which I have already alluded.

The Poor Law Commission of 1832 denounced the abuse of outdoor relief to the able-bodied, a system which Sidney Smith said was "eating out the vitals of the nation." The Commissioners may have been stringent in their recommendations, which resulted in the Poor Law Act of 1834, but they exposed clearly diversion of funds: "it is our painful duty to report that the fund which was directed to be employed in the necessary relief of the impotent is applied to purposes destructive of the morals of the most numerous class and to the welfare of all."

Nearly a hundred years have passed, and the country has but recently reverted to a system of "doles," and is still faced with the unemployment problem; arising sometimes from lack of demand in the world at large, over which there is no practicable control, sometimes from local causes owing to the surplus of labour required in a particular locality for a particular trade. Are we again to revert to the pernicious and demoralising system of "doles," or "something for nothing"? or are we going to try to face the problem with energy? There may be always required old-age pensions for aged persons who cannot work, though the question whether they should come from the State, the industry, the firm, the family, or thrift may be debated by persons according to their views. There may always be necessity for aid to the destitute, to whom in theory the Poor Laws applied and should apply, bringing in under certain circumstances the mother, the infant, the school-child, the sick, the mentally deficient, the aged and infirm, though with many of these, apart from Acts of Parliament intended to be ameliorative, better economic status would permit better aid from the family. There may always be the tramp and vagrant, and those who love "the freedom of the road," as well as the habitual criminals, though every effort should be made to prevent children falling into these classes and adding to their numbers.

Whatever may be the sources of the recruits to the unemployed and the ranks of the poor, it may be noted that in October 1919 there were, exclusive of vagrants, lunatics, and cases of outdoor medical relief, 130 paupers in every 10,000 of the population, or 238,563 paupers (109,816 indoor and 128,747 outdoor cases) in the United Kingdom, with London responsible for nearly 68,000 of them, at a time when the unemployment dole was still running.

What would a business man do if his business was running down through lack of demand, and he saw before him diminished returns or the necessity of piling up stock? He would try for fresh openings, new trade, increased activity from advertisement, agents, and customers, with a view to the maintenance of his business and increased prosperity. The more cheaply he could produce by elimination of waste, by consideration whether quantity would ensure less cost and more clients, by improved appliances, by better work, the more confident he would feel that he might keep or enlarge his market. At the present time, when the whole world is crying out for goods and the home market in many classes of goods is not nearly met; when for years to come the demand seems bound to continue, production is the best panacea for unemployment, but with production continuous care to foresee the developments of the future and so widen the area of trade on every side. The last thing which the business man should think of doing is the creation of unemployment by the lack of assiduity on his part. In the long-run it will be harmful to him and the country. If development and continuous work is in sight, the workman is less likely to have the fear of unemployment before his eyes. Such business care may, and would, largely tend to diminish any lack of demand from the world at large. It is our interest to stimulate demand; to keep and enlarge our markets, to maintain our reputation as a nation of shopkeepers. There is a glorious opportunity as a nation of shopkeepers. There is a glorious opportunity for this country, if it chooses to take it, but without production, without work, opportunity may pass away and not again recur.

However much the world-demand may be the principal factor for a great exporting country, only to be met by keen brains and good work, there remains the difficulty of unemployment at home, through trades chiefly concerned with the home market, or with seasonal trades, like the building trade, which now appears so seriously to hinder the welfare of the community. In some of these trades —though, as far as can be judged, not for a long time in the building trade—there is bound to be fluctuating and sporadic unemployment, or at least such lack of demand as might lead to unemployment. Each instance of it is liable, like a sore hurtful to the whole body, to increase suspicion, distrust, continuance of "ca' canny," and demands for new social organisations which might in their attempted development lead to disturbance, certain to end either in a compromise or in bitter and unwanted strife, and equally certain to be harmful to our trading prosperity.

How is this issue to be met ? It is not an issue that the State can meet suddenly, except by such an evil policy as doles. It is unfair to the State, already overburdened, and to the general taxpayers, who have to subscribe to the State, that the burden of lack of vision or business qualities by employers, or "ca' canny" on the part of workpeople, in sections of industry, should be foisted upon them. It is a common interest of wage-payers and the majority of wage-earners, that the difficulty should be avoided, the hardship minimised. A solution cannot be effected in a day. Every person who has dealt with the Poor Law, or any other administrative law or scheme which affects large numbers of individuals, knows that personal elements, individual examination, sympathetic feeling, the elimination of the unfit, and occasionally a hard rule, are necessary for the achievement of any success. Time and patience, often rendered nugatory by cross-currents of conflicting interests or different theories, are found to be essential for real results. It can only be by hard effort that the evil can be minimised. Even so, it is desirable that the right paths should be followed. With all diffidence I say, on this extremely difficult problem, that the right lines are (1) education, so that youth may have opportunity to obtain a fair chance of advancement, and if obliged to take the position, through lack of opportunity, brain, or initiative, of a "hewer of wood and drawer of water," a fair chance of turning his physical strength fron one business to another; (2) insurance against unemployment, so that during temporary slackness of trade there may be opportunity, without loss of all current income, for change of work or employer, or time to await renewed possibility; (3) unity of purpose and co-operation between employer and employed in each trade, so that in time of prosperity mutual arrangements may be made to deal with persons engaged in the industry in times of adversity, each trade arriving at its own scheme. If any national insurance continues to exist, it ought to be treated as a minimum which has to be bettered or excluded.

The Industrial Council of the building trade has set an example in this direction, though it is not very clear how the payment of contributions is brought home to individuals. They have recommended that, in cases of unavoidable unemployment, the maintenance of its unemployed members shall be undertaken by the industry through its employment committees, and that the necessary revenue shall be raised by means of a fixed percentage on the wages bills, and paid weekly to the employment committee by each employer on the joint certificate of himself and a shop steward or other accredited trade union representative.

Any other system than a system of the responsibility of each trade must lead to doles or subsidies to a particular industry. Doles have been condemned over and over again, by generation after generation. Wherever they have been tried they have ultimately failed and been denounced. Subsidies are generally unfair, taxing other industries; can only be excused for national reasons; are subject to political influence, passing phases of sentiment, or the bias of personal judgment. It is the duty of an industry to maintain its own reserves of labour. If reserves are required, it should pay for the reserve. If it is argued that the co-operation of employers and employed in an industry or in a firm (and wise is the firm which follows the principle) to provide for unemployment, sickness, or old age will lead to trusts and combines against the interest of the consumer, I can only give an opinion. That opinion is that the argument is sheer nonsense. In these small islands, highly developed as they are even at the present time, with a watchful Press, a democratic franchise, and keen competitors, detrimental trusts can be defeated almost before they begin to exist. The scare of trusts is a hypothetical scare of the possible future. The problem of unemployment is a vital, immediate, and urgent question which cannot be ignored.

CHAPTER XXXI

SOCIALISM

PRIOR to the War much was said and written from time to time on the value of co-partnership. The type of co-partnership proposed seems to have been an alliance between Capital and Labour in the sense of giving Labour an opportunity to take a share in the business. It was not the same principle as co-operative production. Co-operative production had led to small undertakings and numerous failures, as in the case of the quarries started after the Penrhyn disputes. They lacked capital and skilled management, and failed to expand into large undertakings. It was also not the same principle on which business was practised by those large co-operative distributive societies which have grown from small beginnings into immense industrial undertakings.

Lord Robert Cecil was specially prominent in advocacy of co-partnership, saying that he was " convinced that the co-partnership system held the secret of the solution of our industrial problems, if any solution was to be found. Co-partnership was not merely profit-sharing; it also represented a sharing of the capital and a sharing of the responsibilities. It was by the adoption of that principle in the industrial life of this country that we might seek and hope to secure a peaceful issue of the present threatening condition of affairs." The co-partnership undertaking which is continually cited as an example for others is the South Metropolitan Gas Company and the scheme of its chairman, the late Sir George Livesey. Lord Robert praised co-partnership at the unveiling of the Livesey statue. The scheme was unfortunate in its origin, being the outcome of a big strike in 1889, which has not endeared it to trade unions. The company's principles are the payment of a percentage bonus, half in cash and half in shares, on all salaries and wages, varying in amount according to the price at which the gas is sold to the consumer. The principle has extended in the gas industry, thirty-four gas companies working on analogous co-partnership plans by 1912. It may be remarked that this industry, working under statutory obligations and possessing monopolies, would generally have no loss, and consequently a bonus is practically certain.

Another salient example is that of Messrs. Lever Bros., at Port Sunlight, where partnership certificates are issued equal in amount annually to 10 per cent. of the salary or wages of those employees qualified to share under the scheme, the certificates participating *pari passu* with the ordinary share scrip, after 5 per cent. has been paid upon ordinary shares.

But, however useful such schemes may be in special and profitable businesses, many of which might possibly undertake them with advantage, it cannot be said that they have had much influence on the general industrial conditions of the country. Only 298 schemes are reported to have been started between 1865 and 1912, and of these only 133 continued to exist in 1912, though they were spread over about sixty different trades and industries. The majority of them do not give the workpeople, particularly the unskilled workpeople, whose share must be small, a sufficient interest in the business to ensure thrift or keen interest in the success of the business. The call of the trade unions and their rules are too strong a force on the opposite side, and the trade unions are generally hostile to any support of them. The schemes may coincide with other advantages which firms may start with a view to co-operation in interests, but can seldom be the "end-all" or "be-all" which would allay unrest. It is certain that any conditions annexed to such schemes restricting freedom to join a union or to strike, or which lead to the belief that the schemes may reduce the ordinary rates of wages, will be bound to lead to failure. It should also be noted that co-partnership schemes must insist on a portion of the bonus payment being reserved for investment in the business, otherwise the recipient may be profit-sharing, but does not tend, however slowly, to become a co-partner. There may be future developments of co-partnership, but I should be loth to say that schemes as at present devised provide an example which, if followed, would satisfy the relations of Capital and Labour. Some of the schemes by different firms do improve the chances of suitable men getting through by merit or initiative, on which I have laid stress, and in that sense and as some inducement to thrift cannot be ignored. They are examples of the various ideas which may be said to be fructifying in the silent ranks of employers with a view to meeting the theories and claims which are so prevalent in the ranks of employees, or at least in their speeches and writings. Although employers are now more and more alive to the value of co-operation, and as a whole desire better feeling, they have been slow in taking steps to answer by argument, and to defend the cause of reward to individual exertion, and the value of initiative, and the greater causes of individual liberty and of ideals higher than the pursuit of mere material gain.

As compared with these minor efforts, the exertions of many theorists and leaders of labour are in startling contrast. The War seems to have acted as a forcing-house, and brought forward old and new plants with rapid growth, far more varied in number than any produced by the employers. Although the chief development has come since the War, they all claim to be the historical or natural result of causes or aims existing before the War. All have certain connecting-links, or may even be defined as varieties of a stock plant generally termed "Socialism," but in view of their variety it is difficult to prophesy which of them, if any, will have a governing influence on the industrial future of the country.

If my account of the big disputes for the ten years previous to the War is correct, the reader may be able to exercise his judgement as to how far these strikes or lock-outs were commenced or carried forward with any idea or set purpose of gaining the acceptance of any particular ideal or theory by the country. That some of the persons engaged in them held one or other ideal or theory is certain. Such persons appeared in every strike, particularly in the Irish disputes, which most nearly approached, or were worked upon, demands for a complete change of social organisation. Mr. Larkin, backed by the clever brain of the late Mr. Conolly, did profess to have ideas, though he could not give them such clear expression as his tutor might have achieved. But Mr. Larkin only supported one theory, a theory which found little support in Great Britain. The trade unions of Great Britain did not aid Larkin or Larkinism, but assisted with food the hungry in Dublin, and sent their deputations to advise that trade union principles should be as far as possible asserted and not injured.

There are many other forms of socialism which have been, and are still being, put forward, difficulty arising from their variety to such an extent that union on any common platform seems almost impossible. Some would leave each state as it is; some would have one uniform type of state, e.g. a "democratic state"; some advocate no separate states. Socialistic theories differ, again, in the extent to which they would bring corporate action to bear on the interests of individuals: some would leave a place for individual enterprise; some would "socialise" all individual effort; some would "nationalise" all industry, others only some industries. Certain socialistic theories would confine corporate action to municipalities, others to political states. Others would concentrate attention on or even interpret the entire life of a community in terms of the economic conditions of a society; others would socialise everything in a community, including all the traditionally accepted "institutions." Certain socialists would secure their ends at once, or as soon as the power is in their hands; other groups are prepared to wait and work gradually for a socialistic community of the future; or, in other words, immediate revolution is the aim of one section; progressive evolution of actual society to the ends of socialism appeals to another. In certain details, as in the acceptance of free education, everybody may have acquiesced in some socialistic views, but the ordinary individual is very perplexed with the many theories continuously advanced. It has been described as a "seething welter," from which, as may be noted in any railway train, the young man takes refuge in *Tit-bits* or other amusing papers, or in the latest news of sport. This fact does not, however, preclude the existence of the position that on matters of business his faith has been made up for him or he has made up his faith, and does not want to worry himself any more upon the subject.

If the results are variable in character, the sources from which the movements originate may also be said to be very variable. Sometimes a theory can be traced to the philanthropic enthusiasm of its author; or, again, to an active personal hostility to existing governments; in another case to a deep sense of the misery endured by many under the prevailing industrial régime; sometimes to reaction against a previous theory; or even to a vivid imagination of what society might be. But, though the "seething welter" be admitted, certain broad divisions are at least to be discerned; and if a general definition is possible, it may perhaps be said that the characteristic feature of socialism, whether as a theory or a practical attitude towards the problems of society, is the exclusive and unrestricted application of the power of the corporate action of the community as a whole to the solution of some or all of the questions which arise out of the conflicting interests, more especially the conflicting economic interests, of the individuals comprising a community.

There is practical intention in socialism. It may be said that, with hardly any exception, all such theories are put forward, not in the interests of mere scientific knowledge of society, but with a view to the practical transformation of social and political life as it is. Even those theories which rest on a materialistic or mechanical conception of social evolution, and which maintain that the course of history is necessarily determined in the direction of socialism, assume that a theoretical statement of the inevitable trend of events will be of practical assistance in hastening or in guiding towards the desired end. There is doubtless an inconsistency in holding on the one hand that the course of history is necessitated, and on the other that human beings can hasten or retard, direct or misdirect, its course. But no socialist is restrained by theoretical inconsistency from giving practical indications how to reach the ends he has in mind, and urging their speedy realisation. It is the practical value of socialistic and communistic theories as guides to social and political action which is their main interest both for those who expound them and for those to whom they appeal.

No one will understand the influence which socialistic theories have exerted in recent days who ignores this underlying conviction of the practical efficiency of socialism as a remedy for social and political ills. Without this assumption, socialism would have no hold on the practical conduct of the disaffected, the depressed, or the disinherited members of an industrial community. Its main interest is directed towards the transformation of the economic conditions of social life; and its interest in political issues is entirely subordinate to the problem presented by the present economic status of the worker, more especially the wage-earner. Indeed, every institution is regarded from the economic point of view. The whole present framework of society is looked upon as supporting the economic system which socialism seeks to alter. Thus certain socialists manifest as much hostility to present political, educational, legal, and even ecclesiastical institutions as towards the prevailing industrial system, and would have these modified and if necessary abolished, if this is the only way to securing the economic ends they have in view. Their aim is material comfort or economic amelioration—everything else is secondary. Hence the so-called "materialistic" character of most socialistic theories, some of which, like those of Marx, explicitly rest on a materialistic conception of human society.

In order to achieve this economic amelioration, it will, I think, be found that, whatever may be the particular origin of any given theory, socialism and communism have been based on three main considerations. The first is the glaring contrast between the lot of innumerable individuals under present social conditions and the claims of those individuals to their full measure of human happiness. The second is the proved capacity of human beings for joint action for social and political purposes, and the immense power both for good as well as evil which can be exerted by combined action for specified ends. The third is the conviction, resting partly on experience and partly on mere belief, that human society is essentially and almost indefinitely plastic, and can be moulded into any form to suit human needs.

If these considerations are examined, it may be said that the first hardly requires comment and explanation. The history of industrial life during the last hundred years supplies sufficient evidence in support of the position, and provides abundant argument to the socialist for proposing some transformation of society. It may be said, in spite of the apparent paradox, that socialism is as a rule more concerned for individual happiness than for a social order. The transformation of society is primarily a means; individual human welfare, as understood by the socialist, is the real end in view. Whether or not it can be attained by socialism has not yet been proved by mankind.

Without the second consideration it is safe to say socialism could never have been suggested as a cure for social and political evils. Corporate action for purposes deliberately adopted is a prominent and most distinctive feature of the life of a community. The pressure such action can bring to bear on individuals is irresistible when it is practically unanimous, and a powerful check to individual caprice even where it is not unanimous. It is argued, therefore, that all that is necessary to secure reforms or social changes of any sort is that the power latent in corporate life should be in the hands of those who have most to gain by social change; and that since under present conditions the majority of individuals making up the community are workpeople who have everything to gain by the use of this power, the workpeople have but to stand and act together and their ends will be attained. The fact that power is not proportionate to numbers in the community is argued to be the precise cause of present evils, a grievance to those who suffer from it, a privilege to those who benefit by it, and an injustice in the constitution of society. Power, it is held, should be adequate to happiness, or at any rate to that form of happiness which consists in material comfort. A social situation in which those who are comfortable are numerically weak and those who are numerically strong have much less, a situation in which the few control the power of corporate action for their advantage and the many who create the resources of the community have no power to control its actions—such a situation, where it exists, is one which has only to be realised in order to be condemned or to demand alteration. The clear and conscious appreciation of this position is the driving force of the socialistic movement.

The third consideration above mentioned is also most important. It is assumed, rightly or wrongly, that the individuals comprising a community can make of a community what they please. This assumption is partly due to the fact that, historically, society, or at any rate political society, has appeared in many forms, and that types of organisation have originated, developed, and passed away. In short, history shows that, while a human society may be relatively stable, its structure and composition may change indefinitely and are not rigidly fixed. The assumption is partly due to the everyday fact that men, by individual action, can and do change the life of a community for the better or for the worse. Human nature and human society are, in a word, plastic. Hence it is supposed there is no reason whatever for accepting any social condition as fatally unchangeable. With effort, more especially with combined effort, a society may be changed gradually or catastrophically, in a generation or in a single day. In that fact or in that conviction lies the hope and the inspiration of socialism. The critic of theoretical socialism may see, in such a contention, paradox, inconsistency, or even absurdity; and in the practical development of socialistic movements he may find the refutation of the assumption on which socialistic proposals rest. Experience constantly reveals that human nature is not indefinitely plastic; that its fundamental elements and instincts are apparently as unalterable as the stars in their courses, and are found alike in the socialists who condemn, and in those who uphold, the established order of society; that human society cannot adopt any form we please, but must, if it is to subsist, follow certain rules, accept certain principles, and find room and place for all sorts and conditions of men. In following a theory the socialist may forget human nature. Experience tells me that the socialist often does forget human nature.

I have said that socialism is, as a rule, really concerned with individual happiness. It might appear that certain socialists, more particularly State socialists, seem to regard the community in its corporate capacity as a kind of earthly providence, and to inculcate unquestioning service for the community as a supreme end of individual action. On the other hand, the majority of socialists seem to treat the community as a machine for obtaining the equalised well-being of individuals, for relieving them from the inequalities which are due to nature or circumstance or chance, and for the prevention of the evils of individual self-seeking and individual competition. When certain socialists advocate the abolition of fixed boundaries between communities, the suppression of patriotic instincts and feelings, and the internationalisation of the interests of the workers, it is transparent that for them, at any rate, any community in its corporate action is a means to the ends of the individuals comprising mankind. Socialism thus seems to speak with two voices. In the former case it advocates the subordination of the individual to the community; in the latter case it desires the subordination of the community to its individual components.

In either case it seeks to secure one result which is characteristic of most, if not of all, types of socialism—the equality of individuals relatively to one another. This is a necessary consequence, as it is the persistent claim of socialism that all individuals should be equal, not merely "before the law," but economically. By making the corporate will of the community alone supreme in power and authority over individuals, it abolishes at a stroke the superiority of one individual over another, which unfettered competition between individuals not only permits but encourages. The hostility of socialism to the capitalist system, and the economic equality of all individuals, are merely two sides of the same general policy. The settlement of the conflict with capitalism or between individual interests in society is not left to the competitive struggle of individuals, either singly or in groups, but would be undertaken by and directed from the corporate will of the whole community as such, purporting to act impartially for the uniform interests of all individuals. It is this corporate will of the whole community as the governing force which distinguishes socialistic action from trade union action, and from co-operative action, as also from State action in the ordinary traditional sense.

A trade union may or may not be socialistic in its policy: but neither in principle nor in facts can socialism be identified with trade unionism. A trade union is a form of combination of individuals within a community for the special interest of the workmen in a particular trade or group of trades: it does not cover all the individuals even in the trade (for it excludes the employers); it does not embrace all the interests of all individuals in the community; and it exercises its functions by the sanction of and within the larger life of the community. It has been recognised that, while trade unions might prepare the way for and could promote socialistic action, they are not in a position to carry through a programme which covers the whole life of society.

Similarly the operation of co-operative societies is distinct from socialism. They concern particular individuals within a community associated voluntarily for mutual benefit; they have due regard to the varying interests and claims of each individual; are subject to dissolution at the desire of an effective majority; and require the sanction of the community for their operations. The only point of resemblance between socialism and co-operative associations is that both seek to secure a common simultaneous advantage for all individuals within the organisation by the distribution of the entire product of this joint effort among the producers. In other respects there is hardly any resemblance; for example, a community is not a voluntary association, it requires no superior sanction for its action, and most socialistic theories would not allow "proportionate" participation, but would require "equal" participation in the product.

Socialism, again, is clearly distinguishable from State action in the ordinary sense. Every State takes some care of its component individuals, and decides between the conflicting interests of individuals in certain defined cases, and must do so for the sake of the order and unity of the community. But socialism holds that the community in its corporate capacity must directly impress its will upon individual interests, so as to secure that no individual shall pursue his advantage at the expense of that of others, that communal action shall take the place of competitive action between individuals, and that the economic resources of the community shall be managed on behalf of the common interest of all, be jointly produced by all, and be distributed on the principle of equality to all. It may be safely said that no historical State has acted on such a principle, and the action of the State on behalf of individuals, however closely allied in effect to certain aims of socialism, as in the cases of State education, State insurance, State inspection, etc., cannot, therefore, be compared with, and has never been accepted by socialists as equivalent to, the position of socialism.

The above remarks tend to indicate the difference between socialism on the one hand and the actions of trade unions, co-operative societies, and the ordinary State.

The difference of socialism from communism and anarchism is much less ; in fact, all three are closely connected. The connection between socialism and communism is, indeed, so close that the terms are often used interchangeably both in ordinary speech and by writers on socialism. But there is an important difference. Socialism is concerned *mainly* with the economic, and secondarily with social and political inequalities between individuals—inequalities of opportunity, inequalities of station inherited or acquired, inequalities of natural endowments, inequalities of political power, inequalities of economic reward for labour. It seeks through the corporate action of the community to control all the powers and resources of society in such manner as to diminish or abolish all these inequalities, and in particular so to communise or nationalise all the industrial enterprises of the community as to produce in effect an equality of income or economic reward for all individuals. In a word, socialism seeks, by the agency of the community as a whole, to substitute unqualified individual equality for unqualified individual liberty, and to establish this principle of equality by a thoroughgoing system of communal control. It therefore shows no hostility to private property, provided this property, both in amount and kind, is regulated by the corporate will of the community. Strictly speaking, no doubt, it insists that there is only one proprietor—the community in its corporate capacity; but by demanding that the entire wealth of the community shall be distributed equally amongst or shared equally by its component members, it tries to do justice to the fact and the need of private property.

Communism, on the other hand, is actively hostile to private property, and is less interested in the distribution of public property to individuals for their private use than in the abolition of private property altogether. Doubtless the abolition of private property cannot be carried out without the abolition of other elements of the present economic régime : for example, property is bound up with contract. But the disappearance of other elements would be consequential on the abolition of private property. It is held that private property is the root evil, and the source of all or most of the inequalities with which socialism is concerned. Moreover, if it were abolished, there would be less need for the exercise of those powers vested by socialism in the corporate will of the community. Communism, therefore, presents two possible attitudes to the corporate action of the community: when private property is abolished, either all property would be held and used by all in common, the community deciding and distributing according to need, immediate or remote; or there is no property in any sense at all, and each takes as he wants and what he wants without supervision: in other words, there is no corporate action on the part of the community required. The first comes very close to socialism in certain forms; hence it is true to say that, while a socialist may be a communist, a communist is not necessarily a socialist. On the other hand, the second attitude comes very near to anarchism.

The difference between socialism and communism regarding the right to private property is thus one of principle. They doubtless may be said to agree that the individual shall be deprived of the unrestricted right to private property. But communism denies the individual's right to private property absolutely. Socialism admits a limited right to private property, subject to the collective will of the community.

While socialism and communism, again, agree that the final authority in determining the individual's sphere of action and his share in the common good lies with the corporate will of the community, they differ in their conception of the kind of community which shall exercise this supreme authority. Socialism invariably understands by the community the whole body of a nation or a state, the community in its widest sense. Hence Socialism has been and is generally identified with social democracy in the political meaning of that term. Communism is not thus restricted. A communistic body may be large or small: it may be a state or a village commune, or even an artificially created combination of individuals acting communistically. Its attitude towards any large type of community like the State is suspicious and distrustful, or openly hostile, mainly because the larger the community, the more is the individual's interest beyond direct control.

The last remark leads up to the anarchist conception of society. This seems at first glance quite alien in principle to either socialism or communism, for both the latter accept as final the authority of a common will, whereas anarchism appears to deny all such authority, or indeed authority of any kind. But such a view is merely a surface view of anarchism, a view which possibly gains much support from the methods of openly violent hostility to any government which have from time to time been adopted by particular individuals claiming to be anarchists. There is no necessary connection between open violence and anarchism. Anarchism, as the term implies, means the rejection in principle of all right to rule or control over the individual by an agency alien to himself or not having his free assent to the exercise of such control. Just as socialism and communism lay emphasis solely or mainly on the principle of individual equality in the abstract sense of sameness of rights or privileges in a community, so anarchy lays exclusive emphasis on the principle of individual liberty. But as in the former case the maintenance of individual equality is held to be not at all inconsistent with the existence of a community, so in the case of anarchism the insistence on individual liberty is held to be quite consistent with a common social life. There is indeed a still closer connection between these three views. In the case of both socialism and communism, the corporate will of the community is brought into action primarily in the interest of the individual, to redress the present inequalities as between individuals and to give equality of status to all. Anarchism carries this concern for the individual to its utmost limit: it takes the individual's interest to be paramount even over any authority exerted by the community. Anarchism will allow no interference with individual liberty of any sort, and maintains that where the individual's welfare is concerned, the individual is the best and the final judge.

The negative aspect of anarchism, which denies the right of interference with the individual by any alien authority, is only one side of the doctrine. The positive side rests on what may be called an optimistic assumption of the inherent goodness of human nature. Anarchism maintains that individuals, left to themselves, will form communities based on mutual interests, mutual co-operation, or mutual affection. In other words, such communities would exist or be permitted under anarchism as the individuals freely establish for their specific individual benefit, and no others would be required. All the ills of society are held to arise from the force brought to bear on individuals by the organised agencies of government. Such organised agencies of force are as artificial as they are harmful. They create evils in their endeavour to prevent evil. A community is but a means to an end more important than the community. The real end of government, it is maintained, is self-government, and the true form of self-government is one where the individual feels no constraint on his action for his own good other than his own will. Self-government at its best reduces to a minimum the pressure of governmental action on the individual; the extreme limit is reached where there is no pressure exerted by government. Such a limit is found where no government exists; and this is the ideal form of community which anarchism defends and inculcates. In short, anarchism carefully distinguishes, whereas historically existing communities always combine or even identify, authoritative government and the community. The latter anarchism accepts as natural; the former anarchism rejects as artificial and unnecessary.

The compulsion which anarchism resents and resists in the case of government is only one type of force—the most prominent, and therefore the most to be opposed. But any type of organised constraint of the individual's liberty is rejected. Thus individuals shall not be constrained to work except at what they like or when they like, or, indeed, shall not be constrained to work at all; all imposed systems of ideas or institutions are to be set aside as illegitimate. Since educational and ecclesiastical institutions exist for the purpose of inculcating or impressing certain ideas on the minds of individuals, they are considered hostile to the individual's liberty. The resentment against authority even passes the bounds of the present world, and the anarchist frankly announces that God has no more authority over the individual than the State, and openly proclaims that anarchism must mean atheism.

The three most influential forms of socialistic doctrines at the present time in this country are those advocated by the Marxian Socialists, by Syndicalism, and by Guild Socialism. A brief account of these may not be out of place. They are important subjects for the consideration of men and women, owing to the notoriety which various phases of them are wont from time to time to achieve.

CHAPTER XXXII

MARXISM—SYNDICALISM—GUILD SOCIALISM

THE theories covered by the terms of Marxism, Syndicalism, and Guild Socialism have much in common, in spite of their differences. They make or have made a strong appeal to the labour world on the same general grounds; for their purpose in each case is first to act as a solvent of the present industrial system, and, secondly, to guide society towards a new industrial order. All three make an attack on capitalism as currently in operation. All are hostile to the political and social conditions which tolerate and support the traditional economic régime of free industrial competition, the subordination of labour in industry, and the accepted "wages system." All are in favour of the transformation, if necessary the exploitation, of industry in the interests of the workers. They are all hostile to bourgeois supremacy.

Apart from details, they differ in three essential respects: (1) in their view of the State and its relation to Labour; (2) in their methods of securing their ends; (3) in their specific interest in the economic situation.

(1) Marxism is a thoroughgoing State socialism. It accepts the State as the necessary instrument for securing social and economic justice. Its function is so to control the instruments of production as at once to destroy capitalism and the capitalistic control of industry, and to give the worker unrestricted enjoyment of the whole product of his labour as his rightful reward.

Syndicalism is hostile to the State, distrusts and resists the interference of all political government in industry, and will have nothing to do with socialism in any accepted sense, least of all with State socialism, which it regards as bourgeois control in another form.

Guild socialism would separate off completely the

functions and operations of the State from all that specifically belongs to industry. It would make industrial organisation in its comprehensive sense a self-contained whole, governing itself by its own regulations and assemblies, and uncontrolled by any interference or, apparently, any assistance from the State. The State is to form a distinct organisation by itself, equally self-governing, and equally independent in its action and procedure from the organisation of industry. These two organisations are to exist side by side within the community, each having sovereignty in its own domain, while the unity of the community's life as a whole is to be represented by and expressed through a congress or council whose business it will be to deal with matters affecting equally the above two primary and fundamental organisations into which the effective life of the community actually falls.

(2) The method adopted by Marxism for securing the transformation of the present industrial régime is twofold. By a thoroughly critical analysis of the nature of Capital and its relation to Labour, Marx seeks to expose the injustice of the capitalist system, and to prove that in principle and in experience the real source of wealth is derived from the labour of the "working class." From this to the practical conclusion that the reward of labour should fall to the worker and not to the capitalist, the step is easy. The claim of socialism he thus maintains is scientifically demonstrable. The second aspect of his method consists in the inculcation of the gradual and complete organisation of the proletariat, so that they shall be able to take supreme control over the instruments of production by the centralised forces of the State. The process of assuming control is not that of sudden revolution, but gradual development of the principles inherent in the economic order, which, in his view, point to the socialistic industrial State as the final goal of human society.

Syndicalism, on the other hand, seeks to realise its end catastrophically, without any appeal to or reliance on history and scientific economics, and without any State assistance. Their instruments of transformation are "direct action" and the "general strike," or, where the general strike is impracticable, sporadic and incessant strikes. Syndicalism relies on violence, using this term in a broad sense to cover any attack on the capitalist class, from petty passive obstruction to widespread destruction. For this purpose it makes the utmost use of local and national trade unionism.

Guild Socialism looks to propaganda and the gradual development of complete organisation of the whole industrial world to bring about peacefully but triumphantly the overthrow of the present industrial system. Organisation is to be by industry and not by craft or specialised trade. and the natural interlocking of industries is to be the effective means of securing and retaining possession and control of the sources, the resources, and the rewards of industry. The past and present development of trade unionism points the way to the final self-government in industry which is the aim of Guild Socialism. This will automatically separate the sphere of State control on the part of the territorial association from the control of all industry by those directly engaged in industry within the community.

(3) Marxism as a form of collective or State socialism concentrates the problem of industrial transformation round the interests of the consumer. Its main concern is with the question of consumption, the ultimate issue of the industrial process. Society is to be changed and reorganised for the benefit of the consumer of the produce of industry. Hence trade unions must be superseded and State socialism installed.

Syndicalism is primarily, indeed solely, concerned with the producer, the worker as the agent for producing wealth. Hence trade unionism is to be supreme and the State set aside.

Guild Socialism lays exclusive stress neither on the consumer nor on the producer, but seeks to do justice to both. It is, therefore, opposed neither to the State as such nor to the trade unions as such. The consumer's interests are relegated to the care of the State as the supreme territorial association. The producer's interests as such are to be under the sole charge of the National Guild, the natural development of national trade unionism. By the two together, the State and the National Guild acting in complete and sovereign independence within their respective domains, the entire interests of the community—consumers and producers alike—will be conserved and secured.

While these three forms of social and political theory have exerted, and still exert, great influence on the labour world, the influence is not of the same kind. The significance of Marxism lies mainly in the region of political and economic theory; its practical influence was possibly greater in the past generation than it is at present. Syndicalism directly controls large industrial movements at the present time. The era of Guild Socialism has still to come; its hopes are fixed in the future. The first professes to have its roots in the past history of civilisation; the second finds its inspiration in the present stage of industrial life; the third in the community that is to be.

Marxism

The most vital and, for the labour world, the most effective doctrines of Marx are to be found in the vigorous and trenchant statement of the socialistic programme contained in his *Communist Manifesto*, first promulgated in 1848; and in the severely abstract quasi-scientific analysis of the relations of Labour and Capital elaborated in his work on *Capital*, the first volume of which appeared in 1867, the second in 1885, the third in 1894.[1]

The *Communist Manifesto* is a pronunciamento addressed to the proletariat. Holding as he does that the course of human history is necessitated and that civilisation must be interpreted materialistically, he maintains that the inevitable trend of modern social movements has been and is towards a revolutionary reconstruction of society. The first revolution was that of the bourgeoisie against mediæval feudalism; the second, still to come, is to be that of the wage-earning proletariat against the capitalist bourgeoisie. Liberation from the bondage of feudalism was brought about by an inevitable struggle between two divergent classes within the community; another class war will be necessary, and will continue till the liberation or supremacy of the wage-earners is assured. This second war has been brought about by the bourgeoisie as a class. The modern factory system has at once created the power of Capital over Labour, and divided the employing class from the workers by

[1] Marx died in 1883. The second and third volumes were edited and brought out by his friend, Engels.

the gulf which separates those who for their own ends can buy labour at a market price, and those whose sole function in industry is to be a means to the ends of others for a price which is a bare subsistence wage. The interests, aims, and persons of the two classes are thus in their natures antagonistic; the employer despotically controls the whole machinery of industry primarily for his own benefit, the worker is but a living part of the machinery, and, in all except name, a slave to a system which he abhors in his heart. The antagonism is bound in time to take shape, and it begins as soon as the wage-earners can unite as a class sufficiently large and cohesive to make a stand against the capitalists. The sole power which the workers can exercise is by combination in their own interests, first for purely economic reasons, and secondly to secure by political means their proper economic status. The proletariat are without property; they can only be supreme if they assail the foundations of all existing forms and conditions of appropriation. "They have nothing of their own to secure and fortify: their mission is to destroy all previous securities for and insurances of individual property." "The theory of the communists may be summed up in the single sentence —abolition of private property." For this purpose they must obtain supreme political power. The battle for democracy, if won, means the supremacy of the proletariat; for this will mean that all the instruments of production will be in the hands of the State as the organised body of the workers. Such a State will not be the State as it has hitherto existed, but it will be a State in the sense of a sovereign power in the community, exercising its will over all its members without division or distinction of class.

The movement is not to be and cannot be confined to a particular State. The interests of all proletarians in every community are identical. The supremacy of economic democracy must mean the disappearance of present state boundaries and interstate conflicts. Socialistic democracy is thus international, not only in the sense that it is the same for all nations, but also in the sense that in the long-run there is but one society—the great society of the proletarian workers. With the establishment of such a society all the institutions which at present make up national States—their peculiar laws, ecclesiastical and educational institutions, etc.,—will forthwith disappear as being buttresses of the old régime and essentially alien to the progress of social democracy. Marx concludes his manifesto with the words, " Let the ruling classes tremble at a communistic revolution " ; and to the proletarians he says, " They have nothing to lose but their chains. They have a world to win. Workers of all countries, unite ! "

The work entitled *Capital* may be regarded as an attempt to justify, in the sphere of scientific theory, the revolutionary social democracy which he considers to be at once historically inevitable and the deliberate aim of the wage-earners as a class. It is doubtless paradoxical to maintain, on the one hand, that a social movement is in fact a necessity which, being mechanically determined, will come about whether it is desired or not, and, on the other hand, to advance scientific reasons why the end should be sought. Men cannot help themselves if they are borne on the tide of destiny, and therefore need no assistance from scientific arguments ; if the change does require, for its initiation or for its success, scientific arguments, it cannot be inevitable. A movement which is necessary may be explained by science, but it cannot be promoted by scientific reasons or retarded for the lack of them. In estimating the consistency of Marx's position, this point is important. His doctrine throughout is a blend of revolutionary propaganda, enthusiasm for downtrodden humanity, a materialistic conception of human history, and abstract economic theory. It is needless to say that the assumptions and principles governing these various aspects of his position are radically inconsistent.

It is not easy to state precisely what is the real aim of Marx's book on *Capital*, and quite impossible to condense his whole argument, which covers an immense field and is, at least in expression, highly abstract and formal. Not only his critics, but his sympathetic exponents, are at variance regarding the object of his analysis. But there can be no doubt that one essential purpose of the treatise is to provide a defence of revolutionary socialism by a scientific, or quasi-scientific, proof that, in the production of wealth in the economic sense, Labour is primary and Capital secondary, Labour is the essence and Capital a superfluity, Labour is the only necessary and enduring substance, and Capital a transitory historical accident.[1] It is this part of his doctrine which has attracted the labour world and given his theory so much influence on labour politics. No statement has become more familiar in labour circles in recent years than the proposition that "labour is the basis of all wealth." However understood or misunderstood as a Marxist doctrine, it is to Marx that it is primarily to be traced.

If we ignore the highly technical language in which Marx pursues his arguments, his main contentions may be embodied in the following propositions. From the point of view of economics, the only value which commodities possess is that which they obtain by the exchange of one commodity for another. In the last resort this "exchange-value" of commodities depends not on the quality of the commodities themselves, but on what is common to the commodities exchanged, viz. the labour involved in their production. Since in the process of exchange we take no account of the nature of the workman or the kind of work he does, the labour which is the basis of exchange is simply labour as such, labour in the abstract. Abstract labour cannot be estimated qualitatively, for it is the same throughout; it can therefore only be estimated quantitatively, in terms of its amount. This amount is calculated by reference to the time taken to produce the commodity, and by the "time" is meant the "socially necessary" time or average time required to produce a commodity under average conditions by a labourer of average ability. Since the sole value of commodities, economically speaking, thus lies in the labour "congealed" within the commodities exchanged, it is transparent that the source of the worth of commodities, i.e. the source of all "wealth," lies in labour. How, then, does a person who is not a labourer, i.e. a capitalist, become possessed of wealth?

[1] His argument is thus rather a thesis which he set out to establish than a conclusion arrived at as the result of an impartial examination of all relevant historical facts. The Manifesto above referred to preceded his work on *Capital*, and may fairly be said to govern the direction of his thought in that work. What was a practical demand in the Manifesto was taken for granted as a fundamental assumption in his theory, viz. that Capitalism must be dethroned and Labour placed in its rightful position as the supreme power in industry. This assumption he tries in his theory to transform into the language of scientific principle. This can only be done either by a *petitio principii* or by ignoring certain important elements in the economic situation. Hence the later contradiction of his theory which he himself admits and which has never been removed.

This can only be by intercepting a part of the total exchange value of the commodities and appropriating it to his own use. But how is this done ? The answer is that under the present wages system the labourer is paid for his work a wage determined solely by reference to his needs of subsistence, and not by reference to what the commodity he produces will bring when exchanged for other commodities. The difference between the price paid for the amount of labour put into the production of a commodity (including in this amount, of course, the labour "congealed" in the machinery or plant and in the "raw" material, etc.) and the amount of labour represented by the commodity for which the former commodity [1] is exchanged goes to the capitalist as his share of the undertaking. It is part of the "value," but a part not acquired by the actual labour of production. It is "surplus value," and it is obtained at the expense of, or in other words by deduction from, the true or total exchange value of the commodity produced by the labourer. "All surplus value is in substance the embodiment of unpaid working-time." It is, therefore, a form of legalised or customarily permitted spoliation.

Marx elaborates his main thesis in great detail and with the utmost use of dialectical subtlety. He supports it by a skilful if arbitrary selection of historical illustrations ; and by abundant denunciation of the abuses under which the labourers suffer from the present industrial régime and the present wages system. But the main doctrine is the point which is now being considered. It may be remarked that the term "surplus value" is not fortunate. The term would imply value not derived from the actual exchange, but in excess of the exchange, whereas there can be no value except through exchange. What it means is "surplus" with reference to what the labourer actually receives by the exchange, i.e. a value not strictly expressed in terms of mere labour. The purpose of using such a term is obviously to convey that the capitalist's share is illegitimate and unnecessary, and this is undoubtedly the sense in which the term has been adopted by those who applied the Marxian theory to practical labour problems.

The purely theoretical and highly abstract character of his argument are apparent even from the above outline,

[1] The exchange takes place generally through the medium of money—but this is irrelevant to the issue.

and have often been exposed by his critics. It is plain, for example, that there is really no such thing as "abstract human labour"; the only labour that has any significance is that of individual workers. Even if there were such a fact, it could not be calculated; and even if it could be calculated, it could not form the basis for exchange. He states that it is the identity of the quantity of labour in two commodities which explains and makes possible the exchange, but if this were really the case there would be no exchange. People do not exchange on a basis of identity, but because of the difference of the commodities exchanged. If each already has what the other possesses, there is no need for exchanging at all. It is because each lacks and wants what the other possesses that exchange is possible. In a word, Marx confuses exchange with equivalence, and hence ignores the many other factors which bring about the transaction of an exchange.

How, again, are we to estimate "socially necessary time"? And what is the time taken by "an average worker" engaged in the production of a commodity? Even if the quantity of time in this sense could be discovered, it is bound to vary from country to country, from locality to locality, and from decade to decade. Yet such variation may not in the least affect the actual quantity of commodities exchanged.

It is equally clear that exchange value is not in actual experience effected on the basis which Marx states. Other factors are involved and are of essential importance. Marx himself was constrained to admit this point when considering the relation of his theory of value to actual rate of profit on capital. On his theory, commodities always sold according to their values (i.e. exchange values), and profits vary not only with the capital (constant and variable), but with the special composition of the capital in each case. In actual fact, equal amounts of capital tend, through competition, to yield the same average rate of profit, regardless of the special "composition" of the capital (i.e. the proportion of constant to variable). His theory of value is thus admittedly "irreconcilable with the actual movement of things, irreconcilable with the actual phenomena of production." And no solution of this contradiction was supplied by Marx or by his followers.[1] Hence, either

[1] See Böhm-Bawerk: *Karl Marx and the Close of his System.*

his theory of exchange value is unsound or, if it be true, it has not yet been proved. In the face of such an alternative, it is certainly not possible to attach importance to his conception of "surplus value," or to suppose that the fortress of capitalism has been undermined by his analysis. It is remarkable that the significance of the operation of the elementary and universal economic factor of competition should have been overlooked by Marx in determining his fundamental economic conception.

In spite of this, his theory has exerted, and will doubtless continue to exert, much influence in labour circles, where consistency of reasoning is of less importance than practical tendencies and practical issues.

Marx has much to say regarding the ways in which capital has been accumulated historically, the wages system, the effect of machinery on wages, and of the factory system on the workers. But with these it is not practicable to deal in this space.

Syndicalism

Syndicalism [1] is in important respects a reaction against Marxism and the social democratic State which Marx sought to defend and establish. The reaction may perhaps best be expressed by saying that, whereas Marx sought to utilise the trade union movement to bring in the social democratic State, to sacrifice the independence of trade unions and the forces of trade unionism to the collectivist community, Syndicalism seeks at all cost to maintain not only unimpaired but in increasing strength the economic forces of trade unionism, and if possible to overthrow the State (whether the traditional or the collectivist State), in order to secure this supremacy of trade unionism in the community.

Syndicalism claims to be revolutionary in its aims, and indeed, if we regard historical society as a relatively continuous constitutional order of mankind, there can be no doubt that the overthrow of society in this sense, which is the object of Syndicalism, must mean revolution. Syndicalism will have no superior force exerted over the individual worker by a central authority, whether that

[1] The exposition and main defence of Syndicalism will be found in the volume by George Sorel, *Réflexions sur la Violence.*

authority be exercised by an oligarchy of the bourgeoisie, by Parliament, or even by the collective proletariat. Hence Syndicalism is opposed to the mere "change of masters" which collectivistic socialism of the proletariat would establish. "It cannot conceive why a revolution, even as far-reaching as that involved in the suppression of capitalism, should be attempted for a trifling and doubtful result, for the change of masters, to satisfy 'ideologues,' politicians, and speculators, who all of them adore and exploit the State."[1] This is merely substituting the power of the proletariat for the bourgeoisie which it overthrows. Syndicalism does not, in fact, believe in the exercise of force in the proper sense at all. By force it understands the imposition, by a governing minority, of the organisation of a certain social order. Instead of force Syndicalism advocates "violence," and violence consists in "acts of revolt" (not in "acts of authority"), and the object of violence is to destroy any such order and any such "acts of authority" imposed by the governing body.

Syndicalism claims that the course of history justifies the exercise of violence, and that, in fact, it is the proper outcome of the socialistic movement properly understood. Violence is the form assumed by the class war, the war of workers and employers who have nothing in common but their mutual hostility. The various forms of violence "can have value historically only as the brutal and frank expression of the class war." It is not a struggle within any particular community: it transcends the boundaries of states and nations, for the division of classes is universal and common to all States as at present constituted. The employer is an adversary wherever found, and with such an adversary it is only possible to have dealings after a war. "There is no more a social duty than there is an international duty."[2]

How, then, are the workers to be in a position to carry on the class war? and by what method is it to be maintained?

The rallying centre for the worker is his trade union (*syndicat*),[3] and the complete co-ordination of trade unions is the sole condition of maintaining effectively the battle with the employer. With State assistance or Parliamentary "constitutional" procedure the syndicalist will have

[1] Sorel, *Sur la Violence*, p. 266. [2] *Ibid.*, p. 89.

[3] *Syndicat* means primarily a *local* union.

nothing to do. These are mere subterfuges or bourgeoisie ways of allaying the strife of conciliation. The business of the syndicalist is not to allay but to keep up the struggle, until he is completely victorious against all opposition. Violence has its own justification, and requires no assistance or support from morality or any established institution. It is almost an end in itself, so far at least as trade unionism is concerned. At any rate, it can only terminate when the employing class have capitulated and the "wages system" has disappeared.

Trade unions must be federated or organised to the utmost extent possible in order to carry on the struggle successfully. This organisation is brought about in different ways in different countries. In France the unit and the vital centre of the syndicalist is the local (and mainly craft) union; the "general confederation of labour" (the C.G.T., as it is commonly called) is now the national organisation of all unions, but its operations are limited by the relative but effective autonomy maintained by the local union.[1] In America, Syndicalism is the policy of the Industrial Workers of the World (the I.W.W.), whose organisation rests on industrial unionism, not craft unionism (which is the basis of the American Federation of Labour). It is in those two countries that Syndicalism has its strongest hold, and of the two the methods of violence have been more terrible and more thoroughgoing in America than in France.

For the attainment of its goal Syndicalism has no belief in theory or argument, arbitration or conciliation. These are palliatives or anodynes, not radical cures for an evil situation which has to be rooted out. Its method is action, immediate and "direct," going straight at the destruction of the citadel of the enemy. That enemy is the capitalist régime which is buttressed by the present organisation of the State. Direct action is, therefore, necessarily political action, i.e. not action by political methods, but action which seeks to overthrow political authority in matters affecting industry and the producers of wealth. Strictly speaking, it would be better to describe direct action as anti-political action; it is action by the industrial workers for their own ends, which are not political but purely economic. It is not reformist, but revolutionary;

[1] The history of this movement will be found in Cole, *World of Labour*, chap. iii.

not evolutionary, but catastrophic. The methods of political socialism retard and endanger the ultimate triumph of the workers. Even anarchist politics are rather a hindrance than a help, just because, being "politics," anarchism is occupied with political issues and Parliamentary action of a kind, and to that extent neglects the main object of Syndicalism, which is the organisation of the class war to be carried on solely by and in the interests of the trade union (*syndicat*). Syndicalism seeks simply to subordinate all unproductive social functions to the productive (i.e. industrial workers). It is, therefore, not in the least concerned with any existing party in the State, and is not concerned to form another party within the State; in a word, it will have nothing to do with the State at all.[1] "Syndicalism recognises neither the elector of any party nor the believer in any religious or philosophical faith." It is for the same reason anti-militarist and anti-patriotic. It has no country, for "country" and "property" are inseparable. "The country of the workers is their own and their family's stomach. The country of the workers is their own class." Action, direct action, anti-political action, is the only sure method of the workers for securing their end. The end is twofold—to give due or complete power to the workers as a class, and to improve the lot of the workers as a class. It aims, therefore, at something more than reform and more than mere revolution. Reform alone would leave us with a mere democracy, revolution alone would be of no ultimate advantage to the workers.

Direct action, then, is the method. It educates the workers in class-consciousness, and it brings about the destruction of capitalism. Its supreme expression is the general strike, a simultaneous strike of all workers, nationally and internationally. It is true the general strike cannot be at once effected; it is a step to be taken "some day." But it is the supreme type and form of all strikes. Each particular or sectional strike is a step or instance of what can be done by the general strike; it helps to teach the workers the power of their class; for each strike is in a measure "general," and it trains them to effectuate the "social general strike" when this can be carried out. In every strike the great social revolution is foreshadowed and anticipated.

[1] In that sense it has a certain affinity with anarchism.

In practice direct action and the theory of the general strike take various forms, from mere passive desistance (" the strike with folded arms ") to open and widespread violence. Many syndicalists advocate *sabotage*, a general expression which covers the use of any and every weapon to combat and overthrow capitalists. Any agreements may be broken, and moral considerations are of no importance: they are bourgeois rules of procedure, and do not concern the workers who are seeking to introduce a new moral code. *Sabotage* appears in the policy of " ca' canny," making an art of a craft without regard to the time and money of the master; carrying out regulations so literally as to produce a stoppage; petty irritations; the boycott; and at its worst wholesale wrecking of machinery. *Sabotage* is, however, not encouraged by all syndicalists; for Syndicalism seeks to make the worker fit to control industry, and that means the exercise of self-control.

Syndicalists have not yet developed either a complete or an unanimously accepted conception of what is to be done, and what form society is to take after violence has successfully destroyed the master-class. They even differ amongst themselves regarding the need for such a scheme for the future.

On certain points, however, the French syndicalists seem agreed. Property is not to belong to the particular union, but to the collective body of all unions; the local union is to be the unit, not the industrial federation; decentralisation is to be preferred to centralisation. But these are French developments, and do not necessarily appeal to syndicalists in other countries. Nor is it clear what is to happen to the State and the non-labouring part of the community when Syndicalism has done its work.

Guild Socialism

Guild Socialism, like Marxism and Syndicalism, equally considers that its doctrine is the true expression of the general evolution of the previous movement of history. With the establishment of guilds on a national basis, the struggle between classes will disappear, and with that " social classes."

Guild Socialism may be regarded either as a compromise between the rival extremes of Collectivism and Syndicalism, or as a combination of the principles on which each of them lays stress. Collectivism stands for the sovereignty of the State as the whole body of consumers; Syndicalism stands for the sovereignty of the whole body of producers, regardless of the State; Guild Socialism stands for the indissoluble unity of the community as consisting of both consumers and producers. Consumers and producers form together the whole community, but each group has its separate interests in the community; and these interests can be, and in principle should be, separately organised and managed. These separate organisations can and should have separate functions assigned to them. Between them they exhaust the whole life and operations of the community. The organisation of the community in the interests of the consumers constitutes the purpose and nature of the State: that of the producers in their own interests, the purpose and function of national industrial guilds. This is, in brief, the main contention of Guild Socialists.

The State is essentially a territorial association; and all forms of State management and control—the devolution of its authority, etc., through county and municipality, etc. —rest ultimately on a territorial basis. The Guild is an industrial association or association of industrials which is not limited to or by territorial conditions, but is determined by reference to the economic fact of production alone. Each is intended to be independent and supreme in its own domain, with separate legislative and executive powers, the one exercised through political and Parliamentary procedure, the other through the Guild Congress or Federation of Guilds. When the true democratic State arrives (and without this Guild Socialism cannot exist) the two will be on a level of complete equality of powers and functions relatively to one another: for then production will be organised by "democratic associations of all workers in each industry linked up in a body representing all industries," and the consumers will be organised into a democratic State operating through national and local governments. In such an ideal situation the State would own the means of production, and the Guild could control the work of production. The two would be in equal partnership for the well-being of the whole community.

The Guild, then, is an industrial organisation whose function is to control production and "the producer's side of exchange" in the interests of the producers, and has to manage all matters concerned in the life and work of the producers as such. It has nothing to do with political questions as political. On the other hand, the State is to concern itself with the needs and desires common to individuals as "consumers or users" of the product of industry. It must not interfere with or control production or producers.

Guild and State must recognise each other and each other's functions. It is not enough that trade unions should be accepted as the channel for the expression of the views and demands of the workers. They must as an organised body have complete control over their work and lives as producers, and must be in a position to recognise the State on the same terms and in the same sense as the State recognises the Guild. Trade Unionism as it is to-day must advance to the higher stage of the greater unionism which the Guild stands for. Craft must no longer be separated from craft nor industry from industry. Industrial Unionism in the form of the Guild means the linking-up of all industries in one association of labour, and must exercise self-government in its own sphere as complete as the self-government exercised by the State in its sphere. In such a situation alone can the two bargain on equal terms.

But it is clear that there cannot be two self-governing authorities in the community absolutely sundered and never co-operating. Mutual recognition implies that they may differ: and the unity of the community's life implies that they have interests in common and require an instrument of mediation. The Guild must favour the right to withdraw labour and lower production; the State will have to check unjust demands and profiteering producers. The mediating agency between the two is supplied by the joint Congress of Guilds and the State. It will be called in where matters affecting both are concerned, and where the whole interests of the community are involved. No doubt in the last resort the fact that the two organisations are absolutely equal may give rise to a deadlock at the Joint Congress. But "it is almost impossible to imagine such a deadlock arising in an equalitarian society." The normal situation will be a balance of power between the industrial organisation and the political organisation, each possessing in its one domain complete legislative and executive authority, and both being in that sense equal.

But there is to be another link between the Guild and the State besides the Joint Congress. The individual, the unit of the community, would have vested rights in both the industrial and the political organisation, and in his fundamental capacity of a member of the community would have duties in both spheres. No individual is wholly and solely in the producer Guild or in the consumer State: everyone is in both. Every individual need not be a member of a Guild, "but he will be a member of some form of a productive association in the widest sense of the word," i.e. an association based on some form of "social service."[1] Thus the individual is a connecting-bond between the two equal complementary organisations, and the division of social authority between these organisations "preserves the integrity of the individual." One would rather say "the division of social authority" *demands* the integrity of the individual in order to make such a division workable. Moreover, the only security for the freedom of the individual is the balance of power between those two equal authorities, which with extreme optimism are supposed not to arrive at a deadlock.

The Guild, as the organisation of an industry in such a way as to give to the producers complete control of all that concerns their life and work as producers, is held to be the natural and necessary development of the trade union movement. Trade Unionism cannot be a mere appanage of industrial activity, a mere instrument for the carrying out of certain temporary ends, however important, such as increasing wages and improving working conditions. It cannot exist merely on sufferance, and have its powers limited by the State, whether the socialistic State or any other. It must advance to its ultimate goal, which is to secure direct and entire control of the industry from top to bottom, on a national scale and in the workshop. It cannot stop short of the possession of legislative and executive authority in the sphere of industry, free from State interference and equal in power with the State. That must be the direction and the aim of trade unionism in the future. National Guildism is to be the historical issue of the trade

[1] See Cole, *Self-government in Industry*, p. 92. This distinction is neither clear nor convincing.

union movement, and thus Guildism will supersede collectivistic socialism and quasi-anarchic Syndicalism. Guildism is the only real democratisation of industry and the State.

It is the modern representative of the mediæval guildism, with this great difference, that, whereas mediæval guilds were associations, generally localised associations, of masters and men in a particular craft, Guildism is an organisation of workers or producers alone, the power of the master or capitalist being eliminated as an industrial superfluity. In modern guildism, therefore, the "slavery" of the present "wages system" will disappear, and, with that, poverty, which is but the symptom, not the cause, of the present slavery of the wage-earning producer class.

Guilds will be many in number, but they will be unified in the National Congress of Guilds, with which supreme legislative and executive authority in industry will lie. Its authority will be exercised through decentralisation, not overcentralisation.

At present the Guild theory is a hope and an aspiration. It has not yet secured the assent and approval of trade unionists, but trade unionism is to be educated into gradual acceptance of the Guild principle.

Methods have been sketched by which the members of the Guild are to be elected so as to secure at once the freedom of each Guild from the workshops upwards, and the complete democratic government of the industry through the Guild Congress.

There is at first sight an appearance of artificiality in the division of organisation between the Guild and the State. It seems, indeed, primâ facie impracticable to have two such equal authorities within the one life of the community. But such a separation of powers is by no means without historical parallel. We may not inaptly compare the Guild proposal with the view which has been often advanced in Western Europe regarding the relations which should subsist between Church and State. It has been maintained that the community in its religious aspect can and should form the single autonomous organisation of the Church, and the community in its secular aspect should form the single and equally autonomous organisation of the State, the connecting-link between the two being the individuals who are members of both organisations. These two organisations are considered to have equally legislative and executive authority within their separate and independent spheres; and both are held to subserve fundamental and necessary interests of the community. Guildism is an application of this principle within the domain of the secular life of the community. The State and the Guild stand to one another in the secular life of society as the Church and State do when they divide between them the religious and secular interests of the community. This parallel, however, does not remove the objection to the Guild theory, but tends to bring out the difficulties which lie in the principle of divided authority. The division of powers between Church and State has been the cause of endless conflict in Western Europe, and that conflict is not yet allayed. If it has not made for peace where the interests are so divergent as those of religion and secular life, there is still less chance of peace in a community when we try to make a sharp division within a community in a sphere where the interests concerned are inseparably connected. If the division between Church and State seems natural, that between producers and consumers is wholly arbitrary. Production is but a stage in a single process which is continuous with that of consumption, and cannot be cut off from it. Moreover, production in one industry is consumption in another, as in the relation of iron ore to the steel industry. Consumption cannot be limited to the case of food-supplies.

Again, if producers are to form a separate self-governing body, why should not other classes in the community equally do so? In a democratically constituted community individuals may be distinguished as at once making laws and obeying laws. Are these aspects to form the basis of separate self-governing organisations? Where are we to stop in the process of separating fundamental interests in the community? Moreover, it is impossible to separate the State and industry into self-governing organisations without creating endless sources of conflict. The authority of the State in a community is comprehensive, and concerns itself with the formulation and maintenance of all the rights of all the individuals. It is the supreme arbiter as between persons, single and corporate. The individual will come to regard the final authority in his life to be either the State or the industrial organisation. One will be subordinated to the other.

They cannot be equal when the liberty of the individual life is at stake. So far from the balance of power between Guild and State securing the liberty of the individual, it will tend to imperil his liberty at every step. And who will determine the individual's liberty in Guild or State? Not the individual himself, but the organisation. In a word, the only guarantee that the Guild and the State under such a scheme would promote liberty would be if the individual's liberty were secured independently of both. Between the two both liberty and individuality could be crushed beyond recognition.

There is, again, no final authority or power vested in the Joint Congress to have its decisions either ratified or carried out. A Joint Congress has by hypothesis no power of legislation and no executive authority. It is a mere addendum to the Guild scheme, although the exercise of its functions might in the last resort be the sole guarantee for the liberty of individuals in both organisations.

These are but a few of the objections and difficulties in the way of this hypothetical reconstruction of the life of the community.

CHAPTER XXXIII

THE POSITION BEFORE THE WAR, 1913–14

THE year 1914 opened darkly. The official report of the preceding year said: "The year 1913 was remarkable for the number of disputes which occurred during its course, far exceeding the number recorded in any previous year. Practically all the main groups of trade were affected by the increase in the number of the disputes, notably the building, metal, engineering and shipbuilding, and textile trades"; and yet no single dispute involving more than 50,000 workpeople occurred in 1913. A leading journal stated:

"A welter of movements is going on within the world of labour, and the only thing certain about them is that they will find some outlet. Perhaps the most salient feature of this turmoil at the moment is the general spirit of revolt, not only against employers of all kinds, but also against leaders and majorities, and Parliamentary or any kind of constitutional and orderly action. . . . There is sporadic action without any regular organisation or parade of principles."

This summing up was, I think, fairly accurate. It was at least reflected in the work of my Department, at the close of 1913 and during the first six months of 1914. Day after day was taken up in travelling to all parts of Great Britain by my officers and myself to answer the numerous calls to preside at conferences, with a view to settlement of sporadic disputes. The coal-porters of London, the furniture-makers of High Wycombe, the London building trade, and the lace-makers of Ayrshire, were only instances of obstinate local disputes, taking up much time and care.

In November 1913, at Bristol, I had endeavoured to

point out to members of the recently formed Cavendish Club some of the points in the position of affairs, which at the time occurred to me as being correct. I remarked :

" There is a spirit abroad of unrest, of movement, a spirit and a desire of improvement, of alteration. We are in, perhaps, as quick an age of transition as there has been for many generations past. The causes of this are manifold. I am only going to indicate a few. One is that the schoolmaster has been abroad in the land, and that, as education improves, the more a man wishes to get to a better and higher position. Another is that the competition in life increases, and must increase, year by year. . . . Again, every man, whatever the actual cost of his livelihood may be, if he has arrived at a particular standard of life, not only desires to improve it, but also would struggle hard before he would give it up. When you come to certain standards of wages and livelihood, and find that particular things that you particularly use rise greatly in price, it affects the amenities of life and the margin of life to such an extent that there is disenchantment and a desire to keep to the standard which may have been achieved. Then there is the spirit of movement throughout the world. We quicken day by day means of transport. You have your tramways, railways, motors, taxis, and fast ships ; and more and more a movement from place to place, and a movement that is taken advantage of by the people at large in increasing millions year by year. In addition to that you have in this country for some years past what I may call political equality. One man's vote is as good as another—sometimes better. If a man has got educated up to the view of considering himself politically equal to another man, he is far more anxious to achieve a greater amount of economic equality ; a desire to reach that economic equality must necessarily exist in his mind. Upon platform after platform there has been preached the doctrine of Imperial possessions and their importance, and men to whom these Imperial possessions have been given are not inclined to think they are nobody in the world. There is also a vast amount of going backwards and forwards to dominions beyond the seas. Men come back from Canada and Australia, and come back imbued with ideas they find there ; and leaven the local feeling in particular localities in this country. That, shortly, sums up some of the reasons why there is unrest, unrest that nobody can be surprised at, and which is bound to continue. Are men to remain in a backwater and do nothing, or to be cast out of the stream and remain as flotsam and jetsam on the bank ? If this unrest of every kind has to be taken advantage of and properly directed, every man ought to put his hand to the helm and do what he can for the advantage of his country, the advantage of his fellow-countrymen, and see that the most economical force, the greatest advantage, should be got out of the movements which are existing.

"The alternative of service by men like yourselves is an increased separation of the so-called classes, and increased want of understanding between man and man. Some men read newspapers that you never see, while you read newspapers that they never see. By newspapers, by magazines, by books, the workpeople are self-educating themselves far more than they ever did a score of years ago. There is the difference of the influence of class upon one side, and upon the other a feeling that education has been different, that there is no sympathy between person and person, that you are a set apart from them, and not of the same flesh and blood as they are ; that you are people whom they would like to overthrow, and of whom they are suspicious, while you stand aside not knowing of them, and enter not into their feelings. This view is fostered by theories of social changes largely imported from the Continent, but with the difference that the Englishman, while the Continent will often talk without translating the talk into actual and practical tests, is apt to prefer action to theory. At the present time there is not only an advisability, but almost a necessity, of campaigning for the better understanding of class and class. I have said we are in a period of transition ; it is a period in which the world is going very fast. That the present unrest will cease I do not believe for one moment ; it will increase, and probably increase with greater force.

"Within a comparatively short time there may be movements in this country coming to a head of which recent events have been a small foreshadowing. Therefore it is no time for you to stand by and do little or nothing, and take no interest in these concerns. I do not believe that any movements of the kind I have indicated can be stopped by force. What I do think is that they can be understood, and any harm to the community mitigated by a better understanding between person and person; an understanding which young men and those who are coming forward as young men may be able to do much to assist. I do not wish to put forward any gloomy forebodings. Far from it. The world and its improvement are going on, and it is desirable that every man in the world should want to improve himself. The more education progresses, the more other factors progress, the more man desires improvement, and he will do his best to get it. But it would be well if he could do his best in the way that is of the greatest advantage to the community at large and himself in particular. As long years ago Sir Philip Sydney said: 'A man is on duty here, but knows not how or why and does not need to know. He knows not for what hire, and he must not ask. Somehow or other, though he does not know what goodness is, he must try to be good. Somehow or other, though he cannot tell what will do it, he must try to give happiness to others.' "

From the description which I have endeavoured to give of actual strikes and lockouts, their course, and the issue arrived at, it may be gathered that the two principal causes of the disputes for the twelve years before the beginning of the War were either economic demands for better wages and conditions, or arose from the pressing forward of organisation too fast in the idea that organisation, however obtained, was necessary to obtain economic improvements. The workpeople wanted to "addle more brass," and no amount of philosophic discussion or philanthropic sectional improvement could make up for the desire for more secure and better pay. The cost of living had either rapidly fluctuated or had gone up for prolonged periods at a time of increasing prosperity without quick resilience by the employing classes to the movements and the ensuing demands. In many cases there was complete ignorance that any change should advisably be made; in other cases there was the contention that time for recovery from lean years was necessary; in some cases an objection to pay out money which would otherwise come to the employers, or to give advances which other people had not given or might not be willing to give; while in undertakings like the railways the argument of statutory restrictions and the impracticability of raising rates against competing lines and shipping, the merchants and manufacturers, or the public, was adduced. In addition, there was general lassitude upon the subject. In answer to this lack of quick resilience, the workpeople saw that organisation increased their power, and that unorganised trades could not hope to fight against employers who, with smaller numbers and larger resources, could combine more speedily. In their eagerness for organisation many trades, especially the miners, struck on the non-union question, which employers regarded as a question outside their scope of action and as one to be decided between workpeople; or only within their scope of action if it was claimed that they were to be compelled to bring non-unionists into a union or not to be allowed to employ any suitable man offering himself for employment. In their eagerness, too, on the same principle, union fought union, while the employers had to suffer passively, in some instances at very heavy cost.

These were the chief causes of strikes and lockouts. On the other hand, there was immense work being done by joint organisation of employers and employed; conciliation boards increased continuously; the conciliation work of the Board of Trade increased, particularly under Presidents who, like Mr. Buxton, aimed, as he himself said in November 1913, at keeping any question of conciliation out of politics, and as far as possible putting it upon a basis where there should not be Government interference from a political point of view, and where no suspicion of politics should attach to the Industrial Department.

The number of disputes avoided or composed by these agencies was very large, and in comparison with the number of mistakes the number of successes was considerable. Trade after trade was gradually being organised on bases of good relationship, so far as the leaders on both sides were concerned. A network of associated employers and of federated trade unions was spreading over the country.

So far as the Government was concerned, Ministers were immersed in constitutional struggles. They had little or no labour policy. The Members of the Government were strangely outside and ignorant of the labour movements in the country; or of any personal knowledge of the principal labour leaders. The interference of politicians in labour disputes, much as many of them hankered to come in, was deleterious, and could be exposed far more strongly than I have mildly indicated. Their best Bill, the Trade Boards Act, was forced on them by a few enthusiasts and by Sir Charles Dilke. Their Labour Exchange Act I have already mentioned. The Trade Disputes Act was carried on grounds of political expediency and contrary to the express statements on certain clauses which the Attorney-General had made in the House of Commons. The Coal Mines Regulation (Eight Hours Act) of 1908 would never have got through if the Parliamentary representatives of labour in the House of Commons had been a negligible quantity. The Old Age Pensions Act and the Children's Act were long overdue. The National Insurance Act of 1911 was almost entirely due to the work of Sir Hubert Llewellyn Smith. The Labour Party in the House of Commons, from 1906 onwards, was a force to be reckoned with, but they were not constructive. Their chief influence consisted in the desire which the Government had to bring in Bills which they would not oppose, or to carry on administration without being subjected to too many unpleasant questions.

It might have been supposed that even under these conditions the proofs of gradual evolution would have appealed to the country at large and prevented useless disputes. There was a strong yearning for peace. The very praise given by the newspapers, in reflection of general opinion, to those striving to make peace and establish bases of future peace, indicated support of the principle of peace. The country was sick of strikes, but though in some senses it was tired, there were beneath the surface bubbles of excitement continuously forming and breaking out.

The labour leaders who had got into Parliament lost touch with the rank and file in their own unions. Some of them were surprised at the outbreaks in the ports of the country. The fervour of organisation led to a desire to make use of the organisation. The collection of funds seemed to produce a purse whose contents should be distributed. The more leisure an Eight-hour Act gave, the more education continuously poured out young men eager for advancement, so much the more time there was for meetings and for thought, the more recognition there was for the conscious or subconscious knowledge that the paths of advancement were narrow, devious, and blocked. Sporadic disputes and "irritation" strikes were the order of the day. There was effervescence, and behind the effervescence there were movements growing, with demands for shorter working-hours, more pay and more power, both over industry and in the government of the country. The young men were ready to move, and did move sporadically. They were also ready to move in support of any large movement, which, if they had realised it, their sporadic movements often endangered and hurt. They did not realise what their leaders knew or by experience slowly learned, that labour marches on its stomach, that large masses of men, particularly in unskilled trades, cannot support long stoppages without privation, unless preparations have been made long before and with adequate foresight.

Although the numerous small strikes seemed to be evidence that men were ready to cease work, workpeople in the more general sense seemed to have a growing feeling of that terrible danger to all workpeople, unemployment and its results. Memory recalled the slumps in the building trades, slackness of work at the docks, stagnation in shipbuilding and engineering. There may have been increase in savings, but the margin for saving in many trades was not sufficient to induce thrift. The atmosphere of thrift was not sufficiently widespread. The amounts, where saving had been effected, were not sufficient to imply security. There was apparent a great growth of the policy of "ca' canny," and in some trades a dead set against piecework, fostered by the belief that the less work done the more employment there would be to go round, or by remembrance of piecework rates being cut if a man earned by his energy much more than his fellows. The margin of piecework rates over time rates was in many cases too small. Where the minimum rate was high and the margin too small, the tendency was to be satisfied with the minimum rate rather than to work much harder, possibly at the cost of some physical efficiency, at the current piecework rates. In shops where the machinery or part of the machinery was out of date, men grumbled at rates which did not give them as much as other men with better machinery could speedily earn. Although there were many employers with vision, who consistently examined their stocks of machinery and were continuously out for improvements and who thought of the welfare of their men in and out of the shops, and strove for good ventilation, cleanliness, amenities, and recreation, it cannot be said that the majority did more than comply with the bare necessities required by Factory Acts, or interested themselves much in extra amenities, the housing of their workpeople, or their social aims of all kinds. There were few who thought of business training of their foremen on lines that would interest them in the business, and make them in their turn better leaders or teachers of the men under them. The tendency to widen the gulf of classes was rapidly making headway on both sides. There was not enough human relationship between leaders of industry and the rank and file, particularly the young men.

Coupled with zest for sport and amusement, and objection to any interference with time available for it, there was a strong and by no means unhealthy objection to overtime, though the objection was sometimes carried to extreme lengths. Where this occurred, there was irritation for the employer who, hampered by "ca' canny," could not get his proper or estimated production, could not fulfil his contracts, and found that his men were more and more unwilling, particularly if they belonged to unions with rigid rules, to give him assistance by overtime, even in instances of great stress.

The difficulties were not due to one side only. Many employers were too fond of hand-to-mouth expedients, without careful thought of planning or of preparation, so that workers might have suitable conditions under which the best that was in them might have a chance of being brought out. If the heads of the firm followed such lines, the example surely spread through the whole firm, through the managers and the foremen, down to the workpeople. Friction, delay, muddle, only lead to waste, bad feeling, and slackness.

I have already noticed the progress of self-education, by books, magazines, and newspapers. Some of them would speak of the power of the Labour Party in Parliament, and by the Trade Union Act of 1913, following upon the Osborne judgment, opportunity was given for subscriptions to be collected to finance elections and support Labour Members of Parliament, in addition to the assistance which payment of Members by the State might afford. The sense of greater strength came, too, by the vast increase of membership in the unions specially dealing with the semi-skilled and unskilled workpeople, a result due partly to systematic organisation, partly to the requirement of the National Insurance Act that wage-earners should belong to an approved society. The Workers' Union alone had 111 branches in 1910, 567 in 1913, 750 in 1916, and 2,000 in 1920. At the same time small unions tended to unite, or to be affiliated to larger associations. Those larger associations became more and more strict in insisting that all persons working in their industry should be members of trade unions. In the most powerful mining centres the federations aimed at the inclusion of all workpeople in the Miners' Federation, and the Miners' Federation only. The growing strength of the miners was proved by their power of enforcement of the Eight Hours Act in 1908, the improvements of the Mines Regulation Act in 1911, and the passing of the Coal Mines (Minimum Wage) Act in 1912. Their intention of considering a triple alliance, miners, railwaymen, and transport workers, was strongly expressed by Mr. Smillie in December 1913. The young men were forcing the hands of the older leaders all over the country, especially in South Wales. They found leaders to their taste in the stern autocracy of Mr. Smillie and the advanced views of some of his chief lieutenants. Their strength was to be exhibited still further at a later date. The claims of Guild Socialism, Syndicalism, and Nationalisation were murmured from time to time, but did not seem within practical possibility so much as since the War, though nationalisation had for some years been regularly passed as a "hardy annual" at Trade Union Congresses. Nevertheless the feeling and the preaching against capitalism grew daily, watered by plenty of literature and speeches to which no adequate answer was given. Capital offered in some disputes a passive resistance, but it made little sign of defence by argument or proof. It was not explained how the vast wealth of Great Britain had been built up by individual effort and energy; nor why the system seemed to be failing in power to satisfy the needs of the time or to obtain better distribution of wealth. It seems to me that there was very great materialism, with few ideals of service or of anything else beyond materialism.

CHAPTER XXXIV

THE BEGINNING OF THE WAR

THE comparative placidity of the summer of 1914 seemed in a measure to be deceptive. It was known that the three years' agreement made in 1912 between the Engineering Employers' Association and the Amalgamated Society of Engineers was drawing to a close, and that claims were going to be advanced for shorter hours, increased wages, and improved conditions which might lead to great differences. Even if federated firms were prepared to make concessions, particularly with regard to hours, non-federated firms would certainly not take the same view with any unanimity. The mining industry was also preparing claims for the autumn. The transport industry had been steadily organising. Those unions, which were principally recruited from semi-skilled and unskilled workpeople, were adding daily to the numbers of their members. The cost of living appeared to be on the upward trend. There was a spirit of unrest which vaguely expressed itself in an oft-heard phrase, "Wait till the autumn." I had decided to try for a long holiday, so as to get some rest before the strenuous time which promised to be forthcoming in the near future. At this juncture a curious dispute occurred.

It must have been a cynical pleasure to those who took part in that meeting at Berlin on July 4, where it is said the decision was taken to give Austria a free hand in Serbia and to support her at all costs, when they heard that on that same day a deputation to the Chief Superintendent of the Ordnance Factories for the reinstatement of a dismissed workman at Woolwich Arsenal had failed, that tools had been thrown down, and that the whole Arsenal, two days later, was practically at a standstill. Prince Metternich had several times expressed a desire to hear opinions of labour difficulties at the house of a mutual friend, saying that he had reported to his Government my views that the disputes so rife in 1911 and 1912 were economic in character, were not anti-dynastic or anti-Governmental, and that the nation at heart was as sound as any nation had ever been. Baron Marschall von Bieberstein, the succeeding Ambassador, during his short term had tried to meet me twice without success, but one of his staff was deeply interested in the dockers' disputes. The next Ambassador, Prince Lichnowsky, did not mention the subject. This sudden outburst in Woolwich Arsenal itself, a Government Department, must have pleased those in Germany who may not have liked Ambassadors' reports contrary to their wishes, and to the theory that unity between Capital and Labour was impracticable in Great Britain.

The Prime Minister sent for me about the dispute, and asked my view, agreeing to the suggestion of a court of inquiry of two employers, two leading labour representatives (Mr. Barnes and Mr. Clynes), with myself as chairman. A few days later, upon the appointment of the court, the men returned to work, which they had left without notice, and without representing their grievances through the proper channels. The strike was an attempt at direct action which had no sanction from the authorities of the trade union, but it presented some difficult features which it is unnecessary to give in detail. Suffice it to say a unanimous report, completed after several days of inquiry, was settled on Wednesday, July 29, but was not then published. That night I went to the country for a short rest, but by the last train a messenger arrived, with a letter saying the situation was grave, and I should return by the first train in the morning. On Tuesday, August 4, we were at war, and the situation had at once changed.

At the beginning of August there were 100 disputes known to the Department to be in existence. At the end of the month there were twenty. The advantage of the principle of conciliation, and in a lesser degree of arbitration, in trade disputes, the gradual work and the example of results during so many years, were in fact wonderfully vindicated at this time of crisis. Throughout the country, when war began, all the great organisations of employers and workpeople sank their domestic quarrels, and united in a concerted effort for the welfare and preservation of the nation.

The London building trade dispute and the threat of a national lockout closed by an agreement on certain points, and the reference of all remaining points to the National Conciliation Board for decision, with the suggestion made at the joint conference that all other disputes in the building trade ought to be settled as soon as possible; the Marine Engineers' Union told their men to proclaim a truce by resuming work; the electrical industry in London on both sides followed suit; the shipbuilding and engineering trades dropped their demands for an eight-hour day; the ship-repairers laid aside disputes, and stated that their whole resources would be placed at the country's disposal; the engineers and boilermakers withdrew their claims on the Great Western Railway; the dock labourers and the General Labourers' Union took the same course with their employers.

The Mersey Dock and Harbour dispute in Liverpool was settled after long conferences arranged by the Department. In the coal trade the trimmers and tippers intimated that they would work by the day or night; the Scottish coalowners withdrew their demand for a reduction of wages; in South Wales the Coal Conciliation Board had unanimously agreed that one hour extra work per day was to be given in all coal-pits producing coal for the navy, and a joint committee was established for the settlement of other disputes.

Besides the general conciliation work by the great organisations of the country and by the Department, and in addition to numerous arbitrations I was asked to take, with rapid journeys to Scotland and the North, an interesting feature of the first two months lay in the number of employers and of union leaders who called informally. Within a few hours of each other, and without each other's knowledge, representatives of both sides would come to request advice or intervention in disputes where a deadlock or a difficult tangle had arisen.

Disputes melted away as fast as the hours of the day, and often of the night, gave time for the hearing of difficulties. Efforts in all parts of the country were endorsed by the resolution of the Chief Committees of representatives of Labour "that an immediate effort be made to terminate all existing trade disputes, whether strikes or lockouts, and whenever new points of difficulty arise during the War period, a serious attempt should be made by all concerned to reach an amicable settlement, before resorting to a strike or lockout."

It seemed that the whole country rose to the height of the King's message of September 9:

> "The calamitous conflict is not of my seeking. My voice has been cast throughout on the side of peace. My Ministers earnestly strove to allay the causes of strife and to appease differences with which my Empire was not concerned. Had I stood aside when, in defiance of pledges to which my kingdom was a party, the soil of Belgium was violated and her cities laid desolate, when the very life of the French nation was threatened with extinction, I should have sacrificed my honour and given to destruction the liberties of my Empire and of mankind. I rejoice that every part of the Empire is with me in this decision."

Yet, with the month of October, the results of the first half-million and then of the second half-million men being withdrawn from industries, the knowledge slowly beaten into some minds that the War would not end without a long and bitter struggle, the hope in other minds that it would soon end and business must be preserved, losses in one business, profits in another, competition for skilled men, efforts to fulfil contracts at any price, all the many dislocations of a sudden and great war, began to have effect. The cry, "Business as usual," which might have been useful in earlier days in preventing panic or calming men, was now out of date. There could not be business as usual, or the satisfaction of ordinary demands. Shortage of labour began to be acute. Contractors were not fulfilling their contracts or producing supplies in anything like the quantity laid down in their contracts, or desired by the continuously increasing clamour of the War Departments for more and yet more material. The requirements of the army and navy were clashing. In their anxiety for labour, employers were bidding against each other to entice skilled labour to their works, or bribing men to remain in their employment. Labour was getting more and more unsettled, and at the same time was not abating the restrictions which kept certain men to certain work, and prevented change of occupation, the entry of new workmen, or the abrogation of a thousand and one rules developed by hostility or in defence during the years of peace.

Early in October the leather trades were in a state of turmoil. There had been depression in the trade after a period of prosperity during the Boer War; new price-lists had been made in 1907; there were differences in systems and rates between Birmingham and Walsall; the unions of these cities were not united, nor were the employers, and there was alleged competition from London. New designs, orders, and requirements poured in for every class of leather equipment. The lines between heavy, light, and fancy leather goods were not clearly defined; the conditions were becoming obsolete; the whole industry required adjustment. As the majority of the work was piecework, adjustment meant revision of an immense list of piecework prices as well as of general conditions, time rates, rates for women who were rapidly diluting men's work, and, above all, uniformity between competing firms. There were long conferences with me over the difficulties, one of them lasting for twelve hours; but it says much for the good feeling on both sides that ultimately an adjustment was made, which with minor changes lasted throughout the War. It may have been a blessing in disguise that this important industry reconstituted itself so early in the War, though at the time the disputes were naturally a source of anxiety.

If adjustments in the leather trade involved the question of smoothing the methods of supply, another problem was presented by the woollen trade—namely, shortage of supply for the requirements of the army. In the middle of November Lord Kitchener asked me to see him, and told me he had not enough khaki and other army cloth to clothe the troops; he wanted more, and a great deal more. Could the production be increased by friendly arrangement? Could cotton operatives be transferred? Would I deal with this, and then he might want to see me on huts.

Cotton had been hit by the War, as were some few other trades. The question of unemployment had arisen, and earnest consideration had had to be given to the form of Treasury grants, or, in other words, "doles," to such industries. An allowance had been given to the cotton industry. In spite of this there was threatened trouble there, owing to difficulties of employment. The previous denunciation of the Brooklands Agreement had left the cotton trade without any authorised method of dealing with disputes; a point on which I was already conversing with their leaders.

I told Lord Kitchener I would inquire at once, and went to Manchester, Huddersfield, Blackburn, and Glasgow. This question of the use of wool involved in principle several cruxes of the War. There was the supply of cloth for the army and navy to which a proportion of the work was devoted. There was the supply of recruits for the army, denuding an important section of labour. There was also the question of home supply of cloth, and how far it should be diminished; of export supply, by which the nation paid its commitments or obtained profits from which taxes could be obtained; and of maintenance of supply in view of the growing shortage of labour. The facts came out in a simple manner. Manufacturers had no idea that sufficient khaki was not being produced, and at once agreed to turn their mills on to increased war production, but said they could not maintain supplies unless temporarily recruitment of great and little "piecers," the latter mostly young men, was restricted. Piecers required education. Cotton piecers were useless for wool. When more piecers were educated, the young men could be released.

Lord Kitchener ordered the report to be carried out immediately, but by that lack of co-ordination which seems to beset Government Departments, the order, never shown to me, stopped recruitment of piecers in textile trades generally, not in wool only, and hindered the cotton trade from getting rid of their piecers, particularly in Oldham, just as young cotton piecers were being actively recruited in Lancashire. It took some time to get a change in the order, but its effect did not do much harm, because it roused the cotton trade in South Lancashire to quick action against the danger of sudden disturbance. *The Manchester Courier* of December 13, although it took no account of the hours of negotiation required to lead up to the result, summed up the position correctly when it stated:

"A new agreement, to take the place of the former

Brooklands Agreement, was entered into yesterday in Manchester by the Master Cotton Spinners and the Lancashire Cardroom Amalgamation.

"The meeting at which the agreement was reached only lasted twenty-five minutes. The text of the agreement is:

> "NOTICES TO CEASE WORK SHALL NOT BE POSTED UP IN A MILL UNTIL THE MATTER IN DISPUTE HAS BEEN CONSIDERED BY THE JOINT COMMITTEES OF THE TWO ORGANISATIONS, BOTH LOCALLY AND CENTRALLY.

"It is doubtful if ever before an agreement between masters and men in the cotton world has been reached in so short a space of time. Both sides, however, felt the need for some such arrangement to take the place of the old Brooklands Agreement, and accepted the suggestion of Sir George Askwith that representatives of both sides should meet in conference, and, if possible, come to some arrangement that would obviate hasty strikes, with all their concurrent difficulties and hardships. The new agreement is on exactly the same principle as that on which the Brooklands measure was drafted, and its simplicity is not its least satisfactory feature."

As the autumn progressed, hints of difficulty in various trades began to show themselves, particularly due to the growing shortage of labour. Rates for seamen on ships taken by the Admiralty, shortage of dockers at Glasgow, hutting disputes (on which I again saw Lord Kitchener) in the West of England, packing-case makers and shell-box makers in London, glass-makers in the North, seamen at Liverpool, printers, several air-craft disputes; all claimed attention, but were more or less solved by conferences and conciliation. In the great armament departments, lack of labour and shortage of production went hand in hand. Additions were made, but in no commensurate proportion to the ever-growing demands and the new contracts; skilled men were required everywhere, either to work or to teach. Many of the best men had gone. Works were disorganised by the loss of "pivotal men." At the same time the competing claims of the Admiralty and War Departments bewildered employers. The country had to meet the requirements of the services in regard to recruits; the requirements of our own country and in part of our allies in regard to munitions of war of every kind; and the maintenance of trade and commerce in order to pay for food, provide finances for ourselves and other countries, keep in work the vast mass of people, and secure credit. It was a heavy burden, of which the adjustment was not assisted by the astounding lack of co-ordination between Departments, one of the chief evils, even in times of peace, of our system of government. As a Minister remarked to me in the middle of the War, "I would give a million pounds (if I had it) to invent a good system of co-ordination between Departments."

As early as October, in the shipbuilding and engineering trades conferences between employers and unions on the subject of production, restrictions, and shortage of men had commenced, but they made little progress. In December conferences between shipbuilders and the big unions in the shipping trade for amended rules broke down. There was a complete deadlock, and something like despair in the minds of those who had been most energetic in attempting to effect an agreement.

In my opinion, if an opinion may be hazarded, the root difficulty was that very few individuals either in this country or in Europe expected the War to last; and it was some time before the result of the first battle of Ypres and its frustration of a quick decision, at least on land, came home to the minds of the people. As one of my greatest friends, the late Dr. Page, the American Ambassador, aptly said, "Who would have dreamed that all Europe could be divided into two camps and fix themselves on each side of a ditch from the British Channel to the Adriatic and beyond?"

It is no part of my purpose to enter into any general disquisition on the War or any general essay upon the many points arising in the relations of Capital and Labour, and the supply of munitions, goods, or workpeople. Remarks must be confined to the comparatively limited sphere coming within an individual's power of observation and special work—a minor scene in the enactment of a great drama. The line of thought directing my mind was that, whether the War was long or short, it was my business to compose differences, so far as practicable, between employers and employed.

It was quite evident to any observer that the armament firms were hampered by shortage of labour and the restrictions preventing them from the best use of the labour still remaining to them; they desired to acquire skilled labour from engineering or analogous firms; the latter firms did not wish to hazard their future by parting with skilled workmen, and thought that some of the work should be given to them; neither contractors nor sub-contractors could fulfil contracts or sub-contracts without more skilled labour; the army did not like any hindrance to recruiting, and spoke of co-operation of employers and trade unions "to secure the employment of men ineligible, through age or other reasons, to become recruits, and of women in place of eligible men who may be taken as recruits"; the navy took and kept skilled labour, particularly for such munitions as torpedoes, and was obliged to have a mobile and large reserve ready to repair damaged ships after any brush with the enemy, much more after any serious action; the trade unions at the same time were not prepared to give up the position obtained after years of struggle, without being absolutely satisfied that adequate reason was shown. Men did not realise the coming long periods of difficulty; the necessity was not explained to them, or so far as it was explained to leaders, those leaders were pledged not to divulge the position, lest it should help the enemy. The rank and file did not and could not know, except by instinct. The whole fabric of effort rested upon spirit and faith, and with the reaction from first efforts, the winter months, the lack of information, the lack of imagination or understanding of the necessity of a long pull and a pull all together, and many disintegrating influences, faith began to fail, wrangles began, and, once beginning, gained force.

The growing lack of faith seemed to me to arise from two main causes: (1) The lack of leadership and co-ordination between Departments, and (2) the lack of agreement between employers and employed as to the necessity of avoiding disputes which hampered that production without which our men and women could not achieve success. The point within my province was principally the second, a very wide field; but while considering with the parties the question of getting rid of the deadlock over amendment of rules which had arisen in December in the shipbuilding trades, urgent request was made by the Board of Trade that negotiations should be extended with a view to improve production of munitions of war generally, and the release of men for skilled work by change in the more restrictive rules of trade unions. The Board of Trade were practically at the end of their resources in the supply of skilled men, and with every effort could at most maintain a stationary number of men, although demands for greater production were increasing daily.

"After the failure of the Sheffield Conference in the engineering trade," says an official report, "Mr. Allan Smith proposed that Lord Kitchener should be asked to make a personal appeal to the unions to suspend their restrictions. The suggestion was forwarded by the Board of Trade to the War Office. Lord Kitchener declined to intervene. He considered that the Board of Trade, as the Department to which the War Office had referred the question of labour supply for armament purposes, should communicate with the parties and seek a settlement. It was then decided (about January 19) that the whole range of questions in dispute with the engineers and with the shipwrights and boilermakers should be dealt with by the Chief Industrial Commissioner, Sir George Askwith."

Faced by this problem, I pointed out that there was no use in one Ministry stepping in unless the army and navy were represented, and could have reported to them what steps were being taken, particularly as they were pulling different ways in the matter of contracts and priority. This proposition was agreed to. The general view was that it was absolutely necessary, in the interests of the nation, that changes should be made in the methods governing the production of articles of war and the restrictions imposed by trade union rules; but in the many interviews held with a view to preparing associations and unions while the Government were deliberating, I was warned on all sides of the difficulties, and can still recall the face of the secretary of one of the chief Employers' Associations when I asked for his assistance, and his remark that the task was impossible. A subsequent official report in the *History of the Ministry of Munitions*, contains the statement that "it would be hard to name a more perilous field for even the most delicate advance of Government interference." I can only say that it had to be attempted; and at last, after some delay, shortened by urgent pressure from Lord Kitchener, the Government settled the reference, and the First Lord of the Treasury appointed a Committee on February 4, 1915, Sir Francis Hopwood (now Lord Southborough), as a Civil Lord of the Admiralty, being selected for the naval side, and Sir George Gibb, then recently made a civil member of the Army Council, for the military side of the Government Departments, with myself as chairman and Mr. H. J. Wilson, of my Department, as secretary.

The Committee became well known under the name of the Committee on Production, and initially received the wide reference

"to inquire into and report forthwith, after consultation with the representatives of employers and workmen, upon the best steps to be taken to ensure that the productive powers of the employees in the engineering and shipbuilding establishments working for Government purposes shall be made fully available so as to meet the needs of the nation in the present emergency."

Instructions were added that, failing agreement, the Committee should report to the Government, adding, if they pleased, statements of what they thought would be a satisfactory settlement.

CHAPTER XXXV

THE SPRING OF 1915

So far as the Committee on Production was concerned, the sphere of work was sufficiently clear. The Board of Trade were already taking up the question of distribution of work to engineering firms other than armament firms, and the release of skilled men, already recruited, from the army. The corollary of these plans was continuity of work and increase of production by removal of restrictions which should enable (1) the best use to be made of skilled men; (2) the utilisation of semi-skilled and unskilled men on such work as they were capable of doing or could be soon instructed to do. Accordingly the question of restrictions was taken up as it had been left by some of the parties in December, and by others in January, after nearly three months, as was stated, of negotiations without any progress.

The chief difficulties of the problem to be faced were: (1) to effect arrangements between employers and the trade union leaders, and (2) to ensure that those arrangements should be respected and have results in the shops and yards.

It was not sufficient to overcome the first difficulty, because, however eager the officials on both sides might be to help in the national emergency, it was useless to have a paper agreement which was not endorsed and worked up to by the rank and file. The union leaders were hindered from accepting the removal of restrictions partly by distrust of the employers, partly by the fear that their own members would repudiate them. There was no time, nor were there sufficient leaders, to talk over and canvass every yard and every shop. The object in my mind was to effect such an agreement as would enable the leaders to tell their men that the trade union position was secured and that any departure was only temporary. If this principal point was secured, then it would be possible for employers and workpeople, according to the requirements of each shop and each locality, without fear of disloyalty to their organisations, to make such changes as were most suitable to the shop and the locality. "Departures from present practice would cover the attendance on machines, overtime restriction, greater utilisation of semi-skilled, unskilled, or other labour," any differences being, if necessary, referred to the Board of Trade for settlement.

If this plan could be carried out, the grave objection to Government interference and the imposition of terms from above would be avoided; but if the agreements could not be made, and after the long and fruitless conferences the prospect seemed to be doubtful, it would be still open to the Government to "put a prepared scheme before *both* sides, hear, and if they chose adopt, any amendment suggested by either side, and then give a decision, intimating that the decision must be taken as a final settlement, at least until the parties could come to a satisfactory arrangement among themselves." My memorandum contained a long schedule of definite terms to be put before the parties, enumerating in detail the restrictions which it was desired to suspend on Government work, and a proposed undertaking by employers for restoration of conditions.

The proposals were accepted by the Government and conferences at once began. There was some hitch owing to the Shipbuilding Employers' Federation objecting to a meeting as a Federation, but they forwarded a statement, and representatives came on behalf of the principal firms as firms. All parties agreed that the point was to go ahead on matters where agreement could be reached, with the result that on February 16 a report on "broken squads" in shipbuilding yards and improvement in methods of dealing with them in different yards was reached, the principle being that employers and employed should settle loyally in manner suitable to the varied local conditions. Four days later there was issued a second Report on Engineering, revising the proposals debated at Sheffield on January 13, and adding that they should apply to the industry as a whole and not to Government work only, and to workpeople employed in the shops or on board ships or elsewhere away from the factory. The employment of female labour was to be extended. Piecework prices in firms producing shells and fuses were to give an undertaking to the Committee on behalf of the Government to the effect that, " in fixing piecework prices, the earnings of men during the period of the War shall not be considered as a factor in the matter, and that no reduction in piece rate will be made, unless warranted by a change in the method of manufacture, e.g. by the introduction of a new type of machine."

These proposals indicated that piece rates would not need to be protected by restriction of earnings and output, but by a definite engagement by the employers to the Government that any departure from practice should only be for the period of the War, and that rules and customs existing prior to the War should not be prejudiced after the War by any change in practice.

The second division of the Report stated that:

" During the present crisis nothing could justify a resort to strikes and lockouts which were likely to impair the productive power of establishments engaged on Government work and to diminish the output of ships, munitions, or other commodities required by the Government for war purposes. The Committee submitted for the consideration of the Government that the following recommendations to Government contractors and sub-contractors and to trade unions should be at once published, and their adhesion requested:

" *Avoidance of Stoppage of Work for Government Purposes*

" With a view to preventing loss of production caused by disputes between employers and workpeople, no stoppage of work by strike or lockout should take place on work for Government purposes. In the event of differences arising which fail to be settled by the parties directly concerned, or by their representatives, or under any existing agreements, the matter shall be referred to an impartial tribunal nominated by His Majesty's Government for immediate investigation and report to the Government with a view to a settlement."

I handed the Second Report to the Prime Minister on Saturday, February 20. On Sunday, February 21, the Government published it, expressing their concurrence, and extending the existing reference to the Committee by empowering them " to accept and deal with any cases arising under the above recommendation." Thus the Committee was established as the chief arbitration tribunal of the country, and remained so throughout the War. The extreme speed with which it was appointed as an arbitral tribunal was largely due to the outbreak on the Clyde which was just commencing. On Monday, February 22, with this new tribunal available for investigation and report, I had to meet the executive of the Amalgamated Society of Engineers upon this very serious matter.

The first division of the Report had cleared up points of disagreement between employers and employed. It was decided that the parties themselves should continue technical negotiations on which they had already embarked, and embody themselves the whole of the different matters, technical and otherwise, in an agreement made by the trade itself. The result, delayed by the Clyde outbreak, emerged on March 3, in the " Shells and Fuses Agreement," between the Engineering Employers' Federation and the A.S.E. and allied organisations. There was, however, one point which could not be effected, and that was adherence to a settlement without a ballot. The A.S.E. ballot takes about twenty days, and has without doubt the advantage of getting the approval or disapproval of the rank and file to any proposals. In view of the extreme urgency of the case, and a confidential return from the War Office showing the condition of contracts for guns and shells, which was perfectly appalling in the proof it gave of shortage in amounts contracted for and the delays which had occurred and must continue before contracts could be completed, I pressed with all the energy I could command that the proposals should be accepted by the executive, and then, if constitutionally necessary, a confirmatory ballot be taken. I had desired that some eloquent Member of the Government, or perhaps Lord Kitchener, should take up this task, but no one wished to do it, particularly under the circumstances that facts as to the position in the war areas were not permitted to be divulged.

Without facts, which I was not allowed to give, the executive were not satisfied; they could not put before their constituents reasons for the extreme urgency; they were impressed themselves, but there were the men outside; the ordinary course of a ballot had to be taken.

There was a third Report issued on March 8, after long conferences with the Emergency Committees of the Engineering and Shipbuilding Trades, dealing with the points on which the unions were specially concerned. This Report dealt at length with proposals for demarcation of work and the use of semi-skilled and unskilled labour. The decision how far to agree with the proposals and the best methods of carrying them out was deferred by the parties until the result of the engineers' ballot was known. If that was unfavourable, there would be no chance of effecting further changes; but if favourable, the principle of every possible assistance would have been decided by the rank and file. The leaders were favourable, but they emphasised over and over again the necessity of the cordial co-operation of the men. Real acceleration could only take place if that was obtained.

The ballot return was ultimately favourable, but before its result was out Mr. Lloyd George had come in with the Treasury Agreement, imposed without a ballot, but remaining practically a dead letter until a ballot had been taken several months after a conclusion might possibly have been reached. As for suspension of restrictions, the Ministry of Munitions were pressing for changes a year afterwards, in a less satisfactory atmosphere, and did not appear to have made any progress. The two plans went upon different principles. My views were that the work-people, not the leaders by themselves, should be enlisted on the side of greater production, less restrictions, and improvement of demarcation rules, even if a few days were necessary to let them know what was happening; and that in the localities, by the people who knew the conditions, the changes suitable to the locality should be made. The other plans were directed to imposing, from above, rules, regulations, and orders, often with complete disregard of the persons in the locality and the character of the place.

Although the discussion on the ballot had not deferred the holding of it, it had the good effect that the leaders of the A.S.E. were determined to do all they could to ensure avoidance of stoppages, and hindrance of work from that cause, a point on which they had at once to suffer a severe test. In the week beginning Monday, February 22, the Clyde burst out into strikes, at the very time when the whole effort of the nation was required.

The cost of living had been gradually rising, but general increase of wages had not been given to meet it. Forty-seven new disputes broke out in February, the largest increase since the beginning of the War. It seemed, too, that the faith to which I have alluded was beginning to wane, and no greater cause of that existed than the fact that it was seen that some people were making money out of the War, without any restraint upon their methods.

Faith, or any great ideal, seems always to be hampered by the suspicion of mercenary motives on the part of individuals engaged in a cause. Profits may come, as in the case of armament firms, from the culminating result of the very work to which they have devoted years of preparation and low results. Profits may also come from the force of circumstances, where the shortage of supply, as in the case of shipping, obliges the shipowner to take the highest bidder from a number of consignors competing for carriage of goods at almost any price. Profits may necessarily arise from many other causes, including individual greed, but whatever may be the cause, it is not unnatural that those who do not get profits should wrangle with those who do, and should demand a share in the profits. Wrangling is likely to be enhanced if those who make profits flaunt their profits or boast of their profits, an element not unknown in the autumn of 1914, and still better known since that period, when the word "profiteer" has become so notorious: A shipowner who stated that he had made profits, was going to make profits, and had a right to make profits, did more harm than a great naval defeat would have done. To name "defeat" would rouse the nation to set their teeth and fight against an alien foe. The profiteer's statement would rouse class against class, and only tend to disruption within the nation itself.

It was this question of profits which assumed a dangerous aspect in the first months of 1915. It caused discontent, and that discontent grew with the competition for skilled workmen, a competition bewildering to the men, and utterly beyond the efforts of labour exchanges, themselves hampered by the loss of their best men. Individual workmen might be receiving very high rates to keep them for particular work, and in that measure were making profits, but the rank and file were not getting increase of pay at a time when it was most apparent that some employers were beginning to make large profits. If the Government had made a pronouncement at the beginning of the War that nobody ought, or should be allowed, to make profits out of the War, or, as they were urged, had so acted even at a later date, or if one of their chief spokesmen, other than by half-hearted remarks, had boldly denounced undue profit-making, or profiteering, as it came to be dubbed, the trouble might have been lessened. When men saw that one class was gaining, and that they, as a whole, got no more pay in spite of increasing prices and cost of living, but were told it was unpatriotic to strike with a view to more pay, they objected.

At a late date, Mr. I. H. Mitchell, reviewing this period, wrote :

"I am quite satisfied that the labour difficulty has been largely caused by the men being of opinion that, while they were being called upon to be patriotic and refrain from using the strong economic position they occupied, employers, merchants, and traders were being allowed perfect freedom to exploit to the fullest the nation's needs. This view was frankly submitted to me by the leaders of the Clyde Engineers' strike in February last. As soon as Labour realised that nothing was being done to curtail and prevent this exploitation by employers, it let loose the pent-up desire to make the most it could in the general scramble. This has grown until now many unions are openly exploiting the needs of the nation. If the work is Government work, it is the signal for a demand for more money. Trade union leaders who, from August last year until February this year, loyally held their members back from making demands, are now with them in the rush to make the most of the opportunity."

This was the situation to be faced in the coming months, and the prospect was not inviting.

It may have been that on the Clyde, in addition to the

pressure of cost of living and the example of profit-making, other circumstances assisted, such as influence by men who afterwards became notorious as "deportees," a breaking away by the rank and file from leaders who were out of touch with them, a movement in the shops, or discontent from crowded housing. In any event, the workmen came out on strike without authority from their unions.

At a conference at York, the North-East Coast employers had settled with the unions for a larger increase than had been given at one time, and to that extent met the rising feeling, but the executive union delegates from the Clyde did not at the same meeting agree to the proposal of the Clyde employers for an advance similar to that on the Tyne. The Clyde wages had for years been lower than the Tyne, and similar advances had been always given. The offer was taken back to Glasgow, and while a ballot was still pending, and without any authority from their union, a large number of men, estimated at 10,000, ceased work and demanded payment of the full claim. If the employers gave more, the Tyne would at once have demanded the extra amount. They adhered to their offer.

The situation was extremely difficult. The whole scheme of the War might be hazarded unless the strikes stopped, and particularly if they spread. After some debate, the Government requested me to interview the leaders of the unions and tell them that they must get the men back by every effort which they could make. The leaders sent messages, without avail. Further emphatic instructions came from the Government that they must be asked to go to Glasgow and put their whole influence into stopping the strikes; and, indeed, their own authority in the future depended upon their success in stopping an unauthorised strike, contrary to all the union rules. I was asked by them whether I could furnish a letter emphasising the insistence of the Government, in order to indicate the mission on which they were desired to go, and aid them in a difficult task. The official notice and letter was in the following terms:

"The strike of engineers in the Clyde district has been under the consideration of His Majesty's Government, and by their direction the following letter has been sent to-day by Sir George Askwith, the Chief Industrial Commissioner, to the Engineering Employers' Federation, on behalf of the employers, and to the Amalgamated Society of Engineers, the Steam Engine Maker's Society, the United Machine Workers' Association, the Amalgamated Society of General Toolmakers, and the Scientific Instrument Makers' Trade Society, on behalf of the men :

" ' SIR,

" ' From inquiries which have been made as to the position of the disputes in the engineering trade in the Glasgow district, it appears that the parties concerned have been unable to arrive at a settlement. In consequence of the delay, the requirements of the nation are being seriously endangered.

" ' I am instructed by the Government that important munitions of war urgently required by the navy and the army are being held up by the present cessation of work, and that they must call for a resumption of work on Monday morning, March 1.

" ' Immediately following resumption of work arrangements will be made for the representatives of the parties to meet the Committee on Production in Engineering and Shipbuilding establishments, for the purpose of the matters in dispute being referred for settlement to a Court of Arbitration, who shall also have power to affix the date from which the settlement shall take effect.

" ' I am, yours faithfully,
" ' G. R. ASKWITH,
" ' *Chief Industrial Commissioner.*'

" On receipt of Sir George Askwith's letter, several of the principal officials of the Amalgamated Society of Engineers left the London headquarters for Glasgow last night."

There could be no doubt that the letter was in stiff terms, but the Government considered that they had to scotch this strike, and with the energetic help of the union leaders it was brought to a close. Whether there was any clear idea of the course to be pursued in the event of defiance it is difficult to say, but far stronger measures than a letter indicating that national necessity required resumption of work, were freely advocated. The claims were heard with speed, after a large majority had by ballot agreed to abide by the decision. The award gave the same amount as the Tyne had agreed to, but also added sufficient to equalise the Tyne and Clyde rates.

The award stated that the advances were "to be regarded as war wages, and recognised as due to and dependent on the existence of the abnormal conditions now prevailing in consequence of the War," a phrase which the committee adopted for all their later awards, and which soon became known. At first it caused some criticism, and the Clyde workpeople applied later for the advances to be made a permanent wage increase; but they and others came to realise that no one could tell when the War would end, and what abnormal circumstances might arise, and what variations in cost of living might occur, so that a measure of elasticity was desirable. Acceptance was, I think, also helped by a message sent by the shipbuilding unions on the North-East Coast after they had received a similar award. This telegraphic message to me ran as follows:

> "At a conference of representatives of the Joint Shipbuilding and Iron and Steel Shipbuilding Societies the report and award of the Committee on Production in Engineering and Shipbuilding Trades was carefully considered. It was unanimously decided to accept the same on behalf of the respective societies, and to urge our members to continue, and improve, where possible, on the timekeeping, and the production of ships, munitions of war, and everything necessary to our national welfare in this grave national emergency.
>
> "(Signed) JOHN HILL (*Gen. Secretary, Boilermakers' Society*).
>
> "ALEX WILKIE (*Secretary, Standing Committee of the Shipyard Trades*).
>
> "FRANK SMITH (*Chairman of the Standing Committee*).
>
> "R. W. LINDSAY (*Member, Executive Council, Boilermakers' Society*)."

While these troubles were occurring, the Government were pressing through Parliament the Defence of the Realm (No. 2) Act of 1915, giving very extensive powers for acquiring various forms of control. There was much talk about "taking over," as if the Government could have possibly run the works by themselves, without the aid of skilled management by persons conversant with each business. Much time was lost in talking about "compensation" on this assumed "taking over." It is a curious fact that the form of industry in this country, joint-stock companies, by which immense capital has been collected from many small streams, and which has allowed a strong river to run and fertilise industry throughout the world, proved a difficult problem in time of war. The legal relations of directors to their shareholders, the position of trustees, prevented them from doing acts which as individuals they might have been prepared to undertake. They required the protection of being able to say that they had to do things to which some shareholders might have objected, under the provisions of the law. Neither "taking over," nor "compensation" for such interference, was a feasible scheme. At the same time, and quite independently, it was being bitten into the minds of the members of the Committee on Production that this question of profits was one of the root difficulties of labour unrest, a view which led up to a Fourth Report, which the Government did not publish, although its publication was strongly and repeatedly urged.[1]

The conditions under which this Report was made and its purport may be quoted from the official *History of the Ministry of Munitions*. It is there stated:

"The emphasis is for the first time shifted from 'compensation' to limitation of profits in a memorandum entitled *A Note on Labour Unrest*, which Sir George Askwith sent to Sir H. Llewellyn Smith on February 24. This document reflected the experience gained by the Committee on Production in its endeavours to secure the removal of restrictions on output. Sir George Askwith wrote that, throughout the country, labour men were interpreting the Prime Minister's speech of February 11, on the rise of food

[1] The Report was sent to the Prime Minister on March 8 and printed as a Cabinet Memorandum. A note to the official *History* states: "It was decided to delay publication until after the Treasury Conference of March 17–19. Mr. Lloyd George then again postponed the publication. On April 15 the Committee on Production wrote to the Prime Minister recommending that the Report should be published. Sir George Gibb again recommended it in a Memorandum to Mr. Lloyd George on June 2. The Report, however, has never been published."

prices, as an intimation that little could be done to curtail the large profits which contractors were believed to be making. They were drawing the inference that labour was entitled to higher wages, which were, in fact, in many cases being received. Unless something were done to correct the view that contractors were entitled to unlimited profits, the workmen would claim corresponding freedom; and they had never been in a stronger position to enforce their demands. They might lower their claim, if they could be satisfied that some control was being exercised over contractors to minimise their profits.

"The same incidence of emphasis on the need for limiting profits is noticeable in the Fourth Report (March 5) of the Committee on Production, which is further remarkable in that it adumbrates the use which might be made of a Government pledge to limit profits in securing the consent of the unions to a suspension of their restrictive rules. It thus contains all the essentials of the bargain with labour which was to be made a fortnight later at the Treasury Conference.

"The Committee proposed that the Government should assume control of the principal armament and shipbuilding firms. They pointed out that the general labour unrest of the previous few weeks was accompanied by a widespread belief among workpeople that abnormal profits were being made, particularly on Government contracts. There were consequent demands for higher wages. It seemed to be thought that limitation of profits might be decided to be impracticable, and the men were claiming the freedom to ask the maximum price for their labour. The unrest would prevail while these ideas were abroad.

"They recommended that the Government should at once issue a pronouncement, stating clearly that they did not acquiesce in the view that employers and contractors must be left to secure maximum prices and profits.

"The control of profits could be effected by the following means: that under the Defence of the Realm Act, with necessary amendments, 'the Government should assume control over the principal firms whose main output consists of ships, guns, equipment, or munitions of war, under such equitable financial arrangements as may be necessary to provide for the reasonable interests of proprietors, management, and staff.'

"An Executive Committee, on the lines of the Railway Executive Committee, should be established (*a*) to search for new sources of supply, and (*b*) to exercise continuous and responsible supervision with representatives of the firms concerned. The executive conduct of each business should be left to the existing management.

"Besides the removal of the suspicion above indicated, other advantages would accrue: (1) trade union restrictions might be more readily removed when it was known that the Government, not private employers, would benefit. (2) The existence of a central executive with wide authority over the sources of supply would make possible the control over the output of the various works, the supervision and co-ordination of sub-contractors' work according to relative urgency, and some general regard to efficient and co-ordinated utilisation of labour on private and Government work. (3) Some private establishments would spare labour, if assured that it would be for the direct benefit of the nation.

"Such control would enable a confident appeal to be made to workpeople, and would restore national unanimity. It would also impress on the nation that the country was at war and industrial resources must be mobilised.

"The recommendations of this Report were adopted by the Cabinet, and Mr. Runciman was entrusted with the task of opening negotiations with the chief contractors."

In the discussion which took place about these documents, it was verbally explained that it was not intended that the subjects dealt with should be co-ordinated or controlled by a Committee (or Committees, as Lord Kitchener insisted), but that a Cabinet Minister must be chairman, who, though not always presiding, would be a link with the Cabinet and give or obtain Cabinet decisions in the event of disagreement. Lord Kitchener for some time was doubtful, because he thought the plan might derogate from his position as Secretary of State for War, and his control of all War Departments—a policy on which he set great store, but which no one man could possibly carry out in detail. However, he agreed when the words "or Committees" were inserted, intending to have Committees confined to the War Office, where he wanted them to be so limited. Mr. Lloyd George may or may not have been influenced by the plans for co-ordination outlined in these reports, but they at least fell in with his views of stepping forward, and that they were extremely useful to him is evidenced by the fact that their tenor and even their language were incorporated, word for word, in the agreement called the Treasury Agreement, and subsequently, again, incorporated in the Munitions of War Act. A memorandum embodying all their points was handed to him by me on March 16, the day before the Conference on the Agreement commenced.

Although the question of profits was the essential point which alone could cause any adequate sacrifice of restriction by the trade unions, and although hints were given in May and June that something was going to be done, nothing was done for several months, except so far as limitations of profits in controlled establishments was enacted by the Munitions of War Act in July. The result was distrust and suspicion. It is true that the Budget introduced in May by Mr. Lloyd George must have been prepared at an earlier date. It contained nothing on the subject of profits. The Coalition Government was formed at the end of May, and another Budget for the end of September was prepared, in which taxation of profits was included, but disclosure of the fact came very late. When a duty was imposed, it was in a form which did not appeal to the working man, who still saw instances of expenditure, evasion, and waste going on upon all sides of him. The tax became a necessity during the War, and had indeed to be increased. When enterprise was intended to be directed to the War, when there was no outlet for it in other countries, and when the tax served a purpose, in showing that all the profits did not go to one class, while other classes were restricted by compulsion, when the nation was absolutely obliged to divert every possible means of wealth into the national purse, the tax was defensible and not unwillingly received. It wears quite a different aspect when the channels of enterprise are open, and reconstruction, the opening of markets, and industrial progress are the first principles to be considered. In peace its continuance throttles industry, and falls most hardly on those persons by whom industrial progress can be best achieved.

Meanwhile the effective influence which, in spite of the

intervening Clyde outbreak, was arising from the reports of the Committee and the intention of both employers and the principal leaders of the employed to work together on lines which continued to be practically agreed, and which would have improved, as soon as the engineeers' ballot was concluded, by means of the constitutional support of the rank and file, was modified by a new design. It was intimated that Mr. Lloyd George, after conversation with one or two labour leaders, more prominent for their interest in politics than in knowledge of the feeling and mind of Labour, proposed to come forward and deal with the trade union leaders. The Cabinet seems to have adopted the proposal on March 11, and letters were dispatched summoning a Conference on March 17—

"to consult with the Chancellor of the Exchequer and the President of the Board of Trade on certain matters of importance to Labour arising out of the recent decision of the Government, embodied in the Defence of the Realm (Amendment) Act, to take further steps to organise the resources of the country to meet naval and military requirements."

After three days' debate, the agreement called the Treasury Agreement was effected. Whether it did in fact hurry matters forward by anticipating by a few days the result of the ballot of the engineering trades and by obliging the leaders to dictate to the rank and file, instead of allowing the rank and file to vote in favour of the propositions put before them, no one can say. It laid the foundation for an Act of Parliament, the Munitions of War Act, passed in July; and had the result of the taking over of the supply departments of the War Office by a new department.

It may be noted that, contrary to the principles of agreement suggested by the Committee on Production, the employers were not invited or present, and had no prior knowledge of the proposals which were made. It may also be noted that certain trades not engaged in the supply of munitions of war were not present and were not parties to the agreement, although, with the interlocking of industries and wage questions, they were or became vitally important in carrying out the successful working of those industries which were parties. The Miners' Federation withdrew at the final meeting on March 19, and were not parties. No representatives from cotton, jute, wool, tramways and other important industries were brought in.

On the final day the representative of the Amalgamated Society of Engineers intimated he was instructed not to sign any agreement or scheme until the Executive Council had considered and endorsed the whole report. Mr. Lloyd George had to hold another meeting with the Society on March 25, and was bluntly told that it was for the Government to prove that any further extension of the recent Shells and Fuses Memorandum was necessary, and that the definite terms of any agreement reached with the employers as to limitation of profits should be laid before them, and the first of four points on which the A.S.E. made their assent conditional was the point of profits. The A.S.E. were tired of hints, and knew the feeling of the workpeople. They did not trust any longer to vague statements, and demanded a definite undertaking in writing. Even then Mr. Lloyd George could not avoid a ballot. The agreement was indeed confirmed by 18,000 to 4,000, but confirmation was not obtained before June 16. The unions had reciprocated the delay in the fulfilment of the Government pledge, which was only partially given in the Munitions of War Act on July 2, by delay on their side. It was reported on June 9 that in the shipbuilding trade the workmen's organisations represented at the Treasury Conference "had not approached their members in the matter at all," and that there were numerous complaints from all quarters. In fact, the leaders had purported to suspend restrictions, but the rank and file were scarcely touched by the bargain. On paper the agreement looked well; in practical result it did not come up to the claims made for it, for the simple reason that the rank and file had not been reached.

CHAPTER XXXVI

THE MUNITIONS OF WAR ACT, 1915

THE Treasury Agreement being only an expression of opinion which had designated the Committee of Production and other forms of arbitration attached to the Chief Industrial Commissioner's Department as suitable means for settling disputes, no more power or authority, perhaps less power, appertained to the Committee and the Department than before the Agreement was made. The Committee on Production was named as the chief arbitral tribunal. It dropped naturally, as I intimated to the Prime Minister on April 1, further work on withdrawal of restrictions and rules for organisation of production, which now rested on the terms of the Treasury Agreement and the approaching advent of the Ministry of Munitions. It had a new and engrossing work assigned to it, developed from its appointment as arbitral tribunal on February 21, but it had no power, except moral influence and consent of the parties, to carry out its supposed functions.

All those persons, whether within or without the Agreement, who objected to a semblance of compulsory arbitration had to be convinced that the tribunals were fair, at a time when the leaders of unions were finding the situation more and more difficult through the restlessness of the rank and file. Many trades preferred conciliation meetings, which occupied much time. Those trades outside the agreement would still come to the Chief Industrial Commissioner, but did not wish to range themselves as having anything to do with the munitions side of production or disputes. And yet they might be closely interlocked with those trades by the effect which their disputes might have on the convenience of munition workers, as in tramway disputes, or by example owing to proximity in the same town or district. There were also workpeople employed by Departments, such as the Royal Dockyards, where Departments had to be consulted before existing methods, far too slow for rapidly changing circumstances, could be altered. Other trades, such as the ship-repairing industry of South Wales, had been accustomed to deal port by port, and section by section, with the engineering and allied trades. The trade had now become, by the course of war, an active and quickly developing industry. The old sectional method became hopelessly obsolete. Agreements had to be effected to consolidate claims and unify representatives on both sides for the purpose of dealing with them. Each trade, district, town, firm, and often each union, wanted separate interviews, hearings, arbitrators, or conciliators. It was only the general goodwill, in spite of sections of persons, often through ignorance, getting out of hand, which enabled the work to be got through with comparatively little real friction. The country, both employers and employed, seemed to desire that differences should be settled, and accorded trust which in time of peace would have been difficult to maintain. Perhaps one may add that many years of work by the Department, which had afforded insight into many trades, and established acquaintance or friendship with many representatives of employers and employed, the element of personal touch, was not without value. " You know all our little tricks," an eminent trade union leader genially remarked to me.

It is not necessary to deal with the separate cases brought to the Department; indeed, they were far too many to mention separately.[1] By June 1 the Committee on Productions alone had given nearly forty decisions on wages questions, covering directly over 750,000 workpeople, and there were a large number of other cases. There was, in fact, a wage readjustment, directly or indirectly, for the whole country. The variety may be illustrated by mere mention of a few cases, ranging in intricacy from a simple change in wages to a code of conditions, rules, or amalgamation. Such cases, taken at random, were Woolwich Arsenal, Pimlico clothing, the Royal Dockyards,

[1] The awards of the Committee on Production and of the arbitrators appointed by the Chief Industrial Commissioner from 1914 to 1918 are all printed as Appendices I–VIII of the Twelfth Report of Proceedings under the Conciliation Act 1896, ordered by the House of Commons to be printed on October 22, 1919, in two volumes, each exceeding 900 pages. They will be invaluable material for any historian who may write on the conditions of industry during the War and the questions affecting every section of work.

the Post Office, the cotton trade, Bristol Channel engineering and ship-repairing, moulders and brassworkers in many districts, railway shops, Walsall casting, the saddlery trade, the leather trade, many building cases, tramways, coal-tippers, chain-cable and anchor manufacturers, Thames lightermen, Midland sheet-metal workers, the Scottish steel trades, London carters, army boots, Scottish smiths and strikers, Drogheda steam-boats, cement companies, coppersmiths, rope-makers, pitwood-workers, explosive works, furnishing trades, Leicester hosiery, etc., and also an award in the Scottish coal trade Conciliation Board, of which I had been elected umpire.

As the course of increased arbitration proceeded, it became apparent that Labour desired equality of treatment, with some bias in favour of the "under-dog." That principle was consistently followed throughout the War by the Committee on Production, and by my Department, grievously hampered as they were by the action of Ministers and other Departments acting on their own. It has formed, too, the basis on which all the subsequent action of the Courts and Councils seems to have been based. It was a case of equal suffering, equal relief, "owing to the abnormal circumstances due to and caused by the War," if one may quote the phrase we invented and which appeared in most of the awards of the Committee on Production.

The difficulty in practice proved to be the mass of cases which were brought forward, and the application of the principle to the varied circumstances of each trade and each firm that came forward to arbitration. There were employers who would never give an increase, although it was known almost to a certainty what the sum would be, without a formal award. There were employers who had arguments, some good, some bad, why an increase should not be general to all their employees, or who had particular circumstances which they desired to bring forward. On the other hand, there were employees taking for granted the general advance likely to be received, but pressing for special advances owing to the alleged position of their trade (iron-moulders, for instance, asking for special treatment), or for the settlement of claims they had been unsuccessfully demanding for a quarter of a century. It appeared to the Committee to be more satisfactory to build upon the arrangements effected up to the outbreak of war than to attempt philanthropic reconstruction or embark on unknown contingencies in the middle of the War.

The work of the Board of Trade and other Departments in dealing with transfers, badges, and diffusion of contracts, and of the Armaments Committees and local organisations, in increasing output during the summer, as well as the start of the Ministry of Munitions in June 1915, are outside the scope of this work. It is sufficient to say that the Government found that they could not get on without more power, with the result that the Munitions of War Act was enacted "to organise the skilled labour of the country for the production of munitions of war." The Defence of the Realm Acts were not sufficient. Amongst the provisions of the new Act, not the least important were those relating to labour disputes. Up to its passing there were no compulsory limits on freedom to stop working by a strike pending settlement of a dispute, nor on the maintenance of restrictive rules. An attempt was made to deal with both, but particularly with the limitation of freedom to stop work.

These conditions and the Act were a novelty. Compulsory arbitration was an extreme novelty, which had not only to be swallowed by employers, but by trade union leaders, some of whom had been consistently opposed to it, and by the rank and file, to whom those very leaders had to explain that they must conform to the decisions of three persons in London, whose names they might never have heard, but whose decision was final. It was a strong order, but acceptance of it was, taking it as a whole, wonderful. Men seemed to desire a composing element which would give a measure of finality, be a hindrance to sudden stoppages, prevent long and tedious negotiations with employers, and bring the majority of employers into line. In 1913 the number of cases referred to arbitration was about forty-five. In 1918, the figures having increased by hundreds every year, the number referred to the Committee on Production and other arbitrators was more than 3,500. During the five years of its existence, either with three members or, latterly, with several courts, the total nearly reached 8,000 cases; and, says the Twelfth Report under the Conciliation Act, "the awards were almost universally accepted."

The terms of the Act itself were a sort of compromise

between pure compulsory arbitration and arbitration if recognised methods, inquiry, and conciliation failed. A difference existing or apprehended, if not determined by the parties directly concerned, or their representatives, or under existing agreements, might be reported to the Board of Trade. The Board of Trade had to consider any differences so reported, and take any steps which seemed to them expedient to promote a settlement of the difference :

"and in any case in which they think fit, may refer the matter for settlement either in accordance with the provisions of the First Schedule or, if in their opinion suitable means for settlement already exist in pursuance of any agreement between employers and persons employed, for settlement in accordance with those means."

The Act added :

"The award in any such settlement shall be binding both on employers and employed, and may be retrospective ; and if any employer, or person employed, thereafter acts in contravention of, or fails to comply with, the award, he shall be guilty of an offence under this Act."

The principal clause for delaying a lockout or strike enacted that :

"An employer shall not declare, cause, or take part in a lockout, and a person employed shall not take part in a strike, in connection with any difference to which this part of this Act applies, unless the difference has been reported to the Board of Trade, and twenty-one days have elapsed since the date of the report, and the difference has not during that time been referred by the Board of Trade for settlement in accordance with this Act."

The provisions of the First Schedule were that differences referred for settlement were to go before tribunals determined by agreement between the parties, or in default of agreement by the Board of Trade. These tribunals were :

(*a*) The Committee appointed by the First Lord of the Treasury, known as the Committee on Production ; or

(*b*) A single arbitrator, to be agreed upon by the parties, or in default of agreement appointed by the Board of Trade ; or (*c*) A court of arbitration consisting of an equal number of persons representing employers and persons representing workmen with a chairman appointed by the Board of Trade.

The differences they were entitled to settle were stated to be—

" differences as to rates of wages, hours of work, or otherwise as to terms or conditions of or affecting employment on the manufacture or repair of arms, ammunition, ships, vehicles, aircraft, or any other articles required for use in war, or of the metals, machines, or tools required for that manufacture or repair (in this Act referred to as munitions work); and also any differences as to rates of wages, hours of work, or otherwise as to terms or conditions of or affecting employment on any other work of any description, if this part of this Act is applied to such a difference by His Majesty by Proclamation on the ground that in the opinion of His Majesty the existence or continuance of the difference is directly or indirectly prejudicial to the manufacture, transport, or supply of Munitions of War."

It was soon found by some trades, especially the engineering trades, that their pre-war methods of district and central conferences occupied too much time. With the quick changes which became necessary, the rank and file would not wait, the representatives of unions and employers were too busy in war-work to devote the necessary time, and the speedier methods of a report, reference, and hearing seemed more conducive to the interests of business. The pre-war methods were suspended. The parties by districts or firms demanded arbitration, and in almost every case settled upon the Committee on Production as the arbitral tribunal. This practice tended greatly to co-ordination, but, at the beginning of the War, every single district and often every firm, particularly if it was a limited liability company whose shareholders had to be taken into account, demanded a separate hearing and a separate award. There was necessarily always a long list of cases to be arranged, parties to be communicated with, dates of hearing fixed, and time given for a patient hearing. The Committee on Production worked as hard as time allowed, but it was difficult to keep the lists within bounds.

With regard to other trades, a great many had to be

heard by single arbitrators. Nobody seemed to want a court under subsection (*c*). Very few were either asked for or appointed. For these courts arbitrators had to be collected; refusals on the ground of other work made nominations most difficult; delay was sure to ensue. The other two types of court were evidently preferred. The difficulty which arose with them was that, although most single arbitrators followed the governing cases settled by the Committee on Production, where such precedents existed, strict co-ordination was not practicable. The tribunals were alternative tribunals. If one arbitrator made a mistake, through lack of knowledge of the interlocking of trades or the intricacy of technicalities, the effects and ensuing discontent might be widespread. Although my predecessor, Mr. Wilson Fox, had been wont to say that only one man in a million made a good arbitrator, the result showed that arbitrators, improving by practice and exercising care and patience, could avoid grave mistakes, and, generally speaking, give awards satisfactory to the parties coming before them. In some cases there were errors, chiefly arising from want of attention to the minute detail which many industrial settlements require, but the appointments being under the Department, complaints were soon heard. The system of appointment being elastic, no arbitrator had a vested interest or had to be employed, if it was found that he could not manage the work of arbitration.

The time allowed for investigation and inquiry before reference to arbitration was short. In a subsequent Act it was reduced from twenty-one to fourteen days, but by that time a shorter period was more feasible. At first there was little consolidation between groups of employers. Correspondence had to take place, posts were delayed, individuals or firms did not answer, or their representatives were absent. Claims sent to the Department had often not even been sent to the persons most intimately concerned. Bogus or absurd claims were not wanting. Conciliation was frequently proposed in preference to arbitration. Evidence had to be collected. In other cases the parties had been negotiating for some time, failed to agree, and at the last moment a claim was sent to London, and then all the blame of the delay previous to the claim being lodged put upon the Department, though they might in no way be responsible. Some absurd instances were proved when complaint was made, the delay being due to the lack of organisation in the offices of the parties themselves, particularly when separate individuals seemed to deal with bundles of letters without knowledge of letters received or previous correspondence. Owing to the shortage and changes of clerical assistance in almost every office in the country, employers and their associations, workpeople and trade unions, as well as Government offices, suffered in greater or less degree.

The Act did not cover all workpeople, but only those engaged in munitions of war as defined by the Act. The miners had been represented for two days at the Treasury Conference, but withdrew on the third. They were not a party to the Agreement, and obtained exclusion from the Act by an undertaking to settle all disputes by arrangement with the owners, or, failing that, to call in an independent chairman with full power to settle. This guarantee proved to be of little practical value. The cotton operatives were also excluded, on their plea that their industry was too well organised to require the Act, under which sections of the trade had subsequently to be brought by Proclamation. Instead of all trades being brought in, freedom to strike continued for all workpeople other than those defined by the Act. Numbers of strikes occurred in these industries, often stopping supplies to munition workers or showing an example in interlocked industries which necessarily reacted. In the following year a wider extension had to be given, but much time and trouble would have been saved if it had been realised how closely every industry is connected with other industries.

It is true that other industries could be brought in by Royal Proclamation, a cumbrous method only mitigated by the courtesy of the officers of the Privy Council. Some wiseacre had propounded that this procedure would be impressive, and it was adopted in the Act; but it proved to be troublesome, caused dangerous delay, and had to be used with caution lest the King's name should be brought without effect into the settlement of trade disputes.

In the second part of the Act there was a provision that an appeal could be made from the decision of the Minister of Munitions in the event of dissatisfaction with decisions he might make on proposed increases in controlled establishments, but this provision was not satisfactory in its working. There was also a provision intended to stop restrictions, drastic in form, but soon found to be of small value. The words ran :

" Any rule, practice, or custom not having the force of law which tends to restrict production or employment shall be suspended in the establishment, and if any person induces or attempts to induce any other person (whether any particular person or generally) to comply, or continue to comply, with such a rule, practice, or custom, that person shall be guilty of an offence under this Act.

" If any question arises whether any rule, practice, or custom is a rule, practice, or custom which tends to restrict production or employment, that question shall be referred to the Board of Trade, and the Board of Trade shall either determine the question themselves, or, if they think it expedient, or either party requires it, refer the question for settlement in accordance with the provisions contained in the First Schedule to this Act. The decision of the Board of Trade or arbitration tribunal, as the case may be, shall be conclusive for all purposes."

In practice employers tried to make use of this section, but they pressed too much. Ca' canny practices and shop rules could not be abrogated by a stroke of the pen. The rank and file could evade the strict letter of the law or decisions, and their leaders could not compel them. Some attempts were made, but conciliation meetings and consent of the rank and file proved to be the only safe chance of arriving at any satisfactory conclusions.

Among the criticisms which may be made is that the effect of the Munitions of War Act, and the importance which should have been attached to it, were initially discounted by the Minister of Munitions himself. The occasion arose during the preparation of the Act and immediately after it had been passed.

It has been mentioned that the miners withdrew from the Treasury Agreement. There was pending at the time a general claim on behalf of all miners for a war bonus of 25 per cent. on earnings. On this matter the Prime Minister, Mr. Asquith, adhered to the principle of the Coal Mines (Minimum Wage) Act, and insisted that the claim must be settled by agreement or arbitration in districts. In South Wales, Lord St. Aldwyn acted as arbitrator, and granted an advance of 17½ per cent. in addition to the 60 per cent. above the 1879 standard at which the wages then stood. As the maximum was 60 per cent., this decision practically abolished the maximum, without interference with the technical terms of the agreement. Coincidently with this general claim, the Welsh miners, on March 3, had given notice to terminate on June 30 the agreement which had governed the coal-field since March 1910. They demanded a new agreement, with a new standard of wages 50 per cent. above the previous standard of 1879, the abolition of the maximum, which had been already reached, and the fixing of a new minimum 10 per cent. above the new standard, to be paid when the average selling price of large coal was at or below 15*s*. 6*d*. a ton, or, in effect, no limit to advances if the selling price of coal rose, a greater limitation of declines if the selling price fell, and a higher basis on which advances should be calculated. Their plain object was to ensure a high wage in the event of a slump after the War, and rapid advances during the War. It was a heavy demand, to which the owners replied on March 9 by asking them to continue the old agreement and offering 10 per cent. bonus on standard rates.

Although Lord St. Aldwyn awarded 17½ per cent. on March 12, the Welsh miners continued to press their original claim, and late in June refused arbitration. As the old agreement was due to end on June 30, chaos was imminent. The Government decided to press for arbitration in accordance with the miners' undertaking when they withdrew from the Treasury Agreement, but the most that Mr. Runciman could effect, on Saturday, June 26, was a consent to allow a report to be made by me, by June 29, into the whole circumstances of the miners' demand. I was summoned in haste on Sunday, June 27, to hear the Welsh miners, prior to hurrying North to act as agreed umpire for the Scottish miners in accordance with their constitution and agreements. My report set forth the facts, and tentatively made suggestions amounting to abolition of maximum and present minimum, but the fixing of a new minimum before any proposal to reduce wages below Lord St. Aldwyn's 77½ per cent. was obtained ;

and that the rest of the details requisite in a new agreement would be so different during and for some time after the War that a wage agreement, admittedly intended to apply to peace conditions, should properly be deferred. While I had to be absent, these suggestions were taken up by Mr. Brace, then Under-Secretary of the Home Office, and previously a Welsh miners' leader, who stated, on inquiries he had made, that with certain amendments he was certain the strike could be averted. He proposed abolition of maximum and minimum, but fixing of a new minimum at once, at 50 per cent. over the standard of 1879, with extension of equivalent advantages to surface-men, nightmen, and hauliers. Mr. Henderson, Mr. Brace, and Mr. Roberts, all Labour leaders, went to Wales on July 1, and by a narrow majority, through the recommendation of the Miners' Council, obtained adhesion to treatment of the general proposals of the Government as the basis for a settlement. On the same day the coal-owners very reluctantly accepted the terms at the express wish of Mr. Runciman.

The Council and its more moderate leaders had so far maintained authority, but immediately afterwards the less moderate men further demanded concessions in the form of interpretations, with the intimation that, unless they were granted, work would be stopped. Mr. Runciman would not give way any farther. He wrote on July 7 to Mr. Lloyd George:

"As the interpretations the men want are really in the nature of a demand for further concessions, and as I have gone very far in compelling the owners to accept conditions which are very distasteful to them, and as my proposals on June 30 were definitely made for acceptance or rejection without alteration, I feel it extremely difficult to reopen the matter."

At first the Minister of Munitions backed up his colleague. On July 8 he replied that he would not hesitate to advise a Royal Proclamation bringing the difference under the Munitions of War Act. When, on July 12, a conference of delegates resolved "that we do not accept anything less than our original proposals, and that we stop the collieries on Thurdsay next until these demands are conceded," the direct challenge was answered on July 13 by a Royal Proclamation, making it an offence punishable under the Munitions of War Act to take part in a strike in the South Wales coal-mining industry; a General Munitions Tribunal was set up for South Wales; and the Proclamation was posted throughout the coal-field. On Thursday, July 15, about 200,000 men stopped work, and the Miners' Council promptly recommended that work should be resumed the following day, although the Miners' Conference took an opposite view. It became a question between the effects of a Royal Proclamation in terms of the recently passed Munitions of War Act, the Ministers of the Crown, and the recommendation of the Welsh authority, the Miners' Council on the one hand, and the limited number of strikers on the other, who, I was confidently informed, would be back at work on the Wednesday or Thursday following at latest. "Don't touch it, Sir George," I was told in answer to inquiry whether anything should be done. "Go away into the country, if you can." And yet the strikers won.

At the beginning of the week, while settling a dispute in the Barnsley coal-field, I was told that Mr. Lloyd George had suddenly gone down by special train to Cardiff, taking Mr. Runciman and many secretaries with him. It was said he had been impressed by the feeling of both French and British in France against the continuance of the strike. If so, he settled it by a complete *volte-face* and yielding to the strikers.

After hasty interviews, he gave way on all the main claims, and even on new claims just advanced at the interviews, only deferring for arbitration some very technical points which possibly were difficult to understand on the explanation of one side only. There was a story that one of the miners woke up a comrade in the middle of the night and said, "I am going to ask George for so-and-so"; and the other replied, "No, you can't have the face to do that. It is a bit too thick"; to which the other said, "Oh, yes, I will, and you will see he will give it us"; and he did. Whether this story be true or not, I am not prepared to say, but it indicates exactly the effect of the settlement. In the result all the difficult technical questions were left over for Mr. Runciman, the Minister whose actions and opinions had been completely put aside; men had won a victory by a strike which their principal authorities told them ought not to be continued ; the example was set to strike first and apply to Mr. Lloyd George, whatever Ministers, officials, employers, or union leaders might say, with a view to allowance of all claims as the reward of violence or pressure.

It was almost a farce to the Minister to wire to Mr. Asquith that "the solution of the deadlock was rendered possible on the lines of agreement rather than of coercion by the public-spirited action of the coal-owners, who placed themselves unreservedly in the Government's hands, for the purpose of securing a peaceful and reasonable settlement immediately." The so-called settlement did more to cause unrest during the succeeding years than almost any other factor in the War, and to lessen hopes of establishing a sane method of settlement of labour disputes. Since the War the same policy has from time to time been followed, the sole restraint being whether the trade is important enough or the unions powerful enough to gain access to Downing Street.

The above points indicate some of the difficulties in working the disputes sections of the Munitions of War Act, but, on the other hand, some trades, although not specifically within its scope, followed its principles and settled disputes by requests for arbitration. The woollen industry followed the principle by taking me, practically as sole arbitrator, to settle the whole basis of the many sections of the trade, both in Yorkshire and Lancashire, during the greater part of the War. The boot trade, after many conciliation meetings, formed a constitution of its own, very similar to the subsequent Industrial Councils, with final reference to arbitration through the Department. During the whole of the autumn the Committee on Production, with the addition of Sir David Harrel, owing to the necessary absence of Sir F. Hopwood upon other work, developed into the principal arbitration tribunal, while there was scarcely a trade in the country which in some form or another did not come before the Department. Almost all these cases were concerned with demands for increase of wages, the adjustment of different trades and firms to the general advances, or the establishment of bases of settlement which could cover wide areas of country or industry.

In October a case at Southampton requires more special notice, as the principles of the decision were largely followed during the War. It concerned the employment of men released from the colours for service in shipbuilding yards. The boilermakers particularly objected to men who were non-unionists working with men who, according to rules of the Boilermakers' Society, must be unionists, but at the same time were very loth to admit new men to their ranks. The crisis became acute when a man sent from a regiment as a riveter not only would not say whether he would join the union, but was reported to have dropped his tools into the sea and to know nothing about riveting, thus throwing out other men working with or near him. Men had been fined for leaving their work, and were very angry, a serious dispute being threatened. Apart from the particular case, I was asked to give a general ruling on the principles, as other cases were occurring daily. As publicity was of importance, I went to Southampton to examine into the matter, and heard evidence and arguments before a large number of boilermakers, to whom, for the sake of future peace, it was also advisable that the firm should explain that, under the Munitions of War Act, they were obliged to take and keep men sent to them, except by special leave of the Ministry of Munitions. In the particular case, it turned out the poor fellow had been an orange-seller on Tower Hill, had been got rid of by a sergeant who, wishing to lose him, accepted his own statement that he was a riveter, and was evidently wrong in his head, probably from shell-shock. The boilermakers themselves saw the uselessness of troubling about him, and dropped any further pressure, while the man was, of course, withdrawn. The storm being over, the decision was well received. Its principle was that in time of war conflicting rights must be subordinated to the major issue of the war, and methods must be used for preventing conflict being brought to determination by strikes for the time being.

The decision was to the effect that arrangements had been made for the transfer to this "controlled establishment" of additional workpeople under two schemes: (1) Volunteer munition workers enrolled under the auspices of the Ministry of Munitions, and (2) men released from the colours.

Considerable numbers of men were sent to the firm under both schemes. Exception was taken more than once by boilermakers to the employment of men who were not members of the Boilermakers' and Iron and Steel Shipbuilders' Society. In one case members of the society left their work without notice in protest against the employment of a man released from the colours who was not a member of the union. Proceedings under the Munitions of War Act were taken by the Ministry of Munitions against fifty of the strikers. The case was tried before a general tribunal under the Act on October 2, and the men concerned were fined. Work was afterwards resumed, and the difference was referred to arbitration in accordance with the Act. The award continued :

" The right of workpeople to combine and to press for inclusion in their union of all the workpeople engaged in the particular craft is admitted. It is equally admitted that an individual workman has a right to object to belong to the union. The right of employers to decline to discriminate in any way between unionists and non-unionists is unquestioned. In times of peace there are methods by which these respective rights, if they are all insisted upon and if they come in conflict, may be tested. The results of such a test in the case of an establishment such as the one in question, where the men are members of a highly organised and powerful trade union, can readily be estimated. But the country is at war, and whatever may be the rights of individuals or firms or unions, such rights cannot be freely exercised if by such exercise the production of munitions of war essential to the safety of the nation is delayed, hindered, or restricted. . . . The differences in this case do not appear to be in fact differences between the firm and their workpeople, but are differences between various classes of employees. Where, as in this case, an exclusively 'union shop' is concerned, the individual should not object to forgo his principles for the time being, to the extent required to maintain harmonious relationship with the remainder of the workpeople, and he can follow this course entirely without prejudice to a reversion to the *status quo* in times of peace.

" It is, however, regarded as a necessary qualification of

membership of the Boilermakers' Society that the candidate should ordinarily have served an apprenticeship to the trade of some years' duration. It is obvious that, if the efforts that are being made to increase the amount of labour available for the production of munitions of war are to be successful, a rule of this kind cannot at present be insisted upon. Workmen who are competent workmen and eligible should in my opinion be admitted as members of the society, either in the ordinary way or, if the society so determine, as temporary members. If the society is not prepared to admit workmen who are considered by the employers to be capable of useful employment, they must not during the War be precluded from such employment by any objection on the part of the union or of its members. If in the case of a particular individual the society object to his joining the union, he should be allowed to work freely and without interference or molestation."

As the year drew to a close, signs of the increasing cost of living were apparent in demands being put forward for general increases before the close of the first cycle of wage advances, as it may be called, was yet complete. Claim began to overlap claim. Restiveness in uncontrolled trades, such as cotton, where a strike was with difficulty averted, jute in Dundee, and dyes in Huddersfield, became apparent. Special demands were being made by comparatively new industries, such as aircraft workers, whose rates had been governed by the rates of the craft to which each worker belonged. Co-operative assistants in Lancashire and Edinburgh pressed forward claims on their societies. Some sections of employers holding contracts and afraid of disputes or loss of men began to give advances beyond the standard amounts which others, not so advantageously placed, already had difficulty in meeting. Two commissioners were sent to Glasgow "to inquire into the cause and the circumstances of the apprehended differences affecting munition workers in the Clyde district."

Clearance or leaving certificates being denied to men; raising of rents for houses; jealousy between union and union; lack of belief in union leaders; influx of women and fear of cheap labour; ignorance of the provisions of the Munitions Act, and alleged harsh and unjust administration of the Munitions Act, or the "Slavery Act," as it was dubbed; fines on three shipwrights who left work without authority or notice; irregular increases granted by certain employers, a fruitful source of discontent on the Clyde; and propaganda, were all cumulative causes of discontent in the Clyde district, while many of them applied to other districts.

The non-union question broke out again both in Derbyshire and Lanarkshire. The building trade, denuded of men by recruiting and with building generally at a discount, professed to be unable to grant increases while other trades were getting them. Last, but not least, the example of the Welsh miners was continually mentioned, and became more and more a covert threat. At the same time the Government were in considerable difficulty about finance. On November 18, Mr. Bonar Law in the House of Commons said "that those who represented the working classes, as well as the commercial classes, should set their forces resolutely against any increased pay by the Government in any shape or form for anything that had to be got in connection with the War."

When the Government were informed of the growth of applications for new advances, they as chief employers were alarmed. A memorandum was issued to the Committee on Production, stating that His Majesty's Government "have come to the conclusion that, in view of the present emergency, any further advances of wages (other than advances following automatically from existing agreements) should be strictly confined to the adjustment of local conditions where such adjustments are proved necessary."

This emergency and solemn statement was a necessary factor in considering some premature demands for a second general rise in wages, but could only delay claims tainted with this defect. The rise in the cost of living necessitated consideration of a new cycle. Legitimate claimants pressed that free arbitration granted by the Munitions Act must not be hampered. The Prime Minister had to minimise its intended effect by a statement in the House of Commons, and finally it was formally withdrawn. The year ended with a difficult situation in which the chance of maintaining industrial peace was shadowed by dark clouds.

CHAPTER XXXVII

1916

It had become evident, soon after the passing of the Munitions of War Act, 1915, that it would have to be amended. There were omissions in it; the Act caused confusion and some hardship. As far as arbitration was concerned, the very existence of the Ministry of Munitions caused delay in arbitration by the applications being sometimes matters for the Ministry, sometimes for the Board of Trade, and sometimes for the Ministry first and the Board of Trade afterwards. The absence of co-ordination, which became so accentuated when new Ministers and controllers were appointed by the score, and which at all times is the curse of efficient administration, increased rapidly.

Changes in arbitration procedure were but a small part, however, of the reasons for an amending Act, for which the questions of the inclusion of Government undertakings, leaving certificates, dilution, increased employment of women, and the necessity of a wider definition of munitions of war, were mainly responsible. Discussion on the proposed Act was quickened by the hostile reception given to the Minister of Munitions at the close of the year at Glasgow, and the remarks he heard in that city on the working of the Act, although his appeals urged them to "rise to the height of a great opportunity," when they would "emerge after this War is over into a future which has been the dream of many a great leader." The Bill passed quickly through Parliament, and became an Act on January 27, 1916.

The building and repair of merchant ships, many classes of material, works of construction in any manner connected with munition work, public utility services, the supply of light and power, tramway facilities, and fire engines, were all, subject to certificates in certain cases from the Ministry, brought under the provisions of the Act. The interlocking of industries had been better realised by practice, and, owing to shortage of men, it became urgent that some protection against loss of men should be available for such essential services.

This extension brought more cases by enactment of law under the Arbitration Courts, while at the same time, with a view to expedition, instead of the Board of Trade having discretion to refer a question to arbitration "in any case in which they think fit," it was made obligatory to refer within twenty-one days any difference which appeared to be a bona fide difference. This provision enabled the Department to impress on any party who delayed answers, would not attend meetings, or pursued dilatory tactics, that time was running and reference to arbitration would certainly be made before its expiry gave free permission to lock out or strike.

So far as arbitration was concerned, other important clauses referred to women. In the early days of the War rates for women and juveniles almost automatically followed the usual practice of advancement in recognised proportions to the rates given to men. As women in trades, like the woollen and cotton trades, where this practice did not rule, got large advances, other women moved for increased rates. As, too, men decreased, women began to take their places. The necessity for workers obliged the Government to make every effort for dilution in trade after trade. The conditions under which they should work or enter the places vacated by men, without exploitation either of their own or the contiguous male conditions, became an important problem. The subject had been mooted as early as July 1915, after some arrangement by Mr. Lloyd George with Mrs. Pankhurst. It was debated, so far as munition workers were concerned, during the whole of the autumn. Administrative steps were taken by the Ministry of Munitions by means of circulars known as L2 and L3, applicable to certain classes of munition workers. These circulars had no compulsory effect, and not being compulsorily applicable, penalised firms adopting them as compared with firms ignoring them. The new Bill proposed to give power to the Minister to give enforceable "directions." There was supposed to be an appeal to arbitration from his directions, particularly if the directions were not properly applicable to any particular workpeople or firms. There were numerous cases where it was a question whether the work was munition work or not, and as to how the difficulties of women in the same factory wholly or partly engaged on munitions, and women not engaged on munitions, could be adjusted. There was also the question of a proper minimum, if such was to be fixed, and whether it ought to be fixed nationally, by districts, by trades or by firms, or sometimes by one method and sometimes by another.

Such matters, with others, came within the orbit of arbitration, if differences arose or both sides were to be heard; or they might come within the orbit of command, if legislation permitted it. At the time the Bill was being discussed, a Committee made some recommendations which the Ministry were requested to endorse. Committees in other parts of the country were also making agreements which they considered suitable to their districts. Officials of the Ministry of Munitions took other varying views. The Minister of Munitions desired to endorse the recommendations of the first Committee, and that the arbitration tribunal should accept it, or similar recommendations, and apply it or them to cases coming before them. My expressed view was that, if such a course was to be followed, it must be made known; arbitration should be unfettered, or must be known to be fettered by instructions; the recommendations would affect the great industries which had not been heard; an appearance of impartial judgment, when restrictions unknown to the parties directly or indirectly affected the court, was not an impartial judgment and would be misleading.

The Minister of Munitions endeavoured to get round the difficulties by establishing two special arbitration tribunals attached to the Ministry of Munitions, and in fact he altered, with that object, the draft Bill on the Treasury Bench. As was remarked, "The Amendment has now been rapidly changed by the Minister of Munitions." It will easily be seen that this improvised expedient tended to establish dual authority. The clause stated that:

"(1) The Minister of Munitions may constitute special arbitration tribunals to deal with differences reported under

Part I of the principal Act which relate to matters on which the Minister of Munitions has given or is empowered to give directions under the two preceding sections, and the Board of Trade may refer any such difference for settlement to such tribunal in lieu of referring it for settlement in accordance with the First Schedule to the principal Act.

"(2) The Minister of Munitions may also refer to a special arbitration tribunal so constituted, for advice, any question as to what directions are to be given by him under the said sections.

"(3) The tribunal to which matters and questions relating to female workers are to be referred under this section shall include one or more women."

The new proposals caused the establishment of two new tribunals, the first for women, the second for certain classes of semi-skilled and unskilled men; but the first tribunal was the most important. Its functions were both advisory and judicial, and in the first capacity it had much investigation and statistical work of a difficult character to do. This work was increased by the number of women flocking into industry, the number in July 1918 being estimated to be 7⅓ millions, as compared with about 6 millions in July 1914. As an arbitration tribunal, on the other hand, it had scarcely been established before it was confronted with the exact difficulty I have mentioned, and requested that recommendations put forward by other committees and laid before the Minister should not be published, as they must interfere with its judicial work and position.

Although every possible case affecting women was referred to the new tribunal, and co-ordination was carried out with fair success, the existence of the two bodies, the Special Tribunal and the Committee on Production, in different buildings, with different officials, necessarily caused difficulties. Trades where both men and women were employed objected to two hearings. Some demanded that the Committee on Production should deal with all the workpeople, on the ground that the interests of men and women interlocked, and that a case must be dealt with as a whole, and not by pieces. Cases governing each other came up at different times, awards could not be held back till one tribunal had expressed an opinion, and it was undesirable that either tribunal should be placed in the position of merely registering the decisions of the other.

The effect of the new Act, owing to the necessity of reference within a specified period, was an increase of the number of claims which had to be referred to arbitration, in place of the more lasting settlements which usually result from conciliation and agreements between the parties. Arbitration was more speedy, gave greater uniformity, and affected more people, but it imposed orders and compulsion, principles never generally acceptable to the British race. It was only recognition of the supreme importance of the War which effected such general adherence to the final decisions of the various courts.

An arbitrator is in a very different position to a conciliator. He sits as a judge, and as a rule the less he says the better, provided that the questions and issues debated before him are clear to him. If he pleads judicial ignorance and asks foolish questions in a trade dispute, he is done. The flow of speech is interrupted to explain an elementary point, and any listeners knowing the trade will regret that so ignorant a man has to decide fateful questions. If he does not understand, it is nearly certain that, before the arguments are finished, trade terms, trade issues, the exact difficulties, will be clearly elucidated without an intervening debacle. A conciliator has to go through the same process, but he must be far more quick at getting at the real point, the real kernel of the dispute, and concentrating upon that, with a view to seeing how it can be dealt with. If the parties crystallise in hopeless opposition, a settlement is doubtful. Unless the parties continue to negotiate, either together or with the conciliator accurately ascertaining and weighing the arguments of each party and conferring separately with them, a breakdown is certain. It is vital to continue negotiations, or, as is usually said, to keep the parties together. Negotiations may continue for hours, and then for the time being resolve themselves for further hours into plans for preventing a rupture. It is impossible for outside people to come in with platitudinous remarks or easily given advice, but without knowledge of the concentrated purpose of the man who has to succeed or fail by his view of all the circumstances of the case, and the personalities of the people with whom he is negotiating, and has to intervene with suggestions at the exact psychological moment. It is easy to see, if these points are considered, that in conciliation the main point is to get the parties together and to keep them together ; and that this main point requires patience as the first, second, and third qualification, and, in a minor degree, tact, judgment of men, ingenuity, courtesy, power of interpretation of the wishes of the parties, and an utter absence of exhibitions of partisan feelings. Irony, invective, or eloquence are unwise weapons to use. They are liable to be misunderstood. Anger on rare, but only very rare, occasions may be justifiable. Its strength lies in unexpectedness. Emotion is out of place ; imagination must be sternly curbed, though it may frequently be a stepping-stone to the sure ground of practical suggestion. If the conciliator is asked for his view, let him give it without fear or favour; but it is at least unwise to take sides, as so many people do, before all arguments have been heard or before every aggrieved person has had a chance of saying what he thinks, whether his point is good or bad. The whole picture must be before the conciliator, but he must be very quick in judging the salient features and continuously keeping those features before his mind, even if many irrelevant matters are introduced. The more experience he has, the greater knowledge of trades, precedents, and personalities will be at his command, and the greater will be the influence of common sense or brain-power, particularly when it is applied at the proper time, at the psychological moment. That common sense, brain-power, or magnetism, as some people allege, is directed to one object, which initially, perhaps, nobody else in the meeting may desire or contemplate ; that object is peace, and, as far as possible, a durable peace.

It will be recognised that this procedure requires time, and although the more haste the worse speed may be normally the best course in difficult cases, it is impracticable when speed, as in time of war, is essential for the furtherance of greater interests than a lasting settlement of the local struggle. The remarkable feature was the general acquiescence or acceptance, when the disciplinary command or decision came from third parties who could only act upon arguments put before them in London or in Glasgow, after a comparatively brief hearing.

There were necessarily all types of representatives of employers and employed appearing before the arbitrators. At a later date, in a lecture, I mentioned some of the qualities useful to men who might achieve a position, either as employers or trade union leaders, in which they would influence or govern others and have to appear before arbitrators or conciliators. My suggestions were that they should have acquired as thorough a knowledge as possible of the men or women for whom they were working and whom they were representing, and an absolutely thorough knowledge of what their real aims and desires were, so as not to put forward aims which, even if granted, would not satisfy their constituents. They should know the work they were talking about, and not go with ignorance, which could only cause contempt on the other side and difficulty to the outsider. They should try to put their statements as succinctly and relevantly as possible; show as much courtesy and tact as possible; and not ask too much, but what they thought was within the obtainable. They should take with them, where possible, some of their colleagues, who could listen to what they said and be able to enforce their opinion of what occurred in the council chamber on the large outside constituency to whom they were responsible. If any of them became conciliators or arbitrators, and sat in the chair, the most important point of any to follow was patience, and if they could combine patience with coolness, it would go far to reduce angry passions and bring an atmosphere of calm into the proceedings. It had to be recognised most carefully by arbitrators and conciliators that they were dealing with men and women with like passions as themselves, and that the note of human sympathy, the note of humour, the note at one time of repressing frothy or irrelevant remarks, and at another time of trying to help a little in getting out of a man what he failed to express himself, were all valuable points for an arbitrator.

Although, as has been said, the effect of the new Act was to necessitate arbitration in cases where conciliation might otherwise have been used, there were cases in which conciliation alone could have been employed, notably in the unionist and non-unionist agreement in the South Wales coal-field. This very difficult question had caused innumerable strikes in South Wales for a score of years, loss of millions of pounds to employers, and bitter strikes and losses to employees. Employers had taken the view that the question had nothing to do with them ; the work-people must decide, they could not dictate. In the old days they were not hostile to the view that the non-unionists were an antidote to the unions, but for years they had dealt, not with individual men, but with organisations which purported to speak on behalf of all the miners. All agreements, wages, conditions, and mutual questions were settled with these organisations, except the question of non-unionism, which the employers would not admit to be a mutual question. It is not necessary to discuss the obvious reasons for the antagonism and hatred of unionists to the presence of non-union men in such a stronghold of unionism as the Welsh coal-field. The trouble increased during the War, when new men were drafted into the mines. Local strike succeeded local strike unless and until these men agreed to join the union, while managers or foremen, in the desire to get men, could not exercise judgement in tactful avoidance of men who were not already in the union, and whose presence as non-unionists they knew would be certain to lead to trouble. The situation became a national danger, particularly when at many collieries, including the Admiralty steam-coal area, notices were being sent in to leave work unless the non-unionists joined up.

Under these circumstances I asked the parties to meet me, when they effected an agreement which most certainly obviated and still obviates a vast number of stoppages. The agreement stated that :

" The coal-owners agree that an intimation of the fact that the workmen employed at the collieries are required to become members of one or other of the recognised trade unions shall be made throughout the coal-field generally, and at the several collieries. If, notwithstanding such intimation, workmen fail to become members, or cease to be members, and it becomes necessary to take special steps to deal with such men at any colliery or collieries, the Miners' Federation are to be at liberty to apply to the Coal Owners' Association for assistance in carrying out the terms of the requirement at the collieries in question.

"In the event of difficulties arising at any colliery in connection with this question, which cannot be amicably settled by the co-operation of the coal-owners and miners' representatives, it is agreed that notices to cease work shall not be tendered, nor shall any stoppage of work take place, but that the difference shall be reported to the Chief Industrial Commissioner for action by his Department.

"On the understanding that the owners agree to supply the local agents of the Miners' Federation with a list of the workmen at present employed, and also to supply a list once a fortnight of workmen who have left the colliery, and of new workmen who have been employed, the Miners' Federation agree that show-cards shall be suspended during the War, without prejudice to their position after the War.

"In this agreement the term 'workmen' does not include colliery officials."

This agreement prevented many stoppages, but, remarkable document as it was, its complete effect was lessened by the subsequent desire of the Miners' Federation that members of other unions, such as the Colliery Engineers, who for many years had had a foothold in some of the Welsh districts, ought to belong to the Miners' Union, when working under ground, and also, in a number of districts, whether working above or under ground. The difficulty of settling these disputes, often centering round the position of one man, or of arriving at the correct facts, was greatly enhanced by the parties being so far apart that the union leaders would not meet each other.

South Wales was, however, again the storm-centre on a claim for increase of wages, and on disputes which had been left over from the ill-starred settlement of 1915. A difficulty on the claim arose over the supposed action of an independent chairman in pre-judging the claim before all arguments had been heard, and on the disputes because neither side would agree to a settlement. Under instructions I had to give a 15 per cent. advance, which in fact was not very different from the amounts being received in other trades, though the owners disliked the speed with which the claim was dealt with. Bound up with it was an agreement by the parties to obtain the nomination of a new independent chairman, and a consent that the outstanding disputes should be referred to an arbitrator. For the time being quiet was restored, but the frequent troubles in Wales, the growing failure of the parties to reach agreements, the impossibility of interference by dictation to an uncontrolled industry, and the necessity of continuous production of coal, were largely the causes which led the Government to assume control of all the coal-fields.

As the summer advanced, and the cost of living increased, there were in addition to the vast number of arbitrations in trades under the Munitions of War Acts, often amounting to five or six a day for days together, disputes in many trades outside that Act. The woollen trade, after an obstinate strike of wool-combers, practically arranged that I should take case after case, either as arbitrator or conciliator. The Federated Cotton trade was more difficult. They did agree finally, after a long meeting, to leave the question to my decision. The operatives were not pleased with the percentage awarded, chiefly because the card-room operatives wanted more than the other branches. If they had known the great difficulty I had in getting the employers to agree to a decision being given on the length of time the award should last, which I pointed out must be far less than the long periods customary to the trade, and the bitter objections and fears of some sections of the employers at the chance of any increase, they would have realised they had been within an ace of a most disastrous lockout. Conditions were very fluctuating, many businesses had poor financial results, and cotton had been badly affected by the War.

Other cases, brought from Ireland, reminded me of 1913, particularly when a spokesman would appear under escort from internment in prison after the Easter disturbances, and with brief instruction proceed very temperately to argue a wages claim.

The second cycle of wage advances, as it may be called, began about the end of June. The time for adjustment of anomalies had passed. An enormous number of adjustments had been made, and as far as possible that policy of equal treatment, which in face of a common difficulty the Department had been endeavouring to give, had been so effected that, when once a figure had been fixed, general advances to large trades or sections of trades could be quickly settled. The increase in the cost of living, with the result of a widening gap between the value of actual and real wages, justified a new general advance. Although such a vast quantity of work was unproductive work, and the supply of goods ordinarily required for the use of men was going down without any decrease in the demand, the country generally would have to face a considerable increase in the wages to be paid.

In the middle of June, I wrote a memorandum to the Cabinet on the subject of rises of wages, and intimated the opinion of the Committee on Production. The difficulty of trying to prevent unrest would increase from day to day, and unless there was grave reason to the contrary, which would have to be published, the Committee intended to meet the situation by further increases, which were bound to be general. Quickness was to a certain extent forced by an extraordinarily large grant allowed to workpeople at Coventry by the Ministry of Munitions, without any apparent reference to the interlocking of trades or to other advances, or for any other reason than the chance of a strike, and without consultation with or notice to other Departments. The Admiralty, on the other hand, were straining the dockyards to breaking-point. They would not say whether they meant to adhere to pre-war procedure, give an advance, or leave the question to the tribunals under the Munitions Acts. If other cases had been heard and decided before these long-expressed demands were dealt with, trouble was practically certain. The position became acute, but thanks to the common sense of Mr. Harcourt, who was acting President of the Board of Trade, the Government decided that the dockyards' case should be referred to arbitration, and it was at once heard, to be followed immediately by cases from the Clyde, where the Commissioners engaged on dilution (Sir L. Macassey, Sir T. Munro, and Mr. I. H. Mitchell) had been pressing for wages claims to be dealt with. As soon as it was seen that new advances were forthcoming, an avalanche of cases came from all parts of the country, of which the North-East Coast, Lancashire, South Wales, and Scotland were the most important. The awards of the Committee dealt chiefly with time-work increases, so that workers engaged on time-work, who had not such opportunity as men on piecework to get payment by results, might be able to meet the cost of living. At the same time, relieving the monotony of claims for the general advance, many cases arose where efforts were being made by employers to introduce piecework in branches of trade where piecework had not been generally employed, and where the conditions were disputed. In other trades various schemes of premium bonus and payment by results were being tried, some with success, some in forms which led to disputes. The claims of the Ministry of Munitions for iron ore led to an interesting case in Glasgow, where the trial of a tonnage rate to dockers unloading the ore, instead of a day rate, at once led to large acceleration in supply. This hearing took place on the Clyde in one of a series of visits to Scotland which it seemed desirable for me to take on behalf of the Committee on Production, when quickening of decisions continued to be necessary, and the difficulties of railway travel hindered journeys to London by deputations of employers and employed. The hearings involved every class of trade and every kind of technicality, from the building of submarines to the heeling of boots, and from instrument-makers to the unloading of iron ore; from cases of a few individuals to general advances involving thousands of men.

In the brief intervals which the other Scottish claims allowed, it may be mentioned that there was gradually settled during the War, under my chairmanship, a National Building Code for Scotland. Its beginnings arose from an obstinate dispute of the master-builders with the architects and surveyors as to the mode of measurement for joiners' work. The dispute, which existed in the early days of the War, was so keenly conducted that it was bound to affect other industries, but none of the parties desired such a result, and agreed to meet. After long conferences they also agreed to my final decision as an arbiter. A scheme of measurement for joiners' work, largely due to the able assistance of Mr. Herbert Ryle, of the Scottish Office of Works, was laid before them, and after discussion settled. This scheme led to other modes in the varied branches of the building trade, together with a model contract and regulations, the whole forming a National Building Code. The better feeling, saving of expense and time, regulation of a great and very technical industry, and lasting results engendered by the existence of this code, the first National Building Code produced by any country, is, I think, not the least of the many achievements produced in Scotland during the War.

It may be said that the period from August to November 1916 was probably the period during the War when the least difficulty arose in the settlement of differences; but the plans for equable adjustment were soon cut across.

It was perhaps to be supposed that interference would arise. The activity of the Ministry of Munitions probably appeared in its most unfortunate form in its dealings with Labour. Its Labour Department was very badly organised, or not organised at all in its initial stages, but that fact did not prevent it, under the guise of efforts towards control and dilution, from constant interference in labour differences or quarrels. Numbers of young men, without the least knowledge or experience, were scattered over the country, without defined authority, or under any definite or adequate leadership. They gave orders, proposed or required changes of wages, and by ignorance, or in some cases lack of judgement, created a great deal of trouble. Their action led to much of the dislike of officials and official interference which is still so prevalent. In time some of them gained experience and became good officers; others who showed themselves unfitted and incompetent were weeded out. They ought never to have been appointed, and much less allowed to exercise the harmful influence which they had in so many parts of the country.

In the autumn, too, the Government, unable to find a fixed office for one of its Members, Mr. Arthur Henderson, appointed him its "Labour Adviser." Instead of dealing with broad matters of policy, he issued a statement, quite incorrect, that the Board of Trade only dealt with cases after a dispute had arisen, but he would deal with them in anticipation. He called himself a Department "with a future." This pronouncement at once led to claims by sections who had not got as much as they desired from the Arbitration Courts or by conciliation, and a reopening of cases. He practically made the employers in the aircraft industry yield to demands, and under a statement, called an award, gave to the workpeople a special status and wages beyond what they had actually sought. This procedure at once raised claims from classes of workers of the same category, such as carpenters and joiners, who were engaged in other industries and possibly more onerous work. The work of arbitration was not rendered more easy by such uncertain actions.

The same result followed when, at the close of the year, Mr. Asquith went out and Mr. Lloyd George came in. A Ministry of Labour was suddenly established. The new Minister, Mr. Hodge, also issued a statement to the effect that he was personally available for hearing all grievances. Every disgruntled person at once flooded him with complaints and demands. Old claims which had been practically forgotten were revived. A decision was given at Manchester to boilermakers which affected the whole trade; and finally, so heavy were the efforts for personal interference, that he had in defence to say that all cases must be referred to the courts constituted by law and the Department authorised to deal with disputes.

CHAPTER XXXVIII

NEW MINISTRIES, 1917

THE Ministry of Labour was settled in a few minutes, or even less, when Mr. Lloyd George heard the conditions under which the Labour Party would be prepared to support him politically. No details were arranged, but it was evident that this new departure would mean the transfer of Departments specially involving labour questions from the Board of Trade to a new Ministry. At the time when assent was given to the proposal for the Ministry there existed a difficult dispute concerning the lightermen in London; the South Lancashire cotton trade had to be proclaimed under the Munitions of War Acts, owing to the desire of the leaders of cardroom hands to anticipate the termination of my award of the summer; a move was being made for an agreement in the engineering trades in favour of consolidation of general demands and periodical hearings; the question of coal control was being debated, owing to fresh demands by the miners; the subject of premium bonus and piecework was being seriously pressed in Glasgow and other places; and the whole of the first week in December was spent by me in settling a very large number of disputes in Scotland. There was plenty of effervescing disturbance in the country, and the situation was not free from serious causes of anxiety. The letter of Mr. Hodge, the new Minister, to which allusion has been made, the resulting predicament in which he found himself, and his effort to exercise a dispensing power in Manchester, did not alleviate matters. It was only the beginning of the era, already commenced by the Ministry of Munitions, when new authorities, new Departments, new Ministries, vied with each other in seeking control over any labour questions affecting them, with little or no regard to each other's vagaries. The system spelt lack of co-ordination.

If the Government had had any labour policy, it ceased from December 1916. No Minister of Labour could have had success when hampered by this absence of policy, the force of disintegration resulting from the maze of authorities, and the opportunist arrangements one or other authority continuously made.

Each new Ministry or Department seemed to desire to start out on its own ideas for dealing with labour. The Ministry of Munitions, almost before the new Minister was supplied with offices at Montagu House, pressed him into adhesion to their young men being authorised to deal with labour disputes in controlled establishments. The Coal Controller followed with the contention that he must deal with the wages and conditions in the coal-fields, as Mr. Smillie and other miners' leaders so desired. With the results the whole country is acquainted, and how the Coal Controller, with an appeal always pending to the Prime Minister, was forced from pillar to post and compelled to give amounts which reflected upon other trades. The Ministry of Shipping followed suit, and within a few months set up a shipping board, which also determined wages without much regard to any other Department. The railwaymen, too, watched events and negotiated with the Railway Executive, again with an appeal always pending to the Prime Minister, having precedents in these other trades or setting precedents without cohesion with other trades. The Air Ministry "out-Heroded Herod," and with astonishing lack of control or system brought the building trade and many sections of workpeople into a state of unrest which has left a lasting mark. The loathing with which bureaucracy has been tarred has been much helped by the development of this bad system.

The chaos thus produced was serious, and it put the Minister of Labour in a difficult position, which was not rendered more easy by the general situation, many people making prophecies that Mr. Lloyd George's Government could not last. Neither did Mr. Hodge receive any particular help from the Labour Party. They had put him there, but some of them seemed to be anxious to use him as their tool. This procedure he resented, and when he tried to be fair, was accused of leaning to the side of the employers.

It is not, however, my purpose to deal with the action

of individuals. In addition to the disintegrating elements fostered by the Ministry of Munitions and soon to be imitated by other Departments, there were, at the time of the formation of the Ministry of Labour, the two questions of consolidation of labour demands and the growing pressure for systems of payment by results which had demanded attention during the autumn, before the Ministry of Labour was thought of. To these questions I continued to direct effort.

The Government, owing to the pressure of overlapping claims, had wisely decided, through Mr. George Barnes, that awards, agreements, and decisions must be upheld, and should not be reopened before a reasonable period had elapsed. In view of the rapid changes in cost of living, a reasonable period, it was suggested, should be short. Four months was proposed. As the second cycle of wage demands was now almost closed, and further claims were continuously being forwarded, it was apparent there would be a block of claims to be heard if each district, union, trade, and association, as well as many separate firms, desired separate awards. No single court could cope with such a number, particularly as decisions by the Committee on Production were being demanded in preference to awards by single arbitrators.

At the same time, such anomalies as the Committee intended to deal with had been settled. Demands became more and more confined to changes of wages, with a view to obtaining equality of treatment under the common trouble of increase in the cost of living. Parties themselves had begun to recognise, largely owing to difficulties of travelling, the value of grouping. Employers were sending two or three persons as spokesmen for a whole group of firms, or as representatives of a big association; and the same reduction of spokesmen was being followed by trade unions, who often waited until a number of claims in their districts were ready. Speed in dealing with the general claims could possibly be effected if there were more courts, closely co-ordinated together and working as branches of the Committee on Production, which experience from visits to Scotland indicated as a proved advantage, and if the hearing of the general claims could be consolidated. The formation of new courts and the establishment of increased staff, which had been consistently and unreasonably kept at starvation level, were matters for the Government and the Minister. Consolidation of claims might be a matter which could be effected by agreement.

The attempt was first made with the engineering industry. After consultation with the leaders of the Engineering Employers' Federation and of some principal unions, the idea seemed to be feasible. A large conference was summoned, at which a draft agreement was put forward for consideration. The parties discussed these proposals by themselves, and after some hours effected an agreement, twelve or more trade unions adhering at once, and others deciding to consult their members.

By the end of January, general adherence had been obtained, and an agreement signed in the following terms :

Memorandum of Agreement between the Engineering Employers' Federation and the Unions connected with the Engineering and Foundry Trades arrived at in February 1917.

"It is agreed that, having regard to the special circumstances of the War, the following shall be the principles upon which wages changes shall be arranged for the period of the War:

"(1) That existing agreements or practice under which applications for general alteration in wages are dealt with shall to that extent be suspended until the termination of the War, or for such further period as may be agreed upon by the parties thereto. This shall not refer to agreements or practices whereby the wages of any trades in any district or department rise or fall with the fluctuations in another district or industry not covered by this agreement.

"Nor shall it prevent the unions bringing forward for special consideration at the hearings referred to in paragraph 2 (*a*) the case of any district in which they claim that the rates of wages are unduly low, or that the total amount of war advances is not adequate.

"On the other hand, the Federation shall be entitled to bring forward for similar consideration any special cases they desire.

"(2) During such period of suspension, the following

procedure shall be observed, provided the consent of the Committee on Production is obtained:

"(*a*) The Committee on Production shall, in the months of February, June, and October, after hearing parties, consider what general alteration in wages, if any, is warranted by the abnormal conditions then existing and due to the War.

"(*b*) The award of the Committee on Production shall be an award under the Munitions of War Acts, and shall be of national application to all federated firms in the branch of trade concerned.

"(*c*) The first award shall take effect in all districts on first full pay in April, and the altered rate shall continue until amended by a further award in accordance with provisions hereof. Subsequent awards shall specify the date upon which the alteration awarded shall take effect."

The following memorandum was also agreed between the parties:

"The Engineering Employers' Federation and the Unions whose signatures are appended hereto recommend to His Majesty's Government that arrangements should be made whereby all employers in the trade or trades affected should be subject to the awards which may be made by the Committee on Production in virtue of the agreement hereto attached."

It will be seen that the agreement provided for periodical hearings every four months, by the Committee on Production, in regard to claims for general advances of wages and also in regard to district claims, and that existing agreements or practices for the determination of such claims were meanwhile suspended. By the end of the year fifty-two trade unions signed this agreement.

Agreements on the same lines were subsequently made by the Mersey Ship Repairers' Association and the Employers' Association of the Port of Liverpool on the one hand, and the Federation of Engineering and Shipbuilding Trades (Mersey District Committee) and the Liverpool District Joint Committee of Engineering Societies on the other; the National Association of Master Heating and

Domestic Engineers and the National Union of Operative Heating and Domestic Engineers; the Chemical Employers' Federation and the National Federation of General Workers, etc., and the Joint Committee of Salt and Chemical Workers; the Soap and Candle Trades Employers' Federation and the National Federation of General Workers and the Joint Committee of Salt and Chemical Workers; the Wages Committee of Explosives Manufacturers and the National Federation of General Workers; the Drug and Fine Chemical Manufacturers' Association and the National Warehouse and General Workers' Union and others; the Scottish Building Trades (Employers) Wages Board and the Building Trades of Scotland Standing Committee; and the Employers' and Operatives' Associations and Federations connected with the Building Trades of England and Wales.

In the case of a number of other trades—for example, Shipbuilding, Scottish Iron and Steel Trades, Dockers (Great Britain), Carters (Great Britain), Clay Industry (Great Britain), Railway Shopmen, and the London County Council—the principle of a four-monthly revision of wages by the Committee on Production, without the other clauses of the agreement, was adopted.

In fact, the main agreement and its various branches form possibly the most far-extending single agreement which has ever been made or obtained force between employers and employed in this, or indeed in any, country. Although specified to be a war agreement, the agreement remained intact till the ironfounders gave notice to secede in August 1919, with an ensuing strike lasting for four months, but the system was continued by the other unions. Dealing with general advances, its chief foundation was to give general advances to meet the increases in cost of living, which, when Germany proclaimed unrestricted submarine warfare on February 1, 1917, was likely to increase, and did increase, by leaps and bounds. It came just in the nick of time to combat these advances, so far as increase of wages could do it, in a manner which was generally understood and accepted throughout the country. It gave certainty instead of uncertainty, treated most classes of workers with equality, and, being followed by the mass of the people, tended to general absence of unrest. After the War, the Industrial Courts slightly altered the principle of their advances. In 1919 they took into account the claim that workpeople should be in a better position than before the War, but at a later date, in 1920, they refused an advance on the ground of condition of trade. In some senses, an observer might think that the two principles had been found to be incompatible, that the awards cancelled each other, and that the workpeople could not be in a better position unless the conditions of trade warranted it. Be that as it may, the workpeople found themselves in the position that they would either have to endeavour to retain the system of equal advances throughout the industry, which socialist theory might deem to be desirable, or to resume the pre-war system of district and general conferences without finality of decision, which would allow different claims to be made in different districts, with some regard to the conditions of trade in each district, and the presumed profits of employers in that district. The executive of such an important union as the Engineers could not come to a decision by themselves, without consulting the rank and file, and accordingly, in July 1920, proceeded to a ballot on the subject, under which the war practice has been dropped. This decision would not prevent the courts being used under new agreements suitable for a period of peace.

The first award given under the new system, and the last wide-extending award issued while I was Chairman of the Committee on Production, was published on March 1, 1917. The award gave to the engineering and foundry trades an advance of 5*s.* per full ordinary week to all classes of workers, and also decided that, where the general advances given in any federated district since the beginning of the War (exclusive of advances granted before August 4, 1914, but coming into operation after that date), amounted to less than 7*s.* per week on time rates, the men concerned should receive such further advances as would make their total advances (apart from the general advance of 5*s.* now awarded) 7*s.* per week on time rates.

The award was deemed by some to be a generous award, but later events, due to the submarine successes and the rapid rise in cost of living, proved its justification. It was given to all the workpeople concerned in face of a trouble common to them all, and was at once extended by the Shipbuilding Employers' Federation to the shipyards, and adopted by trade after trade, although some writers proceeded to discern socialistic tendencies in it.

"This award," a critic said, "is in many ways a 'record' in wage arbitrations. For the first time, a uniform advance of wages has been given to the whole of the men in the engineering workshops of Great Britain, nearly a million in number, they and their families representing one-tenth of the whole population; for the first time, the advance is simultaneously accorded, not only to all the sectional crafts, but also to all the labourers in the shops, of equal and identical amount to all grades (5*s.* per week); for the first time the labourers' unions were admitted to the negotiations and dealt with on equal and identical terms with those of the craftsmen; for the first time the same advance is made to all pieceworkers by an addition of 5*s.* to their earnings on an unchanged scale. Moreover, the award is notable in respect of the magnitude of the sum involved. It necessitates an additional payment to the workmen during the ensuing year of between £12,000,000 and £13,000,000."

The formation of more courts was the corresponding factor to agreements for consolidation of claims. The very acceptance of consolidation demanded speedy hearing of claims in different trades within the shortest practicable time. The Committee on Production was simply overwhelmed with the number of cases, each of which required a large amount of correspondence. Its staff was ludicrously small. Visits to the North and Scotland by a single member could only alleviate, not meet, the number of pressing claims. A glut of cases was dealt with as speedily as possible, not helped by a premature announcement that there were to be new courts of unspecified constitution, until finally, in the middle of May, the Minister of Labour was able to announce the appointment of two, and afterwards three, courts, including representatives of employers and employed, with neutral chairmen. Sir George Gibb and Sir David Harrel, with the later addition of Sir W. Mackenzie, a successful arbitrator, continued as chairmen, and the three courts had a common secretariat. With additions and variations in personnel, these courts continued the work and principles founded by the first Committee on

Production, and in the course of the year gave two further general awards for the engineering and foundry trades, one of 3*s*. per week on July 14, and another of 5*s*. per week on November 6, to both time- and piece-workers.

Upon the question of systems for payment by results no success attended the Minister's proposals. In the maze of conflicting opinions, it appeared to me to be desirable that the subject should be examined. The point was to get at the truth in a number of industries, whose circumstances would vary. If an impartial inquiry was held, objections or fancies might be clearly seen, and if invalid, overcome. The value of different systems might be appraised, or their faults and their consequences discovered. It was, in any event, important that the best advice should be given at a time when the fate of the whole country might depend upon the largest possible production. In February, representatives of all the principal trade unions were convened at a Conference, but the Minister of Labour made no headway. He was too blunt. Instead of proposing an inquiry, he spoke from his own experience of steel, and practically intimated that no other system but that which had succeeded in the steel trade was worth anything. He told the whole of the delegates that they must have payment by results. The usual objection against appearance of dictation at once came to the front from trades such as carpenters and joiners, and the iron-founders. They would not admit the contention. What did a man connected with steel know about wood ? etc. etc. The same objections are rife now, particularly in the building and moulding trades. No proper inquiry has been held up to the present day, and yet it is a matter which is worthy of close examination in all its ramifications, and by many said to be vital to the interests of the country.

Following upon the revision of arbitration procedure, some of my officers transferred with me to Montagu House, Whitehall, where the Ministry of Labour was located, but still had to deal with the heavy work of preparation and reference of cases to the arbitral tribunals, as well as with the conciliation cases and the many causes of dissatisfaction arising from the conflicting action of the new Departments. Very important conciliation cases, as soon as I had left the dull work of arbitration, came from the manufacturing section of the cotton trade in North Lancashire, the woollen and worsted trades in Yorkshire, the dyeing trade, the flint-glass trade, and London omnibuses over the employment of women. It may be remarked that the midday air-raids of June 13 settled one dispute quickly, owing to the parties being anxious to leave such an unpleasant place as London by the afternoon train. The work continuously grew during the rest of the summer. As to the conflicting action of new Departments, complaints came in from every side. Dissatisfaction arose with awards when they did not come up to such amount as had been conceded by one or other Government Department. Appeals were rife, first to one Minister and then to another, and finally to the War Cabinet or the Prime Minister. The situation was brought before the Minister of Labour, but he could do little, and indeed had to concede the requirements of the Coal Controller, himself acting under pressure. Following upon a strong letter of complaint from the Engineering Employers' Federation, the situation was also brought by me, early in April, before the Prime Minister, who agreed it was most important, and proposed to hold an immediate meeting of the War Cabinet to discuss it, but a call to Italy stopped this, and the proposal lapsed.

My memorandum upon the subject at that time contained the following remarks :

"The Engineering Employers' Federation have formally complained to the Prime Minister of the lack of co-ordination and the necessity of one authority on labour matters. This is not the first occasion on which such complaint has been put forward. It is known that the Shipbuilding Employers' Federation hold the same view. Trade unions and employers everywhere are in uncertainty and confusion, and are unable to look to any one central or responsible authority in the number of overlapping Government Departments.

"The prestige and influence of existing Departments are being seriously impaired, and no responsibility is practicable where no finality exists or is even attempted, and where new officers are permitted at will to interfere with the work of existing Departments. The Ministry of Munitions has established a Disputes Department. The

Admiralty has at least two. There is nothing to prevent officers of the Board of Agriculture, the Shipping Controller, the Controller of Mines following the same course. The Ministry of Labour is itself divided.

"Under the plea of being the employers, some of these Departments are seriously impairing the relations and responsibility of actual employers and workpeople to settle their own differences; are causing unrest in the ranks of labour; are weakening the authority of trade union leaders; are spreading bureaucracy throughout the country; are pitting one Department against another; and are impeding unanimity and the progress of the War.

"With a view to remedy of this position, it is submitted that:

"1. One Government authority be solely and entirely responsible for dealing with labour matters.

"2. Any representations other Departments may wish to make respecting delays in the execution of work, the transference of workmen, the substitution of semi-skilled and unskilled for skilled men, the introduction of new methods of production, or the remuneration of labour by payment by results, when the workmen decline to adopt it, should be at once reported to that authority.

"3. All appointments of Trade Unionists, Advisers, Labour Committees, and the convening of Labour Conferences should be arranged by or through the Ministry of Labour.

"4. The settlement of conditions of labour should be left to employers and their workpeople or their representatives, and action by the Ministry of Munitions should be confined to simple approval or disapproval.

"5. As to labour differences, the main producing Departments would be strengthened by rigid refusal to be implicated in such differences. The Ministers responsible should be in a position to say, 'My Department has nothing to do with differences, but the work must proceed as it is.' Ministers are continuously involved in hundreds of petty squabbles. Labour differences should be handled by one Department only. This of itself would reduce the differences at present existing, by the creation of an atmosphere of greater stability and security. Where differences do arise, both parties jointly, employers and workmen, should understand that they must make every effort to settle without delay and without friction. Where they fail to be so settled, both parties should join in referring them to the Chief Industrial Commissioner's Department, and take this course, if at all possible, before they come to a head.

"The authority of that Department should be made known to the country. The Department should be as free as possible from all political influence. If it is necessary for the Department to have support from His Majesty's Government, it should be effected by the appeal of the Chief Industrial Commissioner direct to the Minister of Labour, or to the Prime Minister, or by means of a Parliamentary Secretary representing the Department.

"So far as the Chief Industrial Commissioner's Department is concerned, unless it is put in a position of full responsibility in the handling of labour differences, it cannot be blamed for any disputes that may arise."

CHAPTER XXXIX

TWELVE AND A HALF PER CENT.

As the spring and summer of 1917 passed, the evil of lack of co-ordination became aggravated, but received culminating proof of its bad effect in the well-known grant of the $12\frac{1}{2}$ per cent. That event was a strange comment on a series of reports by hastily improvised Industrial Commissions appointed by the Prime Minister in June, to inquire and report within a fortnight upon the causes of industrial unrest. These Commissions were to use any means for ascertaining the facts, were to see for themselves, make inquiries for themselves, get to know what was happening, why it was happening, and report in fourteen days. With the exception of a report on South Wales, none of the reports were much more than a re-hash of known points or of stale complaints. There was no cohesion between them, as the Commissions had no time. They were not summoned to meet and compare notes or to formulate any considered report. Every conceivable *ex parte* complaint and opinion had been invited and heard without check, hindrance to misstatement, or explanation of facts or circumstances. Some of the chairmen asked leave to apply to different Departments to hear their answers to or explanations of various complaints made about them, but met with refusal on the score of time, the reports being published without any Department being given an opportunity of being heard or knowing what statements had been made about them. The reports bore the mark of a "stopgap" expedient with a view of indicating that something was being done, or that complaints would be heard by new authorities.

There were two points, however, on which all the Commissions laid stress: the objection to the leaving certificate regulations, which prevented men from moving from one firm to another, and the difference in earnings between skilled men (such as skilled tool-makers, mill-wrights, setters-up, etc.) and semi-skilled or unskilled workers who had been enabled, owing to the undertakings not to cut piece prices if output increased, the improvement of repetition work, and their own enhanced skill, to earn in some firms more than the skilled men on time-work. If the leaving certificate regulations were removed, such skilled men would be likely to leave time-work for which they were required, and go upon shell work or the easier production work. The Commissions were generally in favour of a system whereby skilled supervisors and others on time rates should receive a bonus. It was only one of the minor recommendations, and they may not have become aware, after so brief an inquiry, how largely the difficulty had been met by special grants to these men in the majority of firms, whose vital interest it was to keep them contented. The question had several times come up in arbitrations before the Committee on Production, who had made suggestions to that effect and indicated that it had best be dealt with locally and according to the exigencies of each case, possibly of each man. It had been agreed always by the representatives of the unions concerned that no general award and no general bonus would meet the very varied classes of workers concerned. The whole question resolved itself into a succession of special cases, and could only be specially dealt with. It was at this juncture that Mr. Churchill, lately returned to the ranks of Ministers, gave a pledge, or used words which, if not a pledge, as was afterwards said, were certainly interpreted to be a pledge. He proposed to abolish leaving certificates, and to effect equalisation of earnings by favour to skilled time-workers. It was an indication of a sectional advance which was bound to react, just as all other sectional advances of the kind must react, upon surrounding sections and thence to trade after trade.

Powers for giving greater authority to the Minister of Munitions to carry out any plan which might be formed were given by a third Munitions of War Act, passed on August 21, 1917. This Act authorised the Minister of Munitions to give directions with respect to the remuneration to be paid for work paid at time rates, being munitions work or work in connection therewith, or work in any controlled establishment. It was provided that, where a difference arose respecting matters in which the Minister of Munitions had given directions, the difference should be referred to a special arbitration tribunal.

It may be added that this Act also authorised a Government Department to report a difference, provided that arbitration tribunals should make awards without delay and, where practicable, within fourteen days from the date of reference, and empowered the Minister of Munitions in certain cases to make awards binding upon minorities, by the extension of awards or agreements made by employers employing the majority of persons engaged on or in connection with munitions work in any trade or branch of a trade. This last section recalled the proposals made by the Industrial Council in 1913 in reference to extension of agreements, but did not allude to the *quid pro quo* in the shape of agreement to delay strikes which was an essential part of the opinion tendered by the Industrial Council.

Mr. Churchill appointed a small committee of officials under a political chairman, who could not have known anything of the subject, with instructions to find a way of fulfilling his undertaking, not of considering whether the plan was wise or not. They reported in favour of a bonus of 12½ per cent. on earnings to certain categories of fully skilled time-workers in the engineering and, later, the foundry trades. An officer of the Ministry of Labour was a member of this Committee, but an early protest by him to Mr. Churchill and to the Minister of Labour was never sent forward. He was never consulted by the chairman or shown the report before it was issued. As soon as the proposals happened to come to me in October, I wrote a strong minute that they ought to be stopped.

The evils of a sectional advance or of one trade in advance of another had been quite recently exhibited, at the beginning of September. The Coal Controller, apparently without any consultation with the Ministry of Labour or the War Cabinet, had allowed himself to be forced into a large advance to the miners. He excused part of it on the ground that back allowance was due, the miners not having had increases at the same time as other workpeople, owing to the delays consequent on the establishment of control. This argument was not apparent to, and did not impress, other workpeople, who saw a flat-rate war grant of 1*s.* 6*d.* a day given to one particular trade in September, and compared it with the advance of 3*s.* per week given by the new Committee on Production in the middle of July, an advance due to stand till the month of November. It interfered seriously with the allowances agreed to in the railway service and in the transport trades. It was evident that unrest must arise from unequal advances both in amount and date of allowance to one class of workpeople. A member of the War Cabinet and the new Minister of Labour, Mr. G. H. Roberts, had had a warm interview with the Coal Controller on this application of a principle of control without co-ordination, which he had forced from the outgoing Minister of Labour. They had insisted that the Controller must not go so far again without the approval of the Government at earlier stages. Now the Minister of Labour became alive to the fact that another sectional advance was in immediate prospect, of which he had heard little or nothing, and of which the effect was obvious.

During my absence in the North, Mr. Mitchell sent to him some prescient remarks upon the subject. He said :

" While the Ministry of Labour is putting up for the regularisation of wages movements a uniform policy, and the observance of awards and decisions, the spending Departments are openly pursuing a policy of generous wage advances regardless alike of the effect these concessions have upon their own Department or others. The first-fruits of the Coal Controller's concessions to the miners is the demand of the railwaymen for £1 per week advance, in addition to the 15*s.* already received. The Scottish Colliery Enginemen were told by the Coal Controller on August 10 that, in his opinion, no case for a present increase in enginemen's wages had been made out. A week or two later, on threat of a strike, he offered them 1*s.* 3*d.* per shift advance, totalling 29*s.* 9*d.* per week advance since the War began. Now that the miners have received 1*s.* 6*d.* per shift advance, it may be confidently expected that the enginemen will demand a like sum.

" The line followed by the Ministry of Munitions is quite as serious. I understand the recommendation of the Majority Report of the Skilled Day-Workers Committee has been endorsed. This is the more extraordinary in view of the fact that the Admiralty quite recently decided to abolish the 'lieu payment.' The lieu payment was an enhanced time rate paid on jobs where piecework could not be applied. Its abolition was necessitated by the discovery that the system was vicious, retarded output, and was abused; it had, however, the semblance of an excuse, inasmuch as the men were supposed to make extra effort. Now we have the Ministry of Munitions introducing a system which frankly abandons all pretence of extra efforts, rejects the conditional 'payment by result' clause, and offers from 10 per cent. to 15 per cent. advance to skilled time-work engineers. Accompanying this is the abolition of the leaving certificate, which in itself will result in an additional upward jump in wages. To these two concessions is also added an extension of the subsistence allowance. In competition against all this, the Admiralty must, of course, proceed to bid up to the attractions set by the Ministry of Munitions, otherwise they cannot hope to retain their men. The immediate result will, of course, be not only claims for similar treatment by all other time-workers on munition-work, but an agitation amongst the lower-paid pieceworkers, where the piecework balance is small, for similar concessions.

"The chaotic, individual, and competitive handling of labour pursued by the various Departments has resulted in fostering the spirit of unrest: harassing and rendering impotent the employers or management: in addition to vastly adding to the cost of the War and hindering output. The only argument advanced to defend this triumph of the competitive system is that the various Ministers and Controllers entrusted with these Departments are the virtual employers, and are therefore entitled to settle the disputes which arise in the works over which they exercise control. Admitting this for the moment, surely the first duty of modern management is to unite with kindred employers so as to ensure economic working."

The leaving certificate regulations were to die, in accordance with the promise of the Minister of Munitions, on Monday, October 15. The proposals of the report on the 12½ per cent. had already leaked out. If it was to be established, the Ministry were anxious to publish their adhesion before October 15. It was for that reason that on Friday, October 12, the War Cabinet held a full meeting, and finally, after the Prime Minister had remarked that he did not see how they could go back on what would be said to be a Parliamentary pledge, referred the detail of incidence to a Committee of the Cabinet which met in the afternoon. At that meeting, Lord Milner at once remarked that, after the statements about the pledge, the 12½ per cent. was past praying for ; there only remained the incidence, and the question where, if at all, it could be stopped. Formal protest by Sir Lynden Macassey, head of the Shipyard Labour Department, and myself were entered on the War Cabinet minutes. As to incidence the foundry trade, on the advice of Mr. Barnes, was even at this early stage added to the classes supposed to be covered by the loosely worded order. That order came out on Sunday, October 14, the day before the abolition of leaving certificates, and was known as Statutory Rules and Orders 1917, No. 1061.

Its effect was absolutely immediate. On Monday, October 15, representatives of the railways came to see me, to ask what they were to do. Their agreements and arrangements were all upset. It would certainly be claimed in the railway shops, and must spread to the working of the lines. Representatives of the Electrical Union also came, telling me that they would never be able to hold their workpeople in the electrical power-stations, with whose managements I had been endeavouring for a month to arrange a joint scheme of equal treatment within the industry, and of advances equivalent to those granted to analogous workpeople in allied industries. All through the next weeks, trade union leader after trade union leader came for advice under the difficult circumstances in which they were placed, some of their members receiving the bonus and others being excluded from it. Officials of the Ministry of Munitions found themselves immersed in the same difficulties. They were flooded with demands for extension, and it seemed an ironical comment on the scores of millions to be annually then and now expended on the 12½ per cent. bonus that, on October 22, four War Cabinet Ministers made moving appeals to the country to invest in War Savings.

An official account states:

"It was found impracticable in the face of agitation to restrict the advance to the original categories, and on December 11, further Orders 1301 and 1308 were issued, giving the advance to other grades of time-workers employed in engineering and foundry, and in shipbuilding and ship-repairing establishments. The agitation for the 12½ per cent. bonus spread to all trades, and by January it had been secured by workmen employed on munitions work, and paid as plain time-workers in engineering shops, boiler-shops, foundries, shipbuilding and ship-repairing establishments, iron and steel trades, electricity generating stations and electrical contracting trades, nut and bolt trades, brass foundries and brass-works, bridge-building and constructional engineering, hollow-ware trade, spring-making works, hot stamping works, tube works, and wagon-building works. In January, by which time considerable unrest had arisen among pieceworkers, who were not eligible for the bonus, the War Cabinet decided, after obtaining the advice of the Committee on Production, to grant a bonus of 7½ per cent. to pieceworkers and other men on systems of payment by results. Before many months, practically every trade had secured either the bonus or an equivalent. The bonus, intended originally as a compensation to certain skilled men on munition work, failed entirely in its original purpose, and merely became an advance of wages which all trades claimed and many secured. Designed in the first place to allay unrest, this disturbance of comparative rates was a principal cause of much labour unrest."

Another account may be taken as an example of the criticism levelled at the new Order. It stated:

"If the purpose which led to the Order was, as we presume it was, no broader in intention than to level up the time-rate of the supervising craftsmen, it is regrettable that this has not been made plain. The Order ostensibly applies to time-rated 'engineers and moulders,' but these crafts do not comprise all the varieties of munitions work in which dilution has been adopted, and much dubiety exists as to whom exactly the Order covers. Already a circular has been issued, indicating certain trades which were intended to be included, but this, it is to be feared, has not improved, but only still further confused, the situation. There may be also a question upon the interpretation of 'earnings,' upon which the Order allows the $12\frac{1}{2}$ per cent. bonus to be paid. But all these matters pale before the graver question of the seriousness of the new departure in principle. Criticism of the arbitration scheme of the Munitions Act has not been wanting; but the scheme has at least the merit of being a system which aims at co-ordinating and proportioning increases of wages. If the Minister of a Department is suddenly, off his own bat, to make wages Orders, what effect is that to have upon the statutory scheme, which, if it has not pleased both parties—as no arbitration scheme probably ever did, or ever will—has at least ensured that all parties interested have been heard, and that the award is the only thing the parties have to respond to?

"The Committee on Production's national awards of April and August covered the same class of men as this Order does. Under the trade agreement, the national award falls to be periodically revised, and, in the recent third revision, an additional war advance of 5*s*. was being decreed, just at the very moment this Order was being issued. We do not know what this new departure portends; we sincerely trust it does not mean the introduction of the politician element in departmental administration; but even if it does, there seems nothing to be gained, and much to be lost, by departure from existing methods, which, upon the whole, have worked satisfactorily. If the Minister thought that he was bound to fulfil his promise to remedy the anomaly of the disproportionate remuneration of skilled and unskilled labour, he might still have recollected that the Munitions Act had, by an amendment on the original Act, expressly included a Government Department amongst those who may invoke the aid of the arbitration scheme. The principle of removing the disproportion of pay grievance by a uniform percentage bonus is dangerous, and possibly unfair, for there may be many varieties and grades, in different trades, or in different establishments in the same trade, of this disproportion between skilled and unskilled remuneration. The existing arbitration scheme afforded ready machinery for inquiry and discussion and adjustment in each set of circumstances, and to have resorted to it would have prevented the possibility of overlapping and ensured a fair hearing for all interested, and, whether it pleased them or not, employers and workmen alike would have known exactly where they were under an award. Nevertheless, any Order may be amended, or may be cancelled. We venture to hope—and we quite believe—that the Minister of Munitions, if he finds, as he probably will, that this Order has missed its mark, will have the courage to cancel it, and, after conference probably with employers and workmen's representatives, find a workable method of effecting the remedy of an anomaly which everybody wants to see remedied without resorting to a method so foreign to the spirit, and the letter, of the Munitions Acts."

On November 9 a conference representing half a million unskilled munition-workers in the engineering trades was held at York, and they demanded the bonus. The piece-workers began to move, and say that an equivalent should be given to them. Strikes were beginning all over the country. Each attempt to confine it, or each extension, only led to more unrest and more claims. So beset were other Departments by the claims made upon them, at a time when they were ignorant what the Ministry of Munitions were from day to day doing, that I called together, after consulting the Minister of Labour, representatives of all the chief Departments, and suggested a plan of a joint consultative or co-ordinating Committee, which should consider questions affecting all the Departments, and that a smaller Committee of the Labour and Munitions Departments should especially deal with the pending demands for extensions of the 12½ per cent., and that nothing should be done by any Department without the knowledge of this Committee, which could speedily circulate opinions or advice. It was once more an attempt at some form of co-ordination, and some method also in dealing with the 12½ per cent. The Departments almost wholly supported the suggestions. They had suffered too much by the absence of any principle enabling them to deal with wages, and the want of knowledge of action taken by other Departments. The question of this Committee came before the War Cabinet at the end of November. Mr. Churchill still wanted to keep the control, and said, if he was allowed, he could by drastic action, but at the risk of many disturbances, still keep the 12½ per cent. within certain bounds. Every Department and Minister was against him, and the Committee was established, not as I wished it, in close connection with the Consultative Committee of Departments, and equally with it under the control of the Ministry of Labour as a neutral authority, with, if desired, a Cabinet Minister as chairman, who could carry important points of principle to the Cabinet, should that be necessary, but under a Cabinet Minister (Mr. Barnes) as chairman, and the Minister of the National Service (Sir Auckland Geddes), who was admittedly unversed in the intricacies of British labour, as vice-chairman. Under these circumstances, involving that lack of co-ordination which it was expressly intended that the Committees should prevent, if use could be made of the Ministry of Labour as the connecting-link, I would fain have been relieved from serving, but was curtly told to remain as a member.

The reference settled by the War Cabinet to this "Government Labour Committee" was "to deal with questions of wages (including interpretation of the Orders relating to the increase of 12½ per cent. recently granted to plain time-workers in certain industries), and to co-ordinate the settlement of labour questions affecting Government Departments." It would "confer with a consultative Committee consisting of representatives of principal Government Departments concerned with industrial questions," but not supersede the functions of the arbitration tribunals set up under the Munitions of War Acts by the Ministry of Labour.

The Committee held eight meetings between December 5 and 17, but made little progress. Its work seemed to consist chiefly in the registration of demands, which only emphasised more and more the difficulty of finding any ditch at which a line could be drawn, beyond which the 12½ per cent. ought not to be extended. The chairman, Mr. George Barnes, complained that he found deputations waiting in his ante-chamber when he arrived, and on the doorstep when he left. At an early meeting I appealed with some fervour to Mr. Churchill, even at this hour, while there was time, to withdraw the 12½ per cent. altogether, and tell the country plainly there had been a mistake. Although he considered the view carefully, he judged it could not be stopped now, a point of policy to which the Treasury reluctantly agreed. He thought he might confine it in certain cases, but no satisfactory reports came of his efforts in that direction. An attempted settlement at Sheffield only lasted for a few days. The majority of the Committee thought that a broad scheme with clear notification to the country involving a statement of war aims, the necessity of more men, further action against excess profits and against the increasing cost of food, together with intimation that no advances except for cost of living could be afforded, and that the 12½ per cent. must stop, might cause a better feeling and meet pending difficulties. Various drafts were prepared on these lines, but, in spite of many further meetings, the year came to an end without any decision by the War Cabinet. Decision was being hotly demanded by employers. The engineering employers said they must have finality. The Clyde was nearly going up. Sheffield was in a state of disturbance. It was absolutely necessary to clear the air in order to give any chance to the proposed campaign for more recruits. Gloomy accounts were given of the feeling in France and Italy, if the British efforts for increased assistance were not apparent.

On December 31 the situation was further complicated by the complaint of the railway executive that the National Maritime Board, without notice to any other department, had largely increased the wages of seamen and firemen, and had not defined the classes to which the increase should be given. If extended to railway-owned boats, it must spread to coasting vessels, dredgers, tug-boats, estuary boats, etc., some of them manned by men who slept at home nearly every night and were in no danger. Thence it would effect railway wages and agreements of which the National Board seemed to be entirely ignorant.

At the beginning of the new year it was reported, on Friday, January 4, that men on the Clyde were all going on time- instead of piece-work, owing to the pieceworkers having had no grant. The work took twice as long and was twice as costly as if a grant was made. On the following Monday the employers, decision or no decision, were intending to give a flat increase to pieceworkers. On January 5 the railway executive complained again that they must know how to deal with their running-sheds. The men were out on the Great Central Railway, and were coming out that evening on the Great Western and London and North-Western. It was felt that the railways were under the control of the Government, and that in this case there was no logical reason for refusing the grant of the bonus. The decision in this case prevented serious strikes at the eleventh hour.

Contrary to custom, I kept daily notes of the proceedings of this anxious month, but details of the choppings and changes would be of little value now, except as an example of how we are governed. Among them I find two remarks in a lighter vein: recording how Sir Auckland Geddes, new to administration, came out with the correct soliloquy that "no department cares a tinker's curse for any other department, but goes on its own"; and how Sir Edward Carson, in the middle of a long and fluent speech by Mr. Churchill on the importance of getting a good atmosphere for Sir A. Geddes' National Service Scheme, and that he must have "a free field," quietly asked, "Do you expect them to go better to the services if they are paid 2*s.* 6*d.* in the pound (12½ per cent.) more to work at home?"

The railways and the clamour of employers for finality were not the only signs that a decision of some kind must be given. A concession to pieceworkers had already been promised in Belfast, and though there were exceptional circumstances there, the employers demanded that their action should be endorsed. On Friday, January 4, I had pointed out that telegrams had come in saying that the electricians would wait no longer, and were going out at once unless they got the 12½ per cent. Having arranged a meeting with them at Leeds on Friday, January 11, on travelling allowances, I had wired suggesting discussion of the 12½ per cent., but I must know what powers I had; in actual fact it was more than doubtful if any delay was feasible. The Government Labour Committee were all of opinion that this matter must be settled, and should be referred to me to act with utmost speed, but their decision was not a decision by the Government, and without the authority of the War Cabinet any action could be questioned as imposing charges on undertakings which were not under the Munitions of War Acts, and whose representatives could not even be got together without days of delay.

The position with regard to these workpeople was extremely difficult. For weeks past the Electrical Trades Union, or E.T.U., had pressed for revision of wages and conditions, and advances, after much discussion, had been granted as from September 1, and again from December 1, without any dispute coming to a head, although active negotiations had been necessary. Two or more unions with rival claims were concerned in the industry. The principal union had its headquarters at Manchester, whence no effective control was exercised over London and other big cities. The employers themselves were divided into three principal sections with divergent views and interests. These were the great power companies, municipal and private employers, and the electrical contractors. Some of them were under the Munitions of War Acts, some were not. Some were reimbursed by the Government for extra expenditure, others would not be reimbursed. In addition the managers and chief officers of all these undertakings were paid on no organised scale. Some of them received very low salaries. Borough and city councils gave them most varied remuneration. They, too, were moving for increased emoluments. The delays had driven nearly all the men into the principal union, and that union, under energetic leaders, particularly in London, was proceeding to use methods of pressure to bring in all non-unionists and the adherence of members of the rival unions. Again and again I had got their consent to the avoidance of a strike, but such influence could not be exercised indefinitely. On the top of this situation came the $12\frac{1}{2}$ per cent. Electricians might reasonably have been included in one of the Orders of the Ministry of Munitions, but the Order made dealt with the engineering trade, and it was held that only electricians engaged in the repair-shops were covered, and not the electricians in the generating stations or on tramways. Many of these were not under the jurisdiction of the Ministry of Munitions, and no order or decision of the Government had been given. During the whole of December, while a decision had been awaited, the men had been kept, as it were, tugging at a leash. Now they were breaking away.

On the Saturday morning, January 5, the position was found to be more than acute. The Office of Works telephoned that all their men were going out at noon. The officer in command at Woolwich stated that all the electricians in the controlled works in the neighbourhood and at Woolwich were leaving work, which would stop the Arsenal. The same wail came from Enfield and Waltham and from the great power stations. Sir George Riddell called to say the newspapers were holding conferences and all the newspaper electricians were going out. It was of no use to await an endorsement from the War Cabinet, which did not meet till the afternoon. I could only obtain the undertaking of Mr. George Barnes that he would press for endorsement of full powers. Mr. Webb, the district secretary for London, was asked to call, and confirmed the rumours. He said that, even if he wished, he could not have held his men. When the strike began in London that night, all the electricians everywhere would cease work. It would spread like wildfire over the country.

"Mr. Webb," I said, "you have got to stop these men. The Government will give me full powers to-day. A conference will be held on Monday, when the question will be decided one way or the other." "Well," he said, "it can't be done. It is just on twelve now. I can't get to Woolwich in time." "Use my telephone," I replied.

I have heard uncomplimentary remarks about Mr. Webb, who sometimes may be brusque, but he acts with decision. He rang up his delegate at Woolwich, who said the men were putting their coats on, and some had left, with no intention of coming back. There followed instructions to send men right and left and get them back, with some remarks about the heads of Government Departments which would not have pleased them. "Tell the lads I'm sitting at Sir George's desk now, and he's to have the whole show. No more of the others." All that afternoon and evening the wires were kept busy, telling men to resume work at once, notifying the London County Council, the borough councils, the power companies, the electrical contractors, and the union offices, summoning a conference for Monday, wiring to branches in the big cities that work must continue, and preparing Press notices.

In the afternoon a full Cabinet met, but after long discussion came to no general decision, though they did formally agree that the electricians' difficulty was to be referred to me with full powers to decide. It was well that it was so. If the men had been put off again, all munition works would have stopped, and a general upheaval might have been the result. The crux was that it was certain that the $12\frac{1}{2}$ per cent. would have to be given; there was no logical reason against it; but that it would have to go back to the date in October when the electricians were not included in the Ministry of Munitions Order. This retro-action would affect authorities who would not have come under an Order, and who could not recover the money from their consumers on bills already paid. Had the Government any intention of giving recoupment if by their order such payment was made, and what would happen if the companies refused to pay without it? The Chancellor of the Exchequer absolutely refused to pay from the Treasury, but after long debate it was passed that the Treasury, if there was difficulty, would be prepared to advance loans and the Government would support any necessary bills for future higher rates in Parliament.

With these powers, whether strictly legal or not it is difficult to say, I met the London employers and the representatives of the two unions. It was impossible to warn the provincial employers or to get them up in time, but several of the big London companies had important branches in the country. Two hours were wasted over the quarrels of two unions, who would not meet each other, or accept the result of the negotiations conducted by one of them. It became necessary to settle the case of the E.T.U. with the employers, and then either to persuade the other union, before a decision was signed, that their points had been fully brought up, or to hear their arguments independently. In all, nine hours were occupied in discussion and technical points before a practically agreed award could be made. It was only just completed in time. Mr. Webb dashed off with it to a mass meeting in Holborn Hall which had already been waiting for two hours, and copies were rapidly circulated throughout the country. Some few works did indeed stop, but resumed within a few hours.

After stating that it was given under powers from the War Cabinet, the decision ran that:

"All plain time-working employees in generating

stations, sub-stations, and on mains directly concerned in the generation and distribution of electrical energy, including the technical staff and, in the case of electrical contractors, employees engaged on munitions work, including the technical staff, shall receive a bonus as follows :

"(1) All workers who have received not more than 20*s.* war advance, the equivalent of 12½ per cent. on earnings ; any advance given by a pending decision of the Committee on Production or any advance given by agreement or otherwise, equivalent to the advance of 5*s.* granted by the Committee on Production to certain trades from the first full pay-day in December, to be added as a war advance to the advance already given, and to count as part of the earnings from the date of such advance.

"(2) All workers who have received over 20*s.* war advance sufficient to produce the equivalent of the 20*s.* plus 12½ per cent. on earnings—that is to say, any excess in war advances over 20*s.* shall merge in the 12½ per cent. on earnings.

"(3) Workmen who have received the equivalent of 20*s.* war advance plus 12½ per cent. on earnings, or more, are not affected by this settlement. In calculating whether 20*s.* has been received, it shall be taken as 20*s.* for the normal week as recognised in the district.

"(4) Basis rates of wages and conditions of labour shall remain as at present until the withdrawal of war wages and war bonuses. This clause is without prejudice to pending negotiations, if any, which may have commenced.

"(5) This decision shall take effect as from the beginning of the first full pay the next after October 13, 1917."

Discussion arose in many cases how the decision was to be applied in the varying circumstances of different undertakings, when, with the consent of all parties, an interpreting note was added. The decision was that all such questions, including the question of application to technical staffs, must be settled in the locality of the parties concerned, and only in the event of any serious difficulty should the difference be referred for settlement. It speaks well for the understanding of employers that the 12½ per cent. for electricians could not be avoided under the circumstances which had arisen, that, with the exception of a few queries, the decision was accepted throughout the whole country. The decision was accepted, even though representatives from the Provinces had not been able to be present at the hearing and had not known of the difficulties which had occurred.

On the following day I heard that, while I was engaged with electricians, the Cabinet had sat for hours, and finally come to a decision to refer the whole question of the 12½ per cent. to the Ministry of Labour to settle. Mr. Barnes had explained that for five weeks two Cabinet Ministers continuously, and others from time to time, many heads of Departments, a large number of officials and other administrative officers, had been absorbed in this question. They could not go on with it. Time was urgent, and with the New Year, turmoil was sure to ensue. It was therefore got rid of by the simple process of delegating it to somebody else, the resolution being so worded that it swept away the Government Labour Committee and the annexed consultative or co-ordinating Committee. It is possible that all of this was not intended, but neither the chairman nor the vice-chairman called either of these bodies together, and no orders were given for the continuance of either of them. Co-ordination continued to cease to exist.

It is, of course, true that administration should not be centralised, but policy can. Owing to the complexity of business and the relation of employers and employed on the spot, administration, including settlement of trivial or management disputes, must be handled by the persons chiefly and closely concerned. A central authority cannot possibly deal with all such disputes. The delay alone would allow minor difficulties to become great difficulties. The perpetual intervention of a third party would be intolerable. Intervention by the emissaries of the controlling authority, under whom employers were no longer free agents, had caused trouble even in minor disputes. But when employers belong to an association, it is not in order for members to deal with difficulties in a manner alien to the interests and policy of other members of the association, without warning or consulting them. Similarly, trade union officials are continuously urging their members that sectional disputes or cessation of work for which other members have to pay must not take place without the knowledge and the authority of the officials who are placed in that position for the purpose of rectifying grievances, settling unnecessary disputes, and deciding whether the interests and funds of the union are to be put forward for the furtherance of sectional claims. This interlocking of interests is the main object why in a great trade, like the engineers, elaborate machinery of district and general conferences has been established. The same course is pursued in all the large and organised industries, with varying machinery according to the needs of the industry. When the Government comes in, even in war-time, and becomes a large employer it should at least conform to the rules which bind other employers in the industry on which the Government has impinged, or in self-protection, when it is a great employer or controls employers, in a vast number of industries—railways, coal, shipping, munitions, chemicals, dyes, etc.—should follow in its different Departments the policy of the supreme authority, if that authority has a policy. It should act in concert with and at least inform other Departments in all cases where changes, disputes, or settlements must affect those other Departments, possibly in the most vital manner.

My view is that in labour matters the Government had no policy, never gave signs of having a policy, and could not be induced to have a policy. My view also is, and these notes have failed of their purpose if they do not show, that the Departments never followed any policy in labour matters, except a policy of disintegration ; did not act in concert ; did not even inform other Departments of the most vital decisions ; and went on their own way in a manner which cost or lost hundreds of millions of money, precious time, and urgently needed supplies.

The Cabinet, on January 7, also intimated that a percentage grant would have to be given to pieceworkers, but instead of butting in with a random guess at the amount which they were inclined to give, were induced to take the advice of the Committee on Production. They issued as their decision a document stating that :

" As from the beginning of the first full pay week which followed January 1, 1918, a bonus of $7\frac{1}{2}$ per cent. on their earnings shall be paid to all workmen of twenty-one years of age and over, employed in establishments or trades (other than the iron and steel trades) covered by the existing

Orders relating to plain time-workers or extensions thereof, and engaged in munitions work as defined in the Munitions of War Acts, who are pieceworkers or are paid on a premium bonus system, or any mixed system of time and piece or any system of payment by results, including men working at augmented time rates fixed in lieu of piece rates, or by reference to results or to output of work."

There followed provisions for merger, or special conference in the iron and steel trades, and reference of the claims not dealt with to the Committee on Production for settlement.

This document did not end the episode of the 12½ per cent. The matter having been handed over to the Ministry of Labour, the Minister and myself had to ask the principal leaders of the trade unions to urge restraint upon their members, in order to gain time for the many claims to be dealt with, and to give the Ministry of Labour a chance. There were only two methods by which the Ministry could deal with the subject—arbitration or conciliation. Arbitration was possible in those trades where it was a question whether and to whom the 12½ per cent. or 7½ per cent. should be given. Many of these trades had to be interviewed, and, wherever possible, a legal decision was asked for, upon a reference, from the Committee on Production. Some employers recognised that the percentage must come in, others demurred and did not like a reference where they considered the scales were weighted against them. The majority recognised that the percentage or its equivalent had to extend not only to munition workers and controlled firms, but to others. It might be true that the principle was wrong; the advantage went to the higher-paid and not to the lower-paid workers; the expenditure was unknown, uncertain, and vast; its cost was not limited to the Government, but extended to industries and employers of all kinds. In cases where a percentage was given, it could not act as a cost of living advance, as its application was quite unequal, but it was causing trouble alike to employers and to trade union leaders, who had first of all been told to say that it did not apply to their trades, and then found that the pressure of their men obtained it over their heads. Then they had to press in trades where they knew it had not been meant to apply.

One could only put the position before them, that this thing had happened, and they had better make the best of it. Their arguments might be quite correct and might be entirely logical; to discuss whether or not Mr. Churchill or anyone else was right or wrong did not assist the practical position in which they were placed ; the intention of confining the grant had not resulted in the grant being kept within narrow limits ; trade after trade, firm after firm, had had to admit this result, and they must exercise their own judgement whether it was possible for them to stand out. Their position could be legalised, and whatever arguments they thought best for any differentiation or special limitations could be considered before an arbitral tribunal.

It may be noted that the officers of the Department, especially Mr. Cummings, were kept very busy for months with preparation for arbitrations, and another chairman, Judge Walworth Roberts, had to be added to the Committee on Production, in order to cope with the work.

In other trades there were specially difficult questions over the best method of liquidating back pay without reopening vast details of accounts, or where a percentage advance was not desired by one or other party. These points were best dealt with by conciliation. On the first the Ministry of Munitions produced a scheme which could be generally accepted, after explanation ; on the second long conferences were necessary. At these conferences the chief difficulty was to get the adherence of outstanding sections to consent to a national advance, and to estimate in each trade what the fair equivalent of the percentage might be. The various claims were gradually liquidated, but it was not till April 11, 1918, that, with the exception of the building trade, the last claims by workpeople who deemed themselves to be entitled to claim the percentage of 12½ per cent. in some form or another were finally closed.

CHAPTER XL

1918

THE general settlements required by the $12\frac{1}{2}$ per cent., including a most difficult conciliation case in the tramway and omnibus services, where a general strike was narrowly avoided, had closed by about the middle of April, but the aftermath of the percentage was yet to cause trouble in the building trade.

This trade had been very hard hit during the War. Private building and repairs had practically ceased. Almost all the work was Government work. The priority of that work was dealt with by a small departmental Committee arranged by General Smuts, of which I was a member for a short time at the close of the War. There was a second Committee of the Ministry of National Service purporting to deal with the supply of labour. Their efforts were greatly hampered by the number of men who had gone into the services, or drifted into munition work or the shipyards, where there existed a continuous demand for carpenters, joiners, etc. It was not easy, with growing shortage of men, to obtain recruits for remote aerodromes, poison-gas and explosive factories, camps, etc., nor to settle the rates at which they were to be paid. There was also a third Committee, comprising officials of the Ministries of Munitions, National Service, and various other Departments, which worked at finding out the building rates, etc., in districts where the building trade was organised; settling the rates to be offered, by analogy with neighbouring districts, in places where there was no real rate or an entire absence of rates; and either composing disputes or sending them to arbitration.

The difficulties of this Committee were many, because large contractors moving with their special men from district to district would not comply with the local rates or the instructions of the Committee. Government Departments, especially the Air Ministry, also failed to comply. The efforts of the building trade itself, not well organised in large parts of the country, were becoming useless through the rates being continuously changed or set at naught by these offenders. Extraordinary dislocation resulted. An application was made to the Ministry of Labour to assist, with the result that a scheme was prepared by which the building trade, as on the North-East Coast, was to settle its own rates, with the understanding that the Government, acting through the Committee, would see that the rates settled were the rates to be paid by its own Departments, but, as the chief employer in the country, would have a voice in approving or objecting to the rates proposed prior to their final acceptance. An Order, known as Order 742, was to be issued by the Ministry of Munitions, embodying the conditions. Any difference not adjusted by agreement was to be referred to the arbitration tribunals for settlement. The scheme was generally welcomed as at least some attempt to obtain order, was signed by the building trades and the Government, and lasted to December 1919, when, on the passing of the Industrial Courts Bill, arbitration became voluntary, and the treatment of the building trade as an industry subject to the Munitions of War Acts, even though such a result only came from the agreement of the trade, ceased.

The difficulty over the 12½ per cent. arose while I was endeavouring, on becoming chairman of the third Committee, (*a*) to effect co-ordination between the three Committees, and (*b*) to draw up the general scheme and secure assent to its provisions. The Government had been obliged to give the 12½ per cent. on the top of the existing rate in many branches of the building trade. The local builders were naturally pressed by their employees to give the same percentage, or its equivalent in an extra payment per hour. So much was the 12½ per cent. disliked that, in most cases, an equivalent was given in the shape of a flat advance, but it was stated to be an equivalent, and not deemed to be the rate of the district except for those who merged their 12½ per cent. in it. Men could have the old rate plus the 12½ per cent., or the new rate without the 12½ per cent. If this procedure had not been followed, employers who were sometimes doing Government work and sometimes private work would have been paying their men different rates according to the job of the moment, or high rates to Government workmen and lower rates to private workmen in the same shop; and such form of payment would have produced once again the disparity which the increase was intended to prevent. This plan, leading at least towards equality and the avoidance of a vicious circle, was generally accepted everywhere; but at Liverpool a local conciliation board of small builders, not one of whom had any Government work, chose to raise nominally the Liverpool rates as high as London, always the highest rate in the country, and in raising the rate said not a word about the 12½ per cent., although Manchester and neighbouring cities had accepted the plan. The decision was only reached by two employers voting with the men in favour of the increase, the decisions at these boards being by a bare majority. Of these two, the chairman stated he had voted on the wrong side by mistake, the other kept his identity concealed and never disclosed it. The matter was brought before the North-Western District Board, who could only say it was a decision according to the rule that a majority decided, but entered a strong protest. The National Board, however, as well as other district boards, complained that the result would upset the whole of the rates in the country by the extension from one district to another which would certainly result. The shipbuilders and other Liverpool trades also complained, and last but not least the Government, if they accepted the new rate when it was claimed by their employees, as it was claimed, with the 12½ per cent. upon the top of it, put themselves in the position of allowing one unknown voter to dictate a rise which would upset the whole country and cost huge sums. Payment was refused, and arbitration offered, or the opportunity of the Liverpool Board saying how much they allocated to the 12½ per cent. out of the new rate, if it was to stand as a rate. The case led to long discussions and conferences, some of the Liverpool people arguing they would not have any mention made of the 12½ per cent., they had nothing to do with it, the Government could do what they liked, etc. It was at length settled, with a few minor stoppages, which generally ended on explanation, the Government adhering to their position.

This case serves as an instance of the lack of cohesion and order existing in trades, the importance of the Government having a part in the wage arrangements when the Government is practically the only employer, the danger of snatch settlements or changes made by irresponsible persons affecting other districts and other trades, and the continued effect of past mistakes, such as the 12½ per cent. In no trade at the present time is it more important to have care exercised than in the building trade. On that trade the nation have to rely for the provision of needed houses at a reasonable rate, and it is now subsidised by the Government. Absence of organisation in any one district may have serious consequences, but how far the Government at the present time is keeping watch over its own interests and the interests of country in this matter, I am unable definitely to say.

So far as disputes went, a number of conferences were held in the building trade between May and September. There were also visits to Ireland to establish schemes for the collection and preparation of the flax crop in Ireland, where strikes were threatened and Proclamations under the Munitions of War Acts were issued; dock disputes at Belfast and Dublin; a bus and tram stoppage in London and some other towns on the question of the wages of women conductors; a strike of municipal employees at Cardiff, and adjustment of various minor disputes. Larger and more important disputes paused in their incidence. Personally, I doubt whether the fluctuations of the War generally had direct effect upon the number or importance of disputes, but at this period I think the commencement of the Battle of the Somme on May 27, and the German offensive near Rheims on July 15, did directly affect disputes. From May to September there was much greater peace throughout Great Britain. The minds of men were concentrated on the dangers of the War. Consequently, it was with surprise that the country heard, early in September, that the Metropolitan Police had struck. As a great employer in the North remarked to me, "It gave me a blow as if the Bank of England had stopped payment. That and the Metropolitan Police seemed to be pillars of the Constitution." The strike was speedily followed by a threatened strike of the London firemen, a serious strike of Co-operative Wholesale employees, and many other disputes.

It was correctly remarked at the time that

> "an epidemic of strikes and threats of strikes seems to have commenced. Three essential services have been stopped—the Yorkshire coal-field, the London passenger traffic (partially), and the Metropolitan police service—and until September 11 an extensive district of London was gravely inconvenienced by a strike of gasworks employees. Now the Lancashire cotton operatives threaten to cease work on September 14, the London Fire Brigade service is in the mood of revolt, the South Wales miners are menacing, the employees of the Co-operative Wholesale Society are strenuously urging their claims upon Sir George Askwith, the municipal workers in eight London Corporations are loudly proclaiming their grievances, prison workers are unrestful, the temporary postal workers in London are threatening determinedly, and railwaymen are pressing claims with some display of temper. It is a prospect which might afford some comfort and encouragement to the enemy, if the position in France had not so greatly improved."

The subject of the Metropolitan Police was dealt with by the Home Office. The other two principal disputes, in the Fire Brigade and the Co-operative Wholesale Society, chiefly turned on the question of recognition of unions. In the former the C.W.S. had been accustomed to deal with craft unions, but the A.U.C.E. (Amalgamated Union of Co-operative Employees), comprising employees of different branches of trade, had for some time been moving for higher wages and other conditions on behalf of their members. A dispute began with printing employees at two works in the North, and rapidly spread to flour-mills, soap-works, margarine works, hide and skin departments; bacon, grocery, packing, jam, biscuit, and tea departments. Long conferences with the parties were necessary, and as delay hazarded supplies of food, the strike had to be proclaimed and referred to arbitration under the Munitions of War Acts.

The firemen's dispute was, by consent of the parties,

referred to me for arbitration. Preliminary to wages questions, which the Fire Brigade Committee of the London County Council was prepared to settle, the whole point turned on the extent to which any union should be permitted in the brigade, or how far officials of a union other than firemen might represent the men. Almost all the men had, during the last few years, joined the National Union of Corporation Workers. The objection of the majority, at least, of the London County Council was that an outside union or anyone connected with any outside union, of which men in the brigade might be members, should have anything to do with a body where discipline was essential, and on whose skill and discipline the safety of London from fires might depend. The men contended that they belonged to a union, should have recognition of a union, and had no intention of interfering with discipline or management. The decision was not easy, because the Provinces were bound to follow the principles accepted in London, and because the attitude of the Home Office with regard to the police had not been announced. The arguments were heard, the award drafted, its terms shown to Sir George Cave, the Home Secretary, in order that one Department should not settle without the knowledge of another Department engaged on work possibly similar in character, and publication made on September 23.

The terms of the award were:

"There has been referred to me, the undersigned, by both parties, under the terms of a resolution unanimously passed at a conference held between the parties on September 13, 1918, the final decision on a scheme as to the relations between the London County Council and the uniformed staff below the rank of station officer of the London Fire Brigade. Having heard the parties, and considered their verbal and written statements, my decision is:

"1. The present rule 512 (which permitted complaints by individuals) in favour of any individual member of the Fire Brigade who may desire to avail himself of it, shall continue in force.

"2. A collective body, consisting of members of the

Fire Brigade only, who are desirous of bringing under the notice of the Council, or of the Fire Brigade Committee, matters connected with their conditions of service and general welfare other than questions of discipline or methods of management, may also do so through the Chief Officer, who will, if desired, afford them an opportunity of seeing the Committee.

"3. Representations may be made by a committee of such collective body, provided such committee consists of, and is chosen by, men who are members of the uniformed staff of the London Fire Brigade.

"4. The committee, or members of the committee delegated by the committee, may be accompanied on deputations by a 'spokesman,' chosen by the committee, who need not be a member of the London Fire Brigade. Letters sent by the 'spokesman,' if expressed to be by order of the committee, shall be received as communications made by the committee.

"5. The collective body, as a condition of collective representation, shall *not*—

"(*a*) Take part in any labour or industrial dispute, or under any circumstances induce members of the Brigade to withhold their services, but only concern themselves with differences strictly relating to the conditions of their service and welfare in the London Fire Brigade.

"(*b*) Interfere in any way with the regulations and discipline of the service or methods of management, with the sole exception of cases of alleged injustice. The committee may bring such an alleged case before the Chief Officer, but shall forward full particulars by writing prior to asking for any interview. The Chief Officer may refuse in writing such interview on the grounds that the particulars disclose interference with the regulations and discipline of the service and methods of management.

"(*c*) Bring forward any complaints before they have been first examined and considered by the members of the committee.

"And, further, the collective body shall in the first instance, without any stoppage of work, bring any complaints, with which the collective body or the committee are entitled to deal, before the Chief Officer. In the event of a difference arising upon such complaints and no settlement between the London County Council and the collective body being reached, such differences shall be referred to an agreed tribunal. If the tribunal and form of tribunal is not agreed, the tribunal shall be appointed by the Ministry of Labour. The decision of the tribunal shall be final and binding. In the event of a breach of the above conditions, members of the Brigade may be called upon to sever their connection with any union to which they may belong.

"6. The London County Council have indicated, and I decide, that it shall be permissible for the members of the London Fire Brigade to form a London Fire Brigade Union composed of firemen only, to be embodied with the above conditions laid down in its rules, or with such modifications of the above conditions as, after conference with the Fire Brigade Committee, and with me, are admitted to be suitable to the service. Such London Fire Brigade Union, if formed, shall be deemed to be a union with which the London County Council can make agreements, and its union secretary, if acting as secretary for such union only, shall be entitled to act on their behalf without further proof of his authority.

"No further proof of the authority of such union to represent the majority of the London Fire Brigade shall be required other than a list of members to be furnished upon request to the Chairman of the London County Council for the time being. The chairman shall decide whether he is satisfied that the union sufficiently represents the Brigade, or if he thinks fit may refer the matter to arbitration.

"7. This decision shall continue, as agreed by the parties, for three years from its date, and thereafter subject to three months' notice by either side. No notice shall be given prior to June 20, 1921.

"8. Any question of interpretation shall, as agreed by the parties, be referred to me for decision.

"As witness my hand this 23rd day of September, 1918.

"G. R. Askwith."

These terms were loyally accepted by both parties, and I have not heard of subsequent difficulties.

A short time, too, before the Armistice, Mr. J. H. Thomas, largely by his personal influence, averted a railway strike, and it may be mentioned, in view of the public criticism which has been levelled at Mr. Churchill, that over a difficult question whether a special supply of poison-gas was to be delivered in time by the easy method of yielding to a strike and abnormal demands in two factories, or his consent refused to payments demanded by force and likely to ensure far-reaching and bad effects, Mr. Churchill took the risk of handing over the whole case to my Department. His letter of thanks and relief, when a constitutional settlement was effected, is dated October 3.

Notice may also be taken of two Committees, one under Lord Sumner, appointed in the spring, and another under Lord Justice Atkin, appointed in the autumn of 1918. Both were singularly belated, and for that reason their conclusions lost influence and effect. Lord Sumner's Committee dealt with the cost of living, producing a report which might have been invaluable at an earlier date. Although the cost and character of living had varied so greatly during the War, no Government inquiry or authoritative examination had been held. The Board of Trade statistics, useful for statistical purposes, but comparing prices paid for articles in times of peace with prices paid for the same articles, some of them practically unobtainable, in times of war, were used in argument as the real reflex of the increase in the cost of living. They were fallacious for that purpose. In 1914 I had suggested they should be suppressed as useless for the purposes to which they were being put. This suggestion was not accepted, on the ground that it might cause alarm, and interfere too much with the appearance of business as usual. The Committee on Production had to make the best estimates they could on piecemeal argument and data put before them. Representations at length caused explanatory memoranda to be added to the statistical returns, pointing out the limitations affecting the figures and the comparison of conditions, but in every argument and claim the figures alone were put forward, the limitations were passed over. It was not until 1918 that Lord Sumner's Committee made an investigation, and by that time the trade unions had become so accustomed to make use of the ordinary statistical figures in their arguments that they ignored new returns, and particularly a smaller figure. Lord Justice Atkin's Committee arose from questions affecting the wages of women, orders by the Ministry of Munitions, and the relations between the wages to be paid to women and men respectively. Connected with these subjects was a contention by the Ministry of Munitions that orders by the Minister took precedence of or could override decisions of the arbitration courts, a point on which the Law Officers decided that the Ministry was wrong. If these questions affecting women had been previously so important as they became at the time of the bus and tram strikes in August, it was rather late in the day to inquire into them two months before the Armistice.

As regards awards, the Committee on Production, in dealing with the periodical hearing under the special agreement between the Engineering Employers' Federation and the trade unions connected with it, decided on March 5 that "conditions at the present time do not warrant any further general alteration of wages." By that date the effect of awards had been to establish for the engineering and foundry trades a general advance, as compared with pre-war rates, of not less than 20*s.* per week on time rates, the corresponding figure in the case of pieceworkers being 13*s.* per week as a supplement to earnings, in addition to previous advances generally amounting to 10 per cent. or upwards on piece rates. These amounts were exclusive of the bonus of 12½ per cent. on earnings in the case of plain time-workers, and 7½ per cent. in the case of pieceworkers and other workmen not paid at plain time rates.

On July 24 the Committee gave a further advance of 3*s.* 6*d.* per week, a decision hampered by the action of the Coal Controller in doubling the flat rate advances given to miners as from the end of June. On November 9, two days before the Armistice, an advance of 5*s.* per week was awarded to the same workpeople. These advances were generally followed by other trades throughout the country.

Some Ministers had a passion for committees, the number of which greatly occupied the time of hardworked employers and trade union leaders. The Minister of Reconstruction was said to have arranged more than two score. It is not my purpose to criticise the results, but one committee, known as the Whitley Committee, from the name of its chairman, did produce some important reports, and should be mentioned. The Committee had been appointed as early as October 1916, Mr. H. J. Wilson, of my Department, acting as secretary, its reference being:

(1) To make and consider suggestions for securing a

permanent improvement in the relations between employers and workmen.

(2) To recommend means for securing that industrial conditions affecting the relations between employers and workmen shall be systematically reviewed by those concerned, with a view to improving conditions in the future.

An official account states :

" The Committee issued reports of which the best known are those in which they recommend the establishment in suitable cases of voluntary Joint Standing Industrial Councils, consisting of representatives of the Employers' Associations and the Trade Unions, for the purpose of securing the largest possible development of the industry as a part of national life and for the improvement of the conditions of all engaged in that industry. . . . In connection with their inquiry, the Committee also thought it necessary to give some attention to cases in which parties might desire voluntarily to refer some difference that had arisen to arbitration or conciliation, and they issued a report on this subject in January 1918. The Committee expressed themselves as opposed to any system of compulsory arbitration, and emphasised the advisability of a continuance, as far as possible, of the existing system whereby industries made their own agreements and settled their differences themselves. The Committee's conclusions were:

" (*a*) Whilst we are opposed to any system of Compulsory Arbitration, we are in favour of an extension of voluntary machinery for the adjustment of disputes. Where the parties are unable to adjust their differences, we think that there should be means by which an independent inquiry may be made into the facts and circumstances of a dispute, and an authoritative pronouncement made thereon, though we do not think that there should be any compulsory power of delaying strikes and lockouts.

" (*b*) We further recommend that there should be established a Standing Arbitration Council for cases where the parties wish to refer any dispute to arbitration, though it is desirable that suitable single arbitrators should be available, where the parties so desire."

Joint Industrial Councils have been established in a number of industries, and in some industries District

Councils and Works Committees, both of them integral parts of the Whitley scheme, have also been formed. The scheme has not been adopted by the industries of coal-mining, cotton, engineering, shipbuilding, iron and steel, and railways. The great industries standing outside the scheme prefer to follow their own lines of agreement or arrangements. Efforts to obtain force of law for the decisions of Industrial Councils have been advocated in some cases, but have as yet not succeeded. As an example of the objects of the councils, notice may be taken of a council which was alleged to be a success. The Pottery Industry agreed to establish a National Council, giving as their objects :

"The advancement of the Pottery Industry and of all connected with it by the association in its government of all engaged in the industry.

"It will be open to the Council to take any action that falls within the scope of its general object. Its chief work will, however, fall under the following heads :

"(*a*) The consideration of means whereby all manufacturers and operatives shall be brought within their respective associations.

"(*b*) Regular consideration of wages, piecework rates, and conditions, with a view to establishing and maintaining equitable conditions throughout the industry.

"(*c*) To assist the respective associations in the maintenance of such selling prices as will afford a reasonable remuneration to both employers and employed.

"(*d*) The consideration and settlement of all disputes between different parties in the industry which it may not have been possible to settle by the existing machinery, and the establishment of the machinery for dealing with disputes where adequate machinery does not exist.

"(*e*) The regularisation of production and employment as a means of insuring to the workpeople the greatest possible security of earnings.

"(*f*) Improvement in conditions with a view to removing all danger to health in the industry.

"(*g*) The study of processes, the encouragement of research, and the full utilisation of their results.

"(*h*) The provision of facilities for the full consideration and utilisation of inventions and improvements designed by workpeople and for the adequate safeguarding of the rights of the designers of such improvements.

"(*i*) Education in all its branches for the industry.

"(*j*) The collection of full statistics on wages, making and selling prices, and average percentages of profits on turnover, and on materials, markets, costs, etc., and the study and promotion of scientific and practical systems of costings to this end.

"All statistics shall, where necessary, be verified by Chartered Accountants, who shall make a statutory declaration as to secrecy prior to any investigation, and no particulars of individual firms or operatives shall be disclosed to anyone.

"(*k*) Inquiries into problems of the industry, and where desirable the publication of reports.

"(*l*) Representation of the needs and opinions of the industry to Government authorities, central and local, and to the community generally."

These objects appear excellent on paper, and in this industry are reported to have produced some good results. The joint education of representative employers and workpeople by meetings and common objects must be valuable. If a criticism is made, the whole chance of the success of Industrial Councils lies in the way in which they are worked. If the aim is mutual co-operation and joint effort, and that aim is continuously kept in sight and broadly interpreted, an industry in one way or another may be improved by the existence of a council. If the council is used to maintain two camps, and during a period of advancing wages and prosperity only employed for purposes of pressure, with an inevitable deadlock so soon as the demands become greater than the trade can bear, then ultimate disintegration will ensue, and possibly a worse position than before the advent of a council. This position, according to recent accounts, was nearly reached in the pottery industry, for which so much success has been claimed. It will be the spirit which counts, and I do not agree with the criticism that the councils may form combinations to mulct the consumer and hurt the public at large; but many employers will prefer to stand outside the councils and deal with their workpeople on methods which will give opportunity for individual advancement, initiative, and reward, without the possible restrictions which associations are apt to imply.

In the foregoing sketch, partly of an historical character, many important phases and matters have necessarily been omitted. The sketch only purports to deal with the efforts to maintain or restore industrial peace—chiefly so far as they came within the purview of one Department during the changing movements inseparable from a time of great stress, anxiety, and effort. Some of the lessons to be deduced from such a history may be useful if the nation again unites for the achievement of any common purpose.

CHAPTER XLI

THE ARMISTICE AND NATIONALIZATION

AT the eleventh hour of the eleventh day of the eleventh month, November 11, 1918, the Armistice was suddenly proclaimed.

The industrial world, or at least some sections of it, were taken by surprise. It was after a meeting held on November 13 at Caxton Hall, where employers and trade unions had been convened to hear speeches from Ministers on the subjects of stabilisation of wages and the restoration of pre-war practices, that I met the Presidents of the Federation of Cotton-Spinners' and Manufacturers' Association and the Northern Counties Textile Association in a complete quandary as to the course to follow over an imminent dispute in the weavers' section of the North Lancashire cotton trade. The Prime Minister had talked of committees of employers and employed, and had indicated that the Munitions of War Acts, which would include the provisions for proclaiming a strike, would soon be repealed, but they had no knowledge when these steps would be taken and whether any new provisions would meet their case. Meanwhile there was certain to be trouble, unless some settlement could be reached. After discussion, it was agreed that I should act as chairman at meetings in Manchester, in order to attempt a settlement, and with that view conferences were held there on November 20 and 21, and between December 3 and 7.

The settlement was by no means easy, and would not have been effected but for the good-will shown by both parties, men well known to me in previous disputes. The last settlement during the War had been made in June. Large profits had been made by employers up to September, but during the next two or three months trade prospects had worsened, and prices of yarn and cloth had fallen. As soon as the Armistice came, employers deemed the future to be very uncertain, and shrank from the concession of a large advance until the course of the markets became more clear, while the leaders of the operatives contended that their members had not received an adequate share of past gains or sufficient consideration for the increased cost of living. They demanded in the weavers' section an advance of 50 per cent. on current wages, and also a "fall back" or minimum wage in cases where operatives were unable to work, or, in technical parlance, had to "play," owing to shortage of raw material.

Both Associations eventually agreed that the wage claim should be referred to the new Interim Court, which had been meanwhile established to take the place of the Committee on Production, and that the "fall back" question should be examined by a strong committee of both parties with a view to seeing if an arrangement could be made, the matter to be referred to arbitration, if necessary, after a period of months.

It was not till December 3, on the eve of meeting with the weavers, that a mass of papers were sent to me from other officials who purported to have the matter in hand, with the intimation that, even if the weavers' difficulty was settled, the spinners and cardroom operatives were coming out on December 7, and in a short time would hold up the trade. Action—or inaction, because nothing had been done—had broken down. It was suggested I should try to effect a settlement at the eleventh hour, when it ought to have been dealt with days before, the whole case being a curious instance of the lack of co-ordination in Departments, of failure to estimate the right time for intervention, and of the ill effects of unnecessary delay and division of authority.

There was literally only just enough time to induce the parties to hold one meeting on December 6, the notices of 100,000 operatives maturing next day. It appeared that the employers in this section had made an offer of 40 per cent. on standard rates upon November 1, and had reluctantly agreed to renew their proposal, although the Armistice was said to have stopped large profits and there was a fear of industrial confusion. They were not inclined to increase this offer, owing to the uncertainty, and some may have thought a stoppage might steady the market. On the other hand, the workpeople wanted a share of the back profits, and objected to arbitration because a tribunal had endorsed orders of the Cotton Control Board (*a*) for reduction of hours from 55½ to 40, without compensation for the lesser hours in the American mills, where cotton supplies were short; and (*b*) for abolition of a "rota" system of unemployment established under the restriction of output system.

The history of the case was that in June an application for an increase of 30 per cent. on list rates had been compromised by an agreement to pay 25 per cent. increase from June 15, but the rates of wages to remain unchanged up to and including the week ending December 7. This concession had been materially affected in the American mills by the shortening of hours during which wages could be earned. Although these workpeople had secured an advance on list rates of 25 per cent., their actual wages, as a result of working shorter hours, were smaller than they had been before the rise just secured, and yet they were committed till December to the agreement of June. The tribunal, while endorsing the orders of the Cotton Control Board, expressed an opinion that, owing to a change of conditions, there were good grounds for a modification of the wages agreement, which had two months to run, and that, in the circumstances, it would be well if employers and employees were invited to meet, to see if some arrangement could be made.

For some reason or other this suggestion was not acted upon by the officials dealing with the matter. The operatives, particularly the shop stewards and young men, pressed forward and put in notices for cessation of work on December 7, the last day of the agreement, unless their demands were accepted. All negotiations were broken off. No notice was taken of this in London until December 3, when the papers were forwarded to me. On December 6 the parties had the meeting which I had managed to arrange, but failed to settle, and also refused, in spite of argument, to hold any further debates, breaking off with an employers' proposal that:

"In view of the fact that the situation in the trade has changed very unfavourably for the employers since November 1, when their offer of 40 per cent. on list wages, together with other conditions, was made, the employers, although of opinion that they would be entitled on the present state of trade to reduce that offer, are willing, in order to arrive at a settlement, to allow the offer of 40 per cent. on list rates for six months for acceptance to-day. Failing acceptance of this offer it is hereby withdrawn, but the employers are willing that the matter in dispute should be settled by arbitration."

The operatives briefly replied :

" We cannot agree to the acceptance of your offer, and in view of our past experience we cannot agree to arbitration."

All that I could deduce was that the employers, had there been time, might have advanced their offer by 10 per cent. if they could be sure that the operatives would agree, and that both parties would take note of the amount received by the weavers. All that could be done was to hurry the issue of an award to the weavers, and in the result the same percentage for spinners and the cardroom workers was forced on the employers, after an unnecessary strike had commenced, by Mr. Lloyd George in the following week. A cotton strike in the middle of a General Election was not to be regarded with equanimity, as the complaints of the Parliamentary candidates in Lancashire showed.

It was while I was engrossed in the cotton difficulty that the Wages (Temporary Regulation) Act 1918 passed through Parliament and became law on November 21. It was based on a report produced for some reason or other by the Ministry of Reconstruction and not by the Ministry of Labour, and on which the principal Departments concerned with awards and agreements had not even been consulted. This Act was intended to be a temporary measure lasting for six months, with a view to preventing a sudden fall in wages during the change over from munitions to civil work, but was subsequently extended for a further six months. During this period employers were to pay rates not less than prescribed rates (corresponding approximately to the standard rates existing at the date of the Armistice) or such other rates as might be substituted by an award of the Interim Court of Arbitration established under the Act, or by an agreement or settlement approved by the Ministry of Labour. The Interim Court of Arbitration established under the Act was in effect the Committee on Production with certain additional members to meet the altered circumstances.

The clauses of the Munitions of War Acts relating to the prohibition of strikes and lockouts were repealed, as also were the clauses relating to compulsory arbitration, except a difference " as to whether a workman is a workman of a class to which a prescribed rate of wages is applicable, or what is the prescribed rate of wages, or whether any rate should be substituted for the prescribed rate, or what is the substituted rate of wages."

Any difference on these points could be reported to the Minister by or on behalf of either of the parties concerned, and the Minister was required to consider the difference and to take any steps that seemed to him expedient to promote a settlement of the difference, and, where the Minister failed to effect a settlement by such means, he was required to refer the difference to the Interim Court of Arbitration for settlement, or if, in his opinion, suitable means for settlement already existed in pursuance of agreements made between employers and employed, for settlement in accordance with those means.

There were numerous other clauses on powers of examination and inquiry at the premises of any establishment, proceedings for offences before munitions tribunals, and fines upon employers for any contravention of the Act. At a later date the Act, which affected one side only so far as fines went, and confirmed bureaucratic interference, was superseded by the Industrial Courts Act, under which permanent Courts of Arbitration were established for those who might desire to use them.

At the same time, during my absence in Lancashire, internal changes were made in the Ministry of Labour upon which I was not consulted. Officials poured in from the Labour department of the Ministry of Munitions and the Admiralty. A Wages and Arbitration Department to administer the Wages Act and the Conciliation Act was established, and other changes were made, which involved the creation of a huge staff. The results have yet to be awaited. My own connection with the Ministry practically closed with the end of December, when His

Majesty was graciously pleased to confer upon me the dignity of a peerage.

Of more general interest, a very important step was the concession of the Eight-Hour Day, or the reduction of hours from 54 to 47 hours per week, by the Engineering Employers' Federation. This step anticipated the revival of trouble which had been suspended by the War, although the speed with which it was granted caused difficulties in the shipbuilding yards and on the railways, where the principle had to come into force before the mode of application had been considered. The tendency towards reduction had been often manifested. Arbitrators and conciliators had generally favoured, and I had frequently urged, the full Saturday half-holiday, and, where practicable, some reduction in hours. My own view had always been that eight hours a day continuous work, particularly monotonous work, was as much as men and women could well bear; but there is no doubt so drastic a change affected machine production and caused difficulties of adjustment. It was a concession which necessarily spread to other industries, and will have a great and lasting result, by its developments and effects, upon the industrial life of the nation.

In other directions, out-of-work donations or "doles" were introduced for the purpose of dealing with unemployment, feared in anticipation, but not then occurring in actual result. Committees were started on the subject of restoration of pre-war practices in accordance with the pledge of 1915; the Ministry of Health Bill went forward; demobilisation, resettlement of soldiers and sailors, and of workers in national factories, controlled establishments, and firms engaged on Government contracts, were referred to Committees; a very large number of other plans and schemes came into more or less active operation; and the year 1918 ended with a General Parliamentary Election. At the time, the Ministry of Reconstruction claimed to have played its part "in the practical realisation of an idea fraught with infinite possibilities for the future of the nation—the idea of organised thinking and common thinking, as applied dispassionately to the complex problems of social progress and national development in this country." The proofs of its success or the reverse must be judged by later results and opinions. If "organised thinking " could produce nothing better than the payment of doles to workpeople in the manner in which they were distributed, its power of anticipation and skill in meeting contingencies were not creditably illustrated. The very officials dispensing doles confessed that the people were settling down to live on them. Payment to persons who could claim one week's work since 1915 and produce an insurance book to show it, wasted money and endowed the most incapable workpeople. The system as worked was demoralising and unfair. It encouraged the belief that anything could be got from the public purse, and that little or no work, small or no results, entitled men and women to be maintained at the expense of others.

With the opening of the New Year of 1919, a new Minister of Labour, Sir Robert Horne, succeeded Mr. Roberts, who moved to the Ministry of Pensions; but as my official work practically ceased before Sir R. Horne entered the Ministry, concluding remarks must be of more general character than when one was intimately acquainted with the details of disputes during the periods of his predecessors.

In the propositions put forward at this time by statesmen there does not appear to have been uttered, as far as I can trace, any word of warning for the future, with one notable exception. Mr. J. R. Clynes, on January 24, is reported to have said:

" In the main, there was a tendency amongst trade unionists to make demands and to press them, which the trades could not very well afford to meet, and which the country, he feared, would not for some time to come be able to bear. He said this because we had lost so much wealth, and got into such a state of disrepair during the period of the War, that all the energy that we could bring into industry was required for the purpose of enormously increasing the output of our products, and thereby adding immensely to the aggregate wealth of this and other countries. That great increase in production could take place, he was convinced, without any injustice to the masses of workmen, without the application of any tyrannical instrument on the part of employers; it could take place by man making a more successful use of the thing that he could conquer and control—the machine. It could come by better arrangements; by a more successful subdivision of work; by overthrowing those old trade customs and conditions which belonged to the past, and which should be left to the past; by accepting and welcoming the higher and better forms of management that the modern-minded and more capable business men could apply to their interests. In short, it could come by organisation and skill."

With the exception of this one Labour leader, no statesman had the vision to see or raised his voice to point out that before the final coming of peace there must be delay and uncertainty, but that from the moment of cessation of fighting, reaction must begin; that scarcity existed in the world, and that a devastated and wounded Europe required economy, work, production, and security before it could recover. No warning of shortage of material and food, of the weight of national debt, of the evils of inflated currency due to borrowings by the Government, and the long row to hoe before valid recovery could be achieved, came from the Government. Unemployment "doles," distributed with amazing laxity, discouraged work and thrift. A state of unpreparedness, lack of leadership, and the example of state extravagance were to lead up to the "land fit for heroes to live in."

The actual result was that, after the first days of holiday, the Parliamentary Election, and a brief period of reaction, Labour began, with added factors, to resume the claims and movements suspended by the War. The aim of the extremists may be taken from their expressed views at the Election:

"The whole capitalist class stands united in their common desire to exploit Labour. Under capitalism the freedom of the working class consists in the freedom to starve or accept such conditions as are imposed upon them by the employing class. The freedom of the master class consists in their untrammelled freedom to buy Labour to create profit. Thus the workers are not free. Neither owning nor controlling the means of life, they are wage-slaves of their employers, and are but mere commodities. . . . The best Defence is Offensive, and as a consequence the workers must build up their industrial organisation to obtain control over the means of production and destroy the State institution of the master class."

Two main points were put forward among professed aims, viz.: "(1) In home affairs we affirm that all land, railways, mines, factories, means of production, and all other instruments of Social Service shall become the communal property of the people. (2) Social classes thus being abolished, no person shall have the power to employ another person for private profit."

Below these drastic aims there were naturally any number of grades. In times of discontent, or unsatisfied desire, particularly when unfulfilled promises appeared to have been made, men were apt to unite in pressing claims which individually they might not seek or even deem to be feasible. The power of unity had been shown by the War. Organisations had been improved and perfected during the War. Mental unrest had been engendered by the War. By the end of January disputes began to be apparent.

The very 47-hour week, which had been put forward by one section of employers without co-ordination with other trades, proved an early difficulty. Dealing with the situation over the 47-hour week, Mr. Clynes very truly said:

"Here we had an instance, a very outstanding instance, of what at least might be called a great inadvertence, if not a very great blunder. We could not detach any one great trade from the rest of the businesses and the industries of the country, and set up something totally new in that trade in regard to working hours, wages, or conditions of labour. The influence of example was strong, and as soon as a great change took place in any one trade, it was natural that millions of people in other occupations should ask, Why should they not enjoy this benefit too? The engineering employers and the associations in that trade rather suddenly agreed to make a change in the working hours. It only knocked off half an hour a day in the working time, and yet it was beset with all manner of difficulties. The men themselves very soon found out that, in respect of many homes, it did not quite fit in with the domestic conditions, and employers of labour also found that the change was not the perfect thing they thought it would be.

"The troubles which sprang into light at the beginning of the week could be traced, he believed, to certain employers having put up notices announcing the withdrawal of certain privileges that the men had actually enjoyed in their different workshops. There was a misunderstanding on a point of interpretation. The employers naturally concluded that the 47 hours meant 47 hours' actual work; the men concluded that it meant something else, and before there was an opportunity for the two sides to come together calmly to solve these differences of interpretation, notices were put up, shop meetings were held, growing into larger mass meetings, resolutions passed, and strikes at one or two places, or threats of strikes, with the now usual declaration that, if the men were called out at one place, they would be followed by all others. That was the wrong way to do business. Business men in any one trade should be careful of what they were doing, and the associations of workmen should be equally careful, because of the influence of example."

In the first week in February, an official report indicated the nature of some of the disputes which had then commenced to burst out. It said:

"The most serious strike now in progress is that of the motormen on the London Tubes, who are demanding that the thirty minutes' break for a morning meal, which they have been accustomed to under the 9-hour day, shall be retained under the 8-hour day. The Metropolitan Railwaymen came out in sympathy on February 4. An agreement has been made, which it is hoped will result in a resumption of work. The strike on the Clyde continues, although a number of men are already returning to work. In Belfast the situation is still grave. The strikes of boilermakers on the North-East Coast and of ship-repairers on the Thames continue. There are a number of strikes in progress in South Wales, in almost every branch of industry. These include a strike of practically the whole of the South Wales members of the Electrical Trades Union, which began on February 3 in support of their demand for a 47-hour week and a basis wage of 2*s*. and 1*s*. 9*d*. per hour for the various grades. Strikes involving several thousand men occurred during the week at collieries in the Amman Valley (Anthracite District), Llanbradach, and Landore, etc. The Dowlais miners resumed work on January 28, the management having granted all their demands.

"At Barrow, on January 30, about 300 carpenters and joiners were out as a protest against the existence of a premium bonus system. At Birkenhead about 400 riveters, shipwrights, and caulkers struck on January 28 at Messrs. Cammell Laird's. A large number of smelters are out in Lanark. There has been no indication that the strike of the 4,000 boilermakers in the Bristol Channel shipyards has been settled.

"The London electricians threatened to strike in London on February 6 unless the Government brings in a Bill for a national 40-hour week and sets free the Clyde strike leaders. Certain sections of the National Union of Railwaymen, notably London and Liverpool, threaten to strike on February 9 as a protest against the Government's alleged dilatory method of dealing with their national programme."

The burst-out over the 47-hour week, with the subsequent demands for a 44-hour or a 40-hour week in some trades, was only the preliminary to disturbance throughout the country, first of one industry, and then of another. If the general position is considered, it may be deduced that the War had tended to equality in rationing, equality in conscription, and equality in the general advances of war wages to different sections of the community. The War had also tended towards big organisations in both Capital and Labour. In the one case big organisations had been effected by Government action, in the railways, mines, etc., and by control of shipping, engineering, national factories, etc. They had also been effected by voluntary action, with a view to economy of production and greater efficiency, or by the limitations imposed through shortage of managerial power. In the other case, the equality of wage demands had brought unions together, insurance through approved societies and other agencies already acting before the War had increased their strength, dilution or interchangeability had brought trades into close relation.

This was one side of the picture. On the other was the

fact that many of the older trade union leaders, largely through their perpetual work in London, had lost influence, and could not control the huge bodies of which they were the leaders. Sporadic strikes of sections were apt to arise. The rank and file would not submit to discipline. In individual works they aimed at power within the shop without reference to leaders, whom they seldom saw and who were continually busy on other matters. The workshop committees became during the War a real force and had to be reckoned with. Since the War they have become still more powerful, particularly as they afford a mode of expression to the young men.

A disquieting effect of the strikes upon the country was due to the fact that disputes in certain industries—mines, transport, railways—bound more or less closely together under the name of the Triple Alliance, particularly affected the comfort and well-being of the community at large. The common factor noticeable in all of them was the restless pressure and support of the young men in favour of a strike on almost any pretext, until it became almost a farce in the recent voting of the Yorkshire "nippers" in the coal dispute. The stirring of the War, the success of mass effort, the insistent claim and proof by their leaders that the Government could be made to yield, induced large numbers of men in every case to support demands against employers largely without regard to the possibilities of the future of industry. The lavish expenditure and grandiose schemes of the Government could only add fuel to the flame. Men desired to have a share in the assumed millions, which did not appear to be used to reduce the cost of living.

At the same time, many of the young men were determined to have a better time and more of the amenities of life, as they had been vaguely promised, without more work, often with less work, and without production even equivalent to the amount produced per head in the years previous to the War. They desired more pay, less work, a better standard, and more openings, openings which were crystallised in the phrase of more control, or a share in the management of the conditions under which they lived.

On these natural desires there was built the ideal by some of their leaders, particularly the coal-miners' leaders, that both material gain and control could be got by service to the State, and not to private owners. The private owner, as the capitalist, was to be ousted. The advantages of the incentive of personal gain and work, the fact that Capital is generally the aggregation of a vast number of small savings entrusted to a few people, either for investment or speculative purposes, were passed over in favour of a phrase, "nationalization," which has never been clearly explained. In fact, one of the miners' leaders has written that it was not a good word, and that some word like "socialisation" might be more suitable. The damning effect of bureaucratic action was also disowned, but it had never been explained how the State could manage mines without the employment of bureaucracy, nor that any enterprise, development, or cessation from strikes would be more likely to be obtainable under the State than when the mines were worked by an extended unification of the interests of coal-owners and coal-miners. The aim of nationalization was and is quite sincerely held by one of the miners' leaders, Mr. Smillie, himself one of the strongest individualists in the country, and possibly would be claimed by him as an extension of liberty, leading to collective liberty in work through self-government, and individual liberty outside work through the shortening of hours.

Another element in Mr. Smillie's opinions may have been correctly described by his lieutenant, Mr. Frank Hodges, who wrote in March 1920:

"The end he (Mr. Smillie) had in view was service to the bottom dog, and the great thing that he wished to see accomplished was the nationalization of the mining industry, not so much because he felt, as the younger school of advocates feel, that it would bring increased freedom and status to the workmen engaged in the industry, but because of the very concrete issue of increased safety to life and limb, improved housing in mining villages, pit-head baths, and other amenities in the life of a miner. It is a source of great pain to him now that the work of the Coal Industry Commission has not resulted in a single additional working-class home being erected in a mining village, or a pit-head bath being constructed, and that the accident rate in mines has not been diminished."

For the time being, at a time when the consumption of coal had had to be restricted, and when the recruitment of miners after the German advance in 1918, the necessity of export to France owing to the loss of output from the French mines in the Pas de Calais, and influenza epidemics, heavily reduced the available supply from British mines, the movement of the miners, with claims for nationalization, wages, and shorter hours, was very serious. Mr. Smillie was too able a tactician not to realise that force, if it is to be effectual, must be used in a manner which will ultimately persuade, not in a manner which will alienate, the ordinary citizen. He consented to Mr. Lloyd George's proposal for a Commission, of which he became a member, under the chairmanship of Mr. Justice Sankey, and that the strike should be called off. The reports of the Sankey Commission are well known, but the manner of appointment of this Commission, its constituent parts, its method of business, and the subsequent working of the mines, failed to convert the ordinary citizen, or all the miners, or to convince the Government of the necessity of accepting the majority report.

To the ordinary man nationalization was nothing more than a word, or a cry. It was not understood. Its results had not been explained. Its method of working was not shown. Without any clear facts upon which judgement might be exercised, the people were faced with a demand when their burdens were very heavy, and when they did not wish to be hustled into another huge national undertaking.

The miners brought up the question before the Trade Union Congress in September, which endorsed previous annual resolutions in favour of nationalization, but shelved the main question of direct action, and deferred the subject for a special congress in December. It has again been alleged to have come to the front, after a declaration by the Government against it, under the guise of a demand for increased wages and the reduction of the price of coal to the home consumer, which would absorb the Government profits on export coal, and in fact, if not in theory, go far to hand over the mines to the miners.

It appeared to me that, whatever the proposed scheme might be, the nation must receive education on the subject and be prepared to exercise judgement with some knowledge, a view which the miners seemed themselves to take, as they started an educational campaign. With this view in my mind, I wrote, in the interval between September and

December, some remarks in *The Times* upon the position, from which the following passages may be taken :

"Resolutions upon nationalization of industries had become recurrent at Trade Union Congresses in the past, but little result had been attempted or achieved. Owing to circumstances known to the whole country, a call this year has been made upon their colleagues by the powerful mining unions, to put an opinion into force and make it a tangible reality. Their claim is backed by an argument which they know must appeal to many. They allege that they have been let in by the Prime Minister, that at least an implied pledge should oblige the Government to support the findings of the majority of a Government Committee.

"The Trade Union Congress could hardly take any other course than that of support to its previous abstract views. Nobody suggested it should oppose either its own expressed opinion or the demand made by its most powerful section. It may seem futile, under such conditions, to appeal for further consideration before a bitter campaign is launched, or to suggest that a war between nationalizers and anti-nationalizers is unwise, and perhaps unnecessary.

"But there are strong reasons why further consideration should be given to an issue so vitally important to the country as a whole, and why the subject should be approached without temper or recrimination. . . .

"There are two points which beset the minds of ordinary men on this subject of coal. The first is a strong desire for a cheap, plentiful, and regular supply of coal. A man desires warmth and comfort in his home, and facility for maintaining, improving, and enlarging the business or industry in which he is engaged. The second is growing annoyance, even anger, at the perpetual quarrels reported in one or other coal-field, culminating from time to time in national quarrels which upset the plans and livelihood of everyone in the country. The public, if convinced, would accept any reasonable scheme which would relieve their minds of anxiety upon these two points. Other points are subsidiary.

"The miners' leaders appear to say that the course which they are proposing will satisfy these two points, and that in addition the system will ensure the best conditions for the coal-workers. Obviously, unless the country is prosperous, no system will ensure to the miners or any other workers good and improving conditions.

"I have been present at the Trade Union Congress and have heard the speeches made upon the subject. The strong impression left upon my mind by the speeches, and by the opinions everywhere expressed by members of the public, is that the miners, although they claim to advocate a plan which will suit the public, have not taken nearly enough trouble to prove the value of their plan, and have not convinced the public either of the value of their plan or that they mean well by the community. Consequently the issue is serious. . . . There will be worse friction than was even known in the past if nationalization is carried through by the force of one section of the community. A retrocession from the step, once taken, is likely to be impracticable. A reasonable majority of the people ought to be convinced, and those who advocate so far-reaching a plan ought to be able to convince them. There should be time for the nation to examine, criticise, and understand so large a movement. At present little beyond a word is placed before it.

"The miners may contend that resolutions have already been passed by Labour, and that a Government Committee has reported in favour of nationalization and produced a scheme. I sympathise with the miners. A Government Commission should have great weight in guiding statesmen towards a correct course in legislation, but for that purpose it must be a Commission in which the country has complete confidence, particularly on questions vital to the whole community. Rightly or wrongly, the nation has not been convinced by the report of the Coal Commission. . . .

"I do not seriously blame the miners for this development, but, remembering their frequent expression of lack of confidence in the Government, they might wisely have taken great care that any inquiry affecting their industry should have been conducted with the aim of convincing the public that their views are sound, their claims just, that there is no packed jury, nor any feeling that immense power is being used to rush a position for selfish ends. If there is intention to rush the position and press the vague report of this Commission at all costs, if a campaign such as is foreshadowed prior to further consideration is going to be started, it will be taken as an attempt to stampede the people, it will be contrary to the principles of intelligent democracy, and it will create a bitterness absolutely inimical to any co-operation, any unity, or that rest which the majority of the nation so much desire. . . .

"Among other matters, the question of the workers having 'a voice in the management' looms large in the present controversy. It is quite obvious what the extreme labour men intend by this 'voice in the management.' They mean the whole voice. It is equally clear what the mine-owners mean when they object to any interference with management. It is not clear what the Coal Commission Report means or the Whitley Councils mean by the same phrase. Management is a highly specialised business; it is, in fact, the most highly specialised part of any business. Consider the resentment of a skilled miner or mechanic if he was informed of a proposal that someone who knew nothing of the intricacy of his business was to be appointed to have a say as to how the coal was to be got, or how the mechanism of a machine was to be assembled. A skilled workman is supposed to know his business, and no such workman worthy of the name would stand interference. Similarly a manager should know his business, part of which is to keep in close touch with the desires of his workmen and do his best to make their work as attractive as possible. If he fails in this, he fails as a manager. He is, in fact, the connecting-link between the workmen and the employer, a leg of the three-legged stool, and, if he is worthy of the position, would, like his best workmen, resent any interference with his duties. The best managers, while alive to the desires of both employers and men, are as little inclined to submit to officious interference of their directors as to factious interference of the employees. I have in mind many such managers whose success in municipal undertakings or private concerns has been due as much to confidence in their power to prevent such interference as to technical knowledge of their business. Imagine the position of such managers when called upon to consult a workman or a committee of their own workmen elected, not because of the ability he or they have shown in the expert business of management, but because a man has succeeded in securing election by his fellows. Popular election is the worst type of recommendation for such a position. A delegate so elected will sooner or later find himself in the position of losing the confidence of his fellows or supporting proposals for the management of the business which he knows to be wrong. Ill-considered schemes which can lead to such a result are valueless. They are harmful—very pleasing to the theorist, but not practical in their working.

" In order to avoid such schemes and to convince the country as to the best course to be followed, it is necessary that the country should understand the question. The issue is wide and national, the Commission was largely partisan. It is a plain necessity that the country should have far more information upon the subject and proof in support of assertion."

CHAPTER XLII

GOVERNMENT METHODS AND CONCLUSIONS

THE coal-miners were not alone in pressing forward demands. Once again the system of sectional settlement, without any co-ordination, by different Ministers, had full sway. On the railways, in answer to large claims, the locomotive men and firemen obtained advances which only served as an inducement to the other grades to press forward demands for themselves on the same principles, although the locomotive men had pressed for special treatment on the ground of skill. The unrest grew, section after section in different trades demanding more wages and new conditions: and as each section advanced, a patchwork settlement was effected, first by one Department, then by another, with the chance, in every case, of carrying an appeal from one Department to another Department, from one Minister to another Minister, and when the union was powerful enough to cause much trouble, from minor Ministers to the Prime Minister. Co-ordination and system were ignored at a time when peace and rest was of the utmost importance to the welfare of the country. Finally, a petty strike led by one man who could not or would not follow the general, though temporary, settlement in the coal trade, led to a supreme instance of the result of these methods, and illustrated the state of turmoil into which the country was drifting. The whole condition of affairs and the policy which was being followed so moved me that I could not refrain from writing a letter, published by *The Times* on July 30, in heartfelt denunciation of a system, not, as some chose to think, for any political purpose against a party or an individual. A portion of this letter stated:

"Strikes have arisen from the ill-defined recommendations of an opportunist Commission. As a result, the spectacle is afforded of the Prime Minister of the United Kingdom of Great Britain and Ireland coming back, from acting as the representative of the greatest Empire known in history at Conferences designed to settle the most awful war of all known wars and the whole future of the world, to sit surrounded by subordinate Ministers and high officials from many Departments in the famous Cabinet-room of Downing Street for the purpose of arranging the meaning of a report and the piecework rates of one of the Yorkshire coal-fields. It is a spectacle analogous to that of five Cabinet Ministers, with the same man as their leader, wrangling unsuccessfully in 1912 between the parties in a London dock strike. Verily 'a degradation of Government.' And there are many disputes equally big going on, or just coming on, and many far bigger disputes looming in the future. Are there to be more opportunist Commissions and more and more contentious matters drifting to Downing Street, with the chance of an opportunist settlement dictated by the supposed need of the moment and the sturdiness of 'audacious' demands? Why is it? Is there no policy? Has there ever been any industrial policy?

"Meanwhile the burden of the long War is upon us, and with huge debts, restricted exports, swingeing taxation, and continued borrowing, we listen to speeches urging production on those who will not hearken, and work on those who either cannot get it or do as little and spend as much as they can. Demands are made more and more, prices rise as the supplies decrease, efforts to maintain or increase supplies are half-hearted, futile, or purposely not intended, and an orgy of expenditure is the fashion. In this whirl of insecurity and uncertainty profiteering stands out with ugly insistence; there is restlessness and discontent; beneath the surface those with small or fixed incomes form a body filled with ominous and growing anger. The cry is ever, 'Give! give!' to which the Government replies, not by economy or urging restriction of wasteful outlays, but by borrowing more money, ladling out more doles, proposing more place-men, continuing vast subsidies, not even making a pronouncement against profiteering. There is a continuous scramble for money, and more money, at any cost to the nation. The inevitable disturbance results and grows from the least hitch, after a vague settlement of the recent industrial trouble. Is it remarkable that the Prime Minister has to settle piece-work rates of Yorkshire mines at 10 Downing Street?

"The Prime Minister has brought it on himself by a system of opportunism and political interference in industrial business. He is the victim of his own method. From the time when he entered the Board of Trade, through the time when he established and carried on the most lavishly run Department the world has ever seen, down to the present moment, he has been a spending Minister, utterly regardless of economy, guided only by opportunism, and with no Labour policy except political interference for political aggrandisement at the expense of the country. Opportunism has been coupled with spectacular displays, such as the supersession of the responsible Minister in the South Wales mining difficulty of 1915. In that case he left Mr. Runciman to wipe up a maze of vague clauses, and impressed every trade, sometimes employers and more often the employed, with the belief that they had only to push hard enough to receive their demands from the bottomless purse of the nation. Now the nation is reaping the results.

"Again and again the Government was warned, verbally and in writing, that the splendid response of Labour to the War, the abnegation of self, the sacrifice of war, would be swamped if profiteering was not denounced and a lead given which would make those who were living more or less safely at home realise the supreme sacrifice which the flower and youth of the nation were daily incurring for others. They were told, in a report submitted early in the War by the Committee on Production, 'that the needs of the nation in time of war must not be made the means of undue private gain.' That was the only report which was suppressed. That principle has never been adequately acted upon, is not acted upon now, and is flouted by most men who have a chance of flouting it. I venture to say this flouting is loathsome to all the best men and women in the nation, and particularly to those who have risked or lost in the War those who are nearest and dearest to them, even though some in self-protection have had to join in the rush for profits.

"As for Labour, they see the profits, they see the

extravagance. They ask for more. Taking any one of the numerous demands now being made, the employers in one district might be able to meet it out of Government contract prices. If they did, they know that it would spread to every district in the country; and if given in one trade, leap like a prairie fire from trade to trade. They refuse, and a strike results. One Department, out of the many overlapping Departments which have been established by the Prime Minister, comes in. Their official says, 'Give it'—regardless of the efforts of arbitration tribunals, ignorant of the interlocking of trade with trade, ignorant of the ABC of the question, or, if not ignorant, careless. . . . Hundreds of millions of pounds have been thrown away in this manner, the worst instances being the 12½ per cent. and various efforts of the Ministry of Munitions and the Air Ministry, and, in addition, the seeds of future trouble have been continuously laid. Another official in a similar case says: 'No. This involves issues too serious. You cannot give it.' The men's leader says: 'We see the profits; they can pay, and they *shall* pay. They get it from the Government. We insist upon our share. It does not matter to us if the rise spreads to other places. So much the better for our men there. We want our bit, and the cost of living justifies us. If the employers take big profits, we will too.'

"The Civil servant who takes a wide outlook and is more anxious to maintain a sound policy in the matter of advances than to secure temporary peace by opportunist concessions, risks and frequently receives blame. He is discredited by his opportunist political chief. The old Civil Service and its great traditions have been nearly swamped by the influx of new Departments and politicians holding office for a few months, during which they can gain no knowledge of their business, but, following the example of others, see that grandiose plans, vast expenditure, and an army of new men commend them for promotion. The new men imitate their chiefs; the Civil servants, both new and old, find themselves at the mercy of transitory leaders; claims for salaries are based on the size of Departments; the pursuance of any considered plan or policy is rendered abortive; if a line of patience or considered work is attempted, it is ridiculed. . . .

"It is time that some sane lead should be given to the

country. Patience has been preached, but nothing has been done. There is no unity of purpose, no real lead, no thrift in administration or private expenditure, no hindrance to the scramble for money and the continuance of profiteering. War is a time of sacrifice. Many have made it a source of gain, and flaunt their ill-gotten wealth before the eyes of those who risked life on their behalf.

"I have accused the Prime Minister of opportunist prodigality, with which principle he has imbued the colossal staffs surrounding himself and his Ministers; of interfering with good government in the country, and particularly with the *moral* of the Civil Service; of entering into and supporting a systematic interference of the politician in industrial disputes, and thereby achieving the double result of fomenting trouble and degrading Government; and of promoting and condoning lavish waste and expenditure. A system of doles and political bribery for the maintenance of political power can never last, but it may irretrievably injure this country before it comes to a dishonourable end. The Prime Minister has been necessarily absent. He has been weighted with many cares; but the task of pulling the country together and changing the system will brook no delay. Let him tell the people the real situation and preach to them the necessity of economy and thrift, and, above all, act upon it himself. Let him put the settlement of industrial disputes on a sound basis, to be dealt with between employers and employed, only lending, if necessary, outside aid in the event of a deadlock. Let that aid be the one authority whose action shall be final, without interference by politicians and Downing Street, and continuous and uncertain cutting across of its actions. Let him denounce the profiteer, whether he be employer, middleman, or employee, and take steps to stop their profits and nefarious methods. Let him insist on an example being set by all Government Departments, ruthlessly cut down unnecessary place-men, and demand on every side a cessation of extravagance and waste. The country is looking for a lead, craving a lead; and there is yet time to give it a lead. All sane men will wish him God-speed if he will take his chance and act quickly. Failing that——!"

My theory was and is in favour of an avoidance of

disputes by all honourable means, and a just and equitable composing of difficulties when they arise, a policy entirely contrary to the use of the political machine in industrial matters, where its interference has continually wrought harm.

The letter only anticipated the storm by a few hours. During the early days of August the pent-up anger of many men broke out. The Press reflected the opinion of thinking men and cried loudly against extravagance and waste. An official announcement was made that the Ministry of Labour would return to the pre-war method of settling disputes, an announcement which has not been followed. The President of the Board of Trade (Sir Auckland Geddes) introduced an ineffective Profiteering Bill, which the Government stated to be urgent and necessary to carry through at once. The Chancellor of the Exchequer (Mr. Austen Chamberlain) painted in a gloomy speech the state of debt, and called loudly for economy, hinting that the country was on the straight road to bankruptcy. The Government Departments were told by the Prime Minister that staffs must be cut down immediately. A storm of criticism on expenditure and waste ran through the country, but criticism had never come from the Government, or any important Member of it. The feeling was reflected in the Trade Union Congress. Although "direct" action as a means of forcing political ends was shelved, at least for the time, the mere fact that resolutions in the country had caused it to be discussed formally at the Congress indicated discontent, and the Congress also passed strong economic resolutions on such subjects as a levy on capital, as well as for nationalization of mines. Then there was a lull, broken only by a "Foreword" by the Prime Minister to a new paper called *Future*, which led me to write again to *The Times* a series of letters about this hypothetical "New World."

It seemed so absurd to speak of the "new world" when storms were actually gathering, almost immediately to burst out into the railway strike, a case of "direct action" to force the Government to yield to a section of the community, though the Government were the real employers, and a curious comment upon the claims of the miners that service to a Government would be more respected than service to other employers.

The same procedure which had now become so common

was carried out, squeezing the railway executive to get near an agreement, and then standing out for more; squeezing the Minister, this time the new Minister of Transport (Sir Eric Geddes), on the first day of his entry into office, and then in this case striking; and eventually squeezing the Prime Minister to yield still more. The same process, without the strike, was followed on the subject of standard rates in the following December. Whether the claims were good or bad, such a system of settlement seems to me to be thoroughly bad, and brings Ministers, and particularly the Prime Minister, continuously into a false position.

This railway strike, coming quite unexpectedly after the public had been told all was going well, in answer to a promise of a considerable advance, and apparently largely out of pique with a particular Minister, annoyed the public. It was the beginning of winter, when people generally desired some peace in the industrial world. The public did what they could to assist themselves, and the Government obtained their support. It was a very unpopular strike. It was an unwise strike, if the Labour Party, as it was said, desired to achieve political success, because it threw them back for the time being. It did not lead the people to believe in their sense of responsibility. The object lesson was not thrown away upon the transport workers, who agreed to refer their claims to a court of inquiry, or upon the miners, who started the campaign of education which has been mentioned.

In addition, during the autumn, a sectional strike of iron-moulders, refusing to work on piece-work, demanding more for time-work than any allied sections, turning deaf ears to the interests and advice of the many trades dependent upon castings, hindered then, and as an aftermath for many months, that production in the engineering trades which was so necessary to the welfare of the nation. Thus closed the year 1919, with a general feeling that some trade unions were being worked for political rather than industrial ends, and despair at the absence of stability and security in obtaining production or the establishment of efficiency in production when employers and employed were not adequately united in the same object.

In this present year of 1920 it may be noted that an international sense, in a mild form, has been cultivated by the meetings and advisory decisions reached at Washington by delegates united under the fiat of the Treaty of Versailles. This movement may acquire force in the future. At present, so far as this country is concerned, the efforts bring forward no points of great novelty. Great Britain, comparatively speaking, takes the lead, but the importance and success of the proposals depend in other countries entirely upon administration, the most necessary requirement to give effect to paper promises. It is also to be hoped that, under the system of voting, the immense maritime interests of Great Britain will not be hazarded by equality of voting power being given to countries like Switzerland, Czecho-Slovakia, and Poland, whose interests do not lie in the possession of ships. Equality of power seems to have been allowed at the recent international conference at Genoa.

International sense has, however, been followed up in a far more extreme form by the renewal of threats of "direct action" for political ends, and claims that the Government in international politics should follow the decisions of a few Labour leaders. The future of such action it is not possible to predict, but up to the present all the claims for direct action have been characterised by speeches and action so astonishing in the sum of ignorance which they display that Ministers have had small difficulty in meeting the criticism. Understanding of foreign affairs does not come from the mere fact that a man is a successful Labour leader, or thinks that he can stop transport, or has influence to hinder by strikes international undertakings of which he has the most rudimentary knowledge. It is, nevertheless, important to recognise that the real measure of support given to such claims is the firm desire on the part of the whole nation to have peace, and not to be embroiled in war, unless the nation has full cognisance and an opportunity of judging the reasons which may lead to war. With that ideal put before the people, much might happen.

In conclusion, the few months since the Armistice, a brief period in the history of a nation, have been undoubtedly marked by reaction after the War, the desire to have a good time, to relax the tension and the continuity of work. There has been the high price of food and all necessaries of life, continuously rising, with wages not covering in all cases the demands made by increasing costs. There has been the fear of higher prices, the fear of unemployment, and the fear of competition by the influx of more workers and the effects of demobilisation. The better feeling among employers generally was not recognised sufficiently, while, on the other hand, strong dislike of profiteers continued to exist, and the belief that Capital would dominate, with resentment against such a possibility. New men had arisen in the course of the years, who threw over old methods and thought that, by combination of demands and organisation of workers and by strikes, they could force from employers, or if not from them, from the Government, the chief controlling employer, a concession of their demands. Propaganda ceaselessly pressed for a change of social life, a better position for the workers, and more control. Behind all these causes writers and speakers have revived or pressed idealistic views, which now or never it seemed possible to obtain, and which were often held without realisation of the tragedy of the times, the ravages of the War, or the grim results and further strife which might follow by pushing forward doctrines the results of which they could not control. It is easy to be a revolutionist; it is not easy to be a revolutionist who sees where he is drifting or being led. The freedom not to exercise toleration may be a defensible theory, but may also become selfish individualism.

In some districts of the country, particularly large cities, the housing difficulty aided discontent. Men cannot work properly if their homes are thoroughly uncomfortable or crowded, and yet if they go farther away from their work, every increase of tramway or railway fares diminishes earnings, and may even cancel the gain of their own advances in wages. Instead of more amenities in life or the hopes of home which might have been cherished, the fruition, in spite of lavish promise, continued and continues to be lamentably meagre.

The sense of proportion must be exercised when dealing with the views and opinions of large masses of people. Elements of discontent are cumulative. One man is chiefly guided by one reason, another by a different reason, but the result may be the same. The absence of logical reasons is generally more noticeable than their presence. It is probable that the majority of people want to be left alone, and not to have their lives interfered with, particularly by officials: people want to do things on their own, and not in manner prescribed by agents, however benevolent their views of uplifting and improvement may appear to be. In the case of lockouts and strikes, it must always be remembered that the percentage of persons in dispute at any particular time is very small relatively to the large numbers of people steadily working, and not interested in the least in the dispute unless it happens to impinge on their own interests, work, or enjoyment. It is, however, disconcerting to the majority of people, who desire to settle down and live in peace, when an epidemic of strikes, or "a strike fever," as one politician complacently called it, is reported in the Press, and fuel, travel, or supplies of food and articles required in every household are gravely interfered with. Before settling down again into complacency, the public, of whom the majority are other working men and women, want to know the reason, and may feel the direct effects. There are also serious after-effects in restriction of trade and export, increased taxation and increased cost, which they do not fully realise, though they are there, and must affect the wealth of the nation available for distribution among the people, generally out of all proportion to the value obtained by the immediate protagonists in the dispute. The effect, too, on the mental and moral nature of men is bad. All this hatred, bitterness, and jealousy cannot be good. Divergent interests and suspicion and intent almost always arise or remain after these struggles, even though men may shake hands over the particular dispute. It would be better if they did not arise.

Then how is that result to be obtained? It would be useless to say that the waves of the sea are always to be still, or that the movements of ambition, greed, and interests will not lead to clashing from which struggles of strength will arise. The small minority actively engaged in promoting complete changes of society, followed all the more easily by the masses as organisations are enlarged or more closely knit in discipline, would alone be sufficient to prevent such a millennium. The example of other nations, either in political, industrial, or revolutionary movements, is not to be left out of account, although often magnified into undue importance, and although unity at home is surely of more value than a vague alliance with contemptuous and foreign dictators of illegal violence. The preachings of publicists, and one-sided propaganda by enthusiasts urging what they would destroy but not thinking what they would retain, the very workings of the minds of men, must prevent placid contentment. It is vain to think that peace can be got by Acts of Parliament, however orderly the arrangements they propose or the benevolence they breathe, or by pensions, insurance, maximum prices, town-planning, public works, or multifarious devices resulting in heavy and ever-increasing taxation. I find no answer in the interference of the politician in the struggles arising in industry, and in my opinion such interference should be rigidly curtailed.

Let me return to the first pages of this book. If the orderly advance of peaceful development is to be obtained, in place of the surging storms of hatred and strife, there must be more knowledge, so that men should not blindly follow guides who may be blind. There must be simple and plain modes of bringing forward grievances and avoiding disputes by all honourable means, and of composing difficulties when they arise, justly and equitably. There must be efforts to improve the comfort of the workshop and its surroundings, reduce the monotony of work, and by all possible means obviate the fear of unemployment. There ought to be a strong effort by each industry to deal with the question of unemployment within that industry, a difficult but vital task. There must be an attempt at better personal understanding, and chances given to the young to make use of their education, and by means of their brains and energy to have opportunity of service to others and to themselves. There must be desire of common interest, and if possible of unifying common interest, partly by the touch of human and personal sympathy, partly by the joint interest of material gain, with the ideal of joint service. It is the spirit, not paper systems, which alone can prevent war and reduce the reasons for industrial strife.

My work and the work of a zealous Department, fighting through times of sporadic disputes, times of revolution in 1911 and 1912, and times of war, will have been mainly thrown away if it has not shown that bitter disputes can be settled by understanding, that employers and employed can work together, that united effort produces great results and lays the seeds of greater results, and that the peace of the kingdom as a whole is of greater value than success in a petty squabble or the encouragement of hatred between man and man. Peace and good-will among men may have been too high an ideal to obtain, but in the seeking of it it has been possible, sometimes, to lay the seeds of future understanding and a living growth of unity and unified effort between man and man, beyond the material settlement, important though that be, of the wages between employer and employed. "I see two classes," says Margaret Hale, in Mrs. Gaskell's *North and South,* "dependent on each other in every possible way, yet each evidently regarding the interests of the other as opposed to their own." That is the position of the two camps. The unity of the camps is the aim of conciliation.

INDEX